Dialogue & Deliberation

Josina M. Makau
Debian L. Marty
California State University, Monterey Bay

WAVELAND

PRESS, INC.

Long Grove, Illinois

For information about this book, contact:
Waveland Press, Inc.
4180 IL Route 83, Suite 101
Long Grove, IL 60047-9580
(847) 634-0081
info@waveland.com
www.waveland.com

10-digit ISBN 1-4786-0065-9
13-digit ISBN 978-1-4786-0065-7

Printed in the United States of America

7 6 5 4 3 2

To all who endeavor for a
peaceable, just, and secure world,
where people treat one another
with the respect and dignity
they wish to experience themselves

Contents

SECTION THREE
Deliberation   141

Acknowledgments

We are in excellent company in the ongoing endeavor to transform dialogue and deliberation for the realities of life in the twenty-first century. Many scholars, activists, educators, civic leaders, and engaged community members are tapping into humanity's communicative potential in order to address our mutual problems and goals. We share with them—and with concerned people everywhere—a common motivation to connect meaningfully across our differences and disagreements and a commitment to just and wise decision making. We, too, yearn to live in peaceable and just communities. We would like to acknowledge here those who have inspired and informed this current effort.

We owe a special gift of gratitude to Neil and Carol Rowe of Waveland Press, whose enduring support provided a beacon lighting the way throughout the crafting process. Readers familiar with the Rowes' long-standing commitment to visionary work will understand how and why we found their sustained enthusiasm for this project so deeply inspirational. We are grateful, too, for the care, insight, and skillfulness reflected in Carol Rowe's manuscript edits. Not only did she help us to avoid substantive errors, her revisions significantly improved the clarity and overall readability of the volume.

As is revealed throughout the book, we have benefitted from the invaluable work of scholars, commentators, and activists dedicated to improving the quality of communication and civic life. Their words and ideas made this project possible. Indeed, their spirit of inquiry serves as a continual source of hope that humanity can flourish in the twenty-first century and beyond. A special mention is owed to the late James A. Mackin, Jr. Our paraphrase of his thesis from *Community over Chaos: An Ecological Perspective on Communication Ethics* became a foundational insight guiding our work: *The quality of communication affects the quality of the community and our ability to act together in common purpose.*

We are indebted as well to the transformative frameworks for communication, civic life, and decision making made available through cutting-edge professional associations. The National Coalition for Dialogue and Deliberation, the Association for Practical and Professional Ethics, the Association for Moral Education, Physicians for Social Responsibility, the Organization for Research on Women and Communication, the National Coalition Building Institute, the Informal Logic Association, and the National Communication Association's Communication Ethics and Peace and Conflict Divisions provided especially helpful resources.

Numerous colleagues, friends, and family members served as "clear mirrors" during the drafting process. Their insights and suggestions carefully reflected back the strengths and limitations of the manuscript at various stages. We wish in particular to acknowledge the valuable contributions of Sharon Bracci, Sonja Foss, John Berteaux, Kathleen Rice, Clifford Christians, Ron Arnett, Amalia Mesa Bains, Darcia Narvaez, Richard Johannesen, Vic Makau, and Ingrid Makau.

Literally hundreds of students at California State University Monterey Bay became our most engaged and enthusiastic critics. They were enrolled in our courses in interpersonal communication and conflict resolution, ways of knowing, cooperative argumentation, and communication ethics courses and read excerpts or versions of the manuscript in its entirety. Their various interpretations and applications of dialogue and deliberation helped us "keep it real." Their enthusiastic efforts to practice dialogue and deliberation in everyday life also affirmed the significance of this project for us. A Penn State doctoral student also deserves the proverbial shout-out. Craig Rood's invitations to join presentation panels at Rhetoric Society of America and National Communication Association conferences became the tipping point for reinvestigating civility's role in dialogue and deliberation.

Finally, work of this kind demands extraordinary levels of patience and understanding from those most dear to us. We are deeply grateful for the love and support of our friends and family throughout the many months of research and writing required to complete the project. Above all, we thank our partners, Carole Pavlo and Genevieve Marty-Lorick, who have given us the precious gifts of their unconditional love and practical wisdom. Through our lives together, we have experienced the deepest enrichment of being heard, understood, and known. These beloved relationships have served as touchstones of trust. Each of us has grown immeasurably as a result, further inspiring us to share our findings. We sincerely hope that the book our loved ones have helped us to create will contribute meaningfully to readers' dreams and pursuits of living and doing well.

Introduction

At the conclusion of events honoring her extraordinary achievements as host of her award-winning talk show, Oprah Winfrey shared what she described as one of the most profound insights she had gained during her work. Across the globe, in every barrio, city, village, and suburb, she urged, people want to be heard, known, and understood. Winfrey's astute observation is echoed by the findings of scholars in fields as diverse as sociology, political science, psychology, theology, and communication. Being heard, known, and understood are widely recognized as key elements in the fulfillment of human potential.

The same holds true for communities. The capacities to hear and be heard, to understand and be understood are critical to communal well-being. People willing and able to engage constructively across differences offer their communities the promise of working together effectively in recognizing and responsibly meeting the demands of the moment. In James A. Mackin's words, "the quality of our communication affects the quality of our communities."[1]

As the challenges confronting individuals, relationships, and communities become increasingly compelling today, so too does the need for effective communication across disagreement and other forms of difference. And yet, as so many have observed, the fabric of our communities is at risk of being shattered by polarization, acrimony, demonization, and other forms of fracture. Being heard, known, and understood have become increasingly rare experiences for individuals and groups, creating disabling obstacles to people's abilities to work together in pursuit of common purpose.

In this volume, we explore the roots of this crisis, and offer a pathway out of the thicket. The book is divided into three sections. We begin the opening section with an overview of assumptions regarding the human condition that have long been instrumental in compromising people's abilities to communicate and reason well together. Within the United States, the assumption that individual success can be achieved only through relentless pursuit of self-interest without consideration of

1

consequences to others is particularly tenacious. Related is the widely held image of a "dog-eat-dog" world divided into winners and losers. This line of thinking sees individuals who are able to hone their competitive edge as inevitably triumphing over those who pursue a more collaborative approach to decision making.

The idealized approach to adversarialism associated with this narrative has created artificial separations of the self and community and otherwise gravely compromised people's abilities to collaborate in pursuit of common purpose. In response, we introduce research regarding the inevitability of interdependence in all aspects of life, and consider the implications of this interdependence to our interactions with others. This section of the book presents related research replacing the dominant narrative with a more reliable understanding of human nature. Contrary to the dominant myth regarding human nature, people's capacities for connection, cooperation, care, and compassion are vital links to flourishing. People well equipped to engage meaningfully with others not only contribute to communal well-being but are themselves greatly enriched through their compassionate and caring experiences.

Human happiness, as we will see, comes for most people not through relentless pursuit of self-interest but rather through engaged connection and reflective pursuit of meaningful efforts. Development of the skills and sensibilities associated with dialogue and deliberation promises to help individuals and communities fully realize this potential.

Section Two of the volume builds on this groundwork by focusing on dialogic communication as a compelling alternative to adversarialism. Here we explore the nature and purposes of dialogue, drawing parallels as well as distinctions to widely publicized calls for civility and other forms of engagement. The chapters in this section provide detailed overviews of what is required for people to express the thoughts, feelings, and experiences that inform their personal views, as well as the skills and sensibilities required to respond effectively to the cares and concerns motivating others. As this section of the book will reveal, effective dialogic communication enables us to repair the breach between individual and social responsibility, to restore the balance between individual liberty and the public good, and to lay the groundwork for sound personal and communal decision making.

These foundations are especially critical in today's complex and globally interdependent decision making contexts. Perhaps more than ever, the human family faces issues of unparalleled urgency—from environmental perils, to war, hunger, poverty, global terrorism, and economic crises.

The urgent need to understand and responsibly address such issues together informs our discussion of deliberation, the focus of the third section of this book. Our exploration of the art of deliberation begins with a recognition of obstacles to its pursuit. Jonathon Haidt's cutting-edge research in moral psychology has revealed several of these obstacles, including the confirmation bias that inevitably influences individual and group framing of issues, circumstances, and available options. As Haidt and his colleagues have shown, people's minds are designed to maintain alliances and reputations. Most of us acquire expert capacities to manipulate our self-representation. And in the pursuit of "truth," most of us are inclined to "find" only (or primarily) evidence affirming our orientations, perspectives, values, master narratives, and other forms of bias.[2]

The 2012 presidential campaign was marked by a substantial increase in fact checking by the media. Yet voters seemed almost immune to the efforts; there was a tendency to forgive the politicians one supported. "No matter their ideology, many voters increasingly inhabit information bubbles in which they are less likely to hear their worldview contradicted."[3] Frank Luntz, a political strategist, commented: "We don't collect news to inform us. We collect news to affirm us. It used to be that we disagreed on the solution but agreed on the problem. Now we don't even agree on the problem."[4]

While overcoming these predispositions is difficult, Haidt offers words of encouragement. Although it's usually not possible for any individual, group, tribe, or community to get fully out of their own and "into" another's moral matrix, we do have the capacity to train ourselves to subject our ideas to the scrutiny of others. In doing so with as open a heart and mind as human fallibilities permit, we create the promise of being able to move together across our differences in common quests for truth, justice, fairness, peace, compassion, and informed and wise decision making.

Demographic shifts and technological advancements offer historically unparalleled access to others' ways of knowing, being, and valuing. Within the dominant adversarial paradigm, these forms of diversity are often viewed as deficits, obstacles to overcome. When understood within the interdependent model of communication proposed in this volume, however, diversity in all of its forms is recognized as a potentially invaluable asset. Within this framework, tapping diversity's promise is both an imperative and a realizable goal. Section Three introduces tools required to tap diversity as a resource for the exercise of practical wisdom across contexts.

Taken together, the chapters in this volume reveal how people empowered by the abilities to hear and be heard, to understand and be understood, and ennobled by shared quests to pursue justice, fairness, peace, and mutual prosperity may most effectively tap the opportunities made possible in this historic moment. As we will show, development of the skills and sensibilities associated with dialogue and deliberation are key to fulfillment of this potential.

Our approach seeks to be integrative, offering both theoretical grounding and concrete tools required for practical application. In the end, our goal is contribute to the development of knowledge, skills, and sensibilities required to live and do well. To fulfill this aspiration, we offer "real-world" examples from representative situations, as well as composite examples with details altered to convey essential points as clearly as possible. In order to protect people's privacy, we have used pseudonyms throughout our presentations.

Our work on this project has awakened us to the richness and deep complexity of the subject matter we've chosen to explore. As you "take in" the material, we invite you to bring your insights to bear, enriching the material for yourself and for others in your circle. Through these efforts, we hope and trust that you will join us in experiencing the vast reserve of individual and communal well-being made possible through the arts of dialogue and deliberation.

SECTION ONE

Laying the Groundwork

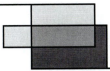

Communication in the "Argument Culture"

Throughout history, communication has been among humanity's greatest resources. Whether through storytelling, information sharing, or argumentation, communication has helped people reach across disagreements and other forms of difference in pursuit of knowledge, truth, and understanding. Families and communities in search of healing turn to communication as their primary resource. Truth telling and reconciliation through communication have been identified internationally as vital resources for pursuits of peace and justice. Through communication, sages are able to share their wisdom, enabling individuals and communities to build on their insights. Scientists, healers, and artists alike depend on communication in pursuit of their crafts.

These are but a few examples of communication's pivotal role in fulfilling humanity's great potential. At the same time, however, history is replete with accounts of communication's central role in fomenting hatred and war, enabling tyranny, fostering injustice, supporting greed, undermining truth, and otherwise compromising pursuits of humane values. Recognition of communication's powers—to heal and to wound, to inspire and to destroy, to uplift and to denigrate, to enlighten and to mislead—provides an important starting point for our exploration of communication within the argument culture.

We begin this exploration by addressing the following related questions: how effectively does today's dominant approach to communication across differences fulfill communication's constructive potential, and what obstacles stand in the way of fulfillment of this potential?

An Introduction to the Argument Culture

In her landmark 1998 work, *The Argument Culture*,[1] Dr. Deborah Tannen provided an incisive analysis of the adversarial condition of public discourse in the United States. Her exhaustive study revealed the pervasiveness of this condition, as well as its corrosive consequences to relationships, to the quality of communities, and to the nation's capacity for reasoned and just decision making. Since then, many related commentaries have described the ways in which such an atmosphere jeopardizes any hope of communication that promotes respect, fosters community, or facilitates reasoned and just decision making.

Despite the broadly recognized need to find pathways for peaceful coexistence and wise deliberations in response to shared problems and despite the growing recognition that constructive engagement of difference offers one of the most important pathways for such pursuits, the argument culture continues to prevail. Talk radio's rancor has spread to cable news and to Internet blogs, political partisanship generates relentless government gridlock, and meetings from the school board to the board of directors routinely deteriorate into hostile shouting matches or shrouded back-room deals.

Academic researchers, political pundits, and community leaders assessing these circumstances confirm Tannen's early conclusion: the argument culture has created a "pervasive warlike atmosphere that makes us approach public dialogue, and just about anything we need to accomplish, as if it were a fight."[2] Consider, for example, the polarizing nature of health care debates in the United States. Nearly everyone involved recognizes that the nation desperately needs to confront its health care crisis: lack of affordable, accessible, and reliable care is driving multitudes into the poorhouse and even the grave. Businesses and public institutions are mired in debt from rising health care costs. Institutions and organizations as diverse as public universities, the Pentagon, and small businesses identify rising medical costs as among the most difficult obstacles they face in meeting their budgetary goals.

And yet, despite the nearly unanimous desire for a responsible solution to this crisis, the nation's political leaders struggle to build on this common ground. Available options are evaluated more for their political viability than for their merits. And while national deliberations regularly entail public poll taking and congressional vote counting, acrimonious discourse severely undermines efforts to pursue creative solutions through sound deliberation.

Reform legislation in this area was passed in 2009, but strictly along party lines. Of the two leading political parties within the United States, one secured enough votes for passage, while the other provided no support for the initiative, with few from either group lauding the process. Following the fall 2010 election, the adversarial climate heightened once again with threats of overturning the results of the previous year's efforts. And since then, acrimony has marked nearly every aspect of the public debate on resolving the nation's health care crisis.

Such divisiveness is typical of the argument culture, laments Tannen, for "criticism, attack, [and] opposition are the predominant if not the only ways of responding to people or ideas" (p. 7). This is how disagreement is confronted within the argument culture: people view one another as adversaries and see differences as cause for power struggles.

Fifteen years after the publication of Tannen's book, the argument culture has become so pervasive within the United States that the nation is in danger of not being able to address pressing problems. Economic crises, environmental disasters, and cross-cultural conflicts are among countless areas of concern urgently requiring collaborative efforts and innovative ideas. Yet, during these complex times, an adversarial mindset not only prevents people from working together on common problems but also promotes demonization and intractable opposition. Throughout the United States, a crisis in communication is damaging the quality of life for individuals as it undermines the common good.

This volume addresses the crisis by offering a viable alternative to the adversarial model. Before presenting the alternative, however, it is important to consider *why* efforts to engage constructively across disagreement and other forms of difference are in so much trouble.

Why Is Constructive Engagement of Disagreement So Difficult?

It can be uncomfortable to learn that others see things differently. The experience is often accompanied by a mix of unwelcome feelings—confusion, vulnerability, and even anger. Disagreeing with someone can add distress to general feelings of uneasiness and insecurity. Reproaches and criticism may permeate an exchange, making for a fractious encounter. Apprehension about conflict leads others to avoid the people with whom they disagree, refusing "even to give them the time of day." As a result of such experiences, feelings and thoughts about disputes often tend toward *negativity*.

While some people respond to disagreement with curiosity or an enthusiasm for learning, most within the argument culture typically cope by "fight or flight"—"getting in your face" or declaring "I'm outta here!" Still others opt out via cynical indifference. "Whatever" is their motto.

The strategies of fight, flight, or indifference may help us cope with disagreement's stressors, but the process is decidedly unsatisfactory. Relationships are often strained, and disputes usually are not resolved. Instead, they simply come to a close because someone exerted more power, or yielded it, or stopped caring. Technically, the disagreement is "over," but with little confidence that the parties understood each other, considered all the available options, or made a wise choice. It's just done—until it compounds the next conflict!

Disagreement is difficult within the argument culture, then, in part because the experience is permeated with negativity. Nevertheless, people routinely engage deeply in disputes—whether confronting one another or rehearsing the conflict in their minds. Significant human needs surface when people disagree. We all *need* to be heard and to *matter* to one another; this is a shared feature of the human condition. Ideally, we could meet these needs by connecting respectfully, making sense of the situation together, and deliberating wisely. Habitual responses to disagreement in the argument culture—fight, flight, or indifference—cannot satisfy these needs.

Constructive engagement across disagreement and other forms of difference fosters conditions for pursuits of knowledge, truth, understanding, and wise decision making. In today's complex interconnected world, such pursuits are both more difficult and important than ever before. Unfortunately, however, conditions within the argument culture often undermine these quests.

Philosopher and political scientist Kristen Renwick Monroe offers insight into one of these conditions. "Given the choice between feeling good about themselves and representing the world accurately," she writes, people often take the first option."[3] This desire to "save face"—even at the expense of mutual understanding and sound decision making—is both most easily recognized and especially challenging in intimate interpersonal contexts. Therapist Jeffrey B. Rubin offers the following observation based on his professional experience working with distressed couples. "In more than 24 years of practice, I've discovered that the biggest source of conflict for couples isn't money, sex, fidelity, child rearing or in-laws. It's the urge to win. Wanting to win, to be right, is natural. It makes us feel strong and safe and gratified. It's also disastrous for a relationship."[4]

This desire to be right is deeply connected with maintaining a positive self-image and a secure reputation. It is "disastrous for a relationship," however, because couples treat each other as adversaries rather than as loved ones. When we perceive each other as opponents involved in a contest to be "won," we become immersed in a power struggle over whose view will prevail. The discord between meeting our needs and solving our disagreements follows. Because we may invest more in being "right" than in listening to the other's perspective, we may judge differences negatively. Or, in an effort to protect our position or reputation, we may blame others for causing the conflict as we defend our own views and actions. Although evaluating the available options fairly leads to the wisest decision, we may manipulate the deliberation in order to avoid "losing" the argument. When we respond to disagreement within this cycle of judgment, blame, and defensiveness, we remain entrenched within the confines of the argument culture.

Whether in interpersonal or public discourse contexts, human beings stand a better chance of working through disagreement if we *extend to others what we wish for ourselves*: if we inquire genuinely about the other's perspective, listen with openness, and evaluate the options fairly. We can request the same consideration and, no matter the response, set *constructive limits for engagement*. If others reciprocate, then more of us could experience a greater sense of trust and, on that basis, make more effective decisions regarding our common needs and shared problems.

The argument culture does not facilitate interactions that meet basic human needs or effectively address our problems. How did the United States polity become so steeped in opposition?

Historical Roots of the Argument Culture

The adversarial approach to disagreement was originally seen in the Western world as fulfilling two critically important goals: the clash of opposing views was meant to help us to discover truth and, based on those findings, to enable informed, reasoned decision making. This idea has permeated core institutions within the United States (such as law, government, and education) since the nation's founding.

For example, the legal system in the United States and throughout many other Western nations is founded on the premise that impassioned and skilled arguments on behalf of "both sides" would help to reveal the truth in any given case. Judges and juries would be well equipped to make reasoned and just decisions about a defendant's innocence or guilt in this adversarial system.

Similarly, adversarial representations of different points of view within the political system were expected to provide citizens the arguments needed to make the informed decisions necessary for self-governance. Candidates for political office were expected to debate the issues before the voters; those elected were then expected to debate policy and legislation on the House or Senate floor.

This form of competitive debate was institutionalized in schools and universities to prepare students for professions such as law and politics as well as meaningful civic engagement and responsible citizenship. The national polity's commitment to this adversarial pursuit of truth and just decisions is manifest in the ways in which democracy is taught, exercised, and upheld through oppositional forms of argument and debate.

In many ways, adversarial truth seeking and decision making highlight important communication skills. *Advocacy* allows us to voice our views, *critique* helps us refine them, and *refutation* steers us away from baseless facts and mistaken inferences. These are invaluable contributions to democratic governance and reasoned decision making. And in the chapters of this book, we will offer strong support for continued development and use of these skills. We will show, however, how *idealizing the conditions of adversarial confrontations* in the nation's history has helped to create obstacles to *constructive* forms of advocacy, critique, and refutation. Following this exploration, we will introduce an alternative model of communication specifically designed to address today's deliberative contexts.

Historically, the adversarial process within the United States took place between privileged men of similar background and stations in life. Whether in the courtroom, legislatures, or the classroom, they sparred as equals, with assurance that "truth would out" and that "the best man would win."

Sometimes it happened that way. More often than not, however, the adversarial approach fell short of this ideal. The legal system, for example, is criticized widely for the gap between the idealized and the actual pursuit of justice. Consider criminal trials. As mentioned earlier, a prosecutor and a defense attorney do their best to persuade the jury of the accused person's guilt or innocence. Theoretically, the two competing sides are equally well represented and the jury is competent to make a reasoned judgment. These expectations reassure us that adversarial courtroom advocacy will lead to a just verdict.

In practice, however, desires for courtroom victories encourage advocates to succumb to unethical adversarial practices, leading to suspect verdicts. Motivated to win, advocates may seek biased jurors, easily manipulated into voting for a preferred decision. Similarly, some attorneys might present evidence in misleading ways or hide possibly damaging evidence from jurors. And these courtroom tactics don't even begin to address the impact on justice from publicly underfunded legal departments or from the disparities in clients' ability to afford competent representation. The gap between the idealized and the actual adversarial courtroom creates grave doubts about our legal system: can it produce justice for all?

Traditional academic programs in argumentation and debate within the United States endeavor to instill a more reasonable path through the argument culture. Students in these programs are taught to select a disputed topic and to develop "cases" for "both" sides. They learn to identify relevant issues, to provide adequate reasons for their positions, and to refute alternatives. Research shows that this approach achieves noteworthy goals, such as sharpening critical thinking and improving advocacy. These skills have served graduates of these programs well, particularly as they entered such competitive professional environments as the law, business, and politics. In light of this record of success, many programs around the country continue to privilege such competitive, adversarial approaches to argumentation and debate.

Although demonstrably successful at fostering important skills, these programs also entail significant risks. For example, although students in these programs develop important abilities to consider alternative perspectives through their research on "both sides" of each issue, much of their research focuses on securing "evidence" in support of a case. Students are encouraged to look for arguments to support one of two "competing" points of view, rather than exploring a multiplicity of perspectives required for understanding and resolving complex issues responsibly and wisely.

Adversarialism in the classroom creates an educational ethos where students learn to relate as opponents competing for the one right answer or the triumphant case. Many believe this approach invigorates class-room dynamics and leads to the rigorous pursuit of knowledge. While this educational outcome may occur at times, adversarialism always undermines *what* students know, for it affects the very *process* of learning. Three scholars of argumentation—Dennis Lynch, Diana George, and Marilyn Cooper—describe the impact of the argument culture on students' relationship to knowledge. "Students have learned to argue vigorously and even angrily," they write,

> but not to think about alternatives, or listen to each other, or deter-
> mine how their position may affect others, or see complexities, or
> reconsider the position they began with, or even to make new con-
> nections across a range of possible disagreements.[5]

These scholars describe specific effects of the argument culture, where students are socialized into ways of knowing and learning that actually diminish their understanding of themselves and their world. Thus, while students are learning the valuable advocacy skills of critique and refutation, their lessons are embedded in harmful communication habits. Students are taught to view those who disagree as *opponents*, habituating them to pit themselves against others, to get locked into their positions, and to reject reflecting on or reconsidering their own assumptions, ideas, and beliefs. These aspects of adversarial communica-tion are counterproductive, for they create a "got'cha" norm of negativity and one-upmanship, wherein "the winner can feel accomplished only at the expense of the loser."[6]

The art of governing in the United States exemplifies these conten-tious lessons. Earlier, we described the argument culture's effect on the national health care debate. But the partisan divide that precluded colle-giality and productive compromise is not limited to health-care legisla-tion. Strident partisanship so consistently undermines the government's ability to address pressing problems that the "polarization between the worldviews of Republicans and Democrats, and the intense negative effects they produce, reach new lows daily."[7] These "new lows" in the political process are reflected in abysmal public approval ratings for both the executive and legislative branches of government. They also are a profound source of concern for many who work there.

These calls echo the voice of Scott McClellan, who served as White House Press Secretary under President George W. Bush. The former spokesman issued a compelling critique of the political environment, decrying the extent to which a "permanent campaign culture" had taken over government functions.

> Washington has become the home of the permanent campaign, a game of endless politicking based on the manipulation of shades of truth, partial truths, twisting of the truth, and spin. Governing has become an appendage of politics rather than the other way around, with electoral victory and the control of power as the sole measures of success.[8]

The Democratic senator from Indiana, Evan Bayh, concurred. His concerns about political process and priorities motivated his unexpected retirement. After nearly twelve years in office and anticipating a likely reelection, Mr. Bayh offered a public explanation for his decision in an editorial. Echoing McClellan's critique, Bayh described the devastating effects of perpetual campaigns on Congress members' ability to reach across the aisle and govern on behalf of the people, rather than political party.

> Today, members routinely campaign against each other, raise donations against each other and force votes on trivial amendments written solely to provide fodder for the next negative attack ad. It's difficult to work with members actively plotting your demise. Any improvement must begin by changing the personal chemistry among senators. More interaction in a non-adversarial atmosphere would help.[9]

Adversarialism permeates the operations of the nation's fundamental institutions, damaging public discourse and obstructing efforts to teach, govern, and uphold democratic practices. The vaunted ideal of adversarial truth seeking and just decision making—where advocates of equal status and skill subject each other's position to critical scrutiny—is not found in the actual practice of law, governance, and education. We have gone too far in idealizing adversarialism as a desirable means for confronting disagreement. Indeed, *we've gone so far with adversarialism that we have come to believe that the argument culture accurately reflects everyday reality and basic human nature.* We approach disagreements as opponents would a fight, because it aligns with a worldview that supports pursuing self-interest and winning over finding common ground and respect for others.

The Argument Culture and Adversarial Individualism

Even though the argument culture does not facilitate interactions that meet our relational and decision-making needs, it proliferates throughout public and private life. The fact that it does so, despite its devastating effects, invites a deeper look. What fosters this cultural reliance on adversarialism as a way of meeting disagreement?

If we examine the basic assumptions underpinning adversarial communication and the argument culture in the United States, we begin to piece together its alignment with aspects of a worldview privileged during the nation's founding. We find that adversarialism intersects with the ethos of rugged individualism—the nation's "can do" spirit of self-reliance.

Frontier icons like Daniel Boone and Davy Crockett personify this rugged individualism. With their wilderness-taming exploits forged amidst pioneering adversity, they symbolize independence and initiative. This folk-hero status was converted into urban success stories through the numerous "rags-to-riches" tales of Horatio Alger and the real-life narratives about self-made men, such as Henry Ford and Albert Carnegie, who purportedly pulled themselves up by their bootstraps and made monumental fortunes.

But as with adversarialism, this pervasive mythic imagination has taken individualism beyond the contours of its nation-building origins. Historian and the twelfth Librarian of Congress, Daniel Boorstin, wrote: "In history, even the great explorer had been the man who drew others to a common purpose."[10] His words encourage us to remember that individuals are always members of communities. Or as essayist Roger Rosenblatt cajoles, "Try to imagine an individual so rugged he could raise a roof beam on his own."[11]

Even President Herbert Hoover, who coined the term "rugged individualism" in 1928 to promote the nation's free market capitalism, acknowledged that a balance should be maintained between individual liberty and the public good. The United States, he cautioned, does not endow individuals with an environment that permits a "free-for-all and the devil-take-the-hindmost." Instead, he asserted,

> The very essence of equality of opportunity is that there shall be no domination by any group or trust or combination in this republic, whether it be business or political. It demands economic justice as well as political and social justice.[12]

Despite these reminders and caveats, the United States has become a nation perceived by many as out of balance, exalting individualism at the expense of community. Journalist Joannie Fischer reports that "a chorus of critics worries that the philosophy of individualism has slipped its original moorings, threatening the well-being of the nation and, ironically, individuals themselves."[13] From the reputation of baby boomers as the self-indulgent "me generation" to the unbridled Wall Street mantra that "greed is good," on through to the 2008 presidential campaign which mocked "community organizers" for not having "any actual responsibilities," the United States appears to have tilted further in favor of an idealized rugged individualism. Combine such pugnacious self-interest with an adversarial mind-set and we create the conditions where it seems it's every man for himself, or what social psychologist Kenneth

Gergen calls "the tragedy of all against all."[14] We can see such adversarial individualism at work in the argument culture's basic assumptions.

Examining Basic Assumptions in the Argument Culture

In an argument culture, the first key assumption is that *adversarial communication is required for truth and justice to prevail.* As noted earlier, this assumption is at the heart of adversarial communication in legal, governing, and academic contexts. While understandable, this assumption is founded on a *false dilemma.* It supposes that there are two views—presumed opposites—and that we must choose between them, elevating one as the truth and rejecting the other as false. While apparently promising clarity, adversarial communication actually promotes a power struggle between oversimplified and mutually exclusive positions. Faced with this false dilemma of having to be either right or wrong, individuals struggle over whose perspective will prevail at the expense of the other.

Consequently, when advocates become pitted against one another as opponents, *winning becomes the goal* in a disagreement. This second assumption follows from the first. If there are two mutually exclusive points of view, and only one can be "right," then successful advocates must ensure that their positions are victorious. "It's the urge to win," discussed earlier, that is "disastrous for relationships" whether the people involved are in a romantic relationship or a public policy debate. When winning is what matters, how victory is achieved becomes less important. This approach to engaging differences, as demonstrated throughout the chapter, opens the door to harmful communication habits, as people resort to defensive and combative patterns in an effort to win or otherwise protect their status and reputations.

The second assumption of the argument culture, that winning is the goal, generates the third assumption. If winning is a primary purpose of arguing, the third assumption is that *there must be winners and losers.* When we take this for granted, we succumb to the belief that disagreements occur within a zero-sum game. A zero-sum game insists that life is like a pie, where if one person takes a large slice, another person is stuck with a smaller slice. This belief thrives on the perception that resources—such as the pie—are scarce and that people must compete to ensure their place at the table and the size of their slice. Even when resources actually are scarce, people need not divvy up the pie competitively. We could negotiate over the distribution of the slices or reasonably determine portions on the basis of need. But cooperative options are difficult to discern or to believe in when this third assumption is expressed commonly in sayings like "First come, first served," or "I've got mine, you get yours," and "nice guys finish last."

The fourth assumption in the argument culture proceeds from the first three. When differences are viewed as irreconcilable opposites, and only one side can win, a belief develops that there must be winners and losers competing in a zero-sum game for the truth. The stakes therefore are high, producing the fourth assumption: *to be effective, we must partici-pate in the argument culture.* It appears as if there is no exit: we must fight for our side and win or else abide by the decisions made by others. Even if we refuse the adversarial approach, we still will be judged by the argu-ment culture's standards. For example, if we consider dissenting views, we may be accused of "lacking backbone" or even being disloyal. We cer-tainly risk having our perspective discounted, so it seems we must either "fight back" or take cold comfort in critique.

Believing ourselves trapped within the argument culture further reinforces our reliance on combative and otherwise corrosive communi-cation habits. As we have seen, we utilize strategies of fight, flight, or indifference in the hope of reducing the stress of adversarial disagree-ment. Yet, these communication strategies—and the accompanying tac-tics of judgment, blame, and defensiveness—end up harming us, for they escalate the conflict without meeting our relational or decision making needs. A worldview that accepts the assumptions that winning is every-thing, that there are only winners and losers, and that we must partici-pate in the argument culture (lest we be judged most harshly by it) leaves us to confront the false choice of feeling good about ourselves or representing the world accurately without vilification of others.

Transforming the Argument Culture through Dialogue & Deliberation

Engaging each other across our differences does not have to be this stressful! We need not accept adversarial individualism as an accurate reflection of who we are or how we must live. Instead, we can acknowl-edge that important human needs cannot be met when adversaries insti-gate zero-sum power struggles to "settle" disagreements. This mismatch between our worldview and our needs produces temporary, pyrrhic victo-ries and endless conflict. Once we confront the harmful impact of this ideological extremism on human relationships and decision making, we may cease to believe in the argument culture as a powerful and desirable model of interacting.

As mentioned earlier, recognizing the limits of the argument culture is an important first step. The growing awareness of the argument cul-ture's negative effects has led to numerous calls for change in public dis-course. We've heard the clamor for national dialogues on pressing issues and the pleas for civility in our discourse. We know the social anxiety produced by our divisiveness and the frustration generated by our inability to address our problems. But how do we change?

Leadership consultant Margaret Wheatley allows that it takes courage. "It is not easy to begin talking to one another again," she writes. "We stay silent and apart for many reasons."[15] Persistent acrimony and distrust have diminished confidence in our collective capacity to communicate. But knowing the source of our troubled discourse will help us answer the call to change.

We propose that adversarial individualism as a worldview and the argument culture as a context for communication are primary sources of our collective inability to address our shared needs or to solve our common problems. However, we need not abandon individualism or jettison argument to repair the damage. To disagree constructively and productively, we *must reunite individual interest with social responsibility.*

Martha L. McCoy and Patrick L. Scully of Everyday Democracy suggest that such a reunion requires "two powerful but unusual marriages:"

> The first union is between two strains of public talk—dialogue and deliberation. The process of *dialogue*, as it is usually understood, can bring many benefits to civic life—an orientation toward constructive communication, the dispelling of stereotypes, honesty in relaying ideas, and the intention to listen to and understand the other. A related process, *deliberation*, brings a different benefit—the use of critical thinking and reasoned argument as a way for citizens to make decisions on public policy.[16]

Like Tannen and so many others, McCoy and Scully call for renewed emphasis on dialogue and deliberation. We concur. When people disagree, we need a reliable mode of inquiry to help us learn, a thoughtful process of reflection to help us make sense of the differences, and a fair and reliable method of deciding what to do. Dialogue and deliberation facilitate interactions that meet those needs. But we must recognize that dialogue and deliberation cannot thrive in an argument culture, buttressed by an adversarial worldview. It's like feeding chum to sharks.

Hence, we need a second "union." According to McCoy and Scully, dialogue and deliberation must be aligned with constructive action and problem solving. Again, we agree. The possibility of "all talk and no action" is unacceptable, especially given the pressing problems we face. But what constitutes constructive action? Mahatma Gandhi, a world-renowned leader of civil rights, taught that the "means are the ends in the making." In essence, he meant that how we go about making social change influences the changes we can create.

With Gandhi's wisdom in mind, we will describe throughout the chapters how *dialogue and deliberation* rely on the practice of *treating others as we wish to be treated.* Most widely recognized as the Golden Rule, this principle forms an ethical and effective means of communication and action. The reciprocity inherent in the Golden Rule encourages us to hear others as we wish to be heard and to extend the respect that we wish to receive. It also guides our deliberations so that we consider others affected by the problems we confront and the decisions we make. When dialogue and deliberation are practiced according to the Golden Rule, they form a communication context that helps restore the equilibrium between individual interest and social responsibility.

This constructive approach to disagreement doesn't mean that every problem can be solved or every strained relationship repaired. We will continue to encounter conflicting interests and perspectives. Nevertheless, we can choose how we relate to one another and to our problems. We are quite capable, too, of making different choices in the face of disagreement, as Roger Rosenblatt observes. "The fact is that the country has consistently shown its best face and best strength when it has defined rugged individuals as those people rugged enough to come to the aid of their fellows, and intelligent enough to recognize when they need such aid in return."[17]

Before we explore dialogue and deliberation, we need to revisit some basic assumptions about everyday reality and human nature. Adversarial individualism and the argument culture have us believing that success is determined by competition and unfettered pursuit of self interest. In the next chapter, we reexamine these beliefs and ask questions anew about their capacity to depict reality and to reflect human nature accurately. The answer lies within us, as we have always known and are newly discovering.

Dialogic Communication within an Interdependent World

Our examination so far has revealed that communication across disagreement and other forms of difference is one of humanity's most vital resources for pursuits of truth, justice, wisdom, and peace. People from diverse backgrounds and perspectives equipped with abilities to hear and be heard are well positioned to contribute to the quality of their communities as well as to their own happiness and well-being.

As we have seen, however, being able to reach out to others in pursuit of mutual understanding and collaborative decision making is fraught with difficulties within the argument culture. Even in the best of circumstances, people often experience negative thoughts and feelings when they encounter others who seem to endorse contradictory views. This ordinary difficulty becomes especially challenging when we bring an adversarial mind-set to our disagreements. Such contentiousness, as expressed through the argument culture, jeopardizes our ability to accomplish anything without resorting to "a fight." As a result, combative and defensive communication habits often strain our relations and leave our shared problems unresolved.

Within the argument culture, people often approach disagreements as opponents would a fight in part because this approach aligns with a worldview of "every man for himself" in a "dog-eat-dog world." The narrative at the heart of this worldview has become so pervasive that adversarial individualism is seen by many as accurately reflecting basic human nature and everyday reality.

As noted in the introduction, however, a pressing number of *global* predicaments—such as economic and environmental crises, cross-cultural conflicts, infectious disease and international terrorism—are exposing the limits of these ideological theories and the monologic communication habits they engender. No one nation or one person has the necessary resources to survive alone. Moreover, individual actions have a domino effect. For example, a trade policy by one country has manufacturing repercussions in another country that, in turn, creates environmental pollution for neighboring countries. The effects ravage local economies and undermine the value of currencies, thereby driving up the cost of the original trading partners' product, making it very expensive to export. It's a small world after all.

Such interconnectedness redefines the boundaries between local and global politics, as it heightens awareness of the fluidity between domestic and foreign policies. One nation's internal actions have consequences abroad and, like a boomerang, the effects reliably return (but in often unpredictable ways). This globalization of twenty-first century life fuels a growing consensus that public discourse and decision making must be improved if we are to accomplish anything. The calls for civility and effective action are numerous from within the United Nations.[1] The renowned physicist Albert Einstein famously declared, "You cannot solve a problem from the same consciousness that created it. You must learn to see the world anew."

Global interconnectedness helps us to rethink the "consciousness" created by adversarial individualism and the argument culture this worldview has helped to cultivate. For instance, in the 1960s, a wildlife biologist named Garrett Hardin warned that competitive human nature made it impossible to share resources equitably and sustainably. If every villager had access to the common pasture, Hardin argued, they would bring as many cows to graze as they could. In the villagers' efforts to maximize their own benefit, the pasture soon would be overgrazed and worthless. Self-interest inexorably leads to collective demise, or, as Hardin called it, the "tragedy of the commons."[2]

In 2009, however, the Nobel Prize in Economics was awarded to Professor Elinor Ostrom "for her analysis of economic governance, especially the commons."[3] Based on decades of empirical research, Ostrom demonstrated that, contrary to the narrative at the heart of the "tragedy of the commons," many ordinary people around the world *do share common resources wisely*. From the alpine pastures of Switzerland to the forests of Japan to the irrigation systems of the Philippines, Ostrom reported on the success of "cooperative institutions that are organized and governed by the resource users themselves."[4]

When asked about the impact of her work on Hardin's theory, Ostrom replied, "People say I disproved him, and I come back and say 'No, that's not right. I've not disproved him. I've shown that his assertion that common property will always be degraded is wrong.'" Importantly, she added, Hardin was addressing a problem of "significance that we need to take seriously. It's just that *he went too far. He said people could never manage the commons well.*"[5]

In light of these findings, what would it take to govern the commons wisely in the twenty-first century? How can humanity in today's globally interdependent environments tap the potential for collaborative problem solving without succumbing to the temptations associated with tragedies such as those Hardin has identified?

To address this key question, Professor Ostrom points to *dialogic communication* and the development of *shared norms and rules for decision making* as especially valuable resources.[6] In particular, to prevent more tragic failures and to govern the commons effectively, we must reunite individual interest and social responsibility within a *dialogic and deliberative framework of connection*. In concert with Elinor Ostrom, a growing cohort of scholars, scientists, and civic leaders are rediscovering the reality of interdependence. The reason to cooperate across differences has been known to humanity for a very long time.

Interdependence

Interdependence is a reality as old as the Earth itself. Its presence is evident in the evolution of life. Take the honeybee. As it feeds on the nectar it extracts from flowers, pollen rubs off onto its body. Then the bee flies to the next flower, spreading the pollen and enabling the flowers to reproduce. The shape of the honeybee's body, as well as the length of its tongue, has adapted to pollinate particular flowers, which, in turn, have evolved in shape and color to attract the bee. The honeybee and the flower depend on each other for survival, as indeed they rely on air, water, and soil to support their entire life cycles.[7]

Human beings, too, depend on the reciprocal relationships between the bees, the flowers, and the environment. Clearly, people eat the honey that bees produce and the blossoming fruits and vegetables they pollinate. So when scientists began recording a precipitous drop in bee populations, known as "colony collapse," worldwide concern was registered over the possibility that major losses would occur in food crop production and wild plant life. Humanity's food supply was threatened.[8]

This is the truth of interdependence. The diversity of life is sustained through a network of relationships, where each affects the other in ever widening circles. Survival and well-being depend on this interconnectedness and its built-in reciprocities. Similarly, when change occurs—as with the collapse of the bee colonies—it casts a ripple effect throughout the system. Thus, each member of this planetary network must endeavor to sustain relationships—balancing individual interests and the common good.

This concept of interdependence has occupied a central place in human consciousness for a very long time. Its expression can be found among Native Americans, who teach: "what we do to everything, we do to ourselves." Similarly, indigenous South Africans adhere to the Ubuntu philosophy that maintains: "I am what I am because of who we all are." And in Europe, nineteenth-century French literature made its declaration through the lighthearted Musketeers motto: "it's all for one and one for all!"[9] Across time, geography, and culture, humanity has consistently acknowledged the interconnectedness between self and community.

Nearly every major religious and spiritual tradition also accepts interdependence as an idea governing human interactions. As a result, many sacred teachings invoke an ethic of interdependence, commonly recognized as The Golden Rule. No matter the faith or belief system, this ethic advocates individual behavior that advances the common good. For example, Christians instruct followers to "do unto others as you would have them do unto you." Likewise, the Islamic faith maintains that "none of you truly believes until he wishes for his brother what he wishes for himself."[10] When Senator McCain urged us all to "treat one another as we wish to be treated," he was summoning the ethic at the heart of these and nearly all other religious, spiritual, and secular ethical traditions.

This interdependent ethic was evident during the groundbreaking 1993 Parliament of World Religions convention in Chicago, a gathering of over eight thousand representatives from diverse religious traditions. The following paragraph appeared in the convention's "Declaration toward a Global Ethic."

> We are interdependent. Each of us depends on the well-being of the whole, and so we have respect for the community of living beings, for people, animals, and plants, and for the preservation of Earth, the air, water, and soil. We take individual responsibility for all we do. All our decisions, actions, and failures to act have consequences.[11]

As we have seen, the concept of interdependence both describes reality and inspires an ethical code of conduct; it also serves as an organizing principle of successful social change movements. Mahatma Gandhi's leadership in securing India's independence from Britain, Reverend Martin Luther King Jr.'s stewardship of the Civil Rights movement in the United States, and Nelson Mandela's conscientious resistance to apartheid in South Africa are all examples of interdependence as practiced in human action. These social change movements succeeded in the most difficult of circumstances—facing the violence and injustice of others—by adhering to the interdependent principles of mutuality and nonviolence. Such principles restore the balance in broken social relationships by treating others as they wish to be treated, rather than by imposing one's will through force.

And so we come full circle. Charles Hauss, a political scientist who specializes in the study of interdependence, writes: "For some time now most ecologists, systems engineers, chaos theorists, quantum physicists, and other natural scientists have based their work on the assumption that *every actor and action directly or indirectly affects everyone and everything else.*"[12]

This scientific discovery entered popular culture through the maxim (with varying locales): "When a butterfly flaps its wings in Brazil it can cause a tornado in Texas." The saying stems from the work of an MIT meteorologist who changed one computation in a complex weather prediction formula from .506127 to .506. "That tiny alteration utterly transformed his long-term forecast" and produced the term known as the *"butterfly effect—*the concept that small events can have large, widespread consequences."[13] Science had confirmed that interdependence governs the laws of nature. Based on this newly affirmed knowledge, human efforts to care for the environment were reinvigorated.

Earth Day began in the United States in 1970, one year after a massive oil spill in Santa Barbara, California. Its bipartisan origins and popular success enabled Congress to create the United States Environmental Protection Agency and to pass the Clean Air, Clean Water, and Endangered Species Acts.[14] Three years later, the United Nations sponsored the first World Environment Day. In 2010, the theme was "Many Species. One Planet. One Future."[15] These annual events have had a profound effect on human consciousness, including the creation of a widely used expression of the ethic of interdependence: "Think globally, act locally."[16]

Clearly, humanity has long understood the reality of interdependence. The concept has informed our cultural beliefs, our faith traditions, and our ethical codes of conduct. It also has served as an organizing principle in successful social change movements and current environmental efforts.

And yet, just as plainly, we can cite numerous violations of these very same core beliefs and sacred commitments. Around the world we witness religious zealots attacking dissenters, racial and ethnic groups warring with each other, and nation-states and multinational corporations vying for dominance through militaristic might and economic exploitation.

"This is the dilemma," said one speaker at the 2009 environmental conference on "Taking Interdependence Seriously." He asked the audience, "Why do we behave in a way that is entirely inconsistent with the reality that [we're] capable of appreciating intellectually? What is it?"[17] We turn now to examine this pressing contradiction between what people know about interdependence and how we often behave in the argument culture.

The Sticking Point

The sticking point refers to the moment in a disagreement beyond which the involved parties will not budge. At this juncture, people often throw up their hands and lament, "I guess we'll just have to agree to disagree." Such is the current moment within the United States, according to the distinguished political theorist, Dr. Benjamin Barber. He maintains that we are stuck between worldviews—between different ways of seeing our common problems and imagining how we might act. More to the point, in Barber's words, "the built-in interdependence of the ecological paradigm runs squarely up against the profoundly significant paradigm of the last four hundred years . . . [the paradigm of] independence."[18]

These two paradigms (models for understanding reality) shape assumptions, beliefs, values, and practices. As described above, interdependence affects assumptions and beliefs about what is real as it promotes a particular ethic and guides actions—as does the paradigm of independence.

As we have seen, the independence model at the root of the argument culture stems from a belief that each of us exists separately and in competition with others. Within this perspective, the state of independence actually signals an individual's maturation and a nation-state's sovereignty—the attainment of an ideal state of being. As a concept, independence also is aligned with the virtues of freedom and liberty. Because these virtues are widely recognized as ideals, it is believed that people would do well to do as they wish apart from the constraints of others. This well-established paradigm, notes Dr. Barber, represents "another set of values that we cherish, that are rooted in our history."[19]

These two sets of values—interdependent values of connection, collaboration, and compassion on the one hand and independent values of freedom and liberty on the other—have framed the nation's rich heritage. Despite this legacy, however, the argument culture sets independence *in opposition* to interdependence, and forces a choice between them.

In the developed Western nations, and particularly in the United States, the staunchest proponents of the primacy of independence base their arguments on the tenets of adversarial individualism. For them, the concept of independence aligns with the presumption of self-interest and the competition for survival.

This view is evident in Hardin's analysis of the "tragedy of the commons." As noted earlier, the possibility that individuals might attempt to maximize their own benefits at the expense of others is quite real. People confront those struggles time and time again. The difficulty with Hardin's theory as well as the insistence on pitting independence against interdependence is not that they lack insight, but that they go too far. Both ideas insist that adversarial individualism represents *the whole* of human experience and potential—and that there is no realistic prospect to cooperate for the common good. Thus, proponents of this view extol the privileging of individual interests as an inherently pragmatic and necessary choice. *This becomes a sticking point.*

For example, consider the adverse reaction to the speech by then Prime Minister Gordon Brown on "Foreign Policy in an Interdependent World."[20] News agencies around the world reported that the British prime minister used the occasion of his first foreign policy address in the United States to call for a new era of global interdependence. Specifically, Brown listed the following challenges in the twenty-first century:

> the globalization of the economy, the threat of climate change, the long struggle against international terrorism, and the need to protect millions from violence and conflict and to face up to the international consequences of poverty and inequality.[21]

These difficulties, he declared, "all point in one direction—to the urgent necessity for global cooperation." We must acknowledge, he insisted, "that our common self-interest as nation-states can be realized only by practical cooperation; that 'responsible sovereignty' means the acceptance of clear obligations as well as the assertion of rights."

Negative reaction from within the argument culture was swift and severe. Joseph Farah, a nationally syndicated columnist, took great exception. Proclaiming the virtues of independence and national sovereignty, Farah denounced Brown's call for an era of global interdependence as "evil." Speaking directly to his U. S. audience, Farah wrote,

> Here's what I want you, as an American, to remember about interdependence. It's just another name for "dependence." If you are interdependent, you are dependent. Instead of being dependent on one entity, you are simply dependent on multiple entities. That's not an improvement over dependence, it's actually worse.[22]

In addition to condemning the concept of interdependence as weakness, Farah contested Brown's characterization of challenges in this century and spurned his proposal for "responsible sovereignty." Farah concluded, "I don't want to live in an interdependent world, I want to live in freedom. I want to live in a nation that protects its sovereignty. I want to live in a nation that reveres its *independence*."[23]

Farah's objections were echoed by another longtime commentator, Phyllis Schlafly. She specifically rebuked Brown for "reject[ing] the traditional concept of national sovereignty," which she defined as "an independent nation not subservient to outside controls." Her disdain for Brown's foreign policy vision was evident. To follow his direction, Schlafly charged, would result in "a surrender of our liberty and our prosperity."[24]

Joseph Farah and Phyllis Schlafly expressed strong reservations, widely held in the United States, about the concept of interdependence and its ethical imperative for cooperation. To dispute Prime Minister Brown's vision of global interdependence, both Farah and Schlafly invoked long-held and revered American traditions of independence, sovereignty, freedom, and liberty. These traditions are to be honored and maintained. Yet, the *particular expression* given to them by these columnists and other critics is problematic, for it derives from the assumptions of the argument culture and the overreaching tenets of adversarial individualism.

Both Farah and Schlafly create a false dilemma based on the first assumption of the argument culture—that truth can only be discerned through opposition. In their rebuttals to Prime Minister Brown, the American columnists depict independence and interdependence as diametrically opposed concepts. To maintain the truth of one's independence, they contend, one must reject interdependence as false and even dangerous. The risks are significant, Farah and Schlafly claim, as they pit Brown's vision of interdependence *against* cherished ideals of freedom, sovereignty, liberty, and prosperity.

In this context, Farah and Schlafly reject interdependence as unpatri-
otic. In a worldview informed by adversarial individualism, they maintain
that interdependence has no place in United States politics. But the
country's political heritage suggests otherwise. Indeed, President John F.
Kennedy gave a speech on the Fourth of July in 1962 (to which Prime
Minister Brown repeatedly referred) that heralded the reliance on both
the Declaration of Independence and the Constitution. The Declaration
of Independence rightly asserted freedom from the *tyrannical rule* of King
George of Britain, but the former colonies still would maintain social,
economic, and eventually diplomatic relations with their neighbor
"across the pond." The Constitution, however, according to President
Kennedy, "stressed not independence, but interdependence—not the
individual liberty of one but the indivisible liberty of all."[25]

To ensure this "indivisible liberty," the Constitution provided for
three interdependent branches of government: the executive, the legislative, and the judicial. These three branches operate based on a reciprocal
system of checks and balances. In this political system, the Declaration of
Independence and the Constitution were not designed to be at odds.
Instead, these foundational documents are meant to function comple-
mentarily as the cornerstones of American democracy.

Nevertheless, an adherence to independence as a primary goal, to
adversarial individualism as a bedrock philosophy, and to monologic
forms of communication as the most effective means of conveying our
ideas appears across the United States' political spectrum. Legal theorists Lani Guinier and Gerald Torres have analyzed this phenomenon.
"Strategists on both the left and right," they say, "despite their differences, converge on the individual as the unit of power." Guinier and Torres explain:

> The conservatives argue that the group, as well as society at large,
> will benefit when more group members achieve power as individuals;
> the best empowerment strategy, they argue, is entrepreneurship and
> individual initiative. . . . Civil rights advocates argue that individual
> group members "represent" the race. . . . When black individuals
> achieve power for themselves, black people as a group benefit, as
> does our society as a whole.[26]

For all the political polarization in the country, these legal scholars
observe, people in the United States share a common vantage point. They
see things from an individual's point of view. Guinier and Torres conclude:

> Here we see both liberals and conservatives endorsing the same
> meta-narrative of American individualism: When individuals get
> ahead, the group triumphs. When individuals succeed, American
> democracy prevails.

Without a doubt, individuals matter. The ethic of personal responsibility and individual initiative are cornerstones of the can-do spirit in the

United States. Yet, a belief system that posits "the individual as the unit of power" to the *exclusion of social responsibility* is inherently problematic. Without the checks and balances between individual interests and the common good, independence and self-sufficiency can be taken to the extreme.

Take the decision made by the city of South Fulton, Tennessee, to impose a $75 fire protection fee on rural residents who live outside the city limits. If residents fail to submit the annual "pay to spray" fee, firefighters are required by law not to respond to any calls for assistance. In the fall of 2010, a Tennessee homeowner called 911 to report that his house was on fire and to request emergency services. Only that year, he had failed to pay the fire protection fee. Firefighters did not respond until neighbors, who were current on their "pay to spray" plans, called for protection for their property. When firefighters arrived on the scene, the homeowner offered to pay the $75 on the spot. The fire chief refused, and the crew stood by as the house—with the family's four pets inside—burned to the ground.[27]

The event ignited a national debate over whom to blame. The International Association of Fire Fighters condemned their colleagues' decision to let the house burn as "incredibly irresponsible" and chastised the "pay to spray" city policy as "ill-advised" and "unsafe."[28] Nonetheless, the city and the fire department had many defenders. *Time Magazine's* coverage summarized their views, disseminated over various media. A typical response, posted on the Internet, said, "The loss of the home to fire was indeed a bad situation (for the homeowner—not for anyone else)." That person's view was echoed by two columnists for a national online publication. The first acknowledged that "letting the home burn was 'sad,' but he argued that it would 'probably save more houses over the long haul' since people will now have a strong incentive to pay their fees." The other writer was more critical. He denounced the Tennessee homeowner and his family as "jerks, freeloaders, and ingrates." This harsh appraisal of the family was shared by a national television commentator, who declared that loss of home and property was necessary "to prevent people from 'sponging off' of their neighbors."[29]

The "pay to spray" defenders and the International Association of Firefighters were divided over the meaning of the Tennessee house-burning incident. The event could be seen as "either an extreme example of how personal responsibility should be the basis of American democracy or a nightmarish incident that proves how far the country has strayed from its purpose as a place where people care for one another."[30]

This tension over how to balance individual and social responsibility in a democratic society escalated dramatically when it came to making sense of a number of economic scandals. The Enron accounting scandal was among the first to draw extensive commentary and analysis.

Enron was a phenomenally successful multinational energy corporation based in Houston, Texas. For years, top executives had been "cooking the books": they inflated corporate earnings and assets and hid debts and liabilities. Their deceit initially produced amazing short-term gains and generated widespread investor enthusiasm. But the "sleight-of-hand" accounting schemes required to maintain the deception drew increasing suspicion. Eventually, a courageous whistle-blower revealed the depth of the organization's corruption. Enron collapsed within a few months and declared bankruptcy in 2001. The resulting financial fiasco was devastating.

Enron's shareholders lost nearly $11 billion dollars. Over twenty thousand employees lost their jobs, while thousands more saw their life savings vanish with now worthless retirement and pension benefits.[31] The multitude of investors, employees, and retirees demanded to know what had happened and why. They were joined by Enron's international customer base, who had been victimized by its price gouging and market manipulations, another facet of the corporation's fraudulent practices.

Dean Robb, a business consultant, points to Enron's corporate culture. His analysis represents a consensus view. "Enron's internal world was one of individualistic opportunism and exploitation." Its corporate culture was, in Robb's words:

> characterized by exaggerated individualism, low social cohesion, unpredictable changes in markets, and constant organizational restructuring, downsizings, and closings. The rules changed constantly. Since [in this culture] there is low group belonging, people are thrown back on their own individual wits and resources. Operating in this environment is somewhat like living in a chaotic jungle or swimming in a pack of sharks.[32]

Robb's analysis concluded that the *unchecked self-interest* of Enron's leadership—in the pursuit of extreme wealth, ambition, and fame—*created a disastrous corporate environment for making sound, ethical business decisions.* Not only did Enron's corporate culture allow for breaking the law in the pursuit of profit, but *it also promoted utter contempt for the welfare of others.*

During a summer heat wave, Enron's stock traders had manipulated the supply of electricity to energy markets in California. Faced with electricity shortages and rolling blackouts, the state paid nine billion dollars for energy at exorbitant rates; consumers struggled to pay their soaring power bills. The situation was disastrous for California's economy. Despite the dire circumstances, audiotapes revealed Enron's stock traders laughing about California's quandary and exchanging congratulatory expletives for the blithely chosen titles of their trading schemes, such as "Death Star" and "Get Shorty."[33]

Eventually, this unrestrained ideology of adversarial individualism accompanied by a monologic model of communication produced the (then) worst financial collapse in U.S. corporate history and a human "tragedy of all against all." The corporation's fraudulent business practices and bankruptcy filing produced tremendous suffering for its many victims and provoked a federal investigation. Enron's chief executives were arrested. They turned on each other. Each publicly denied all wrongdoing and accused the others of malfeasance. As events unfolded, the consequences were severe: ruined reputations, a suicide, an untimely death, and lengthy federal prison sentences.[34]

Lest people think that this scandal was simply the fault of a few (powerfully) bad apples, Sherron Watkins, the whistle-blower who exposed Enron's corruption, warned: "Enron should not be viewed as an aberration, as something that can't happen anywhere else, because it's all about the rationalization that you're not doing anything wrong."[35] Within less than a year, her prediction came true, as the telecommunications giant WorldCom, another corporate perpetrator of accounting fraud, crashed even more spectacularly than Enron.[36] Still, the worst was yet to come.

In late 2007, the "bubble" burst in the U.S. housing and mortgage loan markets. An encyclopedic summary provides a now oft-told version of the story:

> It was triggered by a liquidity shortfall in the United States banking system and has resulted in the collapse of large financial institutions, the bailout of banks by national governments, and downturns in stock markets around the world. In many areas, the housing market has also suffered, resulting in numerous evictions, foreclosures, and prolonged vacancies. It contributed to the failure of key businesses, declines in consumer wealth estimated in the trillions of U.S. dollars, substantial financial commitments incurred by governments, and a significant decline in economic activity.[37]

The enormous scale of this Great Recession can be measured in part by the record bankruptcy established by the investment banking firm Lehmann Brothers in 2008. The company was $600 billion dollars in debt, far outpacing Enron and WorldCom's former record losses of about $100 billion each.[38] Lehman Brothers utilized fraudulent accounting schemes and was criticized for its hypercompetitive corporate culture.[39] After the government bailout of other financial institutions, a national controversy broke out over the "bonus culture" that continued to issue exorbitant executive compensation and huge cash payouts to employees. One international banking regulator claimed that those U.S. corporations "were having massive private gains at public loss."[40]

There are richly diverse perspectives regarding the nature and sources of this economic crisis. There is little if any disagreement, however, regarding the instrumental roles that corporate corruption coupled with limited governmental oversight, regulation, or consumer protection played in creating the global recession. And yet, "the 'individualistic' convictions of Americans" remain strong.[41]

The Pew Research Center found, for example, that large majorities of United States voters are convinced "that they, and not government or big corporations, control their own destinies in the midst of the current recession."[42] While this belief is a testament to the country's resilience, it also defies the empirical evidence. In 2009, the United States Census Bureau reported, for example, that "the income disparity between the wealthiest and poorest Americans expanded to a record high."[43] Comparative economics also demonstrate that this income gap is the largest between the rich and poor in any Western industrialized nation. Professor Timothy Sneeding, an expert in the study of poverty at the University of Wisconsin, explained: "More than other countries, we have a very unequal income distribution where compensation goes to the top in a winner-takes-all economy."[44]

Other Pew surveys document that U.S. Americans believe, by a margin of six to one, that "when people don't get ahead, it's their own fault."[45] This view holds considerable appeal in its call for individual accountability, as well as in its promise of just deserts for all who are willing to work hard. At the same time, however, this perspective rests on the vision of a "level playing field," at odds with compelling empirical evidence to the contrary. Research reveals, for example, that people across the nation's economic landscape have widely differentiated access to available resources and are more or less advantaged by dominant norms and institutional structures. As a large percentage of people's personal experiences reveal, the "playing field" is skewed heavily in favor of the privileged few. Close examination of the adversarial individualist framework exposes these and other questions about the bases of unfettered individualism. Further, as we've seen, the framework's encouragement of unchecked self-interest and disregard for the welfare of others has devastating consequences.

At the same time, however, our examination does not tell us what the city of South Fulton, Tennessee should do to pay for its fire department. Nor does our analysis of the individualist framework's flaws draw a clear demarcation between private enterprise and government regulation in financial markets or health care. Later chapters will provide an overview of resources available to engage such important questions skillfully.

For the moment, the most important outcome of our examination of the argument culture worldview is an understanding that *beliefs have consequences.* The extreme focus on competitive individualism precludes the possibility of cooperating across differences and undermines governance for the common good. This recognition has led to a growing concern that "the philosophy of individualism has slipped its original moorings, threatening the well-being of the nation and, ironically, individuals themselves."[46]

Columnist Ira Chaleff has identified a particularly compelling example of this phenomenon within the legislature. "Members of Congress," he writes "are engaged in a tragedy of the commons. It is in each member's electoral interest to rail against the ineptitude of government and to run 'against Washington.'" Chaleff notes that this is "frequently a successful strategy for an individual member. But it is a disaster for the standing of the institution in the public mind." Chaleff goes on to observe that the price paid for these pursuits of self-interest is the corrosion of public trust and related democratic safeguards against tyranny and autocratic rule.[47]

Getting Unstuck

One answer to the conundrum raised earlier—why do we behave in ways that are inconsistent with empirical evidence—lies in the fact that we understand our experiences through a distorted version of a treasured philosophy. Adversarial individualism, defended by a combative argument culture, contorts the honorable tradition of individual freedom and liberty in the political heritage of the United States. Instead of a system of checks and balances, this extreme ideology breaks the bond between self and community and then pits individual "independence" against the common good. As a result, people understand life's experiences and problems from the point of view of "every man for himself."

When someone—or some organization—believes that adversarial individualism and the argument culture accurately reflect *all* of human experience and potential, unchecked self-interest and disregard for the welfare of others appears as a realistic and even responsible choice. So, for example, members of Congress continue to use populist demagoguery to pursue their political interests even if doing so compromises the public good. And business executives continue to exploit vulnerabilities even if doing so imperils the environment and countless peoples' economic well-being. Yet, time and again, this approach fulfills Hardin's prophecy of the "tragedy of the commons."

Importantly, many of the most ardent advocates of unfettered individualism point to the economic philosophy espoused by Adam Smith—one of the founders of the nation's market-based framework—as a supporting resource. Close reading of Smith's work reveals, however, that he strongly rejected an economic model driven by pursuit of self-interest alone. Smith recognized that such an approach would be devastating to individual and communal well-being, and stressed the importance of compassion, empathy, social bonds, and related humane values as drivers within the marketplace. Smith's insights underscore the important lesson echoed by today's scholars: relentless pursuit of self-interest without care for and at the expense of others inevitably compromises pursuits of truth, justice, and peace, and otherwise poses obstacles to human flourishing.

In light of these findings, what can be done to heal the breach between self and community? How might individual interest be reunited with social responsibility? David Korten is a cofounder of the nonprofit organization, Positive Futures Network. The network highlights the innovative changes people make to meet twenty-first century imperatives for a sustainable future. From this work, Korten has learned that "getting out of our current mess begins with a conversation to change the shared cultural story about our essential nature."[48] The cynical view about human nature, as expressed by philosopher Thomas Hobbes, is that life is "solitary, poor, nasty, [and] brutish."[49] This view needs to be trans-formed. We need, as Korten says, to *change the story in our head.*"[50]

The Hobbesian "story" shapes beliefs about individual abilities and collective potential. According to Korten, a narrative that human nature is "competitive, individualistic, and materialistic"[51] leads followers to rely primarily on formal military actions and impersonal market forces for security and prosperity. This same account fosters an ideology of adver-sarial individualism and an antagonistic argument culture. By giving more weight to the negative aspects of human behavior and by deriding our cooperative and caring qualities, the Hobbesian story precludes serious investigation about humanity's communicative and relational choices.

Recent neurological and social science research invites us to recon-sider this long-standing story about human nature. The research demon-strates, says Korten, that humans are "wired to reward caring, cooperation, and service."[52] Neurological studies show that the brain's pleasure center is activated by helping others and by positive emotions, such as compassion. This is a "rather remarkable finding," says psycholo-gist Dachner Kelter. "Helping others brings the same pleasure we get from the gratification of personal desire."[53] Recent research makes an even stronger assertion: psychologists found that spending money on others made us happier than if we had spent it on ourselves.[54]

Social science findings about life-satisfaction rates in different coun-tries reach a similar conclusion. They indicate that "beyond the mini-mum level of income essential to meet basic needs, membership in a cooperative, caring community is a far better predictor of happiness and emotional health than the size of one's paycheck or bank account."[55] In other words, around the world, people's well-being depends more on the quality of our relationships than on our status or "stuff."

These research findings tell a new, *more reliable story about human nature*. The new narrative acknowledges the competitive and cooperative dimensions of human behavior but also highlights the latter's role in an interdependent reality. This revaluation is based on compelling evidence. As biologist Frans de Waal asserts, "bonding has incredible survival value for us."[56] Bonding, or the quality of our connection, helps us meet our needs for acceptance, for belonging, and for meaningful contribu-tions to a community. Bonding is critical to human survival and success. We are at our best when we work together to fulfill our common needs—when we treat others as we wish to be treated ourselves.

But "human communities are only as healthy as our conception of human nature."[57] Changing the story about human nature so that it situates both our competitive and cooperative capacities in an interdependent reality is much easier said than done. The Western world has been living with the Hobbesian description of human nature for hundreds of years. Countless social, political, economic, and educational institutions have been based on the belief that humans naturally compete against and exercise power over one another to accomplish their goals. Yet necessity is the mother of invention. Our global predicaments demand that we "see the world anew."

Changing the Story

One way to reunite self and community is to reframe the human story to align more fully with available evidence. For many years now, scholars have described how adversarial individualism is expressed through competitive metaphors. Daniel Cohen recaps the well-known observation: "We routinely speak," he writes, "of *knockdown*, or even *killer arguments* and powerful *counterattacks*, of *defensible positions* and *winning strategies*, of *weak* arguments that are easily *shot down* while strong ones have a lot of *punch* and are *right on target*." These expressions, he continues, "characterize how we think about arguments, talk about arguments, and engage in arguments."[58]

Adversarial individualism partners with the argument culture to produce competitive frames for how we talk and interact with one another. As Deborah Tannen asserts, "The argument culture urges us to approach the world—and the people in it—in an adversarial frame of mind."[59] To align the story with available evidence, we need to change the metaphorical frames that structure how we think and how we relate to others. Communication scholar Ronald D. Gordon concurs, asserting that "the next breakthroughs in communication thinking and theorizing are likely to come as a result of further exercising our metaphorical imaginations."[60] Competitive metaphors do not have to be abandoned, but their influence will need to be moderated by consciously adding cooperative and interdependent frames.

Cognitive linguist Pamela Morgan provides an overview. She describes three "metaphor families": *competition, cooperation, and connection*. These metaphorical frames, she notes, "help people reason about how the world does and should work."[61] They structure how people and events are perceived and what people can imagine doing in response to a given situation. Competitive metaphors, as noted above, pit people against one another to accomplish goals. These metaphors structure human experience around the basic assumption that there are only two sides to a particular situation; moreover, one side is right, and the other is wrong.

Accepting these assumptions encourages people to engage in power struggles to determine who is right and to "win." Morgan elaborates:

> In our work on foreign policy, [we] found that when people were primed with competition-based reasoning, they tended to move toward a self-interested approach to international issues: Is the US doing more than its share? Why aren't other nations doing more? By contrast, when we could move Americans toward more cooperative thinking—"we're part of a team, we're partnering with other countries"—we were often able to overcome the fear that any intervention in another country was bullying, unwanted or inappropriate. And when primed with interdependent or connection thinking—"we're all on this planet together"—people were much more likely to want to invest in other countries' educational and social institutions.[62]

Competition is "characterized as having two separate 'entities,' a 'goal' that both want to achieve, and a situation in which *only one of the two entities can achieve the goal*," explains Morgan. This metaphorical frame sets up a win-loss dynamic. Cooperation metaphors, such as "Family, Friends, Partners, Working Groups (including Sports Teams and Military Units)" also involve two entities and a goal. But, says Morgan, "in this model the entities *choose to work together* to gain the goal."

The third metaphor family is structured around connection or interdependence. These are systems metaphors, where "the whole is more than the sum of its parts, and all parts are necessary to achieve wholeness." What makes the connection family of metaphors unique, says Morgan:

> is the sense of *equality* that is *built into it*. All of the subparts, no matter how similar or distinct, are equally important to the stability or functioning of the system. Remove one part and the system fails: it comes apart, or it stops working. That equality of parts that form the whole is the basic form or idea of this metaphor family.[63]

The environmental and nonviolence social movements tap directly into connection metaphors. Slogans such as "Love Your Mother (Earth)" and "Use Words, Not Weapons" express connection between self and other, founded on an equal regard for all. To help change the story in our heads so that it aligns with reality, we need to change the words we use to frame our thoughts, feelings, and experiences. While connection metaphors serve this purpose most directly, they also can interact with the messages framed by competition and cooperation, with equal regard. In contrast to the argument culture's cynicism, connection metaphors give greater weight to constructive information, to the possibilities of integrating self and communal interest.

A Positive Rationale for a
New Dialogic Model of Communication

Although humans repeatedly have chosen to believe in and act on the false promises of power and control, we also have worked together to sustain self and community. Over the millennia, our cooperative efforts have sustained and preserved us through both human-made and natural disasters. Though we face daunting challenges in the twenty-first century, the human family has a rich heritage of thought and action to redirect efforts toward global peace and prosperity.

We have seen from the exploration above that a central problem occurs within the ideology of individualism, its promise of self-control, and its adversarial assumptions because of the *artificial separation between self and community*. This breach contradicts the common understanding that "no man is an island" nor are many men ever just an anonymous collective. Realistically, therefore, we cannot choose between self-interest and mutual responsibilities. We must look for a way to integrate them.

We need to find a way to come together, respectful of our differences and diversity, even in the midst of deep conflict. One voice of wisdom calls to us from Central America. In an effort to help heal a nation long divided by civil war, Archbishop Oscar Romero asked El Salvadorans to consider the question "What is a people?" He called on rich and poor, the political right and left, the status quo and the forces for change to recognize the inescapable truth: "A people is a community of persons where all cooperate for the common good."[64]

An ethic of interdependence does not eliminate the personal or privilege the collective. Rather, our interdependent reality requires us to restore the relationship between the two, to *repair the breach between individual interest and social responsibility*. In the twenty-first century, we can choose to face our mutual reliance and interconnectedness and to join our efforts in an ethic of cooperation. Fulfilling this promise will require, however, a different mode of communication than that offered by the argument culture. We will need a model of communication in which, in the words of theologian Sharon Welch, "disagreement," can be seen "as an invitation to a deeper relationship."[65]

In sum, we will need to communicate in ways that foster understanding, respect diversity, and enable decision making that is responsive to the needs of all. We will need a dialogic model of communication for an interdependent world.

Adoption of such a model paves the way for us to tap the collective wisdom in pursuit of common purpose. Realizing this promise will require us to replace research driven by adversarial impulses with a deliberative approach to inquiry. The next chapter lays the groundwork for understanding and developing such an approach.

3

Deliberative Inquiry

The previous chapter underscored the importance of communicating in ways that foster understanding, respect diversity, and enable sound decision making. This chapter features a related pathway to fulfillment of communication's constructive potential in today's complex and polarized world. Deliberative inquiry, as we will see, builds on the foundation of dialogic communication and provides the promise of overcoming obstacles to sound deliberation so endemic to the argument culture.

In his forward to the Kettering Foundation's cutting-edge publication, *Democratizing Deliberation*, CEO David Matthews offers insights into the meaning of the term "deliberation," and a window into understanding the nature and role of deliberative inquiry. In the public sector, he observes, the term "deliberation" evokes a spirit of "balancing or weighing," of "thoughtfully considering a matter, in consultation with others, in order to make a balanced decision."[1]

Communication Studies scholar James Klumpp's contribution to *21st Century Communication: A Reference Handbook* provides further insight. Deliberation, he observes, "is a pattern of communication tailored to provide a particular outcome: wise and accepted choice." Klumpp goes on to note that "deliberation is a process of creative thinking and critical testing as well as a method for choosing alternatives."[2]

The art of deliberation is marked by a spirit of critical inquiry and a common quest for informed and wise decision making. By its nature, deliberation is thoughtful and thought provoking. In the private realm as in public arenas, individuals and communities may be said to be deliberative *when they tap all available resources in pursuit of the most informed and wise decision possible.*

Few people aspire to make decisions based on misunderstandings, distortions, false information, and other forms of misperception. In general, people would prefer to base their decisions on reliable, verifiable information and insights. Unfortunately, adversarial communication norms reinforce the natural inclination to confirmation bias. In the argument culture, people are strongly motivated to pursue only what is *confir-*

matory. Rather than risk being wrong or otherwise losing ground in the constant battle for stature, power or other forms of control, adversarial advocates seek support for their perspectives at the exclusion of evidence for contrary views. When confronted with information at odds with their own views, they find themselves in the difficult position of either having to give up hallowed ground and sacrificing their standing on the one hand, or clinging to a perspective in conflict with available evidence on the other.

Fortunately, recognition of our interdependence and its practical implications enables us to pursue an alternative framework for inquiry. Jonathon Haidt's dual terms "confirmatory" and "exploratory"[3] provide a helpful introduction to this framework. Within an interdependent framework, people have strong motivation to pursue an *exploratory* approach to inquiry. Although none of us has the capacity to overcome the natural inclination to confirmation bias completely, recognition of our interdependence and its practical implications encourages us to seek information and insights likely to enhance the prospect of informed and wise decision making.

Within such a framework, deliberative rather than confirmatory inquiry is both an imperative and a realizable goal. Only by opening ourselves to information and insights guided by a spirit of exploration will we be able to subject our ideas to the scrutiny of others. And only through such scrutiny will we be equipped to contribute to the collective wisdom.

Deliberative inquiry provides a critical resource for realization of this goal. This form of inquiry involves several related steps: engaging disagreement, questioning deliberatively, assessing the credibility of information, and thinking critically.

Engaging Disagreement

Earlier discussions have revealed that disagreement is seen by many in the argument culture as a threat to security and a possible obstacle to harmony and peace. It is easy to understand how and why such perceptions persist. We cannot ignore the enduring legacy of conflict experienced by countless victims of violence around the world. It is important to recognize, for example, that the previous century alone saw 227 major military conflicts, resulting in over 107 million deaths. Given this global tragedy, it is understandable that many people seek to avoid overt disagreement, conflict, and controversy.

There are times when avoiding confrontation may be necessary based on safety concerns or to circumvent lopsided power imbalances. In such circumstances, the need to ensure security or to retreat and reassess one's resources supersedes an obligation to address a conflict or engage other disputants directly. Typically though, avoidance behaviors produce little benefit. Rather than avert unwanted situations or consequences, avoidance more often serves to deepen resentments, anger, frustrations, and other sources of tension between disputants. Whether within families, organizations, or nation-states, *efforts to suppress or otherwise avoid addressing disagreements almost inevitably lead to even greater conflict.*

The globe's greatest conflicts and the tragedies associated with them provide unparalleled evidence for the need to develop tools for confronting disagreement peacefully, ethically, and effectively. As Ronald Arnett notes, dialogic ethics require "balancing relationship sensitivity and a willingness to encounter conflict in resolving a problem."[4] Constructive engagement of disagreement helps to achieve the balance to which Arnett alludes. *Disagreement,* as we will see throughout this book, is an invaluable resource for sound personal, social and communal, familial, and professional decision making. When confronted directly, honestly, respectfully, responsively, and thoughtfully, disagreement has the potential to illuminate issues otherwise not apparent on the surface.

Few deny the urgency of crossing boundaries to identify, understand, and mutually resolve issues of global concern in today's world. People who reside in the United States of America are especially well situated to contribute to this quest. Among the nation's greatest assets is its rich cultural diversity resulting from communities of heritage and affinity.

At the same time, however, moral disagreements resulting in part from clashing of incommensurate worldviews can pose challenges. In their landmark book *Democracy and Disagreement,* for example, political theorists Amy Gutmann and Dennis Thompson argue convincingly that these are formidable challenges, ones that can be addressed only if people learn to "reason together" to reach a "mutually acceptable decision."[5] Indeed, Gutmann and Thompson suggest that the very survival of democracy depends on "citizens reasoning beyond their narrow self-interest and considering what can be justified to people who reasonably disagree with them."[6]

As Gutmann and Thompson suggest, sound decision making draws on diversity as an asset and engages differences of perspective with thought and care. Constructive engagements in pursuit of sound decisions profoundly affect the quality of our personal lives and are critical to the preservation of democracy, central to peaceful coexistence across the globe, and vital to our capacity to work together with others in the service of humanity.

Earlier, we noted that fulfillment of this promise requires recognition of important differences between confirmatory and exploratory inquiry. At the heart of deliberative inquiry is a mode of questioning that reflects the spirit of exploration. In the discussion below, we feature skills and sensibilities associated with this form of questioning.

Deliberative Questioning Skills

Unlike confirmatory selection of arguments to support a chosen position, deliberative questioning involves a spirit of exploration. Deliberative questions are framed to elicit insights and information relevant to understanding issues. Such questions are defined by their clarity and ability to evoke critical thought—essential elements for addressing issues responsibly. Within the argument culture, deliberative questioning is sometimes seen as threatening to one's position or status. An interdependent dialogic communication framework allows participants to reach a shared recognition that the quality of our lives depends on our abilities to *make discerning judgments together.*

The development of deliberative questioning skills requires practice and attention. In the example below, for example, we see Kim asking questions that obscure rather than clarify the issues raised by Darren:

> **Darren:** I think that the United States should send more money to help alleviate hunger in refugee camps around the world. After all, we have much more food than we can possibly consume. Sometimes we even pay our farmers not to produce.
>
> **Ruth:** I see what you mean, Darren. But the fact is we don't even adequately feed people in the United States. Just yesterday I read an article about severely undernourished children in Chicago.
>
> **Kim:** What did the undernourished children look like? What nationality were their parents?

Ruth's observation about undernourished children in U.S. cities was relevant to Darren's point regarding the nation's obligation to provide greater assistance to displaced people around the globe. In contrast, it is not clear how answering Kim's questions would have helped decision makers consider whether the United States should send money to help alleviate hunger in refugee camps. Suppose, however, that Kim had asked the following question:

> **Kim:** Ruth, how long have the children you read about lived in the United States? It was my understanding that the children cited in the article had just arrived in Chicago and that the local authorities were making sure the children were properly nourished.

Framed in these terms, Kim's question is *relevant, thoughtful, and thought provoking.* As such, Kim's revised question potentially contributes to a clearer understanding of the relevant issues, strengthening the promise of sound decision making.

As we learned from our opening explorations of the argument culture, the pursuit of adversarial goals often mitigates against effective use of deliberative questioning. In his book, *The Audacity of Hope,* Barack

Obama explains this phenomenon. People "trained either as lawyers or as political operatives" within the argument culture, he notes, tend to "place a premium on winning arguments rather than solving problems."[7]

The classic example of a prosecutor questioning a defendant in a murder trial graphically illustrates how this mentality encourages legal advocates to *use questions in service of adversarial goals*. The defendant has been accused of domestic violence. The prosecutor confronts the defendant with the following question: "When did you stop beating your wife?" Framed in this way, the question is designed to "trap" the defendant, rather than providing jurists the information they need to assess the individual's guilt or innocence. By compromising our pursuit of truth and justice, this form of questioning undermines sound decision making.

Most of our discussion thus far has focused on the importance of deliberative inquiry to decision making within the body politic. However, questioning skills are similarly important in personal contexts. For example, Alma would like to breast-feed her infant, but she is unable to do so. The baby also reacted badly to cow's milk during the first few days of his life. The pediatrician advised Alma and Qun to use a soy-based formula for the first year of his life. Alma has read two recently published, peer-reviewed reports that indicate some researchers are challenging prevailing views on infant nutrition. The reports suggest, for example, that a poor early performance on cow's milk does not necessarily predict a baby's long-term reaction toward it. The reports go on to say that some babies who initially do poorly on cow's milk later thrive on it.

As is so often the case in the context of personal decision making, Alma and Qun have limited time available to pursue additional information and insights. Given their circumstances, they will need to make the best possible use of readily available resources. They will need to ask themselves, "what do we need to know in order to make a good decision?" and "how can we acquire this knowledge as efficiently as possible?" Among the most important resources available for informed decision making in this and nearly all other deliberative contexts are *facts*. The discussion below provides an introduction to this deliberative resource.

Facts

When we speak of *facts*, we are referring to statements that are *empirically verifiable*. Statements of this kind are open to inquiry and scrutiny through the *use of our senses—either on their own or enhanced by experiences and the tools of science—to establish the claim's accuracy*.

"Simple" factual claims are relatively easy to verify or refute through these means. When Henry asks how many people are in a particular room at a given time, and Julia responds that there are 25, empirical verification of her claim is uncomplicated. So long as we can agree on how and what to count, this type of inquiry does not often lead to dispute.

Similarly, when someone states, "it is raining outside," we are able to verify (or refute) this statement using our senses. The statement, "Asha teaches philosophy at a public university" is empirically verifiable as well. So long as we share an understanding of who we have in mind and what we mean by "teaches philosophy," we can verify (or refute) this statement empirically.

Generally speaking, significant common ground regarding how to assess the truth of each of these claims enables us to "settle" the question of their accuracy with limited difficulty. This does not mean, however, that we will never disagree on "simple statements of fact." Our senses can deceive us. The philosopher Descartes noted, for example, that a stick in the water appears curved. Further examination would reveal that the stick is straight, but initial impressions, relying on perception alone, could result in disputes about the nature of the stick.

Many claims about the natural world fall into this category. Prior to the development of telescopes and related instruments, many people believed that the earth was flat. From the vantage point of sitting on the beach at sunset, the earth's horizon looks decidedly "flat." We can certainly understand why people believed that a ship sailing too far from land would "fall off" the earth. With the aid of scientific instruments, space travel, scientific reasoning, and mathematics, however, humanity's understanding of the earth's shape has evolved. Today, few remain wedded to the idea that the earth is flat.

However, many scientific claims about the natural world are not considered "simple" in this way. For example, establishing the truth of *causality* claims is more difficult even with the aid of scientific resources and reasoning. When scientists assert that global warming is caused primarily by fossil fuels, for example, they are expected to present compelling evidence in support of this complex claim. Not only must they establish that global warming exists (a factually verifiable or deniable claim), but they also must present compelling evidence that the cause of this phenomenon is fossil fuel (rather than the countless other possible causes put forward by scholars on the subject).

Once a scientist or group of scientists has presented evidence in support of a causal claim, others collaborate in assessing the reliability of the available evidence. If a strong majority of qualified scientists find the evidence compelling, the claim is (typically) considered "true" until (or unless) compelling evidence is provided to the contrary.

While natural scientists contribute facts such as these regarding the natural world, social scientists contribute facts about the human condition. Sociologists, for example, offer research findings about the nature of society. Some of their findings are "simple," such as those identifying the number of adults within a township who do not have employment outside the home at any given time. This type of social scientific finding is relatively easy to verify or deny. More often, however, social scientific findings are complex, such as findings related to the *reasons why* so many people in the village remain unemployed outside the home. Determining the reliability of this type of finding requires more complex deliberative inquiry.

Importantly, in this and every other decision making context, it is not enough simply to *find factual claims or other forms of information.* Consider, for example, that a person "surfing" the World Wide Web today will encounter more information in an afternoon than the average person living the Middle Ages encountered in a lifetime! Factual claims and related forms of information are in plentiful supply to people fortunate enough to have access to the Internet. Fruitful insights and reliable information, however, are not so readily available. Given these circumstances, the abilities to *discern more or less credible sources* and to *assess the reliability of information* take on special importance.

Source Credibility

The discussion below introduces tools for discerning *source credibility,* a particularly important form of deliberative inquiry. Discerning the credibility of a source can be as mundane as deciding whether to ask one's boyfriend, one's sibling, or one's parent, "do I look good in these jeans?" Based on your personal insights regarding each of these possible sources, who among them would be more or less likely to provide a loving but honest assessment? Which, if any, of these sources comes equipped with an especially refined sense of fashion? These are among the factors to consider as you discern the credibility of these sources.

Source credibility also can affect significant matters of public policy, such as the health care debate within the United States. What weight should decision makers give physicians, nurses, insurance companies, patients, politicians, and pundits as sources in determining what to do about health care policies?

At times, source credibility even can become a life-and-death matter. This is especially true in end-of-life care decisions. Definitive assessment of source credibility is rarely possible in such cases, and yet there are key indicators available to those to whom we must turn for a judgment.

Importantly, for example, *vested interests* and *partisanship* potentially compromise the credibility of otherwise expert witnesses. When a tobacco company pays a researcher to "test" the safety of their products, for example, the resulting testimonial must be subjected to special scrutiny. Deliberative inquiry of sources must take careful account of such potential conflicts.

But these are not the only potential challenges to a source's credibility. Discerning the *relevance* of a source's *expertise* is another important feature of critical inquiry. Consider, for example, the role Chief Justice Roberts might be able to play in assisting policy makers assigned the task of framing policies related to capital punishment. On the one hand, Justice Roberts would be highly credible in articulating relevant legal precedents. He would not, however, be able to serve as a credible source of information regarding the strengths and limits of capital punishment in deterring crime.

As this example reveals, discerning a prospective source's *credibility* is both an important and complex part of the deliberative inquiry process. In general, pursuing peer-reviewed reports, articles, and books from scholarly sources at accredited academic institutions provides a useful starting point for inquiry. In general, these resources tend to provide the most reliable information available on a given subject.

Importantly, however, identifying credible sources is only one of several steps required to assess the reliability of available information. Among other things, all sources are inherently partial in ways to be explored in future chapters. As we will see, even the most thoughtful, competent, and careful researcher is vulnerable to the limits of vision associated with individual and group partiality. Further, as experts in every field are aware, even the most credible sources are fallible. No person or group is immune to these shared human traits.

Assessing Information Reliability

To help minimize the risk of error in the face of fallibility and partiality, credible sources collaborate with colleagues within and across disciplines to develop and apply standards for the assessment of findings. Tapping reliable information from credible sources requires basic awareness of these standards. To illustrate, consider the following example.

In July 2009, scholars from a number of "highly respected international peace institutes" challenged one another's findings regarding whether "war is becoming more or less deadly—or even on how to count the dead." According to newspaper accounts, one prominent group of researchers found that "the true body count over a half-century was at least three times higher than" another renowned group's finding. Meanwhile, yet another researcher raised the tally "to 41 million people slain since the end of World War II." According to this respected scholar, 231 million people lost their lives as a result of warfare during the 20th century.[8]

In part, the different findings reflected diverse research methodologies. The initial group of researchers, for example, "relied on estimates by demographers, historians, and epidemiologists, supplemented by figures from the media, governments, and nongovernmental groups." This group did not include "one-sided violence increases" such as the Rwanda genocide, or "deaths from disease, hunger, and criminal and organized violence." In contrast, the "challenging" researcher's data were based "on statistics by U.N. agencies and humanitarian and human rights groups." According to this scholar, even these statistics are inadequate because they "omit more than 70 million deaths from executions, repression and starvation in Stalin's Soviet reign of terror and the politically engineered Ukraine famine, Hitler's genocidal campaign against the Jews, and Mao Zedong's 'Great Leap Forward' from 1959–61."[9]

This example vividly illustrates different approaches to fact-finding. Within the argument culture, the researchers' diverse accounts might offer partisan political advocates ammunition in support of their cause. To win their case or to gain allies in their quests for victory, these advocates would be likely to choose the studies that most fully supported their causes. For example, peace activists seeking to prove humanity's evolutionary progress might be inclined to adopt the initial group's findings. In contrast, defense contractors might be inclined to use the challenger's findings to support their calls for increased military funding.

In a book aptly titled *How to Lie with Statistics*, Darrell Huff exposes readers to the multiplicity of ways statistics can (and are) used to serve adversarial goals within the argument culture. As Duff's account reveals, statistics by their very nature may be used, either unintentionally or intentionally, to mislead.[10]

Cynics within the argument culture might use these examples to illustrate the naïveté of anyone who turns to research of this kind in pursuit of untainted knowledge or truth—making the case that all fact-finding research is designed to provide tools for manipulation and exploitation of the masses. An interdependent culture of engagement, however, enables decision makers to use deliberative inquiry to make informed assessments of researchers' findings. In the case at hand, for example, deliberative inquiry enables us to assess the measures and related methodological underpinnings of each study. We can *distinguish* a researcher's *partiality* (an inevitable feature of the human condition) from *partisanship* (a product of the argument culture). Partiality informs us of the source's perspective—how everything from personal upbringing to professional training can influence a source's particular inquiry. But partisanship leaps over particular forms of inquiry toward predetermined conclusions that serve one's "side," without much regard for fact-finding or thoughtful assessment. We take in and *assess the multiplicity of sources representing a diversity of voices and stakeholders* available on the subject. Recognizing partiality without succumbing to partisanship enables us to enhance the prospect of securing reliable information and insights.

As this exploration reveals, assessments of statistical findings and related research require not only confidence in the researchers' credibility but also other assessments. Within an interdependent culture of engagement, statistical data and related research findings should satisfy at least the following standards: It should come from the *most credible sources*; rely on the most *valid measurements* available; be *current*; and be *representative*.

The discussion above reveals both the importance and the complexity of securing verifiable factual information. Through deliberative inquiry, decision makers are able to question source credibility, to discern and assess the validity of diverse research methodologies, and to apply related means for assessing the degree to which they can trust the verifiability of factual claims.

Deliberative inquiry must also uncover and address beliefs outside the empirical domains explored thus far. Often, even when we agree on the facts in a given situation, we find ourselves disagreeing on *values*. Sound deliberative inquiry requires cultivation of the ability to discern and understand this grounding source of beliefs.

Values

The term *value* is difficult to define. Sociologists, political scientists, philosophers, psychologists, communication scholars, and anthropologists are among those who have sought to bring clarity to this important, but complex, construct.

Argumentation theorists Karyn Rybacki and Donald Rybacki provide a fruitful overview of common definitions:

- Values are intangibles linked with the vision people have of "the good life" for themselves and others.
- Value is a general conception of what is a good way to live or to behave.
- Value is an enduring belief that a specific mode of conduct is personally or socially preferable to another way of being.
- A *value system* is an enduring organization of beliefs concerning preferable models of conduct or being along a continuum of relative importance.
- Values may be defined as concepts that express what people believe is right or wrong, important or unimportant, wise or foolish, good or bad, just or unjust, great or mean, beautiful or ugly, and true or false.[11]

As this overview reveals, *values* are those commitments to elements in life, whether intangible, relational, or material, that we associate with *flourishing*. Examples of commonly embraced values include security, peace, liberty, privacy, fairness, and friendship.

Value beliefs include a broad range of *perspectives regarding what is right and wrong, good and bad, more or less important, and so on.* Examples of commonly embraced value beliefs include the views that fairness is right, integrity is good, cheating is bad, abusing children is wrong, and moral courage is admirable.

Unlike statements of fact, value claims fall outside the domain of empirical verifiability. Consider, for example, the following value statements: "People should be kind to one another." "Peace matters deeply." "Children are precious." In each case, verification of the "truth" or "falsity" of the claim does not depend on empirical verifiability. Indeed, generally speaking, value statements are not appropriately assigned qualities such as "true" or "false."

Value Hierarchies

The elusiveness of verifiability regarding the reliability of value statements is even more evident in the context of value hierarchies. A *value hierarchy* is an *ordering of values*. In many deliberative contexts, the most contentious differences are attributable not to different values but rather to conflicting value hierarchies.

Conflicts regarding the best way to respond to public safety threats in the United States illustrate the problems caused by value hierarchies. Following 9/11, the government suspended a number of civil liberties previously held dear. Surveillance of communications without warning, violations of privacy through invasive screenings at airports, and the use of interrogation techniques illegal under Geneva Convention rules were among the casualties of the government's efforts to insure public safety.

Importantly, these shifting policies did not reflect a shift away from the nation's commitments to privacy, the rule of law, or freedom from governmental surveillance. These values continue to hold sway in the United States, even among those who support the policies in question. However, in the face of perceived grave dangers to public safety, the ruling administration privileged security over other cherished values.

Among the most passionate opponents of these policies were those people whose value hierarchy places rule of law and related civil liberties above other values. From their perspective, compromising these liberties is a costly and potentially grave error. In support of this view, they offered historical evidence that violation of civil liberties in the name of security nearly always risks tyranny, injustice, and corruption. In light of these concerns, they admonished the nation's leaders to restore the rule of law, even in the face of security threats.

Conflicting value hierarchies of this kind are at the center of nearly all policy disputes. Health care, environmental and energy policies, economic policies, immigration policy, and foreign policy are among the many deliberative contexts in which the greatest source of conflict is found in competing value hierarchies, rather than in different values.

Importantly, this phenomenon is not limited to deliberative contexts involving governmental policy making, or even difficult decisions facing two or more people. The most difficult personal decisions are often traceable to sets of cherished values in conflict with one another as well.

Consider, for example, personal decisions routinely facing air flight travelers. As the methods used to screen passengers have become increasingly invasive, people must decide whether to forgo the benefits of air travel to protect their privacy or vice versa. A significant number of people faced with this set of options have decided to abandon air travel.

A majority, however, have continued to use this mode of travel despite the cost to their privacy.

Thus far, we have identified questioning skills and information competencies (such as the abilities to acquire and responsibly use reliable information and insights) and assessing the credibility of information (such as the abilities to discern facts, values, and value hierarchies) as key elements of deliberative inquiry. At the heart of these and related processes is critical thinking, an art vital to successful deliberative inquiry.

Thinking Critically

Critical thinking skills are widely acknowledged as central to sound deliberative inquiry. But the term has proven difficult to define. Educator Edward D'Angelo defines critical thinking as "the process of evaluating statements, arguments, and experience."[12] Philosopher John Chaffee adds that thinking critically involves our "active, purposeful, organized efforts to make sense of the world."[13]

While D'Angelo and Chaffee's insights provide a helpful starting point, they do not fully convey what we have in mind when we invoke the concept of critical thinking. In the following paragraphs, we will provide a brief overview of the many related elements that make up the critical thinking process. Taken together, these elements enable us to *identify, articulate, and apply reasoned, responsive assessments of issues, assumptions, facts, values, inferences, beliefs, perspectives, orientations, frames, and ultimately available options.*

Critical thinking is important, says cultural critic bell hooks, because it empowers people to evaluate and improve their life circumstances. Whether a person is wealthy or poor, hooks asserts, "thinking critically is at the heart of anybody transforming their life."[14] The abilities to seek out and evaluate relevant information on a given topic, to question and assess the value of different perspectives and to draw reasoned conclusions involve processes by which people meaningfully change their minds and their lives. While we cannot control all the external circumstances that shape daily living, we can relate to them proactively through critical thinking skills.

Cultivating critical thinking skills depends on several basic characteristics. Foremost among them is a willingness to take other people's perspectives seriously, especially when their positions differ from our own. Although much in the prevailing argument culture appears to undermine this view—as evidenced by the explosion of hostile radio "shock jocks" and sensationalistic television talk shows—there are nevertheless at least three very good reasons to consider alternative perspectives with care. First, as noted earlier, it is important for us to recognize that *every perspective is necessarily partial.* This means that each person's point of view represents one "side of the story." Each person's side is potentially important and may even be valid when tested or otherwise subjected to scrutiny, but it is inevitably only a part of the whole story.

As a result of our inherent partiality, *alternative viewpoints enhance our own understanding by representing other sides of a story.* Thus, we actually depend on each other for the fullest understanding of any complex, controversial issue. Given the necessarily partial nature of a point of view and the need for a thorough understanding of complex issues, the third reason to take alternative perspectives seriously is *our fundamental interdependence.*

As we learned from the book's opening chapters, not only do our perspectives on complex issues develop in interdependent ways but also our ability to survive on an everyday basis depends on collective efforts. Taking other people's perspectives seriously is a basic necessity in peaceful coexistence.

Given this mutual reliance, critical thinkers in a culture of engagement express a commitment to respectful and constructive decision making. This commitment entails critical thinkers being self-reflexive about their own values and assumptions and responding thoughtfully to others. It also means that critical thinkers respectfully engage emotional, creative, and intuitive sources of their own and other people's knowledge. The critical thinker is someone who communicates his or her ideas utilizing the skills explored throughout this book. It is through constructive engagement that the critical thinker is able to subject ideas to other people's scrutiny.

When we apply our critical thinking skills, we convey to others that an issue or decision matters to us and that we are willing to engage it seriously. Yet, the argument culture often discourages us from embracing critical engagement. For many, these experiences lead to a common and especially harmful misconception. Within the argument culture, critical thinking is often confused with cynicism.

The Challenge of Cynicism

Cynicism is a common substitute for critical thinking. As a mode of response, cynicism dismisses the need for thoughtful decision making by adopting the argument culture's "interpretive framework" that sees "greed, corruption, hypocrisy, competition, and the like [as] permanent and pervasive in human affairs."[15] People who accept this framework often view attempts to reach across differences in pursuit of mutual understanding as naïve and foolhardy.

When we consider the sometimes overwhelming sense of helplessness often felt when we take in the news of the day, it is not difficult to understand the appeal of this mind-set. Stories about entrenched and violent conflicts, poverty, greed, and corruption at home and abroad can be devastating to morale. We can certainly understand why many turn to cynicism as a defensive measure.

Given these circumstances, it is not surprising to encounter at least one person in our circle of family and close friends who responds cynically to most situations. Annette finds herself confronted with this phenomenon daily as her life partner, Alex, approaches nearly all political issues with an air of cynicism.

Recently, for example, Annette learned of an opportunity to participate in a town hall meeting exploring the risks and benefits of a plan to expand offshore drilling activities in the coastal region she and Alex call home. When she mentioned the chance to participate in this gathering and invited Alex to join her, his response was contemptuous. How, he asked her, could she possibly imagine that convening a town hall meeting would do any good? No amount of discussion would make any difference because, in his words, "powerful oil companies and politicians have already decided what to do through 'back room deals.'" Alex asserted that "the real world operates via corruption and greed." He concluded with "Wake up Annette, it's all rigged anyway!" and urged her to save her energies for pursuit of her own (and his) self-interests.

Annette wavered in her determination to go to the town hall meeting. She could just stay home, order pizza, and watch their favorite reality show with Alex. But deep down inside, she didn't feel right about it. She went to the meeting. There she heard community members speaking out—some enraged, some in tears, some seemingly only wanting the spotlight of attention. At times during the meeting, she found herself reflecting on Alex's sentiments. Listening to some of the most powerful figures at the event openly denigrating environmental activists as anticonstitutionalists, for example, Annette was struck by the prevalence of partisan language.

But she chose to stay; eventually she learned that some neighbors were forming a local grassroots coalition. They planned to have information tables at the neighborhood grocery store and park, as well as at the elementary school, to educate the community about economic and environmental impacts of offshore oil drilling and what they could do about it. Annette felt excited about participating in information gathering and dissemination. She discovered too that she enjoyed talking one-on-one with people and feeling a sense of connection with others.

Annette and Alex's responses illustrate some of the significant differences people bring to specific situations. When we consider the seemingly debilitating circumstances confronting those pursuing environmentally conscientious decision making, Alex's response may seem to reflect a healthy realism. And yet, ironically, this pessimistic response guarantees that entrenched powers remain. Civic engagement, community building, and informed decision making can lead to social change. Refusing to participate, despite the validity of some negative concerns, allows the status quo to continue.

As we have learned, many within the argument culture cling to a Hobbesian worldview in which people inevitably pursue self-interest at the expense of other values. Despite compelling evidence to the contrary, the "dog-eat-dog" narrative of humankind continues to hold sway within the argument culture. Through this lens, fear is privileged, disabling prospects of hope. Replacing critical thinking with negativity, the cynic within the argument culture obscures feasible options. With an air of arrogance and superiority, the cynic diminishes the prospect of dialogic communication. In these and related ways, the cynic's orientation sabotages the very possibility of civic engagement, deliberation, and constructive change.

Although seemingly justified given the compelling challenges confronting humanity in today's complex world, unthinking and habitual pessimism harms public policy making. This despairing response, though understandable, poses tragic and lasting threats to the very fabric of democracy. In sum, this posture fuels the very corruption and greed it is designed to address! Philosopher Martha Nussbaum offers related insights. She notes, for example, that cynicism creates disabling obstacles to our abilities to unmask prejudice and expose and uproot injustices. As a result, cynicism "is the best recipe for continued oppression of the powerless."[16]

Among the other negative effects of cynicism is that it can prevent individuals from taking responsibility for changing what affects them directly. Another is that it perpetuates the argument culture's narrative regarding humanity's inevitably "nasty and brutish" nature. This phenomenon can prove especially debilitating to those committed to pursuing a more reasoned, just, and peaceful global environment.

In a moving speech directed to the Muslim community around the globe, President Obama addressed this phenomenon. "The cycle of suspicion and discord must end," he noted, lest we continue to "empower those who sow hatred rather than peace, and who promote conflict rather than cooperation that can help all of our people achieve justice and prosperity."

President Obama went on to propose a "new beginning between the United States and Muslims around the world; one based on mutual interest and mutual respect; and one based upon the truth that America and Islam are not exclusive, and need not be in competition. Instead, they overlap, and share common principles—principles of justice and progress; tolerance and the dignity of all human beings."[17]

Cynicism fails to account for such interdependence. Accepting the Hobbesian narrative, the cynic is driven by an uncritical pessimism. This orientation in turn fosters negativity, arrogance, and related strategies for avoiding meaningful connection and personal responsibility. Through these habits and practices, the cynic subverts critical thinking and otherwise compromises sound decision making.

Importantly, however, the "opposites" of cynicism are equally problematic. Nonreflective agreement, unqualified submission to others' perspectives, groupthink, and acquiescence to authority pose obstacles as harmful as those associated with cynicism. In many ways, these seemingly diverse responses to complexity mirror each other in their failure to reflect critical thinking—and hence in their subversion of deliberative inquiry.

Groupthink and Related Phenomena

Earlier, we discussed the argument culture's discomfort with conflict. As we have seen, this worldview has limited options for responding to passionate disagreements: potentially destructive forms of confrontation, self-interested advocacy, or acquiescence to a dominant individual or group. People struggle with how best to respond. Some individuals and groups abandon their positions to avoid conflict. Other people use a variety of adversarial strategies to prevail. Earlier chapters underscored the debilitating consequences of both of these approaches.

Within the context of deliberative inquiry, *nonreflective conformity, acquiescence to a dominant individual or group, uncritical loyalty, and related efforts to belong* can be especially harmful. Many of us can recall a time during our youth, for example, when a sense of *belonging* was particularly important to us.

During her first semester at Robert Fulton Junior High School, Megan was determined to avoid being an "outsider." She soon discovered, however, that being an "insider" sometimes required her to violate her basic sense of what is right. For example, group members sometimes made fun of people whose dress or demeanor differed from the accepted norm. It was expected that Megan would participate in the mockery, despite the risk of causing emotional suffering to an innocent classmate. Megan decided that the cost of being "in" was too great. Rather than participate in the mainstream group's hurtful behavior, Megan chose to remain faithful to her sense of humanity. By not conforming to unacceptable demands, Megan not only gave up the status of being an insider but also became the object of ridicule herself.

It is easy to understand why, under such circumstances, a large number of students at Megan's school elected the path of acquiescence, conformity, and unwavering loyalty to the dominant group. And yet, upon reflection, we can see how and why many of those who gave in to the pressure would later have cause for regret. National Public Radio's "pick of the day" recording on May 10, 2010, underscored the anguish so often associated with such experiences. In "Caught in the Crowd," singer Kate Miller Heidtke described a time when she turned her back and "just walked away" from a high school friend being bullied. Her chorus conveys heartfelt remorse: "If I could go back, do it again; I'd be someone you could call friend. Please, please believe that I'm sorry. Please, please believe that I'm sorry."[18]

Social scientists have identified this type of acquiescence to groups and related phenomena as significant obstacles to human flourishing. One especially harmful form of such behavior is known widely as *group-*

think. Psychologist Irving Janis defines this phenomenon as *"a collective pattern of defensive avoidance."* As you read Janis's list of eight groupthink symptoms, consider how embracing an interdependent culture of engagement might help to prevent these conditions:

1. An illusion of invulnerability, shared by most or all the members, which creates excessive optimism and encourages taking extreme risks

2. An unquestioned belief in the group's inherent morality, inclining the members to ignore the ethical or moral consequences of their decisions

3. Collective efforts to rationalize in order to discount warnings or other information that might lead the members to reconsider their assumptions before they recommit themselves to their past policy decisions

4. Stereotyped views of enemy leaders as too evil to warrant genuine attempts to negotiate, or as too weak and stupid to counter whatever risky attempts are made to defeat their purposes

5. Self-censorship of deviations from the apparent group consensus, reflecting each member's inclination to minimize to himself or herself the importance of his or her doubts and counterarguments

6. A shared illusion of unanimity concerning judgments conforming to the majority view (partly resulting from self-censorship of deviations, augmented by the false assumption that silence means consent)

7. Direct pressure on any member who expresses strong arguments against any of the group's stereotypes, illusions, or commitments, making clear that this type of dissent is contrary to what is expected of all loyal members

8. The emergence of self-appointed mindguards—members who protect the group from adverse information that might shatter their shared complacency about the effectiveness and morality of their decisions.[19]

Janis has documented numerous perilous decisions resulting from groupthink. He writes:

> Year after year newscasts and newspapers inform us of collective miscalculations—companies that have unexpectedly gone bankrupt because of misjudging the market, federal agencies that have mistakenly authorized the use of chemical insecticides that poison our environment, and White House executive committees that have made ill-conceived foreign policy decisions that inadvertently bring the major powers to the brink of war.[20]

The decision-making processes prior to the preemptive attack by the United States on Iraq in 2003 illustrate the vulnerabilities outlined by Janis. Many officials in the administration publicly expressed a sense of invulnerability. Research reveals that few within the leadership circle appeared to have posed deliberative questions regarding the potentially complex moral, social, and political issues associated with the proposed action.

Groupthink is not limited to any single political party or partisan position. The Republican administration's decision-making pattern explored above mirrors Democratic President Kennedy's nearly catastrophic handling of the Cuban Missile crisis several decades earlier. Researchers have unearthed groupthink as the single most salient cause for the decision making that brought the United States to the brink of a nuclear war.

Similarly, former Secretary of Defense Robert McNamara testified about his efforts to raise questions about Democratic President Johnson's approach to the Vietnam War. A primary architect of the administration's war strategy, McNamara eventually came to question the legitimacy and effectiveness of his own counsel. After carefully consulting available information, McNamara's conscience convinced him to urge that the administration change course. In particular, he counseled the president "to negotiate peace." McNamara's efforts to shed light on and to question his political party's war strategy reportedly succeeded only in "hastening his own ouster from the Cabinet."[21]

One of the primary factors motivating these symptoms of groupthink is the desire to create and maintain group cohesiveness. As groups form, members naturally want to develop a sense of community. Within the argument culture, however, people often confuse argumentation between group members (particularly if it involves challenging a leader's views) with disloyalty toward the group and as a potential threat to the group's achieving their desired outcomes.

Janis points out that if "group members had been less intent upon seeking for concurrence within the group they would have been able to correct their initial errors of judgment, curtail collective wishful thinking, and arrive at a much sounder decision."[22]

Critical thinking through deliberative inquiry offers an antidote to groupthink. When groups commit to thinking critically, they question assumptions, inferences, information, and perspectives. They encourage disagreement and the expression of diverse views. They seek wise, well informed decisions, rather than a false sense of cohesion. They reward community members who introduce relevant new information and encourage open sharing of alternative perspectives. They deplore censorship in any form, even if it is self-imposed. They value deviations from apparent group consensus because they understand that such discussion protects them from judgment errors and premature confidence in the group's decision.

Had "insiders" in the Bush, Kennedy, or Johnson administrations been receptive to diverse perspectives and had they engaged in deliberative inquiry, they might well have spared countless people terrible suffering and saved the nation's taxpayers hundreds of millions of dollars in war expenditures. Had they pursued deliberative inquiry and dialogic communication throughout their tenure, these national leaders might have helped to usher in an era fulfilling humanity's great promise.

Context

Throughout this chapter, we have focused on the role deliberative inquiry can play in helping to tap collective wisdom in pursuit of the best possible decision in any given context. Among other things, we have featured questioning skills and related critical thinking skills needed to discern more or less reliable sources of information and insight.

We've learned, for example, that when encountering complex issues, decision makers position themselves well by asking deliberative questions informed initially through the following frames: "What do we need to know to make a reasonable and responsive decision in this case? Where can we turn for the most reliable information and insights? How can we best equip ourselves for sound decision making?" And in the process, we've uncovered important differences between inquiries of this kind within an interdependent ethic and inquiries framed within an individualist argument culture.

There is, of course, much more to be said about the nature and role of deliberative inquiry in informing sound decisions. Future discussions will illustrate, for example, how deliberative inquiry informs advocacy and decision making in concrete contexts. Before moving to these steps, however, another key feature of deliberative inquiry remains to be introduced. Perhaps more than any single variable, *context* profoundly influences the nature of the choices available to decision makers at any given moment.

To begin, it is important to recognize that all decisions within the practical realms of our personal, civic, professional, and social lives are *situated*. Available options exist within a place and time. How we frame the relevant issues, circumstances, and options is contingent, in part, upon where and how we are situated, and the collective wisdom available to us at any given moment.

The ancient philosopher Heraclitus once famously said that you cannot step into the same river twice. As the water flows, he observed, the river changes. Similarly, with each passing moment, circumstances evolve, insights change, issues are reconceptualized, people's needs and interests change, and so on. In this sense, each moment in human history is unique. Deliberative inquiry requires that we be mindful of contingencies and that we make realistic assessments of circumstances and constraints. There are many factors that define any given moment, and we must consider all of them carefully when using the resources outlined in this chapter.

Dialogue, the subject of the next chapter, offers an effective means of addressing these challenges. As we will see, dialogue connects inquiry with reflection and responsiveness, fostering conditions for overcoming the obstacles and realizing the promise inherent in deliberative approaches to inquiry.

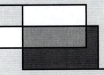

SECTION TWO

Dialogue

Dialogue and Civility

Calls for dialogue are not new. We have heard the entreaties for national dialogues on a variety of subjects from improving race relations to civility in politics to ending bullying in schools. Yet we hear much less about what these well-intentioned initiatives produce. Perhaps dialogue's effectiveness is underreported in the media, or possibly it manifests over the long term rather than in the here and now. But more often than not, the calls for dialogue appear only as momentary flashes in the public sphere. In the absence of demonstrable accomplishment, dialogues are perceived as events channeling "sound and fury, signifying nothing." Why, if dialogues seemingly fail so often to help us bridge diverse perspectives or work through shared difficulties, do we keep calling for them?

The Need for Dialogue

In the opening chapters, two major obstacles to dialogue and deliberation were identified: adversarial individualism and the argument culture. We discovered how the worldview inherent to adversarial individualism inadequately describes human nature and reality. Its competitive "me, me, me" orientation, when taken to extremes, becomes an ideology promoting unchecked self-interest and disregard for the welfare of others. As we've seen, these hyperindividualistic beliefs and behaviors are reinforced by claims that life entails a relentless striving for survival, to be "won" only by the "fittest." It is no surprise, then, that this "reality" demands that people pit themselves against one another in endless power struggles.

To cope with the tension of living in an apparently nasty and brutish world, we address our differences and disputes through the argument culture. Using this lens, we rely on a range of confrontational communication habits—primarily judgment, blame, and defensiveness—to promote our interests and to protect our reputations. We expect others to be similarly strategic and combative in their efforts. Unsurprisingly, then, the strain of ever-present antagonism leads many to seek social refuge. Most immerse themselves in homogeneous, like-minded groups, righteously separated from others by wedge issues and buttressed by polarizing leaders and a partisan media. Others withdraw altogether. Mired in apathy or cynicism, they become resigned to "bowling alone."[1]

Together, the argument culture and adversarial individualism produce an increasingly uncivil and undemocratic society. Social relations deteriorate and intractable problems persist, making it difficult to govern ourselves wisely or well. Public events can spiral into violence and tragedy. On March 3, 1991, Rodney King, an unemployed construction worker on parole, had been drinking and speeding. After a high-speed chase, police pulled him from his car and beat him with batons. He suffered a fractured skull and damage to internal organs. From his balcony, George Holliday observed and videotaped the attack. The acquittal in 1992 of the police officers accused of assaulting King sparked riots in Los Angeles, which caused 53 deaths, thousands of injuries, and extensive damage to property. On the third day of the riots, King addressed the public and uttered the plea, "Can we all get along?" His plea seemed to be asking for a resolution to centuries of racial strife. Georgetown Professor Michael Eric Dyson comments: "It was a critical question at a moment of crisis that forged our human bonds with one another. It grew up out of the hope and the desire, especially of people of color, to see this nation come together."[2]

The rioters paid no heed to King's plea. Indeed, some commentators derided him for helping the entrenched powers that had allowed police brutality and racial profiling to flourish. In such contexts, dialogue stands little chance of success. Even under less traumatic circumstances, ideological extremism that legitimizes incivility and a "take no prisoners" partisanship leaves people with no rational reason to communicate.[3] Why risk an open exchange with one's "opponent?" What "real" gains could a conversation produce? Without cogent answers, skeptics reject dialogue as "all talk and no action" and a "touchy-feely" waste of time.

Ironically, contentious conditions—leading to situations where communicating across differences is unlikely—often generate repeated pleas for dialogue. Unfortunately, those very conditions also raise enormous barriers to the opportunity for meaningful change. Why do people in times of stress and difficulty still reach out to one another for a conversation, despite the purported failures of dialogue to accomplish something concrete? The answer emerges from a more comprehensive understanding of the intersections among human nature, social reality, and communication.

Throughout this volume, we assert the importance of individual liberty and personal responsibility. But we also maintain that an ideological adherence to a competitive human nature and an antagonistic reality distorts the truth. This distortion prevents the crucial recognition that, while capable of independent thought and action, humanity's common welfare requires cooperation. In short, people need one another.

The Harvard Study of Adult Development can attest to that. Since 1937, researchers have tracked a group of male Harvard graduates, interviewing them at regular intervals about their lives and well-being. Dr. George Vaillant, director of the study, has witnessed the participants' adult lives unfold over the last several decades. The study's significance, he found, did not revolve around individual successes or failures but rather in how these 268 men responded to the vagaries of life. Even for these talented and elite Harvard graduates, all of whom had the brass ring within their grasp, Dr. Vaillant concluded, "the only thing that really matters in life are [their] relationships to other people."[4]

The human need to connect with others in meaningful ways reflects our social nature. This fundamental fact about the human condition is confirmed by international surveys on life satisfaction and happiness. These studies document that the ability to meet basic material needs such as food, shelter, and medical care is vital to people's sense of well-being. However, this research further reveals that when human beings achieve the economic stability required to meet their basic material needs, obtaining more income and possessions does not increase their experiential well-being. In country after country, people report greater satisfaction with their lives based on the quality of their social relationships than on the acquisition of material wealth.[5] In essence, these surveys consistently find that rather than status or "stuff," it is our relations with families, friends, and coworkers that—as one advertising campaign asserts—are "priceless."

This international research underscores what was stated most eloquently by the 17th-century poet John Donne: "No man is an island, entire of itself; every man is a piece of the continent, a part of the main."[6] This famous verse proclaims humanity's fundamental interconnectedness and thus our entwined prospects for a happy and satisfying life. With this understanding of our social nature and interdependent reality, we realize a compelling reason to communicate: what we think, feel, and do affects our own and each other's happiness and well-being.

Consequently, we need communication practices that facilitate self-expression *and* meaningful connection, especially across our differences and disagreements. As we have learned thus far, such practices need to include honestly sharing thoughts and feelings, listening with an open mind, and a sensible and sensitive mode of responsiveness. Were we to communicate this way, we would experience a greater sense of engagement in our communities and also improve our ability to act together in common purpose. Thus *the calls for dialogue continue, for we yearn for a means of communicating that promotes both individual interests and the common good.*

The problem for dialogue, therefore, is not that the concept is deeply flawed or that the process is a waste of time. The sticking point emanates instead from the tensions between our lived experiences and social needs on the one hand and our ideological beliefs and behaviors on the other. We need to belong and to contribute meaningfully to caring communities, but we tout our independence and communicate combatively.

Despite this mutual need for connection and cooperation, too many people rely on the "my way or the highway" approach to communication. It doesn't work. We may feel gratified at the short-term prospect of "being right," but the trade-off results in social isolation and intractable problems. Moreover, when faced with significant differences or disagreements, adversarial communication escalates directly to intransigent conflict. This approach is untenable because, although sanctioned by ideological norms, we now know that the divisive language of "judge, blame and defend" cannot serve our relational needs nor resolve our shared problems.

We need to redirect the incentive to win at another's expense. But in a combative and competitive culture, what could be more important than winning? Psychologist Michael P. Nichols tells us that "few motives in human experience are as powerful as the *yearning to be understood*." This desire is so strong, he explains, because the experience of "being listened to means that we are taken seriously, that our ideas and feelings are known, and, ultimately, that what we have to say matters."[7] Given our social nature, human beings thrive when our needs for acceptance, recognition, and belonging are met in meaningful relationships. As the Harvard study and the international research cited above attest, the basic human desire to know and be known is more important than surplus material wealth or privileged status.

The human need to know and to be known keeps returning us to the art of dialogue. We turn to a dialogic exchange because it allows us to say what is on our minds and in our hearts and to find out what matters to those who see things differently. As we interact, we may express the thoughts, feelings, and experiences that inform our personal views and respond to the cares and concerns motivating others. This capacity to integrate self-expression with responsiveness to others makes it possible to link individual interests with the common good. *Through dialogue, then, we can engage in ways that value our relationships as much as we do our convictions.*

And yet, even as dialogue brings individuals together for a sincere and mutual exchange, participants still may succumb to the adversarial habits of the argument culture. Interactions can deteriorate into competing monologues, where individuals vie for attention and "air time." When the topic truly matters, the oppositional impulse to win can distort the dialogic process. Participants may fall back on judging differences negatively, blaming others for the "problem," or defending their own positions or reputations.

To overcome this combative impulse, we investigate the contested concept of *civility*. Like dialogue, civility is oft called upon and regularly scorned. Typically, the pleas for civility ensue when public debate becomes too polarized or an important social norm is transgressed.[8] But, in the argument culture, the call for civility is often strategic, serving as a "cudgel one side uses to smack the other." As a result, the entreaties to treat others respectfully are reduced to political gamesmanship, with "opportunism posing as high-mindedness."[9]

When the concept of civility is not being exploited to feign the moral high ground, it has been employed to keep others "in their place." One need only think of the countless public reminders to be "ladylike"[10] or to refrain from being "uppity."[11] Historically, this brand of civility has aimed "to effectively silence and punish marginalized groups"[12] in order to maintain inequality in a democratic society. In numerous ways, then, the concept of civility has suffered both the whims of partisanship and the abuses of power.

Partisans and cynics alike may bid civility "good riddance." But Professor A. C. Grayling cautions that "the loss of civility means that social feeling has been replaced by defensiveness" and a "breakdown of mutual tolerance and respect."[13] The consequences for societal well-being are severe. As noted above, the judge-blame-defend cycle of the argument culture obscures the many rational reasons to communicate. By the same measure, a lack of civility diminishes the very opportunity for communication. Everyday slights, rudeness, and disregard create a reluctance to engage others at home, school, the workplace, and in the public square. Moreover, incivility's pervasiveness has so strained relations that it has changed the quality of our personal and public lives.

Recent studies confirm increasing rates of social isolation in the United States. One such study found that "intimate social ties—once seen as an integral part of daily life and associated with a host of psychological and civic benefits—are shrinking or nonexistent."[14] Researchers learned that one of every four U. S. residents has no one with whom they can talk about personal troubles; most others claimed only one or two close confidants. People "may have 600 friends on Facebook.com and e-mail 25 people a day," says sociologist Lynn Smith-Lovin, "but they are not discussing matters that are personally important."[15]

In fact, social media is a site of cyberstress for many. A 2011 survey found that "Incivility causes Americans to change their online behavior— 49% report that they have defriended or blocked someone online, 38% stopped visiting an online site because they were uncomfortable, and 27% dropped out of a fan club or online community or forum."[16] In short, these and similar studies have found that we're lonely and that we are losing confidence in civil society to help us reconnect.

Despite these struggles, civility can be reenvisioned to serve our social nature and interdependent reality. We begin by moving away from the historic emphasis for civility—decorum, manners, or rules. In their most benign guise, these traditions of propriety and protocol may facilitate cordial interactions. But a concept of civility-as-etiquette is not robust enough to be effective in the divisive combativeness of the argument culture.

Civil Communication

To repair social ties, a revitalized civility must transcend the boundaries of relating only to one's own "kind" whether determined by identity or ideas. It also should go beyond the superficial "niceties" reserved for small talk and strangers. To be worthwhile, civility should serve as a baseline of conduct and, where feasible, facilitate cooperation, particularly across differences and disagreements. Significantly, too, civil behavior must be practicable even within the divisive confines of the argument culture.

We reframe the concept of civility to address these concerns. In this and the following chapter, we envision *civility as a means of communicating respectful regard for each other as human beings.* Civil communication, therefore, represents a *choice* to interact respectfully on the basis of personhood, rather than on preferences or partialities. It does not depend on attaining agreement, nor is it sacrificed to discord. Civility, thus defined, is a fundamental commitment to act as if each other matters. It is, according to philosopher Megan Laverty, "the practice of interacting communicatively with others while remaining sensitive to their dignity."[17]

This respectful regard may be conveyed through a variety of expressions that treat others as they wish to be treated, that is, as human beings. These expressions may be as simple as an acknowledgement or important as a refusal to demonize. Civil interactions may be fleeting, as when a teenager with only a few grocery items nods "thanks" to the man with a fully loaded grocery cart who allows her to go ahead in the checkout line. Or they may even be lifesaving, as when elderly neighbors keep tabs on one another or drivers refrain from road-rage retaliation.

Civility, when defined as the respectful regard for human dignity, also shapes nonviolent social action. For example, theorist and social activist Kay Whitlock describes how civility informs acts of protest. "We can challenge that which we experience as violent and unjust," she explains, "without degrading, humiliating, or silencing others." Whitlock maintains that a commitment to restraint does not constrain effective protest. "We can express strong viewpoints and confront one another in principled ways without trying to eradicate one another."[18] These and other forms of nonviolent communication enact Mahatma Gandhi's moral stance mentioned in chapter 1—"the means are the ends in the making."[19] We must choose to be civil in order to bring about a civil society.

Thus reframed as communication's Golden Rule, *civility empowers people to become allies in a common cause of mutual recognition.* This effort fuels prosocial interactions as well as social change. And though "recognition doesn't put food on the table," psychologist Michael Bader asserts, it is a powerful incentive to act together in common purpose. He reminds us that, historically, the social movements that "had the most staying power and the most impact" motivated people not only on the issues, but also on the basis of their "needs for connectedness, recognition, and agency."[20] At their best, these nonviolent social movements formed a "beloved community."[21]

Civility matters, as A. C. Grayling concludes, because it "fosters a society that behaves well toward itself, whose members respect the intrinsic value of the individual and the rights of people different from themselves."[22] As an expression of human dignity, civility also lays the groundwork for dialogic communication. For if dialogue is the means whereby we know one another as we wish to be known, civility makes the *knowing* possible. Therefore, the public calls for civility and dialogue continue because people need an ethical and effective means of communicating for social connection and mutual understanding.[23]

In the next section, we reenvision dialogue and civility to address humanity's social needs and interdependent realities. This realignment necessitates an evaluation of dialogue's definition and purpose as well as its reliance on civility. We begin with a recent media report that highlights dialogue's potential.

Reenvisioning Dialogue

A popular San Francisco newspaper columnist recently offered a moving account of a neighborhood dispute *gone right*. He began with the following introduction:

> Everyone knows how neighborhood disputes play out in San Francisco. It starts with a difference of opinion. There's an exchange of correspondence, which becomes increasingly confrontational. Somebody complains to a city agency and the ensuing maze of red tape frustrates everyone. The next thing you know, it's a blood feud. People pick sides, neighbors glare at each other, and everybody lawyers up. Today, on Geary Street, we would like to offer another path. It is a message of hope, understanding, and the *awesome power of conversation*.[24]

The rest of the column was devoted to presenting the facts of the case. The owner of a coffeehouse and a neighborhood resident disagreed as to whether tables and chairs could be set out on the sidewalk in front of the café. The resident held that sidewalk seating would violate local fire codes and thus present a safety hazard. The dispute unfolded in the typical manner and predictably, over the course of the next seven months, tensions steadily increased. The columnist noted that, "Frosty letters were exchanged. A City Hall hearing was scheduled . . . and things were getting ugly."

When the columnist first took up the matter in the newspaper, "anger and hard feelings [had] built up" between the café owner and the neighborhood resident and "mutual distrust" had become entrenched. But though they were separated by only one city block, the two disputants had never met. After the newspaper column appeared describing their plight, the resident walked over to the coffeehouse and talked with the owner. "It made all the difference," the columnist later declared.

Seated together in the café, the resident began the conversation by offering an apology to the owner. "I didn't realize it was going to be this Kafkaesque journey" that "ended up putting you through hell." In response to this overture, the owner quickly surmised that the resident "was sincere and not malicious." The resident remained adamant that the owner comply with fire safety regulations, but he regretted "the way he expressed his concern." Despite "all the emotion and misunderstanding," the coffeehouse owner "accepted the chance to bury the hatchet." The conversation ended on a positive note, with the resident announcing that "I'm going to do my best to drum up business for your store . . . and I'm going to come in for coffee." "Hopefully," the columnist concluded, these two neighbors will "keep talking."

Human-interest stories like these usually focus on the successful outcome. Indeed, the café owner complied with the fire code and, once given the go-ahead from the city, will be able to provide sidewalk seating for customers. But the dispute's resolution wasn't the main point, and it wasn't what ultimately made for a satisfying "feel-good" story. The moral of this story goes beyond the successful outcome of safely providing sidewalk seating at a café. Though public safety and profits for a small business clearly matter, the central "message of hope [and] understanding," as the columnist indicated, emanated from the act of dialogue.

By talking face-to-face, the disputants *came to know one another* and, in the process, *repaired their damaged relationship*. Had they waited for City Hall to issue a ruling, there would have been a resolution. But a bureaucratic decision would have been imposed—for better or worse—without attending to the mistrust between parties. Neighborhood tensions would likely persist and perhaps even escalate. Instead, as they talked through their disagreement, these San Francisco neighbors transcended the usual impasse of asserting convictions *or* expressing care. They utilized the "awesome power of conversation" to reunite individual interests and the common good.

Characteristics of Dialogue

When we use the term *dialogue*, we have in mind a *process of communicating with others—a sincere and mutual exchange involving inquiry, reflection, and responsiveness.* Dialogic communication involves interacting with one another—as did the coffeehouse owner and the neighborhood resident—rather than the monologic modes of talking *to, at, or for others*. These one-way patterns of communication may appear in contexts such as a lecture delivered "to" an audience or a warning issued "at" drivers to buckle up or risk a ticket. Similarly, a politician may speak "for" her constituents, just as a judge may rule on behalf of people residing within the court's jurisdiction. Each of these unilateral speech acts is familiar and serves a purpose, but none are designed to support a sincere and mutual exchange between people.

Communicative interactions count as dialogue if the participants endeavor to know and understand one another as each wishes to be known and understood. This emphasis on sincere, mutual inquiry is central to identifying dialogue. It also distinguishes dialogue from other communication practices more germane to the argument culture, such as competitive debate. In the table below, several key distinctions between competitive debate and dialogue are highlighted.[25]

Competitive Debate . . .	Dialogue . . .
Is oppositional: two sides oppose each other and attempt to prove each other wrong	Is collaborative: two or more sides work together toward shared understanding
Has winning as a primary goal	Has a mutual commitment to know and be known as a primary goal
Assumes one right answer and defends it as one's own position	Assumes fallibility, seeks balanced partiality[26] and investigates differing views
Listens for flaws and to develop counterarguments	Listens to learn and understand
Challenges others' views, including values, assumptions, and beliefs	Inquires about others' views, including values, assumptions and beliefs, and reflects critically on one's own
Prioritizes factual assertions as truth	Integrates facts, feelings, values, interests, and beliefs to discern meaning
Seeks closure by gaining compliance with one's views and position	Comes to closure when participants experience being heard and responded to meaningfully

This table depicts significant distinctions between the formats of dialogue and competitive debate. The obvious difference occurs in the way that people relate to one another and to each other's ideas. Traditional competitive debate, as a method for argumentation, draws on the rhetorical tradition that truth emerges from a clash of views put forth by opponents. The issue with mainstream adversarial approaches to debate is not that people argue about their disagreements; rather, the negative aspects of a competitive model of debate flow from the following characteristics.

> A conception of communication that focuses on the individuals and, thus, pushes the notion of community aside; that focuses on the end effect and, thus, ignores the means; and that presumes the possibility of certainty and, thus, denies the open-ended creativity of communication.[27]

Dialogue is also a means of communication that allows for disagreement and conflict. Participants still may assert their own positions and question the positions taken by others. They can argue, offering principled refutation for consideration. But the "defining characteristic of dialogic communication," write W. Barnett Pearce and Kimberly A. Pearce, "is that all of these speech acts are done in ways that hold one's own position but allow others the space to hold theirs, and are profoundly open to hearing others' positions without needing to oppose or assimilate them.[28]

For over twenty years, the Public Conversations Project (PCP) has applied skills developed in family therapy to heated public controversies. In 2001, the organization facilitated ongoing dialogues between committed activists on opposing sides of the abortion conflict. The participants were willing to talk with one another (which made dialogue possible), but they had to overcome years of seeing each other as the "enemy."[29] PCP helps those with opposing views learn how to know and understand one another.

Sociologist Kenneth Gergen describes the process. "The meeting began with a buffet dinner, in which the participants were asked to share various aspects of their lives other than their stand on the abortion issue."[30] Following the dinner, those present were invited to speak as unique individuals—rather than as representatives of a position—on the topic. They were encouraged to describe their experiences and ideas, to share their thoughts and feelings, and to ask questions about which they were curious. To help in this process, the PCP facilitators asked participants to respond, each in turn and without interruption, to three major questions:

1. How did you get involved with this issue? What's your personal relationship, or personal history with it?

2. Now we'd like to hear a little more about your particular beliefs and perspectives about the issues surrounding abortion. What is at the heart of the matter for you?

3. Many people we've talked to have told us that within their approach to this issue they find some gray areas, some dilemmas about their own beliefs or even some conflicts . . . Do you experience any pockets of uncertainty or lesser certainty, any concerns, value conflicts, or mixed feelings that you may have and wish to share?

Answers to the first two questions typically yielded a variety of personal experiences, often stories of great pain, loss, and suffering. Participants also revealed many doubts and found themselves surprised to learn that people on the other side had any uncertainties at all.[31]

As a result of this dialogue and extensive follow-up efforts, the activists experienced "a more complex understanding of the struggle and a significantly rehumanized view of 'the other.'"[32] The sincere interest and respect expressed during the process made for more productive interactions and more informative exchanges. While the participants remained committed to their original positions, they were not as polarized around the issue, nor were they "demonizing" those with whom they disagreed. They related to one another as allies, seeking to know and understand their different views.

The Public Conversation Project provides an important exemplar, as does the earlier exchange between the coffeehouse owner and the neighborhood resident. Both examples demonstrate how dialogue helps to connect people as they express their differing views. These exemplars, too, underscore the need to distinguish dialogue from other means of communication. We have learned that dialogue is *not* designed to make choices about specific actions, although it often serves deliberation and decision making. Nor is dialogue intended for persuasion, although people may change their minds in the process. A sincere and mutual dialogue does not even depend on finding common ground, although shared interests and agendas may be discovered. *Dialogue is meant to facilitate mutual recognition and understanding*—deterring expectations of advocacy and action.

Dialogue's Purpose

With all the conflict over the planet's pressing problems, why bother with dialogue? Shouldn't we just do something instead? As noted earlier in this chapter, critics typically dismiss dialogue as a waste of time, producing "all talk and no action." With such widespread disdain, the question, "why dialogue?" is rarely taken up.

And yet, as we have seen, people have compelling reasons to communicate, including the nearly universal wish *to know and to be known.* This desire for mutual recognition and understanding is crucial in creating a happy and satisfying life, for nearly everyone needs relationships where they experience acceptance, belonging, and being able to contribute meaningfully to community. At the same time, disagreement and differences are also part of the human condition, generating special needs to communicate in the face of conflicts.

One of the primary reasons we engage in dialogue, then, is to meet our relational needs of mutual recognition and understanding, particularly when confronting issues produced by dissent and diversity. With this overarching purpose in mind, we next address three interrelated processes inherent to dialogic communication.

In the face of differences and disagreements, a primary reason to dialogue is *to encourage greater awareness and understanding of diverse perspectives*. Every person comes to a dialogue with a complex set of identities, worldviews, and experiences that "both enable and inhibit particular kinds of insight."[33] The term *perspective* refers to how these particular insights interact to shape an individual's views on a given topic or situation.

For example, many divorced fathers have lost custody cases, but not all draw the same conclusions from their experiences. A father may be heartbroken over the court's decision, or he may be resigned to the outcome because he is convinced that children "belong" with their mother. He might possibly be satisfied, because he is using the custody battle as leverage for retaining his stock portfolio. Although each man is relating to the same circumstance—the lost custody case—his perspective on what that loss *means* may vary.

This variation in meaning-making requires conversationalists to become *aware* of each other's outlook as well as to *understand* diverse views. Consider the basis for Gerald and Alicia's disagreement. The two students were sitting in the university's cafeteria, looking over the course schedule for the upcoming semester. Alicia was distressed that the required course she needed was offered only at night.

"I can't take the course at night!" she exclaimed.

"Sure you can!" said Gerald, "you don't have another class and you're not working nights."

"You don't understand," Alicia protested. "It's a long walk from the classroom to the bus stop and I don't want to wait alone for it at night."

"The campus shuttle comes every fifteen minutes," replied Gerald. "What's the big deal?"

Seeing Alicia's frustrated expression, Gerald thought a moment more about what she had said. He looked at her and asked sincerely, "Are you really afraid to walk alone at night on campus?"

"Gerald," Alicia said, "didn't you hear Octavia and me talking earlier? She walks to the parking lot with her car keys between her fingers. We're taking a women's self-defense class in the fall."

"I never thought about night courses that way before," said Gerald. "I've just always taken whatever classes I could get into."

Gerald and Alicia's disagreement started from a place of ignorance—they were each unaware that the other *could* or *would* see things differently. Gerald wasn't aware that campus safety was a concern for women and so didn't anticipate Alicia's objection to a night course. For her part, Alicia had assumed that Gerald heard her conversation with Octavia and so knew about their worries and their plan to take a self-defense class.

The disagreement intensified when Alicia and Gerald reacted defensively to each other's perspective. "Whenever we are defensive," explains communication consultant Sharon Ellison, we "create a reality that revolves around a *power struggle*." She continues, "A power struggle is essentially a fight in which we use our words, tone of voice, and body language . . . in order to gain control."[34] One way to interrupt an emerging power struggle is to slow the conversation down. Then we can stop the cycle of "judge, blame, and defend" long enough to calm ourselves and consider another response.

After thinking for a moment, Gerald asked a sincere question in order to understand Alicia's point of view. Though still a little riled, she was able to provide more information about her assumption and concerns. Gerald's reply that he hadn't "thought of it that way before" increased the opportunity for understanding. A sincere inquiry conveys curiosity, not judgment. Gerald and Alicia could describe their different perspectives without insisting that only one of them be right.

The lived experience of feeling defensive and feeling understood is quite distinct, according to communication professor Ronald D. Gordon. "When people feel defensive, they want to *strike* out," he explains, "when they feel understood they want to *reach* out."[35] In the upcoming listening chapter, we describe responsiveness as a verbal "reaching out" that communicates understanding and being understood. For example, we can convey that we understand others by acknowledging their point of view. This small act of responsiveness matters. "Even when opposing parties are reluctant to express agreement with each other," conclude three Stanford University researchers, "the sense that grievances were noted and taken seriously can be a meaningful outcome."[36]

Our efforts to increase awareness and understanding of diverse perspectives lead to one inescapable conclusion: "There is always more than one side to every story!" This means that alternative viewpoints hold the promise of enhancing our own understanding of a contested issue or situation, precisely because they represent other sides of a "story." A willingness to explore all sides reveals another important reason to dialogue: *to learn more about ourselves and the world in which we live.*

We can expand our horizons because dialogue goes beyond individuals simply exchanging previously formed views. The fact that there are always "two" sides to every story is but another way of saying that *meaning-making is social.* If we examine individual views more closely, we can see larger societal forces at work. As noted above, a person's perspective is formed from the intersections of identities, worldviews, and experiences. But identities are themselves social phenomena. For example, what does it mean to be a woman? Each individual woman doesn't decide in a vacuum. Definitions of womanhood vary over time, place, and culture. They also are affected by public institutions—such as education, the marketplace, and faith traditions—and by relationships with one's family, friends, and social networks. In essence, then, learning about a person's point of view is akin to being able "to see the world in a grain of sand."[37]

Another way that meaning-making is social is that it is shaped through language. Examples abound in daily life. If we heard gossip that described casual sex as having a "friend with benefits" or as promiscuity, would the different accounts affect our opinion? What do we believe we know about a person who identifies as a fan of *Jersey Shore* or of *Masterpiece Theatre*? Does it matter if we declare the glass half empty or half full? While it may be widely recognized that naming things influences what we can know about them, we are not always aware that such interpretive framing[38] is in effect—until we encounter someone else who sees things differently.

These encounters help us to learn about ourselves and the world. Although this is an essential reason to dialogue, we are not always prepared for what we discover. We may find ourselves deeply challenged, as did Gordon and Frank when they first heard that a Pennsylvania Amish community had forgiven the gunman who shot to death five girls in their one-room schoolhouse, before killing himself. The media reported that an "Amish neighbor came that very night, around 9 o'clock in the evening, and offered forgiveness to the [gunman's] family."[39]

Gordon sighed. "Wow, I don't get how they could do that—I don't think I could ever forgive someone who shot my child."

Frank was quiet. Tersely, he said, "I know what I would do."

Gordon shook his head. "Now Frank," he said, "you know that retaliating doesn't solve a thing."

Frank defended himself. "It sure does. 'Vengeance is mine,' sayeth the Lord."

"The Bible also says to turn the other cheek," said a piqued Gordon.

"Well," Frank retorted, "you said that you're not going to do that, are you?" The two men were silent for a moment. "I wouldn't hurt anyone," Frank announced. "But I still don't know how they could forgive a killer."

"Neither do I," admitted Gordon. "I wonder what that says about us?"

Gordon's question captures the challenge of learning about oneself and the world from a different point of view. "Human beings may think individually as well as in dialogue," explains philosopher Trudy Govier, "but we seek to confirm our thoughts, our words and reasonings about the world together with other people."[40] In short, we feel more confident about our perspective when others validate it. When a person encounters someone "who has an entirely different way of viewing and experiencing the world," maintains an expert in interfaith dialogue, it "unsettles my sense of security with regard to my own worldview."[41]

It takes courage, therefore, to ask the question, "I wonder what that says about me?" and to reflect honestly about the possible answers. But Stephen Nolt, a specialist in Amish history and culture, found that people around the globe did just that. In an interview given one year after the tragedy, Nolt relayed that the Amish community's moral example inspired international interest in reexamining the concept of forgiveness. People were "not necessarily imitating what the Amish did exactly," he said, but they were "thinking about forgiveness as a complex and difficult but important process and trying to apply that to [their] own lives, [their] own context . . . [It] has really been a heartening development."[42]

How might we develop the courage to cope with the "unsettling" experience of seeing oneself and the world differently? In such circumstances, individuals typically perceive a choice "between feeling good about themselves and representing the world accurately." Unfortunately, as noted in chapter one, "people often take the first option."[43] To save face or to defend a position, we may use judgment and blame to distort the meaning of others' perspectives. At times, too, people may react with prejudice or bias out of a fear of the unknown.

Initially, such self-protective efforts prevent many people from seeing things from another point of view. Differences and disagreements appear too threatening. But as the renowned education scholar Parker J. Palmer reminds us, "to learn is to face transformation."[44] And though many of us explicitly value the growth that comes from learning, we may hesitate "to enter into relationships requiring us to respond as well as initiate, to give as well as take."[45] But should we choose such reciprocal interaction, we might experience the third interrelated reason for dialogue: *to strengthen relationships and build trust.*

It isn't easy, but people continue to call for dialogues as a trustworthy way to connect across differences and disagreements, especially when the stakes are high. Tio Hardiman is director of Crisis Mediation at Ceasefire, an antiviolence program. In a radio interview, he described dialogue as an integral component in the organization's efforts to prevent gang violence in Chicago's neighborhoods:

> We have guys, we call them violence interrupters and outreach workers. The violence interrupters are like the first wave of guys that go out. They get wind of conflicts in the community and they go and *they talk to guys on both sides.*[46]

Ceasefire workers effectively engage community members in conversation because many are former gang members and some are ex-offenders. They understand gang culture and have credibility within the community. They utilize dialogue to help others, as Hardiman says, to "make sense out of the madness."[47] The dialogic skills alone can pay off. One young drug dealer explained that an outreach worker "taught me how to look at things from different points of view." That's why, when faced with a conflict, he called his Ceasefire contact rather than retaliate.[48]

In 2007, Ceasefire's violence-interrupting conversations were a first step in working with 900 "high-risk" youth to help them get off the streets and back to school, jobs, and social services. Studies conducted by the United States Department of Justice and the Johns Hopkins Bloomberg School of Public Health have proven that Ceasefire's model reduces violence. Their success is being replicated in neighborhoods across the nation and even in war-torn Iraq.[49]

When it comes to healing social divides, many communities rely on dialogue. They experience sincere and mutual exchanges as "talk with a purpose."[50] For example, interfaith groups regularly hold dialogues to "pave the way for peaceful coexistence."[51] For the same reason, interracial dialogues have been indispensable for reconciliation: "face-to-face interaction can reduce conflict . . . and dispel stereotypes."[52] Dialogue has a role in helping us develop the courage to see the world anew because people "develop trust through interaction and conversation, in relationships *with* each other."[53]

Despite these constructive outcomes, many people hesitate to engage in dialogue. They may be convinced that everyone is out only for themselves in this nasty, brutish world, or they may not have much experience communicating outside the cycle of judge, blame, and defend. If the ideological dominance of adversarial individualism and the argument culture isn't difficult enough, there's the fear of the unknown or anxieties over the possibility of change to dampen dialogic enthusiasm. But the chief obstacle to dialogue is not any of these concerns. It derives instead from their cumulative effect. *The problem,* to paraphrase the feminist scholar Audre Lorde, is that *we have few patterns for relating across our human differences as equals.*[54]

We don't know how to act. It's quite understandable, for we typically don't witness dialogic interactions in our communities, our workplaces, or even in our households. Nor do we consistently name dialogic communication as something desirable, ethical, or effective. The absence of such everyday experience is mirrored by a lack of role models. Who are the societal leaders showing what it means to be different and equal? What famous interracial allies do we celebrate? Is the "war between the sexes" over? The absence of role models or dialogic norms dims the collective imagination.

To fill this void, many scholars and practitioners have turned to the contested concept of *civility.* However, as we have seen, this enduring effort raises as many problems as it purports to address. To aid us in relating across differences as equals, we focus below on adopting the reframed concept of civility introduced earlier in this chapter.

Reframing Civility for Dialogic Communication

As noted earlier, the concept of *civility* is distorted in a social environment dominated by adversarial individualism and the argument culture. Take, for example, the effort generated by two prominent men—one a conservative, evangelical Republican and the other a liberal, Jewish Democrat—to promote civility among government leaders. Mark DeMoss and Lanny Davis, respectively, developed a "civility pledge" comprised of the following three points:

- I will be civil in my public discourse and behavior;
- I will be respectful of others whether or not I agree with them;
- and I will stand against incivility when I see it.[55]

Over the course of six months, DeMoss and Davis approached each member of Congress and every state's governor for their support. From this group of 585 politicians, exactly *three* signed the pledge.[56] In an editorial, DeMoss explained why he thought the civility pledge project failed to secure more commitment from these elected officials. He wrote, "I've thought long and hard about the lack of interest among our leaders. I can only conclude: too many people *equate civility in public life with unilateral disarmament*."[57] He elaborated,

> Some have wrongly concluded this project was a call to end partisanship (we support partisanship), to limit free speech (I wouldn't try), to surrender personal beliefs and convictions (I would never do that), or for unity (I submit that civility and unity are not the same thing)[58]

This resistance to civility, writes DeMoss, was summed up by Bill O'Reilly on his Fox News show when he said, "I wouldn't sign [the civility pledge] if I were in Congress, [for] I'd be afraid that if my opponent attacked me I wouldn't be able to attack him back."[59]

Government leaders and media celebrities are not the only people leery of civility. Although DeMoss and Davis reported that thousands of U.S. Americans individually signed the civility pledge, the vast majority align with the skeptics. Indeed, to comport oneself with civility with those who differ or disagree is so unusual that the rare instances of comity circulate widely in the public sphere.

In April 2011, for example, a freelance writer shared a "life story" about her unexpectedly close friendship with a woman who was her political opposite. The missive, entitled, "I Can't Believe My Best Friend is a Republican,"[60] went viral on the Internet, even generating "copycat" reports, such as "Help! My Best Friend is a Liberal Democrat!"[61] Relating civilly across differences apparently is so novel it recently merited a celebrated TED talk, where the speaker instructed the (global) audience on how to "Take 'The Other' to Lunch."[62] Similarly, the subject often is seen as newsworthy, making headlines such as "Mikulski Makes History While Creating 'Zone of Civility' for Senate Women"[63] or declaring the "Obama-Bush Relationship: 'Collegial and Cooperative.'"[64]

Public fascination with civility as it is extended across clashing ideas or "rival" identities underscores the point raised above—we lack established patterns for relating across differences as equals. But what does this mean? And why does it matter?

Newspaper columnist Cal Thomas connects civility to relating across differences as equals. While speaking at the Conservative Political Action Conference, Thomas issued a personal attack against a liberal media commentator, Rachel Maddow. He later regretted his statement and so telephoned Maddow to offer a "heartfelt" apology. Writing about the incident, he states that, "Ms. Maddow could not have been more gracious." She not only fully accepted his apology, but also his invitation to lunch.[65]

Thomas wrote his mea culpa in a column entitled, "Rachel Maddow and My Lesson in Civility." The lesson was twofold. First, he states, "When one writes about moral convictions, it's probably a good idea to consistently live up to them." As the author of *Common Ground: How to Stop the Partisan War That Is Destroying America* with his "liberal Democratic friend, Bob Beckel," Thomas asserts, "One of the principles in which I believe is not to engage in name-calling; which, to my shame, I did."[66] Civility, then, is minimally a commitment to refrain from ad hominem statements (attacking the character of another rather than addressing the content of his or her comments) when relating across differences.

The second lesson speaks to the capacity to relate across differences *as equals*. The conservative columnist asserts that he has many friends across the political divide. "They became my friends," he writes, "because I stopped seeing them as labels and began seeing them as *persons with innate worth*."[67] Civility matters, therefore, because it enables us to recognize the fact that people can be different and *equal in their basic human dignity*. This recognition leads us to treat each other with respect, which often is well received.

Thomas and Maddow met for lunch. Maddow described the occasion on her television show that night. With a photograph on screen showing the two of them standing arm in arm at the restaurant, she said, "A sincere apology . . . is like magic." Maddow elaborated:

> A good apology, a real apology essentially erases the mistake. I mean, you don't forget it happened, but you really do forgive it. It's not hard, you move on, you learn from the experience. And you sometimes get a nice lunch with a big tall conservative guy who turns out to be very nice and very funny.[68]

The meeting and, more importantly, the behavior of Thomas and Maddow, was reported widely across multiple media outlets. One online commentator concluded, "Now the challenge is to get other influential people . . . to understand the value of civil discourse."[69]

Such public exchanges affirm the transformative dynamic described earlier. Compare the previous examples of the feuding San Francisco neighbors and the polarized participants in the Public Conversation Project's dialogue on abortion with the dispute between media celebrities. In each circumstance, sincere and mutual *communication with* others created allies in the common cause of knowing each other as we wish to be known.

To form this alliance, we need not validate another's ideas or actions, change our positions, or find common ground on the issues. Dialogue simply requires that we be willing to share our thoughts and feelings and to consider the concerns of others, based on our shared human dignity. But it is precisely such brave willingness to engage across dissent and diversity that is in such scarce supply. For encouragement, we propose a reconsideration of civility.

A new understanding of civility is emerging—that of *civility as communication*. As described above, this changes civility's historic emphasis on manners, decorum, or rules. Instead, as rhetoric professor Thomas W. Benson recently asserted, "Civility as a behavior is fundamentally about communication."[70] A number of scholars have been advancing this view.[71] Many come to the conclusion, as does philosophy professor Cheshire Calhoun, that civility involves an ethics of communication." Civility always involves a display of respect, tolerance, or consideration, for it "is an essentially *communicative form of moral conduct*."[72]

In dialogue, communicating *with* others presumes a willingness to exercise *civility*—which we define as *the expressive act of granting another's dignity*. We assume the truth of each other's basic worth, because dignity is "something that dwells within us, part of what it means to be human, something no one can give or take away."[73] Civility, then, serves as the Golden Rule of communication, for it is the expressed means of treating others as we wish to be treated, based on humanity's intrinsic worth.

Granting one another's dignity is the source for successful dialogue, as well as its most elusive practice. As a result, many have tried to explain its enactment more definitively. Some explain civility in terms of "do's and don'ts." For example, when we can encounter another and accept her as a "distinct self, an independent person in her own right," we do not relate to her as "a tool to prop up [one's] self-image or an instrument to be used in [one's] plans and projects."[74] Civility requires that we don't use each other for strategic purposes. Eighteenth-century philosopher Immanuel Kant advised that the traits of affability, sociability, courtesy, hospitality, and gentleness in social interactions lead to a virtuous attitude that can inspire others to follow the example and help create a universal ethical community where all people are treated with equal respect and dignity, which is humanity's central moral task.[75]

Over two hundred years later, another prominent philosopher wrote extensively and thoughtfully on this essential aspect of dialogue. Martin Buber distinguished the dignity experienced in an "I–Thou relation" from the objectification rendered in an "I–It relation." Communication scholar Richard Johannesen concisely summarizes Buber's perspective. In his words, the "I–It relation" is "characterized in varying degrees by self-centeredness, deception, pretense, display, appearance, artifice, using, profit, unapproachableness, seduction, domination, exploitation, and manipulation."[76] When an "I" relates to an "It," there need not be any recognition of shared dignity or valuing of differences. In contrast, writes Johannesen:

> In the I–Thou or dialogical relationship, the attitudes and behavior of each communication participant are characterized by such qualities as mutuality, openheartedness, directness, honesty, spontaneity, frankness, lack of pretense, nonmanipulative intent, communion, intensity, and love in the sense of responsibility for one human for another. In dialogue, although interested in being understood and perhaps in influencing, a communicator does not attempt to *impose* his or her own truth or view on another and is not interested in bolstering his or her own ego or self-image.[77]

Others, such as Professors Cornel West and bell hooks, describe the same quality of interaction as the willingness to "give one another that subject-to-subject recognition."[78] In dialogue before a Yale University audience, these public intellectuals emphasized such granting of dignity as an "act of resistance"[79] to the dehumanizing effects of oppression. To engage the full humanity of persons subject to institutionalized discrimination is to reject the unjust judgment of inferiority. A "subject-to-subject recognition" then opens the possibility for treating one another with equal regard as we *exchange our different views.*

Civility, thus characterized as enacting an I–Thou relation or as subject-to-subject recognition, is the premise for a successful dialogue. It also is experienced in dialogic interactions as *respect*. Yet even this everyday idea is surrounded by contrary connotations. Sociologist Sara Lawrence-Lightfoot explains. "Respect is commonly seen as deference to status and hierarchy . . . as involving some sort of debt due people because of their attained or inherent position, their age, gender, class, race, professional status, accomplishments, etc."[80] This conception of respect, requiring "expressions of esteem, approbation, or submission," is not an expression of civil dialogue, as it is aligned more with a subject-to-object or I–It relation.

The type of respect needed for effective dialogue communicates that each one of us matters. Participants in a dialogue may acknowledge the different roles, responsibilities, or status people inhabit, but our regard for one another rests on our shared humanity. In this context, we are entitled to a frank exchange of views and to direct, thoughtful responses. We also are responsible for reflecting carefully on our own and others' perspectives. Professor Lawrence-Lightfoot describes this type of respect as creating "symmetry, empathy and connection" even among people whose relationships would be seen as hierarchical, such as doctor and patient or employer and employee.[81]

Although our identities and ideas may be mired in hierarchies of credibility, civility is possible—even in interactions with very high stakes. Vice President Joseph Biden attributes his long-term political success to practicing a type of civil regard. His more experienced peers in Congress "taught him that, no matter how reprehensible another senator's views, his job was to figure out *what was good in that person*, what voters back home saw in him."[82] During his nearly four decades in the United States Senate, Joe Biden's ability to see the good in his colleagues helped him become one of the most effective senators for passing legislation in Congress.[83]

Granting one another's dignity also can be found operating in the highest court in the United States. Justice Ruth Bader Ginsburg has described how *respect* enables the United States Supreme Court to function effectively. Justice Ginsburg "noted that despite their differences, the nine justices of the Supreme Court function as a unified body because of their mutual respect for each other." The Court institutes rituals to affirm this regard. "Our routine gatherings," she says, "begin with handshakes, 36 of them to be exact. It's a way of saying 'even though you circulated that nasty dissent yesterday, we're in this together, and need to get along with each other." "At the end of the day," she asserts, all nine realize that "the institution preserved is far more important than the ego of justices who are on the bench at a given time."[84]

Those who endeavor to look for the good or offer respect express civility, for they recognize the dignity in another human being and act accordingly. Whether such regard is extended in the halls of power or on city streets, it overcomes an attitude of "us versus them" with an orientation of "we," based on our shared humanity. But civility is incomplete if it only extends outwardly to others. It also must apply to one's self.

The Golden Rule establishes that what we do to others, we do to ourselves. Therefore, when we treat others with dignity, we enhance our own *self-respect*. "When we respect ourselves," explains philosopher Marguerite La Caze, "we both think and feel our own worth as persons, and act with a sense of that worth."[85] An awareness of one's own dignity also affects how an individual enters into dialogue with others. Self-respect, states La Caze, "means that we believe we are worthy of consideration, of being treated decently at least, if not well, and of being taken seriously by others."[86]

Whether granted in others or experienced internally, "civility enhances communication by affirming human dignity."[87] Human dignity is the cornerstone for trustworthy relationships, as evidenced by the Universal Declaration of Human Rights. Adopted in 1948, the Declaration was an international response to the atrocities committed during the Second World War. In an effort to prevent any repeat of such "barbarous acts," the Declaration states that "*recognition of the inherent dignity* and of equal and inalienable rights of all members of the human family is the foundation of freedom, justice, and peace in the world."[88]

Dialogue isn't easy, but it is essential to human happiness and well-being. It starts with civility—the recognition and respect for innate personal worth—that allows us to begin to know one another. This basic human need is fulfilled through three interrelated dialogic processes: the capacity to increase awareness and understanding of diverse perspectives, to learn more about ourselves and the world around us, and to strengthen trustworthy relationships. Taken together, these are compelling reasons to turn to dialogue. An ethical and effective means for reuniting individuals within community, dialogic communication provides urgently needed tools to live and reason well together.

Now that we have explored dialogue as a means of engagement designed for mutual recognition and understanding, we need to hone the communication tools necessary for its skillful practice. In the next chapter, we examine a set of dialogic skills and sensibilities that allow for meaningful connection and constructive limit setting.

5

Dialogic Skills and Sensibilities

Introduction

Dialogue can be an effective means of communication when aligned with its proper definition, purpose, and orientation. As described in the last chapter, dialogue involves sincere and mutual exchange, inquiry, reflection, and responsiveness. Dialogue is "talk with a purpose," for it fulfills the human need to *know one another as we wish to be known*. To make knowing one another possible and to ensure dialogue's ethical potential, we practice a robust form of civility. Our combined definition of civility from chapter four is: a means of communicating respectful regard for each other as human beings that empowers people to become allies in a common cause of mutual recognition. Constructive conversations strengthen the trust in our social relations necessary for individual happiness and the common good.

Even with this proper conceptual alignment, dialogue can be a difficult interaction. We have explored the myriad problems that jeopardize the dialogic process, particularly in the context of differences and disagreement. The beliefs and behaviors associated with adversarial individualism and its winner-take-all mentality pose significant obstacles, as does the argument culture's communication cycle of judge, blame, and defend. Power differentials, derived from social stratification and histories of harm and wrongdoing, also strain and sometimes undermine the process. Together, these difficulties create cynicism regarding our very capacity to connect (think of the reaction to the term "Kumbaya"[1]) and generate a deep-seated skepticism about dialogue's practicality. Tensions between concept and practice produce the literal truism: *dialogue is easier said than done*. Nevertheless, the need for dialogue outweighs its potential hardships. So where do we go from here? In the last chapter we identified *civility* as a source for successful dialogue. Lacking widely recognized patterns for relating as different and equal, we struggle to hold subject-to-subject conversations. Now the question becomes: how do we actually have a respectful dialogue, where people communicate with one another through sincere inquiry, considered responses, and thoughtful reflection?

Empathy, compassion, and critical self-reflection[2] are the social skills and sensibilities that join with civility to make dialogic communication possible. We communicate *with* others through these capacities for they enable us, respectively, *to take a sincere interest in others as they are, to suspend judgments and exercise consideration, and to apply this same process to ourselves through introspection.* This trio of skills enable a variety of "speech acts"' that "are done in ways that hold one's own position but allow others the space to hold theirs, and are profoundly open to hearing others' positions without needing to oppose or assimilate them."[3] As was the case with *interdependence, dialogue,* and *civility,* the skills of empathy, compassion, and critical self-reflection are contested concepts. Before describing how to implement them, we first address possible misunderstandings about the terms.

Widely circulated definitions such as "walk a mile in someone else's shoes" (empathy), pity for the "less fortunate" (compassion), and denigrations such as "navel gazing" (critical self-reflection) do not apply here. None of these connotations is suitable for dialogue because they do not facilitate communication with others. The well-intentioned metaphor of walking a mile in someone else's shoes extends the imagination but also risks imposing one's interpretation on another's experience.[4] Compassion is not simply feeling sorry for supposedly unlucky or undeserving others. And while the colloquial term, *navel gazing,* may rightly point to individualism's excesses, its disparaging judgment distorts the value of self-reflection in everyday life. These are not the qualities that can communicate respect for self and others.

To understood the terms more fully, let's look at empathy, compassion, and critical self-reflection in practice. For example, a recent Canadian study asked the question, "What makes a physician an *exemplary communicator* with patients?"[5] The researchers studied the communication skills of forty primary-care physicians who regularly address sensitive issues in adolescent sexual health. The physicians were videotaped interviewing teenagers who were trained to simulate medical visits concerning birth control, sexual orientation, sexually transmitted diseases, and sexual abuse. Each topic requires a frank exchange between patients and physicians in order to care for adolescent health and well-being.

Researchers found that the interview skills of the "most exemplary" communicators differed significantly from those designated as "least exemplary." High-performing physicians consistently demonstrated the dialogic capacities for "empathy, nonjudgment, and self-reflection," while low-performing doctors did not.[6] Empathy and nonjudgment (to use the researchers' terminology[7]) were expressed by the exemplary physicians in post-interview comments such as "I noticed the patient's discomfort and decided to acknowledge it but not push it" and "I watched to see patient cues in body language and waited before I made statements." The least exemplary physicians did not attend closely to patient communication. Instead, these doctors "tended to either change the subject or to respond forcefully to sensitive information," as is apparent in their remarks: "I notice that she's concealing something but I'm not responding to this. I am going through my line of questioning of 'what do I want to get out of her'" and "I don't know if she's lying or not [so] I'm pushing her so she reveals who raped her."[8]

Similar differences existed in the physicians' capacity for critical self-reflection. Skilled interviewers reconsidered their communicative choices. They questioned their choice of words or gestures and pondered dialogic alternatives, such as inviting a patient to rehearse how he might tell his girlfriend about having a sexually transmitted disease. The least exemplary communicators "were less likely to reflect on their performance without considerable prompting . . . and more likely to either excuse their behaviors or blame the patient" with observations such as the "patient was unresponsive and too evasive."[9]

The researchers concluded that the most exemplary physician communicators "were able to conduct a patient-centered, relationally competent approach to medical consultations without sacrificing medical accuracy, efficiency, or mutual understanding." These doctors conversed *with* their teenage patients and effectively served their health needs. The exemplary interactions became "a dialogue between two people driven toward a common goal."[10]

In contrast, the least exemplary physician communicators "tended to *overlook the patient's perspective* and focus on biomedical information. . . . They were also *less likely to respond* to patient cues, which led to difficulty in uncovering the patient's principal reason for the visit."[11] This communicative disengagement led to medical interviews grounded more in "I–It" (subject-to-object) relations. Consequently, these interviews were much less effective in establishing rapport with the patient or in accurately diagnosing the adolescent's health needs.

Empathy, compassion, and reflection are innate sensibilities that permit us access to the meaning-building processes in ourselves and others. These sensibilities are also social skills, in that their practice can be developed and honed. The ethical cultivation of these dialogic skills is vital, for they can serve both constructive and destructive ends. Consider that con artists exploit their empathic awareness of others' vulnerabilities, that compassionate impulses can produce paternalistic actions and that egotism can limit introspection's gaze. To serve communication constructively, these relational capacities must be oriented by civility. Communication's Golden Rule of I–Thou relations needs to guide the intimate powers of knowing and being known.

Below we explore this set of dialogic skills and sensibilities in more depth. The conceptual tensions will be addressed, definitions articulated, and ethical communication examples provided. Empathy, compassion, and critical self-reflection also serve dialogic encounters by fostering connection and, when necessary, setting constructive limits.

Empathy

President Obama's nomination of Judge Sonia Sotomayor for the United States Supreme Court[12] ignited a national debate over the concept of *empathy*. The president declared empathy an important quality in choosing a nominee because "understanding and identifying with people's hopes and struggles [is] an essential ingredient for arriving at just decisions and outcomes."[13] Reactions were swift and vociferous, demonstrating not only the political stakes involved, but also some wildly divergent definitions of empathy.

Critics denounced the presidential emphasis on judicial empathy, initially equating it with emotional bias. "The old-fashioned virtue of objectivity," wrote one commentator, "is giving way to an inherently politicized notion of judging based on feelings."[14] A congressman declared that empathy was "code" for a plan to pick judges based on their "perceived sympathy for certain groups or individuals."[15] His critique was echoed by another detractor. Supreme Court nominees chosen by this criterion, he asserted, would be beholden to "the downtrodden, the powerless, and the voiceless" and thus ready to "discard the rule of law whenever emotion moves them.[16]

The critics earned vigorous and pointed rejoinders from other pundits. "Empathy in a judge does not mean stopping midtrial to tenderly clutch the defendant to your heart and weep," retorted one columnist. "It doesn't mean reflexively giving one class of people an advantage over another because their lives are sad or difficult."[17] Another commentator concurred, adding, "let us remember that empathy is not sympathy. It doesn't require that we take sides."[18] These rebukes were underscored via contrast. "A *lack* of empathy," warned one advocate, "a willful refusal to connect words with the reality of human experience, is its own form of bias and can work its own form of injustice."[19]

Some supporters steered clear of the dispute over emotions and took a different tack. One law professor, for example, sought to establish an "intellectual empathy." He explained that the "importance of empathy for the Supreme Court is not how it makes judges *feel* but how it makes judges *think*." Since judges hear cases involving people from all walks of life, the professor elaborated, "a Justice's intellectual ability to appreciate the situation of someone from a different background or in a different situation is essential."[20]

President Obama himself extended the definition of empathy beyond the emotional and the intellectual. For him, empathy also included moral action. In *The Audacity of Hope*, he wrote that empathy "is at the heart of my moral code and it is how I understand the Golden Rule—not simply a call to sympathy or charity, but as something more demanding, a call to stand in somebody else's shoes and see through their eyes."[21] The extent to which we can "stand in somebody else's shoes" remains problematic as discussed earlier,[22] but the empathic engagement described by the president—to consider the perspectives of those who will be affected by our actions—represents a moral responsibility.

Of all that was written and spoken during the debate, perhaps the most astute statement was: "Empathy is an attractive idea, but it requires some careful unpacking."[23] Ironically, such "careful unpacking" did not occur much during the political fracas, as the disputants mostly refrained from expressing empathic interest in differing points of view. The national rancor can be ascribed in part to the debate context, which was situated at the intersection between legal and political discourse— the heart of the argument culture.

Law professor Lynne Henderson explains the argument culture's impact on the concept of empathy, particularly for lawyers and lawmaking politicians. "The resistance to empathy may be attributable to the *adversarial ideology* acquired during law school." There, she maintains, students are taught that "understanding the adversary is not important unless it serves one's instrumental purpose." Such legal training is validated, moreover, by "the fact that little in the professional culture and scholarship encourages development and use of empathic skills."[24] The emphasis, instead, is on winning.

Ultimately, the national argument over whether empathy is based in emotion, thought, or morality[25] matters less than the fact that, as a means of communication, its consistent goal is to understand. When we want to say what is in our hearts and on our minds and to find out what matters to those who see things differently, we may rely on empathy. *Empathic engagement expresses our sincere interest in others—as they wish to be known— and invites a mutual exchange of the feelings and facts that inform our perspectives.*

Empathic interest manifests in a number of ways. Professor Lynne Cameron, who studies the role of empathy in discourse dynamics, identifies two general types of empathic activity. One she describes as *automatic empathy*. This is "the visceral response we have as human beings to something which is happening to someone else." Think about how moviegoers laugh and cry with the plot twists or how sports fans gasp when a player goes down hurt on the field. "We cannot help this response," Cameron says, "although we can inhibit it." The second type of empathy can be chosen and is referred to as *deliberate* or *cognitive empathy*. In dialogue, deliberate empathy manifests as interest in another person's feelings, thoughts, and experiences in an effort to try "to understand how it is to be them in their world."[26]

But to engage empathically, we first must be paying attention. It may be obvious, but the simple act of truly attending to another person matters. Take, for example, the frustration revealed by a relatively new word in the English language. The term, according to psychologist Dan Goleman, describes "the moment when the person we're with whips out their Blackberry or answers that cell phone and all of a sudden we don't exist. The word is *pizzled*—it's a combination of puzzled and pissed off."[27]

As social creatures, humans require attention. We try hard to secure it and need affirmation that we have it. That affirmation may be expressed, says sociologist Charles Derber, through a variety of "support-responses" that communicate interest in a conversation. He describes three types. *Background acknowledgments* such as "'uh huh,' 'yeah,' 'oh really,' and 'um'" convey a modicum of interest in another's view and encourage a speaker to continue. Another type of response goes further and indicates active involvement with the topic. These *supportive assertions* "are complete declarative responses" and "include evaluative statements." Examples include "That's awesome," or "You make a good point," or "I wouldn't put up with that either." Finally, *supportive questions* provide the fullest engagement.[28] These questions emanate from genuine curiosity about another's perspective. Generally, a question is truly supportive when we really want to hear the answer, rather than to make a point.

Empathy also is expressed by the art of *appreciation*. Appreciation requires awareness of another's positive qualities or an understanding of their efforts. It can be as straightforward as thanking someone for being a good listener or acknowledging that it took courage to "tell it like it is." Empathic interest also allows us to appreciate divergent views. Roger Fisher and Daniel Shapiro of the Harvard Negotiation Project assert, "Even if you disagree with the other person's stance on an issue, you can acknowledge their reasons for seeing the world as they do."[29] To be effective, appreciation must be specific and, above all, sincere.

Empathy can be communicated skillfully in dialogues when we respect others, expand awareness of different and dissenting views, and endeavor to understand the thoughts, feelings, and experiences that shape various perspectives. Motivation comes from the profound human need to be known and from recognizing that "we are all in this together." Recent studies, however, show that empathic engagement is on the decline.

Over the past three decades, college students in the United States have been scoring lower and lower on a standardized empathy test. Researchers report that "scores have dropped 34 percent on 'perspective taking' (the ability to imagine others' points of view) and 48 percent on 'empathic concern' (the tendency to feel and respond to others' emotions)."[30] Another current set of studies document disparities between wealthy and poor people regarding "empathic accuracy." The findings indicate that wealthy people—as determined by income, occupational prestige, and material wealth—were much less adept than the poor at reading emotions in facial expressions.[31]

As might be expected, a lively debate has ensued over the existence or possible causes of this "empathy deficit." Whatever the reasons for the decline or whether there is actually a gap, concern over the potential loss of empathy is widespread. Experts in the study of empathy worry for they know that "an understanding of others' needs is a prerequisite for the transformation of empathy into compassionate action."[32] As one scholar succinctly put it, "No society can long sustain itself unless its members have learned the sensitivities, motivations, and skills involved in assisting and caring for other human beings."[33] Given its significance in human interactions, we turn next to exploring the concept of compassion and to describing its important role in dialogue.

Compassion

Like empathy, the concept of *compassion* has been subject to vigorous debate in the argument culture. As with the clash over empathy, the national disagreement escalated after a presidential invocation of the term. Long before President Barack Obama called for judicial empathy on the Supreme Court, another president had made compassion a centerpiece of his politics. President George W. Bush campaigned and governed based on a political philosophy known as "compassionate conservatism."

The philosophy was an approach to addressing poverty issues in the United States. A critic of government welfare programs, President Bush advocated an alternative "faith-based initiative."[34] This proposal called for legislation to allow federal funding for religious organizations to serve the needs of the poor. Toward the end of his second term in office, the president reflected on his rationale:

> This approach was compassionate, because it was rooted in a timeless truth: That we ought to love our neighbors as we'd like to be loved ourselves. And this approach was conservative, because it recognized the limits of government; that bureaucracies can put money in people's hands, but they cannot put hope in people's hearts.[35]

Few would challenge the assertion that compassion is grounded in the Golden Rule. His implementation of compassionate governance, however, generated years of conflict.

Here, too, political calculations affected the debate, but conceptual rancor over compassion has much deeper roots in the U.S. culture. A nation that prides itself on self-reliance may regard compassion suspiciously. The concern we feel for another's welfare may be viewed as a charitable impulse or as "bleeding heart" sentimentality. Conversely, an extreme adherence to independence can be internalized, for example, in maxims such as "if you don't succeed, you have only yourself to blame" or in circumstances where asking for help feels weak or shameful. A skeptical attitude toward compassion may foment social distrust too, as when we believe that no one helps another without first asking, "What's in it for me?" These ideological tensions deeply affect the ways in which people exercise consideration for one another.

Dr. Rachel Naomi Remen has witnessed various expressions of compassion in her many years working with cancer patients. She has identified three different methods that people—from medical practitioners to supportive family members and friends—use to respond to a patient's suffering. She characterizes these efforts as *helping, fixing,* and *serving.*[36] Each approach is well intentioned but differs in its effectiveness to express consideration or care.

Efforts to help another can flounder, says Remen, because a "helper may see others as weaker than they are, needier than they are, and people often feel this inequality." No matter the material benefits received, Remen asserts, "the danger in helping is that we may inadvertently take away from people more than we could ever give them; we may diminish their self-esteem, their sense of worth, integrity, or even wholeness."[37] Similar risks are entailed in the fixing approach.

"In fixing," Remen explains, "we see others as broken, and respond to this perception with our expertise."[38] "Fixers" may consider it their personal or professional responsibility to apply their knowledge to other people's problems. Yet confidence in one's expertise may lead to numerous impositions, such as unsolicited advice or unilateral actions based on knowing "what's best." Like the Canadian doctors who were deemed the least exemplary communicators, experts may insist on a course of action without adequately consulting the people affected by their decisions. In some circumstances, fixers may not even know or consider those whose problems they are "fixing."

When faced with suffering, helping and fixing responses usually are genuine efforts to express concern. These efforts fall short, however, because the relationship between the "one who cares" and the "cared for" parallels that of the "have" and "have nots." Compassion, however, cannot begin from such subject–object regard. As Remen points out, compassionate action arises from "a relationship between equals."[39] This is compassion as *service.*

Diana Rehling, a professor of communication, encountered these different approaches to compassion as she shifted from *the point of view of serving* to that *of being served.* After being diagnosed with a brain aneurysm, Professor Rehling found herself "experiencing one of the most emotionally devastating aspects of serious illness . . . a sense of being alone."[40] Now, after fifteen years of teaching classes in effective listening, she found herself in need of being heard. Considerate responses, however, ran the gamut of helping, fixing, and serving.

There were listeners who tried to help by understanding Rehling's experience. Their sincerity notwithstanding, they could not breach the divide. They listened from the stance of the healthy, trying to understand the ill. Rehling writes,

> Many of those around me tried hard to understand what I was going through. But it was wearisome to me to always be trying to explain the inexplicable, and although I greatly appreciated the care and concern they demonstrated, I did not feel less alone.[41]

Others addressed the illness as a problem to be fixed. This attempt to care for Rehling also created unanticipated effects. "Having friends or family members," she writes,

> listen to me talk about my health issues from a position of the situation as a problem that needed to be solved, was not generally helpful to me. Neither I nor my friends could solve this "problem" of bleeding in my brain or the consequences of it. . . . Yet, to the degree the listener approached my health issues as my "problem," I was left feeling isolated and somehow flawed or problem ridden.[42]

Despite their best intentions, those who listened as helpers or fixers *remained separate from the suffering* they encountered. Such separation often occurs as listeners attempt to handle the stress inherent in a given situation. Distracted or overwhelmed by their own reactions, helpers and fixers cannot concentrate fully on the other. Like so many of us, they turn instead to common coping responses. The following are a few examples:

- Advising: "I think you should . . ." "Why didn't you . . . ?"
- Consoling: "There, there, now, don't worry, things will get better."
- Storytelling: "That reminds me of the time . . ."
- Shutting down: "Cheer up. Don't feel so bad."
- Sympathizing: "Oh, you poor thing."
- Interrogating: "When did this begin?" "Did you take all your medicine?"[43]

These responses may be adept choices in different interactions. But they fail as compassionate expressions because they uniformly shift attention away from the speaker's thoughts and feelings towards a more manageable topic for the listener.

Although helping and fixing were the most common approaches to compassion that Rehling experienced, she did encounter a "few, very special people [who] did listen to me in a way that made me feel less alone." These listeners *connected with* Rehling, as they talked about what "went beyond my specific situation, to see what there was to learn about being a human—suffering and struggling."[44] Rehling elaborates:

> Approached from this perspective, my illness and health problems
> became not my "unique experience" or "my problem" but rather a
> site of human struggle and suffering that acquires a kind of dignity
> and that can generate a connection that can be explored for meaning
> and insight about what it means to be human and to suffer.[45]

Even though they did not have Professor Rehling's ailment, the compassionate listeners courageously allowed themselves to experience the
distress inherent in illness and confronting mortality. As a result, the "listener" and the "listened to" could learn from one another about this shared
aspect of the human condition. Compassionate listening made it possible
for people to connect as *dignified equals* and *to care across their differences.*

The ability to connect compassionately can extend beyond the circle
of those we already know and care about. Witness the global outpouring
of care for victims of natural disasters or a nation's concern for wounded
and disabled military veterans. But we need to address the predicament of
judgment. When we judge wisely, we utilize a process of critical thinking
and reflection known as discernment.[46] But we also are capable of being
judgmental. Here, we may believe with certainty in our determination
that others are wrong or bad. These types of moralistic judgments impede
compassionate connection, for they impose a subject-object relation.

Philosopher Martha Nussbaum holds that judgment is inherent to
practicing compassion. According to Nussbaum, compassion is a

> Three-stage cognitive process that involves judgments about the suf-
> fering of others—whether the suffering is seen as significantly harm-
> ful, whether it is undeserved and out of the control of the sufferer,
> and whether we feel connected to the sufferer in some way.[47]

Nussbaum describes how many people actually experience and
express compassion in daily life. But as demonstrated throughout this
section, a judgmental approach that prioritizes whether the behavior of
the sufferer was wrong or bad triggers blame and promotes criticism and
condemnation. These moralistic judgments also contribute to the helping and fixing approaches that routinely diminish human dignity.

A compassion that is "restricted to certain kinds of sufferers and to
certain kinds of suffering," cautions communication scholar Lisbeth
Lipari, also "is vulnerable to ideological beliefs about who is deserving
and who is worthy." For example, ideological judgments can "separate the
worthy poor (widows and orphans) from the unworthy poor (unwed
mothers and their children)."[48] In dialogue, such judgmental convictions
can confuse and offend, for these statements separate people into "better"
and "worse" social hierarchies. As a result, these compromised forms of
compassion tend to generate conflict more than they alleviate suffering.

While it is not possible to stop judging completely, we can soften its
negative impact on our efforts to connect with and understand others.
When in dialogue, we can learn to suspend judgments. First, we need to recog-

nize the judgmental "mental chatter" (likes, dislikes, preferences, etc.) that surfaces in our minds. Next, we interrupt the desire to respond reactively to the mental chatter. Instead, we label judgmental thoughts as "thinking"[49] and return our attention to the other person. The more visually inclined might choose to see judgmental thoughts in a cartoon bubble and then metaphorically pop it. Others might turn to the contemplative touchstone, "There but for grace (or fate or chance) go I" to return to a more peaceable mental state. The point of suspending judgments in these and other ways is to create a space where we can know others as they wish to be known, rather than according to the "shoulds" in our minds.

When we refrain from judging another's struggle or suffering, it "doesn't mean that we approve of everyone, or that we won't fight hard to rectify injustice or challenge harmful behavior."[50] As described in the last chapter, a commitment to restraint does not constrain effective protest. Later in the chapter, we explore how empathy, compassion, and critical self-reflection can help to establish constructive boundaries and to confront wrongdoing. Here, we focus on exercising compassion in order to connect with others and to express consideration across our differences. To help realize these dialogic goals, we *set aside comparisons that judge the fundamental worth of self or another* in terms of being better or worse, or as different and *un*equal.

Katherine I. Miller's research findings on compassionate communication support this approach. "Although there is no single definition of compassion that will suffice in all situations," asserts Miller, "both scholars and laypeople would widely agree that compassion involves 'connection' to others . . . and 'caring' for those others."[51] This definition of compassion is realized when we *suspend judgments and respond with consideration* of life's difficulties and disagreements. The expression of compassion may range from consideration to concern to heartfelt care, but it is based consistently on the premise that human beings are different from one another yet equal in their fundamental worth.

Though empathy and compassion overlap in practice, these sensibilities and skills can be distinguished for the purposes of dialogue. Thus far we have defined empathy as *a means of sincere inquiry* and compassion as *a form of considerate responsiveness*. Both communication capacities typically focus on others. To fully learn through dialogue, however, we also must bring empathic interest and compassionate engagement back to the self.

Critical Self-Reflection

Nearly everyone has been introspective at times, looking within for answers that lead to greater self-awareness and self-knowledge. *Critical self-reflection* is the *process of observing and thoughtfully assessing the "meaning-building" going on in our minds*. We practice this type of introspection to cultivate deeper understanding about what we think and feel, to know more about who we believe ourselves to be, and to articulate clearly what matters to us and why.

Despite Socrates' widely acclaimed proclamation, "The unexamined life is not worth living," the virtue of self-reflection has suffered numerous indignities. In the argument culture, where being "right" and "winning" disputes are prized, introspection is a liability. Just as empathy is equated with irrational bias and compassion with "bleeding heart" sentimentality, self-reflection is regarded as detrimental. The possibility of revisiting one's positions or beliefs, or perhaps even admitting mistakes, jeopardizes argumentative success. To avoid this vulnerability, the argument culture stigmatizes the practice of self-reflection.

The campaign to diminish the inward gaze is multifaceted. For example, self-reflection is often characterized as uncertainty or indecisiveness. From this perspective, self-reflection is equated with debilitating self-doubt, as is evident in the admonition: "He who hesitates is lost." Even if not perceived as mental disarray, self-reflection is often derided as idle contemplation. Here, the self-absorbed indulge in the proverbial and irrelevant practice of "navel gazing." Alongside indecision and indulgence, introspection may lead people to dwell too long on the negative or to wallow unproductively in the unchangeable. Poet Theodore Roethke expressed this concern succinctly when he wrote, "Self-contemplation is a curse / That makes an old confusion worse."[52]

In dialogue, critical self-reflection is vital. One may encounter different positions, new information, strong feelings, and spirited exchanges, any of which may challenge participants' perspectives or stress their interactions. Reflecting on a conversation allows us to sort through the layers of content and the multitudes of meaning in a disagreement, beginning with our own views and values. We can search beyond our initial reactions and consider the most meaningful and constructive ways of responding. Skillful self-reflection, therefore, allows us to *integrate self-expression with responsiveness* in dialogue.

Just as importantly, critical self-reflection makes it possible *to learn from dialogic encounters,* for the practice can "begin the work of liberating the mind from previous conditioning, enabling it to hold something new."[53] Recall from chapter 4 the efforts of the Public Conversations Project to bring together those with opposing views on abortion. One of the questions they asked participants was: "Do you experience any pockets of uncertainty or lesser certainty, any concerns, value conflicts, or mixed feelings that you may have and wish to share?"[54] Critical self-reflection invites a rich exploration of such uncertainties, indecision, or doubt, permitting us to learn from changing circumstances and mistakes. It all begins with increasing awareness of our reactions.

When we engage in dialogue, we inevitably react to what others say and do. Sometimes those reactions produce judgmental thoughts, as discussed earlier. Typically, we believe our reactions provide accurate information about other people, as in "She's so rude" or "He's not making any sense." However, others may not find her communication style abrasive or experience his rendition of events as baffling. What accounts for the differences? Our reactions—including our impulses, feelings, and opinions—become our most accessible resources for discovering why we think and feel the way we do.

The issue becomes more complicated when we attribute the *cause* of our reaction to others, as in the common retort: "You make me so angry!" As with judging others based on our reactions, blaming others for our responses is equally misplaced. "We are never angry because of what someone else did," explains Marshall Rosenberg, author of *Nonviolent Communication*. "We can identify the other person's behavior as the stimulus, but it important to establish a clear separation between stimulus and cause."[55] Self-reflection facilitates this very distinction.

Take for example, an instance of a friend showing up late for a social engagement with three other close friends. He apologizes and provides a brief explanation for the delay. The first friend shakes his head and laughs, thinking, "That Otis marches to his own drummer." The second resents Otis's lack of punctuality and remarks under his breath, "He must think his time is more important than other people's." The third friend is indifferent to Otis's behavior but feels anxious about getting everyone out the door in order to make the movie on time.

For all three, Otis's tardiness was a common stimulus. But *the content* of each person's reaction emanated from the thoughts, feelings, and needs of the specific individual. The differences in their reactions may stem from the fact that the amused friend values autonomy, the resentful person needs consideration, and the anxious individual prioritizes order. Their responses to stimuli provide information *about them*, not Otis. Through critical self-reflection and discernment we can learn to "own" our reactions and, in the process, find out more about what matters to us.

Becoming more aware of our reactions can lead to deeper self-discovery. Assumptions fundamentally "structure our way of seeing reality, govern our behavior, and describe how relationships should be ordered."[56] Various assumptions about socializing and friendship (including ideas about time, acceptance, and behavior) as well as dissimilar personal values (such as independence, thoughtfulness, and security) likely drove the differing reactions of Otis's peers. Yet because assumptions "are so embedded in our ways of thinking . . . we typically do not notice they are there."[57] Therefore, critical reflection contributes to self-knowledge through "a deliberate, consistent, systematic effort to uncover assumptions."[58]

Reflecting on our reactions and their underlying assumptions is a complicated process, particularly if we bring adversarial attitudes to our introspection. Tendencies to judge, blame, and defend during a self-examination lead us back to the tension "between feeling good about

[our]selves and representing the world accurately." Critical self-reflection, practiced with empathy and compassion for oneself, can help to work through these conflicted internal dialogues. Dr. Kristin Neff describes her own thought process:

> I slowly came to realize that self-criticism—despite being socially sanctioned—was not at all helpful, and in fact only made things worse. I wasn't making myself a better person by beating myself up all the time. Instead, I was causing myself to feel inadequate and insecure, then taking out my frustration on the people closest to me. More than that, I wasn't owning up to many things because I was so afraid of the self-hate that would follow if I admitted the truth.[59]

Critical self-reflection is most productive when we apply empathic understanding and compassionate consideration. We can appreciate how we came to hold certain assumptions and beliefs and accept both our strengths and shortcomings. We can choose to change, if needed, because we have seen ourselves and our behaviors clearly—and courageously.

This clarity enabled Van Jones, while director of The Ella Baker Center for Human Rights, to confront an internal contradiction between his values and his conduct. He describes the introspective experience in an interview, as well as the lesson he drew from it:

> Usually whatever the external thing is that we're fighting, there is an internal manifestation of it. For instance, I'm challenging the incarceration industry. But there are ways in my own life that I'm punitive and unforgiving. So I want society to be rehabilitative and give people second chances, but I'm not that way myself.[60]

Because Jones looks inwardly without any predisposition to deny or rationalize, he observes his own behavior objectively and can identify the very qualities that he opposes in his quest for a more equitable penal system. Denying or excusing truths about himself would be contrary to his vision of justice. From this heightened self-awareness, he now can contemplate how to align his vision and his behavior. For Van Jones, an empathic, compassionate reflection "opens up a different world of possibilities in terms of how I am going to relate."[61]

The dialogic skills and sensibilities of empathy, compassion, and critical self-reflection—oriented by civility—enable people to communicate more ethically and effectively. When we are open to the possibilities of a subject-to-subject encounter, we are able to express sincere interest in and appreciation for another's views, to extend consideration, and to reflect constructively on the exchange. Dialogue practiced in this manner increases our awareness about a subject's intricacies as it helps us engage others with dignity. As a result, both individual happiness and the common good can be served. Despite these significant benefits, dialogue still may be derailed.

Relating to Incivility in Dialogue

Given the pervasiveness of adversarial norms, dialogic contexts remain infused with entrenched habits of judging, blaming, and defending. Their expression can shut down dialogic interaction and alienate participants. To prevent a return to I–It interactions, we need to "open up a different world of possibilities" in terms of how we relate to incivility.

Even without a context informed by an argument culture and adversarial individualism, each and every human being is capable of being judgmental, accusatory, and defensive. These fallible qualities typically emerge when we struggle with vulnerability and uncertainty. But we have learned that our fundamental needs to be accepted, to belong, and to matter to one another cannot be satisfied through judgment, blame, and defensiveness. These adversarial habits won't go away, but we can *choose how to relate* to them.

In certain situations, one choice for relating to incivility is to *choose not to engage*; we can decide to walk away from a verbal slugfest. Disengagement, under certain circumstances, could be the best preparation for dialogue when tempers have calmed. If one wants to stay engaged, the dialogic skills and sensibilities described in this chapter can direct a wayward conversation back toward the "high road." Empathy, compassion, and critical self-reflection can help set *constructive* limits on combative behavior, while civility maintains *respect* for the fundamental worth of each human being.

Scholarly literature most often examines adversarial communication as "defensive communication." In a classic article on the topic, Jack R. Gibb describes a typical situation where a person perceives or anticipates a threat in the group and becomes defensive:

> The person who behaves defensively, even though he also gives some attention to the common task, devotes an appreciable portion of his energy to defending himself. Besides talking about the topic, he thinks about how he appears to others, how he may be seen more favorably, how he may win, dominate, impress, or escape punishment and/or how he may avoid a perceived or an anticipated attack.[62]

A defensive person is so consumed with self-protection and so absorbed in strategizing that she disconnects from the dialogic interaction. This separation allows her to return to an I-It mode of communication. Once there, she will employ incivility—judging, blaming, and defending tactics—to exert control in a given situation.

Such defensiveness, according to communication consultant Sharon Ellison, impacts dialogue negatively. When feeling defensive, she explains, people tend to (1) build emotional walls; (2) hide information about feelings, thoughts, beliefs, or actions; (3) see the other person as an adversary; and (4) engage in power struggles.[63] Each aspect of defensive communication—whether face-to-face or through a print or visual medium—impedes the dialogic goals to know, understand, consider, and learn about each other.

Though defensive communication is quite common, we do not have to respond in kind. Khaleel Mohammed, a veteran of numerous interfaith dialogues, affirms the *possibility of choice*. Given that many faith traditions generate deeply held beliefs (including, at times, the duty to convert) and that religious conflicts persist worldwide, defensiveness is a pervasive feature in interfaith dialogues. In this context, Mohammed writes, "people can be rude, arrogant, and ignorant" when confronting differences or disagreements. Yet, in response to such defensive communication, he maintains, "I do not have to react in the same manner. . . . One has to deal with difficult questions and interlocutors in a gentle manner."[64] Civility—in concert with empathy, compassion, and critical self-reflection—offers participants constructive choices for responding to defensiveness while supporting the goals of dialogic communication.

For example, Indra Nooyi, the chair and CEO of PepsiCo, describes how "the best advice I ever got" helped her utilize civility in her efforts to be less defensive. The counsel, she says, came from her father, "an absolutely wonderful human being." He taught her "to always assume a positive intent. Whatever anybody says or does, assume a positive intent." Nooyi elaborates:

> In business, sometimes in the heat of the moment, people say things. You can either misconstrue what they're saying and assume they are trying to put you down, or you can say, "Wait a minute. Let me really get behind what they are saying to understand whether they're reacting because they're hurt, upset, confused, or they don't understand what it is I've asked them to do." If you react from a negative perspective—because you didn't like the way they reacted—then it just becomes two negatives fighting each other.[65]

Acting on her father's advice, Nooyi has adopted a positive intent and now recommends it to others. She assures us:

> You will be amazed at how your whole approach to a person or a problem becomes very different. You don't get defensive. You don't scream. You are trying to understand and listen because at your basic core you are saying, "Maybe they are saying something to me that I'm not hearing."[66]

Like Khaleel Mohammed's decision to be gentle in response to defensiveness, Indra Nooyi follows her father's advice to look for the good in people during misunderstandings or disagreements. Their examples demonstrate that we are not limited to adversarial responses in difficult circumstances. We can practice a robust form of civility so as to limit uncivil behavior and, where possible, renew cooperation.

When we choose civil communication in response to uncivil behavior, we are guided by the desire to "respect the intrinsic value of the individual and the rights of people different from [our]selves."[67] Philosopher Megan Laverty explains that civility

> balances self-directed thinking with other-directed thinking; it balances concern for another's feelings with concern for his or her well-being; it balances a commitment to being truthful with sensitivity for the situation and individual.[68]

In other words, civility offers a "both/and" option. We can think of ourselves and others as we choose how to respond. We are not confined to an "us versus them" mentality. "While it is true," Laverty acknowledges,

> that even robust civility cannot automatically assure ethical personhood or a just democracy, it can, unlike conventional civility, provide the *kind of ethos* in which people can cultivate character and justice.[69]

In effect, we become the civil society we've been waiting for.

Gibb advises that civility works in concert with empathy. "Communication that conveys empathy for the feeling and respect for the worth of the [defensive] listener is particularly supportive and defense reductive."[70] His assertion is illustrated by Jon Katz's experience practicing empathic communication in a hospice setting.

During a volunteer training session, Katz participated in a role play designed to simulate a typical hospice situation. In the role play, he was assigned to represent a hospice volunteer, while another trainee was designated to be a caregiver. As the volunteer, Katz wrote, "my job was to listen, to affirm the feelings I was hearing, not challenge them or add my own or try to change anyone's mind." Katz was being instructed to engage in empathic dialogue: to be sincerely interested in another's experience or point of view. The other trainee, in her role, expressed what many caregivers experience as their loved ones are dying: they blame themselves for not being able to prevent the impending death. "'I'm not doing enough,' she lamented, 'I feel like I'm not doing enough, no matter what I do.'"[71]

Katz thought that "under normal circumstances I surely would have reassured her, told her that of course she was doing enough, and urged her not to be so tough on herself." But as a hospice volunteer, he made an empathic choice. He asked, "[H]ow long have you felt this way, that you're not doing enough?" Katz explained this decision, stating that his "neutral question [was] meant to allow her to communicate but not to talk her out of what she was feeling or to dismiss it by suggesting it wasn't really true.[72]

Jon Katz's decision to refrain from offering reassuring statements enabled him to keep his focus on the caregiver's experience, so she perhaps could break through the "emotional wall" of self-blame. No matter how well-intentioned, the typical expressions of comfort he considered—such as telling her to worry less or to be more positive—would shift attention away from her suffering, which could communicate to the caregiver that her feelings had been misunderstood or dismissed.

Katz's empathic choice to inquire further about her feelings checked his impulse to "help or fix" the caregiver's distress. In this instance, empathic dialogue set constructive limits on his well-intentioned response to her self-blame. His empathic inquiry, moreover, communicated sincere interest and expressed a respect for her that she may not have been experiencing at the moment for herself. This effort aligns with the recommendation to engage empathically to support another. Empathic interest should remain focused on the experience of a person behaving defensively, accepting emotional reactions at face value." Gibb clarifies:

> Abortive efforts to deny the legitimacy of the receiver's emotions by assuring the receiver that he need not feel bad, that he should not feel rejected, or that he is overly anxious, though often intended as support giving, may impress the listener as lack of acceptance. The combination of understanding and empathizing with the other person's emotions with no accompanying effort to change him apparently is supportive at a high level.[73]

Empathic interest is complimented by compassionate responsiveness. By engaging others empathically and compassionately, we may imagine subject-to-subject options, even across diametrically opposed views. Joanna Macy's narrative exemplifies this point. On a cross-country flight, she became engaged in a heated exchange with another passenger. He was a "security expert working on a military contract" and she was actively opposed to a nuclear arms buildup. Their dispute followed the expected lines of disagreement emanating from the perspectives of a "hawk" and a "dove."

> Weary and frustrated, I subsided into silence. As we began the long descent into Newark, I glanced at his averted face—father, he had said, of two young sons. I felt a sudden compassion. "It's a grim outlook," I said, "that your kids and mine will have to live their lives under the constant threat of extinction." "It's worse than you think," he replied, "a lot worse—it will come before my kids can even grow up." "That's a hard knowledge to live with," I said. Nodding in agreement, he began slowly to share what it felt like—and he did it with a quiet and infinite sadness. "Usually I just shut it out," he said, but for those moments he hadn't, and we had connected on a far deeper level than our conflicting views of national security.[74]

Although neither Macy nor her seatmate relinquished their deeply held beliefs, compassion allowed them to converse. Macy's moment of "sudden compassion" enabled her to offer a respectful presence, communicating as one parent to another. This subject-to-subject regard allowed the seatmates to suspend their judgments about each other as "hawks" and "doves" long enough to connect regarding their shared concerns about their children's futures. For a moment, they communicated as allies, rather than as adversaries. They were able to share feelings and beliefs they might otherwise have hidden strategically from one another. Their exchange wasn't meant to resolve their differences, but a compassionate response did open a way through their judgmental impasse.

Julia Chaitin refers to such dialogic progress as "working through." As a member of To Reflect and Trust—an international organization that sponsors dialogues for individuals from opposing groups, such as the descendants of Holocaust survivors and of Nazis—Chaitin affirms how dialogue helps people work through their defenses in order to engage respectfully.

> People carry with them all kinds of things, all kinds of attitudes and fears and stereotypes of the other, and a lot of this gets passed on to their own children. . . . "Working through" means not to overcome the past, not to put it behind you, but to learn to live with it. "Working through" is a process, and it's a lifelong process. . . . A good way to learn to live with it is by facing that other, who's willing to face you also, and to enter into dialogue, and to talk about these things.[75]

Compassion is an appropriate response to suffering and a constructive limit to the sufferer's defensive communication. By extending care and connection, people strengthen relationships and build trust. The significance of encouraging such relational integrity in dialogue cannot be overstated. As philosopher Sissela Bok attests, "*Whatever* matters to human beings, trust is the atmosphere in which it thrives."[76]

A third choice for relating to incivility and adversarial communication is critical self-reflection. Khaleel Mohammed (whose experience in participating in interfaith dialogues affirmed the possibility of communicative choice), explains how self-reflection moderates one's own defensive attitudes and expressions:

> I have never ceased to point out the problems that besiege Islam from within. I never fail to point out the anti-Semitic commentaries or the disparaging concepts of "the other" in exegeses. . . . I explain that I have to criticize my own beliefs if necessary, because the Qur'an compels me to do so as long as it is to establish truth.[77]

Stoic philosophers also emphasized self-awareness. In *A Guide to the Good Life: The Ancient Art of Stoic Joy*, William B. Irvine summarizes the view of the Roman emperor and Stoic, Marcus Aurelius:

> Marcus recommends that when we interact with an annoying person, we keep in mind that there are doubtless people who find *us* annoying. More generally, when we find ourselves irritated by someone's shortcomings, we should pause to reflect on our own shortcomings.[78]

Marcus Aurelius's recommendation contains within it a version of the Golden Rule. When we treat others as we wish to be treated, it "will help us to become more empathetic to this individual's faults and therefore become more tolerant of him."[79] Stoic emphasis on self-reflection, moreover, also understands that what we do to others, we do to ourselves:

> When dealing with an annoying person, it also helps to keep in mind that our annoyance at what he does will almost invariably be more detrimental to us than whatever it is he is doing. In other words, by letting ourselves become annoyed, we only make things worse.[80]

Critical self-reflection—acting in concert with empathic interest, compassionate responsiveness, and civility—offers constructive choices to defensive communication. In each instance noted above, this set of communication capacities acted to *limit adversarial encounters* and to *facilitate respectful engagement*. We can choose to relate to expressions of judging, blaming, and defensiveness in dialogue without entering into power struggles over who is right and who will win. As Dr. Martin Luther King Jr. advised his brother, who was angered at discourteous drivers and was tempted to retaliate, "Somebody got to have some sense."[81] When disagreement is intense, however, or habits of incivility are deeply ingrained, other constructive alternatives may need to be applied.

Constructive Confrontation

"Responsiveness to others does not always mean harmony," observes Sharon D. Welch, a former project leader with the Difficult Dialogues Program. "It is sometimes necessary to set things reeling."[82] When dialogue is bogged down in defensive dynamics and participants are stuck in I-It mode, Welch's proposal resonates. Even in such difficult moments, however, we may find opportunities to relate constructively. Dialogic skills and sensibilities serve the most challenging circumstances. For example, Henri Nouwen, an internationally renowned Dutch Catholic priest and writer, advocated *compassionate confrontation*.

Nouwen and his coauthors of *Compassion* state, "Honest, direct confrontation is a true expression of compassion."[83] The intersection between the seemingly opposite qualities of confrontation and compassion is fraught with hazards. Confrontation demands an explanation or points out wrongdoing, while compassion expresses consideration of humanity's shared vulnerabilities. For the act of confrontation to convey this respect, we need the "reality check" of the Golden Rule. Are we able, in the words of peace activist Susan Van Haitsma, to "confront an adversary while simultaneously preserving the adversary's dignity"?[84]

Others also urge consideration of this interdependent principle when challenging the conduct of others. Communication ethicist Ronald C. Arnett states that "caring confrontation" involves "the dual motion of standing one's ground and attempting to confirm the other's humanity by being open to his view of the world."[85] The Confucian concept of *jen* maintains that "one should treat others as the self." A person of *jen* character, therefore, "brings the good things of others to completion and does not bring the bad things of others to completion."[86]

Similarly, Leonard Felder states that the central theme in the Mussar teachings "is to treat one's fellow human beings (especially during a disagreement or a power struggle) in the mutually respectful way you would want to be treated."[87] This tradition in Judaic scholarship, Felder asserts, offers a "much more effective and profound way of speaking up for justice and fairness than the self-righteous name-calling and reflexive demonizing."[88] All these theorists of confrontation emphasize a robust civility and a regard for dialogic skills, which work together to protect the dignity of both the confronter and the confronted. By safeguarding self-respect and mutual regard, constructive confrontation reduces the chance of a conflict escalating as it maximizes the possibilities of understanding, consideration, and learning from the encounter.

Two of the recommendations to ensure constructive confrontations made by the Mussar scholars are:

1. Try a dignified one-on-one first: Rather than attempting to crush the soul or spirit of someone whose actions you would like to change, it's far more effective and ethical to deliver your feedback or suggestions [in private] with such delicacy that the other person feels supported and encouraged (rather than attacked or shamed) by your comments.

2. Make sure you aren't trying to blast someone for what you yourself need to be working on: When you have connected with your own imperfections, manipulation tendencies, and human-ness, you can begin to have a less self-righteous or patronizing tone in your one-on-one dialogues with the person you are hoping to understand and impact in a positive way.[89]

Whichever traditions or theories inform one's approach, constructive confrontation is most assured of success when it begins with critical self-reflection.

Probably the best criterion for determining whether our confrontation is compassionate rather than offensive, and our anger righteous rather than self-righteous is to ask ourselves if we ourselves can be so confronted. Can we learn from indignation directed at us? When we can be confronted by a NO from others, we will be more able to confront with a NO.[90]

Whether confrontation is modified by the terms constructive, compassionate, or caring; or whether it expresses jen character, Mussar theories, or peace activists' principles, *civil confrontation limits adversarial behavior as it communicates one's view.* These efforts do not guarantee any outcome, but they contribute to a clearer conscience. We may still struggle with a situation. We may remain dissatisfied with another's conduct, but restraint from retaliation can nurture self-respect. When faced with incivility, often the only choice we have is how we will respond. Everyone benefits by adhering to the Golden Rule of communication, even if all don't practice it.

There are times, though, when we are reluctant to challenge the conduct of others, because we perceive that "the cost is too great for confrontation or there is insufficient justification to take action."[91] In these circumstances, many would rather avoid confrontation altogether. When people wish to avoid conflict, they often choose from the following:

1. To withdraw: "I politely ended the conversation because I didn't want to talk with the other person," and "I left the scene."

2. To pretend: "I tried to fake that I wasn't upset," and "I ignored the conflict and behaved as if nothing happened."

3. To exit: "I tried not to see the other person."

4. To outflank: "I wanted to take our problems to our boss so that he/she could solve it," and "I said bad things about the person behind his/her back."

5. To yield: "I backed down to solve the problem," and "I accepted whatever the other person said."[92]

While any of these options initially help people cope with the stress of conflict and the strains of the argument culture, they all inevitably prolong interpersonal or intergroup tensions. Avoidance can be a constructive alternative, if it is chosen to allow for a cooling off period or as a measure of safety. But it requires dialogic capacities to discern whether avoidance is warranted or rationalized in a given situation.

Another method for dealing with the need to confront others is to make space for strong emotions, like anger, while setting limits on hostile or aggressive expression. For example, Audre Lorde acknowledges anger's constructive use against injustice and oppression. She writes that "anger is loaded with information and energy. . . . Focused with precision it can become a powerful source of energy serving progress and change."[93] As Lorde describes it, anger can be seen as a productive resource rather than as a source of aggression. "For anger to be a resource," explain Jean Baker Miller and Janet L. Surrey,

> We need a context of relationships in which we are safe to express anger and, most importantly, the real reasons for it. We need relationships in which we are safe to hear the other person's anger without experiencing it as an attempt to attack or diminish us. Anger, seen in this way, notifies the people in the relationship that something is wrong and needs attention, and moves people to find a way to make something different come about. Anger, then, can be the energizing initiator for transforming the relationship to something better.[94]

To engage others through compassionate confrontation, we also may balance righteous anger with what Sharon Salzberg calls "the force of kindness."

> Kindness is compassion in action. It is a way of taking the vital human emotions of empathy or sympathy and channeling those emotions into a real-life confrontation with ruthlessness, abandonment, thoughtlessness, loneliness—all the myriad ways, every single day, we find ourselves suffering or witnessing suffering in others.[95]

For kindness to work as a compassionate force in dialogue, it must be translated from the connotations of *weakness* or *pushover* imposed by the argument culture. Like the trio of empathy, compassion, and self-reflection, the meaning of kindness has suffered distortion.

Take for example the *New York Times* editorial, "Is Ken Salazar Too Nice?" The editorial expresses concern that Senator Salazar may not be the right person to be the Secretary of the Interior Department, a cabinet position for which President-elect Obama had nominated him. "The word on Ken Salazar," the editorial begins, "is that he is friendly, approachable, a good listener, a genial compromiser, and a skillful broker of deals. That is also the rap on Ken Salazar." The *Times* editorial board proposes instead that the scandal-ridden Interior Department needs "someone willing to bust heads when necessary and draw the line against powerful commercial groups."[96]

The *Times* editorial board presents a false dilemma: leaders must choose between constructive relationships or organizational effectiveness. But compassionate confrontation, based in constructive anger and the positive force of kindness, bridges this divide. It is a dialogic process that attends to people's dignity *as* it sets constructive limits on behavior. Ken Salazar's communication skills, as enumerated by the *Times*, could model leadership behavior that is trustworthy, in that it is both responsive and just. The Interior Department need not choose between a pushover and a tyrant.

Empathy, compassion, and critical self-reflection provide choices in relating to incivility. Their skillful expression can transform a defensive power struggle into the potential for mutual regard and understanding. Communication scholar Ronald D. Gordon has written on this transformation in "The Difference between Feeling Defensive and Feeling Understood."[97] He concludes, "When communicators feel understood, they want to **reach** out; when they feel defensive they want to **strike** out. When they feel understood they want to do something *for* the other person; when they feel defensive they want to do something *to* the other person."[98] To further foster the sense of feeling understood, many dialogic facilitators and participants turn to the establishment of communication guidelines.

Dialogic Guidelines

As mentioned in the last chapter, dialogic guidelines are used widely to ensure productive, respectful exchanges. The intention is to generate openness and inclusiveness and to establish constructive limits in the communication of participants. Too often, though, dialogic guidelines have had unintended consequences.

At times, participants have experienced guidelines as carrying a hidden agenda, ranging from the promotion of particular views to preferred outcomes. In other instances, guidelines may be perceived as methods germane solely to the "manners police" who enforce conventional conceptions of "civility." Other dialogic practices promote conformity by relying on dominant or culturally specific communication styles. In such cases, the guidelines fall short of their intended goals because the dialogic structures inadvertently reinforce the anxieties and inequities of the argument culture and adversarial individualism.

Any set of guidelines should express the core values and needs of the dialogue's participants. Ideally, they would craft the guidelines together and make decisions about whether and how to have facilitation. The context of the dialogue also prompts different concerns. For example, people in interfaith dialogues must commit to refrain from any attempt to convert others to one's own faith tradition. Romantic couples in conflict may want to take great care with invoking exchanges about relationship dissolution. Co-workers interacting across ethnic or racial lines need to consider carefully whether to tell an ethnic joke or to use a racial epithet in jest. Even trustworthy relationships may not be able to bear the unexpected strain. These and countless other examples demonstrate that nearly every context has a "point of no return" where the power of expression establishes a subject-object interaction. Whenever possible, parties should identify these conversational boundary lines at the outset.

In this text, dialogue has been defined as the process of communicating **with** others—a sincere and mutual exchange involving inquiry, responsiveness, and reflection. The central and most basic guideline for such a dialogue is to establish a mutual commitment to hear and to be heard. This commitment focuses on full inclusion of the participants and highlights the reality of how we co-construct the complex meaning of any particular topic, issue, or situation. This commitment does not deny or overlook the power disparities that occur among individuals nor does it try to enforce an "equal" proportion of airtime. It simply asserts that the participants agree to the intention to hear and to be heard and to some process of checking in to determine whether they actually experienced reciprocity in recognition and understanding.

A second important guideline is to ensure that people are aware that dialogue searches for *meaning*—for how individuals make sense of their lives, their experiences and their differences—rather than for definitive truths or absolute rights and wrongs. This should not be taken to mean that truth does not exist or that "anything goes." Rather than instigate existential angst, this guideline simply seeks to reinforce dialogue's goals of understanding, consideration, and learning. Consequently, contributions to dialogue are based typically on *personal experience or are expressed as personally held views.*

The third core guideline pays homage to our interconnectedness and recognizes the human capacities to feel with others and to see ourselves reflected through others' eyes. This guideline recommends that participants plan for and practice ways of *getting comfortable with being uncomfortable.* Here again, this guideline does not direct participants to suppress disagreement or conflict or to deny feeling vulnerable or defensive. Instead, the idea of getting comfortable with being uncomfortable explicitly anticipates all these conditions and urges participants to prepare publicly and to practice together how they might *meet and work through* these circumstances.

Most importantly, this guideline depends on a robust form of civility to function effectively and ethically. We need to look for the good in each other, to know that we will fall short of our aspirations, and to try to learn from the experiences. After all, we share the human condition that gives rise to our vulnerabilities and our struggles. Ultimately, we are in this together.

Conclusion

Li Xiaojiang, a Chinese scholar who for years has worked with academics from other nations, has become a practitioner of dialogue out of necessity. She has labored long to exchange ideas and to generate mutual understanding in dialogic contexts containing cultural differences and conflicting theoretical commitments. During the course of her experiences, she developed new insights about the process and purpose of dialogue.

> The starting point of a dialogue derives from "differences," while the ongoing process of a dialogue should clarify these "differences." The goal of a dialogue has in fact never been the sort of deceptive, utopian "Grand Unity," which we have eulogized. Rather, the goal is for both parties to understand their "differences" in order to make corresponding adjustments and coexist peacefully. "Retaining differences" may very well be the most direct goal of a dialogue.[99]

Li's conclusion expresses the practical spirit of dialogue. We have learned that the communication capacities of empathy, compassion, and critical self-reflection help to realize the dialogic goals of *communicating sincere interest in others as they are, suspending judgments and extending care, and applying these qualities to ourselves through introspection.* This dialogic trio, oriented by civility, brings people together in mutual regard and understanding and sets constructive limits on adversarial communication and incivility.

A good conversation across differences and disagreements requires respectful engagement and skillful communication. The same dynamic holds for deliberation and decision making. More often than not, our ability to know one another, to weigh our options, and to take constructive action all rely on a relatively unsung communication skill. It is the art of listening. In the next chapter, we describe how listening serves as a bridge from dialogue to deliberation.

6

Listening

Our discussions thus far have underscored the important role that dialogic skills and sensibilities play in enabling us to reach across disagreements and other forms of difference. As we've seen, the quality of our communication with one another profoundly affects the quality of our communities and our ability to work together in pursuit of common purpose.

In the previous chapter, we discussed how dialogue and a reframed understanding of civility help to realize communication's constructive potential. In the following discussion, we build on this foundation by focusing on the art of listening. As we will see, listening well is an especially important pathway to ethical and effective dialogue.

An example from a popular television show, *The View*, illustrates the compelling power of listening well. In one especially dynamic episode of the program, a tense exchange occurred between cohosts Elisabeth Hasselbeck and Whoopi Goldberg. The topic was prompted by a black politician's controversial use of a racial epithet (the "n-word"). Hasselbeck, who is white, expressed the view that everyone, regardless of race, should refrain from using harmful words because they affect the entire culture. "We don't live in different worlds," asserted Hasselbeck, "we live in the same world." Whoopi Goldberg, who is black, objected vehemently:

> We do live in different worlds . . . what I need you to understand is the frustration that goes along with when you say we live in the same world. It isn't balanced, and we would like it to be, but you have to understand, you have to listen to the fact that we're telling you there are issues, there are huge problems that still affect us and you've got to know this if you want to know us.[1]

Disagreement that occurs between people of different races about race-related topics generates some of the most defensive and combative communication among people within the United States. Having such a disagreement in front of millions of viewers certainly escalates the social pressures to protect one's image and to defend one's perspective. Media coverage compounds a difficult situation. Headlines read: "Fight! Whoopi,

Hasselbeck Slug It Out" and "Whoopi Whoops Hasselbeck" and "Is Elisabeth Hasselbeck Afraid of Whoopi Goldberg?" Despite this recipe for communicative disaster, Goldberg and Hasselbeck's exchange demonstrated moments of sincere engagement.

In the midst of strong emotion and facing an apparent impasse, the two women were willing to continue. Near tears, Hasselbeck asked, "when we live in a world where pop culture then uses that term, and we're trying to get to a place where we feel like we're in the same place, where we feel like we're in the same world . . . how are we supposed to then move forward if we keep using terms that bring back that pain?" Goldberg replied, "You must acknowledge the understanding of what it is and why it is" that black people may use the n-word to different effect. Only after that acknowledgment, Goldberg stated, would it be possible to go forward.

Predictably, the media characterized the exchange in the starkest terms, such as "Goldberg's Tirade" and "Hasselbeck Cries Over the Use of N-Word." One radio and blog commentator, Cenk Uygur, had a different reaction. He felt that both Hasselbeck and Goldberg raised important points. "How do we resolve this?" he asked, "because I think they're both right." He played the clip of their exchange, discussed the salient points, and then answered his initial question. Implicitly, Uygur recognized that two levels of disagreement were taking place.

The first was over the stated topic: who could use the n-word? The second level of disagreement was more subtle, involving the belief whether white and black Americans "lived in the same world." He recognized that Hasselbeck's assertion had the unintended effect of erasing important historical differences in the experiences of black and white Americans.

Uygur concluded that the next step in the exchange should repair that breach, so that the two women could continue to address the controversy over the "n-word." He suggested they try to continue by saying, "Now that you've acknowledged that we come at it from different perspectives, let's try to find a common perspective."[2]

Goldberg, Hasselbeck, and Uygur engaged in a very different type of exchange than the one portrayed by the media, which was based on the argument culture's constructions. One need not share any of their positions or interpretations to notice that they engaged a different *process* of communicating. Goldberg and Hasselbeck's dialogue contained disagreement, strong emotions, and passionate conviction. Within the argument culture, such an occasion might have generated harsh judgment of the differences, blame for the perceived causes, and strident defenses of one's views. Neither Goldberg nor Hasselbeck indulged in these combative habits.

Watching the entire exchange reveals that they *engaged one another by listening*. This dialogic engagement is evident in the many reassurances each woman uttered, such as "I don't want to take that from you," and "I know you don't." They also demonstrated engaged listening by respond-ing to each other's points directly and honestly. Additionally, they showed that they were paying attention through self-reflection, as when Hasselbeck wondered how to address the issue with her daughter, and Goldberg discussed how she grew up. Self-awareness led Hasselbeck to pose a sincere question about how to move forward and Goldberg to state clearly that she needed acknowledgment of their differences. From the video clip, it does not appear that Goldberg and Hasselbeck came to an agreement about who might use the "n-word." But it is evident, as Uygur points out, that their exchange allowed the audience a greater understanding about what each woman thinks and feels.

The quality of the exchange took many by surprise, including com-mentator Uygur. On his news blog, he wrote, "Who would have thought that Elizabeth Hasselbeck and Whoopi Goldberg would begin the racial healing in this country? But I think they did start down that path. They had an interesting discussion about race on *The View*."[3] Uygur's reaction also contributes to this different process of communicating. Unlike so many media outlets, Uygur's headline simply reported the fact: "Elisabeth Hasselbeck and Whoopi Goldberg Have Emotional Race Discussion."

Uygur heard the insights and thoughts offered by both women. He was able to "be in touch with both sides" as recommended by peace advo-cate Thich Nhat Hanh (see chapter 7). Uygur's willingness to listen to both women, without being for one or against the other, allowed him to be open to understanding. As a result, he could hear the two levels of conflict and suggest a mutual way forward. The communication process modeled by Whoopi Goldberg, Elisabeth Hasselbeck, and Cenk Uygur illustrates how we might listen to one another as a means of dialogic engagement and deliberative inquiry. Rather than standing outside and observing from a chosen sideline, we can learn to be receptive to understanding.

Listening to engage is a distinct, first step taken for the purpose of understanding the nature and grounds of our disagreements. It expresses respect, making it possible, as suggested in chapter 2 by theologian Sha-ron Welch, "to take disagreement as an invitation to a deeper relation-ship."[4] Yet, much like other pathways to deliberative inquiry, respectful dialogic engagement does not commit us to adopt specific positions or to take particular courses of action. Instead, listening to engage one another across our disagreements and other forms of difference lays the ground-work for mutual understanding, more informed deliberations, and sound decision making. Below we explore what is required to fulfill this promise.

Listening Receptively

Constructive engagement and deliberative inquiry require listening receptively to one another. What exactly does this mean? Let's first identify three approaches that are *not* part of the process. First, listening receptively is not the same as being uncritically tolerant. The latter type of response expresses tolerance with statements like "everybody has their own opinion," or "you can't debate someone's experience; that's just how it is for them." While seemingly respectful of different perspectives, this uncritical tolerance actually dismisses disputes by refusing to engage other viewpoints. *An open mind is not indifferent.*

Nor does listening receptively entail embracing an uncritical subjectivity. This attitude—often expressed as "I'm okay, you're okay"—seemingly offers unconditional acceptance. It promotes an "anything goes" attitude, without the capacity to discern truth from falsehood or right from wrong. *An engaged, receptive mind is not indiscriminate.*

Listening receptively is also often associated with an idealized objectivity—where we engage "impartially" without any trace of personal bias or preference. And yet, it is not possible to completely eliminate personal values, interests, and emotions in any situation; nor is it usually desirable to do so. Every communicator in an exchange has a rich history of attitudes, beliefs, and experiences. Everyone's interpretive lens is distinctive; everyone is partial. Striving for fair-mindedness is not the equivalent of absolute objectivity, which does not exist. *A receptive mind is not a blank slate.*

Rather than commit us to the impossible, listening receptively allows us to engage one another for the purpose of understanding our differences. To do this skillfully, we rely on three human capacities: *the capacity to be present, to be curious, and to be self-reflexive.* Each capacity is introduced below, as are signals for knowing when an open mind is closing, when it may be time to take a break, or when it is important to set limits or to end the interaction altogether. The goal, as described by consultants at the Public Conversations Project, is to have people "listen openly and respectfully to each other," so *"their relationship shifts from one of opposition to one of interest."*[5]

Rachel Remen, the medical director of the Commonweal Cancer Help Program in California, has learned a great deal about the importance of listening. "Many people with cancer talk about the relief of having someone just listen," she writes, yet "this simple thing has not been that easy to learn." Physicians struggle to express a professional demeanor in an increasingly hectic and stressful work environment, and patients often feel alienated by the impersonal treatment of being seen as a "medical case." Effective medical treatment and healing depend on meaningful communication between patients and their doctors. Dr. Remen concludes, "the most basic and powerful way to connect to another person is to listen. Just listen. Perhaps the most important thing we ever give each other is our attention."[6]

In short, listening receptively calls simply for the quality of *being present—of offering our full, undivided attention.* Think about how it feels to receive someone's full attention. Generally, people remember such experiences as extremely satisfying. The receptive engagement may not have "fixed" the problem or solved a dilemma, but we likely felt closer with the person who listened intently. Similarly, in formal negotiations, listening to engage helps encourage cooperation among the parties.

Being present and offering our full, undivided attention means that we are not multitasking when another person is speaking. We do nothing else physically and mentally except listen. We should cease any activity and quiet any mental "chatter" in order to concentrate on the speaker. This focus allows us to notice more fully not only what the person is saying but also how she or he is saying it. Nonverbal communication constitutes more than half of the meaning inherent in a person's message. Noticing body language, facial expressions, and tone are therefore very important factors in understanding. Once we are able to be present with the speaker, we need to bring sincere curiosity to what is being said.

Sincere curiosity is an important element of listening to engage. As sociologist Sara Lawrence-Lightfoot discovered, "curiosity cannot coexist with a judgmental attitude."[7] This nonjudgmental quality is what we experience in toddlers who continuously ask "Why?" Why does it work that way? Why does he do that? At the moment she asks "Why?" the child isn't evaluating. She simply wants to know and understand what she is experiencing in her world. The same willingness to engage "what is" rather than to determine whether it is what we want or think it should be is at the heart of curiosity. This sincere willingness to explore and learn is the reason curiosity is an integral component of listening with the goal of understanding and deliberative inquiry.

To be fully attentive and curious, we must be physically and mentally present, which takes concentration. It takes consistent effort to listen. Naturally, our minds might wander, or we may get distracted. That's alright. Under these circumstances, we simply can bring our attention back. More likely than not, though, our effort to listen will be interrupted by our *reaction* to what we hear and notice. Because we are not blank slates, we are not indifferent, and reaction is natural. Listening to engage, it might be said, is like a "full contact sport." It involves our whole being—our thoughts, feelings, emotions, and experiences. This is why we need to know ourselves in order to listen well to others and to understand—we need to distinguish our reactions from the speaker's message.

The *capacity to reflect* is a complex and deeply important confluence of abilities and processes. In chapter 5, we looked at the role of critical self-reflection in making dialogic communication possible. Future chapters will be offer fuller explorations of reflection as a critical pathway to constructive engagement. In this chapter, we look at the role of *self-reflection* in listening well.

Self-reflection is understood as a process of looking inward and cultivating self-awareness about who we are, what we think and feel, and what matters to us. Self-reflection enables us to recognize our reactions and their effect on our capacity to listen with an open mind. Relating to others with sincere interest requires us to explore the roots of our responses.

People in the helping professions understand the importance of self-reflection to relationships and to reasoned and just decision making. For example, mediators are professional listeners who help people understand their disagreements and to work toward a mutually satisfying solution. In order to do their jobs fairly and with integrity, mediators develop a professional ethos of impartiality or neutrality. However, the mediation field recognizes the caveat mentioned earlier—no one is a blank slate. Everyone's interpretive lens influences how they take in what they encounter; everyone is partial.

Given this facet of the profession, John McConnell suggests that mediators "must listen in such a way that we are aware of the processes of meaning-building taking place in our own minds as we listen."[8] In future chapters, we will explore influences shaping how individuals and groups make meaning. As these discussions will reveal, self-reflection helps us to discover our own governing interpretive frames. This process in turn enables us to recognize our limits, as well as to monitor the extent to which we are fully present to the other.

Self-reflection helps us discover what might drive our curiosity or repel it. If we listen to our inner voice, we can hear the myriad ways we close down. Closing down need not be positive or negative on its own. Our attention may drift because of fatigue or awareness of significant external factors, such as time constraints. Our curiosity may wane from boredom or be piqued by fascination. Most often we close down based on our reactions to what we hear. Recognizing the reasons for shutting down offers us essential information and lets us know when we are near or have reached the limits to being open. Karen and Charlie's interaction offers an example.

Karen believes that people who have secured large homes, significant capital, and other material resources throughout their lifetimes may be deemed successful. She believes further that, at the end of one's life, making sure that one's family is left with as many resources as possible reflects a particularly strong sense of responsibility and fulfillment of one's overarching purpose. Charlie, on the other hand, believes that success is measured by an individual's record of service, communion, environmental sustainability, and civic engagement. Further, from his perspective, we have a moral obligation to use as few material resources as possible throughout our lifetimes.

It is easy to imagine how, within the argument culture, Charlie and Karen may have difficulty engaging one another's perspectives constructively. It is likely that they will soon find themselves talking at and across one another, succumbing to forms of judgment and condemnation, and shutting down with little sense of connection.

While a culture of engagement provides more constructive avenues for communicating across differences, it is nevertheless important for interlocutors from such fundamentally different orientations to recognize the substantive nature of their differences. As they engage with one another, both Charlie and Karen will need to monitor how they are feeling. Through self-reflection, each will be able to recognize the limits of their capacities to remain open, thereby helping them to retain their integrity without compromising the quality of their engagement with one another.

There are a number of common reactions impeding receptive listening across differences such as these.[9] Often, these reactions are interrelated, and more than one could be happening at the same time. Some examples include: (1) judgments—determining whether the speaker is right or wrong; (2) distortions—our personal biases and preferences change the meaning of what the speaker said; (3) stereotype—pigeonholing speakers or ideas based on our preconceptions; (4) resistance—focus on faultfinding; and (5) attraction—believing what we hear because we find a person attractive or an idea popular.

These and other types of personal reactions are not about the person or position that we are trying to understand. Instead, our reactions express *our* own feelings and thoughts. This tendency would be evident if one surveyed other listeners who heard the same message and experienced different reactions because of *their* own feelings and thoughts. *When we react, we gain access to information about ourselves.*

For example, within the United States, the public is asked regularly whether they approve of the president's job performance. How do we account for the different reactions about the same leader? Our reactions, be they largely positive or negative, tell us about our own priorities and belief systems. During President George W. Bush's administration, for example, some held a more favorable view because they saw the president's leadership style as "decisive" or "resolute," while others saw the same qualities as "stubborn" or "simplistic."[10] Did they react positively because they felt reassured by confidence or because they valued clarity in purpose? Did others experience negative reactions because they wanted more flexibility in addressing changing circumstances or because they believed that issues are complex and nuanced? The answers would identify what the *respondent* held important—be it security, steadfastness, responsiveness, or contemplation. As each of us considers our reactions, we learn much about our disposition, our individual moral map, our belief system, and other factors framing our meaning-making processes. *Our reactions tell us who we are and what matters to us.*

Self-reflection plays an important role in our efforts to listen respectfully and to understand accurately. Self-reflection is key to engaged listening, for we must listen to ourselves respectfully in order to be present, fully attentive, and sincerely curious about others. Our reactions also are important guides to when we may have reached our limit, need to take a break, or to end the interaction. As we practice listening to understand, we will find that we are better prepared for making sense of the interaction with those who hold different points of view.

Listening to Make Sense of the Interaction with Others

The reality of interdependence motivates us to make sense of our interactions with others, whether we have similar or different perspectives. Recall the scientific definition of interdependence from chapter 2: *every actor and action directly or indirectly affects everyone and everything else."* [11] The same is true of communication. Our perspectives on issues may develop in oppositional ways—pro and con, point and counter-point—as they do in debates. Our points of view also evolve cooperatively, as when study partners work together to solve a problem, or jury members review the evidence, or an advertising team brainstorms about marketing ideas. Whether we communicate competitively or cooperatively, we affect each other's perspectives during the process.

When we observe that communication develops interdependently, we increasingly become aware that *every perspective is partial.* Each of us sees things from our own point of view, which necessarily means that there are some things that we do not see and others to which we may attach differing levels of significance than does someone else. This partiality is important for it expresses our individuality, "our side of the story." Yet, our necessarily partial perspectives also mean that we must depend on others for the fullest understanding of a given topic or issue, particularly when we disagree. When we have made ourselves available to take in someone else's point of view by being present, curious and self-reflective, we have taken an important step in the allied pursuits of understanding and deliberative inquiry.

Importantly, our partiality extends to our listening styles. Human beings tend to develop different listening patterns. For example, some of us listen for the "big picture," while others focus keenly on specific details. Different approaches to listening affect what information we take in, how we understand it, and what we bring back to the interaction. As we listen with the goal of understanding, we develop an awareness of our own styles of filtering and processing, which in turn helps us to recognize how our approach to listening affects what we hear and notice.

Communication researchers have identified *four basic listening styles* for taking in oral information: *people oriented, action oriented, content oriented,* and *time oriented.* [12] *People-oriented* listeners are generally inclined to tune in to the speaker's values, feelings, and emotions. They "tend to search for areas of common interest with a speaker" [13] and often emphasize sympathy or empathy in their responses. *Action-oriented* listeners "prefer logical, organized speakers and direct, to-the-point messages." People who use this listening style "tend to scrutinize incoming messages for errors and inconsistencies."[14] People who are oriented toward *content listening* also have a tendency to dissect incoming messages but are "more likely to focus on the speaker's supporting evidence." They tend to "welcome complex and challenging information, listen to facts before forming judgments and opinion, or favor listening to technical information."[15] Finally, *time-oriented* listeners are inclined to prioritize the amount of time an interaction takes. They tend to perceive lengthy or "wordy" speakers as "wasting time" and will be more likely to interrupt others in order to manage the time involved.[16]

Recent studies found that cultural background influenced listening styles. One group of international researchers determined that young adults in Germany tended to prefer the action orientation, while many Israeli youth favored the content style. In the United States, a significant percentage of Americans embraced both the people and time orientations to listening.[17] Listening styles also may impact deliberation and decision making. When asked to assess negligence and damages in a mock case involving a failed savings and loan, a communication researcher found that jurors with a people orientation tended to find the defendants less at fault because they learned about their "good faith" efforts and actual experiences, but they knew the plaintiffs only as a "corporation." Conversely, time-oriented jurors favored awarding higher damages for the plaintiffs, either to express how the jurors tended to value their own time spent at the trial or to punish the guilty for apparently "wasting their time."[18]

Although anyone can utilize any of the different listening orientations, most people tend to stick with one pattern across various contexts and situations. While this may not always be helpful (think of the action-oriented listener growing frustrated with his partner's emotional outburst) or even healthy (imagine the stress a time-oriented person experiences listening to a long, technical explanation of what went wrong mechanically with her car), people usually employ one listening style. No matter which style we prefer, we can enhance our ability to take in and understand what people say to us through attentive listening.

Attentive Listening

Attentive listening is a practice that brings awareness to the different levels of listening and facilitates understanding what we hear. When we listen attentively, we recognize *three levels of input*: the speaker's *content* and *empathic meaning* as well as *our own critical response*. On the content level, we primarily gather factual information—to know precisely what the speaker said. The empathic level helps us identify what the speaker's message means by identifying salient feelings, attitudes, or interests. When we shift our attention from what the speaker is saying to our own reactions and evaluations, we are listening on the critical response level. Here our reactions may be positive or negative. We experience a response to the content of the message, its apparent meaning, and any inferences we may discern. Distinguishing the three levels of input helps us sort through and gain perspective on what we take in, experience, and understand.

In the example below, Teresa gives an oral presentation on the sentences of life without parole for juveniles. One of her college classmates, Mary, is assigned to report back on the presentation, using attentive listening. In this first exchange, Mary reports back on the content level of Teresa's presentation:

> **Teresa:** The Supreme Court ruled in *Miller v. Alabama* in June 2012 that life without parole for juveniles was cruel and unusual punishment; the Court did not specify if the ruling was retroactive for the 2,570 people serving sentences of life without parole for crimes committed before they were eighteen years old. Maurice Bailey is one of those people. He was fifteen when he killed his 15-year-old pregnant girlfriend and has served almost 20 years in prison. He is a different person today. Western Europe has shown its moral superiority by not imposing the death penalty on juveniles—which the United States did until 2005—and by not imposing life without parole sentences on juveniles— which the United States did for non-homicide cases until 2010. With the *Miller* ruling, the United States has finally risen to Western European standards—except for the more than 2,500 people languishing in prison because they were sentenced before 2012, It is time for us to find a more humane alternative for anyone who committed a crime when they were not yet 18 years old. They were not capable of reasoning as an adult, yet they were sentenced as if they were.

> **Mary:** Teresa has reported that there are currently 2,570 people serving sentences of life without parole for crimes committed before their eighteenth birthdays. Maurice Bailey is one of these people. She claims that America's image abroad has been harmed by its treatment of juveniles until notable Supreme Court rulings in 2005, 2010, and 2012. She would like us to find an alternative for people sentenced to prison without the possibility of parole before the most recent ruling.

Mary demonstrates her ability to listen on the content level by providing a clear and accurate account of the facts and positions reflected in Teresa's speech. Mary only reports on what Teresa actually said. As someone focused on listening to understand, Mary does not add any personal interpretation or reaction to the facts and positions she heard from Teresa.

Listening for content is important but does not by itself generate a full understanding of a person's message or purpose. Mary needs to go to the next level and listen for empathic meaning. At the empathic level, we listen for a number of clues to detect a speaker's meaning. We listen for the speaker to convey any specific attitude, belief, value, feeling, emotion, need, or interest to reveal what matters to her. Here, Mary's first effort to understand Teresa's meaning goes a bit awry:

> I really don't see the big deal, Teresa. After all, the Supreme Court
> ruled that the United States will no longer sentence juveniles to
> life without parole. Lawyers will eventually get around to
> addressing the cases of people sentenced before 2012.

In her report back, Mary shows she has not fully understood the essence and purpose of Teresa's speech. Mary did not convey Teresa's distress about the people serving prison terms without the hope of parole for crimes they committed when they were children. If Mary takes an *open interest* in how Teresa experiences this situation, Mary would hear that Teresa is deeply moved by what she believes is the suffering of people who have changed. She also is intensely concerned about what she believes is a symptom of U.S. moral inferiority to other Western nations. Had Mary listened empathically she might have contributed the following to the exchange:

> Teresa is very concerned about the suffering of the more than
> 2,500 people serving sentences without the possibility of parole.
> She thinks the moral standing of the United States around the
> world suffered because of its treatment of juveniles in the past.

In the rephrasing above, Mary identifies the empathic meaning of Teresa's speech. Mary picks up on Teresa's feelings—hearing concern and distress. Mary also recognizes Teresa's conclusion as a statement of belief about what should be done next.

At both the content and empathic meaning level, the listener focuses exclusively on the speaker's message. Mary's initial empathic response went awry not only because she missed important aspects of what the topic meant to Teresa but also because Mary added her own reaction and judgment to her report. The listener's personal reactions and evaluations are not relevant on either the content or empathic level of listening, only the speaker's content and feelings should be reflected there.

Importantly, listeners do not come to an interaction as blank slates or indifferent to what they hear, even when they sincerely want to understand. As a result, we too often impose our own meanings on the message we are trying to understand, diminishing accuracy and straining the interaction. Attentive listening creates a third level where we can hear our own reactions and evaluations. When our goal is to understand, it is best to express the critical level only *after* demonstrating effective content and empathic listening and *when* the speaker is ready to listen openly to us. The critical assessment of a message, while an important third level of listening, does not need to be conveyed immediately. In addition, it is not necessarily positive or negative. In this instance, Mary's critical response expresses doubt, raises other issues, and asks clarifying questions. Mary and Teresa need an opportunity for extended conversation simply to understand each other's perspective on Teresa's topic. Their success in understanding their disparate concerns will be greater if they can listen to one another with open minds and engage each other consciously on the three different levels of listening. One last set of skills can improve interactions dramatically.

Verifying through Responsiveness

The *purpose of responsiveness* is to maintain the communicative connection between listener and speaker and to insure as accurate a reception of the message as possible. Responsiveness is communicated, in part, when we *acknowledge, summarize, and paraphrase* the communicator's contributions.

When we *acknowledge* something someone says, we let them know we have heard a particular point or specific concern. Acknowledgment is the equivalent of saying, "so this is what's real for you." When we *summarize* someone's perspective, we try to repeat their main points and their conclusion. Summarizing is like coming to a bottom-line assessment: so this is what is important, and this is what it means to you. *When listeners acknowledge and summarize, they focus on the speaker's message.*

Paraphrasing is somewhat different from acknowledging and summarizing. When we *paraphrase* someone else's view, we try to *represent the listener's understanding* of what the speaker said. When we paraphrase, we may include more of our interpretation of the empathic meaning, the inferences we drew, and, to a lesser extent, our critical reactions. In effect, we tell the speaker more about what we're hearing in an attempt to verify the accuracy of our listening. We're saying, this is what it sounds like to me. Is that what you mean?

The skillful use of acknowledging, summarizing, and paraphrasing complements our efforts to listen receptively and to engage another person sincerely. When we respond in these ways, we demonstrate that we are trying to understand and that we are interacting respectfully. Two friends having lunch together discovered that they needed to employ responsiveness to help them work through a difficult conversation.

Ernesto and Mariela, both first generation descendants of Mexican immigrants to the United States, were debating whether they would refer to themselves as Hispanics or Chicano/as. Ernesto feels deeply committed to the term, "Hispanic," because it signifies to him the successful integration of Mexicans and their children into the U.S. main-stream. Mariela, however, feels that "Chicano/a" better expresses her pride in the cultural distinctiveness of the Mexican-American community, especially its indigenous roots, which she is deeply committed to preserving. The exchange is rather tense:

> **Mariela:** You said that the term "Hispanic" better represents us because it integrates us into the mainstream. But you're wrong! That term celebrates the conquerors of our indigenous ancestors, it's not ours. The United States government imposed that term on all Spanish speakers for the 1980 census.
>
> **Ernesto:** At least the U.S. government included us! "Chicano" was invented by sixties radicals who were trying to separate themselves from the mainstream. We'll never be successful if we adopt that kind of in-your-face politics.

In this exchange, Mariela and Ernesto are each taking in the other's perspective exclusively through their own interpretive lenses, "hearing" only on their one terms. To understand one another's perspectives, they would each need to take a breath, get curious about what is going on for the other person, and soften their own reactivity through self-reflection. At this point, they may reflect that they are feeling very passionate and possibly somewhat angry. If they want to truly hear one another, they will need to relax their strong feelings in order to make enough space to be present and to listen.

As they listen attentively, they will continue to be aware of the other person's content and meaning, as well as their own critical reactions. To work through the complexity of the interaction and to take care of their friendship, they practice responsiveness. They need to begin by acknowledging their different priorities—Ernesto's emphasis on successful integration and Mariela's interest in preserving cultural distinctiveness.

Acknowledging what matters most to each other could open the possibility of being able to take in more. Mariela could listen carefully and summarize Ernesto's argument by repeating his key points—the examples of successful politicians, businesspeople, and community organizers who refer to themselves as Hispanic; polls that mention greater acceptance of the term by non-Hispanic Americans; and its common usage in the media—and by restating his conclusion that "Hispanic" better represents their community because it symbolizes successful integration. When Mariela finishes her summary, she *verifies* its accuracy with Ernesto. Did she capture the gist of what mattered to him? Does she understand what he wants her to know and what he thinks should be done about it? Ernesto may confirm the accuracy of Mariela's summary or offer clarifications or corrections. Mariela would then try to summarize his perspective more accurately until they both agreed it was satisfactory.

After listening attentively to Mariela, Ernesto could paraphrase her position by describing the passion he hears when she talks about cultural pride and expressing sorrow at hearing how angry she is about racism and imperialism. It would be helpful for him to say that he is not trying to change her mind or to minimize her anger; rather, he admires her resolve and knows that she wants to protect the Mexican-American heritage that is so important to her. Checking with Mariela will enable Ernesto both to verify the accuracy of his understanding of what she is seeking to convey and to receive feedback on his interpretation and critical response.

Mariela and Ernesto may or may not come to an agreement; the topic may become a long-running dispute. However, when they listen with open minds to one another, when they engage each other with respect, and when they make sense of their interaction together, they stand a better chance of understanding each other and remaining friends. They will have taken good care of their relationship by honing their understanding of both their own and each other's perspective. Through respectful engagement, both Mariela and Ernesto will be better equipped to contribute to reasoned and just decision making.

Caveats

Lisbeth Lipari identifies listening as among the most important avenues to responsiveness and fulfillment of our human potential. At the same time, however, Lipari cautions that "among the innumerable ways I can fail to respond ethically, the communicative subjection of the other to myself is perhaps among the most hidden. This is when I insist on understanding on my terms only and hold fast to my cognitive preconceptions and categories and simply assimilate what I already know, or think I know, about the other or his or her point of view." Lipari goes on to counsel a giving up of "our attachment to our familiar and already understood certainties and cognitions about the world in order to fully recognize the other."[19]

Lipari's exploration of *listening otherwise* emphasizes the importance of "listening that is fully present, embodied, and centered. It is an internal but not an isolated state—it is fully within reach of and open to receive the other." She goes on to caution against insisting on "understanding, or familiarity, or shared feelings." Responsible and responsive listening, she adds, is a "kind of looking and listening without objectification or appropriation but with a kind of awareness that makes space for the unthinkable, the unimaginable, the other."[20]

In a phone interview regarding his book, *Why Can't We Be Good?* philosopher Jacob Needleman offered a different, but related, "take" on what Lipari identifies as the art of listening otherwise. After a life of observation and reflection, Needleman has concluded that people know deep down what it means to be good but often lack the bridge to translating that knowledge into their behavior. We know what it is to be good, he said, "but when we go out into the street and meet with difficulties or even minor irritations, suddenly we betray our values." After carefully pondering this inconsistency, Needleman reported "a great discovery:"

> I found it in my classroom— . . . with *the work of listening to another person—that listening becomes a deeply moral action.* And this is something we can all practice . . . there is an actual spiritual discipline and work of listening to another person, particularly when they disagree with us. [It] requires that we step back from our own ego, from our own opinions, and let the other person in, not to agree with them, or disagree, but simply to let their thought into my own mind, and when I step back from myself in that way, I begin to be a much more moral person. There's a relation that establishes with another human being which is a definite, concrete step toward really caring for another person. It doesn't last, perhaps, the moment we get out into the street, maybe it's no longer there, but it's a step.[21]

Conclusion

In this chapter we have discussed how listening for the purposes of meaningful engagement and deliberative inquiry helps to repair the breach between individual interest and social responsibility. Listening well lays a groundwork required to hear and be heard, to understand and be understood. To listen in this way, we attend to the other receptively and attentively, using our human capacities to be present, curious, and self-reflexive. As we develop our capacities for receptive, engaged listening, we become better prepared for making sense of interactions with others who hold different views.

Making sense together necessitates further development of our listening skills. We need to become aware of different listening styles and how they filter incoming messages. To compensate for our particular filters, we employ an attentive listening process which disciplines the "taking in" of messages by distinguishing three levels of input: the content and empathic meaning of the speaker and the critical response of the listener. Finally, listeners need to verify engagement through responsiveness. We respond to others by acknowledging, summarizing, and paraphrasing what we have heard, and by seeking clarity and confirmation with the speaker on his or her terms.

Listening well provides a critical pathway to mutual understanding and deliberative inquiry. The next chapter builds on this foundation. As we will see, the art of understanding is itself often misunderstood within the argument culture, creating obstacles to our abilities to tap into collective wisdom in pursuit of common purpose. Reframing understanding for dialogue and deliberation within an interdependent world enables us to overcome these obstacles.

Understanding

The opening chapters emphasized that most people—regardless of background or experience—desire to be accepted, to belong, and to live meaningfully within a community. Nearly everyone desires to be heard, known, and understood. In addition, most of us seek to make wise decisions and do the right thing most of the time. The argument culture and adversarial individualism, however, often undermine our efforts to relate ethically with one another. Set apart from one another through competitive opposition, we often struggle to balance self-interest and the common good.

As we have seen, living well in today's globally interdependent world—where actions increasingly impact others directly or indirectly—requires renewed effort to address this struggle. We have introduced the interrelated ideas of a culture of dialogic engagement and an ethic of interdependence to illustrate that we can choose to relate to disagreement in ways that integrate constructive connection and effective decision making. Rather than remain entrenched in zero-sum power struggles, we can reach across our differences in pursuit of common purpose.

The previous chapter underscored the role that listening well plays in fulfilling communication's constructive potential. However, fulfillment of this potential rests in large part on the associated art of understanding. In the discussion below, we will focus our attention on this critical resource for skillful dialogic communication.

We begin by uncovering widespread misconceptions about the pursuit of understanding. Like the concept of interdependence, the concept of understanding, ironically, is fraught with misunderstanding. Below we address commonly held concerns and misconceptions about its nature and purpose, reframe the art for dialogue and deliberation, and highlight its importance to engaged, interdependent communication.

Misconceptions about the Art of Understanding

Understanding is a complex art. It is often difficult to know, for example, whether we have truly achieved understanding—whether of a situation, an issue, or of another's perspective. And while there are a number of strategies available for enhancing our capacity to achieve understanding, a simple definition of the term remains elusive.

In relational communication contexts, understanding includes, but is not limited to, *grasping the meaning of what another is seeking to convey.* In our exploration of listening well we noted, for example, how empathic listening moves beyond listening strictly for content. Being able to paraphrase what someone else has said in such a way that she or he experiences a sense of being heard is one of several means available for helping to insure that we have grasped the other's meaning.

Each of us welcomes the sincere efforts of others to understand us and our points of view; we feel more closely connected with those who make such efforts. We know too the frustration—and sometimes even despair—we experience when others misunderstand what we are seeking to convey. In short, we recognize in our own experiences how important understanding is to the quality of our relationships.

Similarly, being able to gain *deep, reliable insight into an issue or problem*—the heart of understanding in the context of decision making—is critical to reasoned and just decision making. Our explorations of listening and other forms of deliberative inquiry have revealed, for example, how the ability to understand issues, problems, and others' perspectives enables people to tap the collective wisdom in pursuit of knowledge and truth.

This insight provides strong grounding for our shared commitment to freedom of expression. Through the free exchange of ideas across our disagreements and other forms of difference, we have the opportunity to discern what is more or less true, just, wise, and reasonable in ways impossible without such openness. Understanding the ideas and insights of others helps us to assess the strengths and limits of our perspectives through different lenses.

We have the potential for understanding one another even across vast divides in part because we share a *common humanity.* As the Dalai Lama observes, no matter who we are or where we live, most people want to be happy and to avoid suffering.[1] Although the human condition is experienced differently across the globe, most people share these basic inclinations. Speaking to *The Women's Conference 2007* in Long Beach, California, Queen Rania Al Abdullah of Jordan expressed optimism that these and related sources of common ground create the possibility of cross-cultural understanding:

> I am convinced that we are all much more alike than we are differ-
> ent . . . that the experiences that shape us, no matter where we grow

up, bring out the same very human responses—of tears and laughter, fear and courage, uncertainty and enlightenment. My hope is that you will see part of yourself in me, just as I have seen myself reflected in other women's lives around the world.[2]

Human beings, though unique and distinctive, nevertheless share a common existence and, with relatively few exceptions, have the potential to engage openly with one another. Yet, we recognize that people at home and abroad have experienced violent conflict and social antagonism in part because of a failure to understand or even accept one another's humanity. Some of this failure can be attributed to widespread misunderstandings of what it means to understand others across our differences.

Common Misunderstandings about Understanding

Thich Nhat Hanh, a Vietnamese Buddhist monk, advised: "When we want to understand something, we cannot just stand outside and observe it. We have to enter deeply into it and be one with it to really understand."[3] He practiced this approach to understanding as an international advocate for nonviolence during the Vietnam War. Neither the Communist nor the non-Communist Vietnamese governments welcomed his ideas; both governments relied on violent methods for convincing the populace to endorse their competing ideologies. Nhat Hanh was exiled from his country because both governments were threatened by his practice of nonviolent understanding. One year later, in 1967, Dr. Martin Luther King Jr. nominated Thich Nhat Hanh for the Nobel Peace Prize in recognition of his leadership in the international nonviolent movement.

Today, Thich Nhat Hanh's approach to nonviolent understanding and peacemaking is "world renowned."[4] Over the decades, he has highlighted the role of listening to understand as a means of resolving conflict and practicing peace:

> In order to help reconcile a conflict, we have to be in touch with both sides. . . . We have to have a non-dualistic viewpoint in order to listen to both sides and understand. The world needs persons like this for the work of reconciliation, persons with the capacity of understanding and compassion.[5]

Despite widespread acceptance in theory, Thich Nhat Hanh's nonviolent understanding may be difficult to practice. When we disagree, we often see ourselves as separate from and competing with one another, making it challenging "to listen to both sides." In fact, the argument culture and adversarial individualism offer little motivation for "entering deeply" and "really understanding" each other. Instead, we are taught to judge differences, to look for blame, and to defend our positions and reputations. These adversarial practices encourage us "to stand outside and observe" the other in disagreement.

The costs of this adversarial stance are high. As we observed in ear-lier chapters, approaching others as opponents intensifies the likelihood that the reasons for disagreement will be misunderstood and that the conflict will escalate. When we invest more in being "right" than in lis-tening to a different perspective, we risk poor judgment or flawed analy-sis. In an effort to protect our status or reputation, we may reject an honest exchange, even though we find mutual understanding extremely gratifying. To prevent "losing" the argument, we may manipulate the decision, although we know evaluating the available options fairly leads to the wisest action. All these "trade-offs" end up as counterproductive choices. They strain our relationships and diminish our decision making. In the process, these adversarial tactics also reflect significant misunder-standings about the concept of "understanding."

Genuine understanding is produced through *connecting* with each other by means of an open mind, an honest exchange, and fair evalua-tions. Sincerity, honesty, and fairness are all commonly regarded as vir-tues. Within the context of the argument culture and adversarial individualism, however, such virtues may be subsumed to the central goal of controlling the outcome and winning. Under these circumstances, the same virtues may be used strategically or even become liabilities. In this state of competitive opposition, a call to truly understand differ-ences—like the concepts of interdependence and cooperation discussed earlier—generates much controversy. The following sections address some common misinterpretations about understanding others with whom we disagree.

Misunderstanding Number One:
Listening to Understand Equals Assent

Many within the argument culture worry *that listening to understand conveys agreement or validation.* As we noted in earlier chapters, however, this assumption is inaccurate. On the one hand, a culture of engagement encourages the free exchange of opinions. In fact, as we will see in the next chapter, the engagement of others' ideas on their own terms provides the very grounds needed for deliberative inquiry. And as such, reasoned and informed decision making depends on the ability to listen for under-standing. *However, the act of listening itself does not grant assent or validation.*

Close friends since childhood, Louisa and Gail share many values and beliefs. However, they disagree strongly on the topic of abortion. Louisa has spent much of her adult life devoted to insuring women's right to choose, while Gail has worked for years as a pro-life advocate. Recently, they've both been asked to contribute to development of abor-tion policy legislation in their home state.

Afraid to destroy an otherwise beautiful relationship, Louisa and Gail have carefully avoided discussing this highly contentious topic with one another in the past. In light of their opportunity to assist lawmakers in framing a reasoned and just state abortion policy, however, they have decided to make an effort to hear and understand one another's points of view.

The results proved invaluable to their abilities to contribute meaningfully to the legislative deliberation process. Through attentive listening and deliberative inquiry, Louisa and Gail were able to identify compelling common ground. They learned, for example, that they both feel sorrow in the face of women's abortions; neither of them is "pro-abortion." At the same time, they have discovered that they both strongly support women's autonomy; neither of them is "anti-choice."

These revelations have helped Gail and Louisa identify the "true" sources of their disagreement. Among these, perhaps the most salient are their different perspectives regarding when life begins. Gail believes that life begins at conception. Given this conviction, Gail views abortion at any point in a pregnancy as the taking of an innocent life. From her perspective, this terrible violation of human rights must not be permitted, even if preventing an abortion risks compromising the pregnant woman's needs and interests.

Louisa shares Gail's sense that all abortions are tragedies. Like her friend, she feels sorrow for everyone involved in a situation involving an abortion. She does not believe, however, that an abortion before viability involves the taking of a life. In her view, life begins at viability (or later). Given this assumption, Gail does not believe that the state has a compelling justification for compromising women's rights to their bodies' autonomy at any time before viability.

Through sincere and attentive listening, Louisa and Gail have opened themselves to understanding one another's views. This process in turn has enabled each of them to contribute more fully to the legislative deliberations. Together, they have been able to assist others in identifying points of convergence and divergence, enabling all of the decision makers to gain greater insights into the strengths and limits of various policy options. Importantly, however, neither Louisa nor Gail "acquiesced" or "assented" to each other's positions at any point in the deliberative process.

As this case illustrates, pursuit of understanding does not equate with agreement or assent. And yet, within the argument culture, people often resist efforts to listen for understanding out of a concern that their open engagement may inadvertently convey acquiescence. This misconception gravely compromises our abilities to reach across our disagreements and other forms of difference in pursuit of sound decisions.

Misunderstanding Number Two: Willingness to Understand Equals Lack of Conviction

A related misunderstanding is the common misconception that efforts to understand divergent perspectives demonstrate a *lack of conviction or authority*. As a reflection of this view, many within the argument culture believe that listening will be taken as a signal of uncertainty, suggesting a willingness to yield too easily.

Louisa's close friend Robert, for example, urges her not to engage openly with Gail. He is worried that any effort to understand the "other" perspective will be seen by the legislators as a sign that Louisa is second-guessing her position and should therefore not be taken seriously. In Robert's words, "For heaven's sake, Louisa, don't you realize that by giving the impression you are taking the proabortion perspective seriously, you will be undermining your authority?"

Fortunately, Louisa does not share Robert's interpretation of the circumstances. She trusts that the legislative committee will value her willingness to engage respectfully with those whose views differ from hers. Further, she sees open engagement with Gail as an opportunity for everyone involved to identify points of convergence and disagreement, to identify available options, and to assess the relative strengths and limits of each. Unlike Robert, Louisa has come to understand that proponents of choice are not "proabortion." This important insight is invaluable to the deliberative process.

At the World Affairs Council in Los Angeles, Republican Senator and presidential candidate John McCain issued a call for a "League of Democracies" where "like-minded nations [are] working together in the cause of peace." The United States would maintain its sovereignty, asserted Senator McCain, but the League's "democratic solidarity" would require that "Americans must be willing to listen to the views and respect the collective will of our democratic allies."[6] The Senator's proposal was rejected by columnist Star Parker. The heart of her objection reflects the argument culture's concern over maintaining the strength of one's convictions and authority.

> We, of course, should strive for peace and seek commerce with all. But let's not forget who we are and seek some pseudo-tranquility by compromising ourselves and becoming more like others.[7]

Ms. Parker elaborated, expressing concern that the "moral uniqueness" of the United States would be compromised by efforts to understand and respect other nations. Such efforts, she maintains, would cede the nation's moral authority to foreign countries and generate only a pyrrhic victory of "pseudo-tranquility"—not peace. She chides the senator, saying, "Remember, John, 'For what is a man profited, if he shall gain the whole world and lose his soul?'" Parker's preferred foreign policy requires that the United States be "free" from the constraints of considering other perspectives in order to maintain national interests and sovereignty.

The problem of conflating the pursuit of understanding with agreement and lack of conviction is so widespread that it has resulted in what journalist Bill Bishop calls "The Big Sort." The poem by Emma Lazarus engraved on the Statue of Liberty describes the United States as a beacon to the tired, the poor, and the huddled masses from all over the planet. In the last thirty years, however, the country has moved away from celebrating our unique diversity and toward creating more and more homogenous communities. This nationwide "sorting," asserts Bishop, is happening because:

> The old systems of order—around land, family, class, tradition, and religious denomination—gave way. They were replaced over the next thirty years with a new order based on individual choice. Today we seek our own kind in like-minded churches, like-minded neighborhoods, and like-minded sources of news and entertainment.[8]

This sorting is different from earlier patterns of enforced segregation or mass migrations for economic mobility (such as the Dust Bowl migration to California during the Depression or the Great Migration north of African Americans during the twentieth century). This recent migration, explains Bishop, is propelled by a desire to live in "communities of interest—enclaves defined more by similar beliefs or ways of life than by age, employment or income."[9]

This phenomenon appears to be replicated by cyber-communication patterns. Preliminary research suggests, for example, that "the vast majority of bloggers link only to like-minded blogs." One study in particular suggests that "when 'liberal' bloggers comment on 'conservative' blog posts, and vice versa, a plurality of comments simply cast contempt for opposing views."[10] Harvard Law Professor Cass Sunstein notes further:

> Only a quarter of cross-ideological posts involve genuine substantive discussion. In this way, real deliberation is often occurring within established points of view, but only infrequently across them.[11]

Sequestering ourselves in "like-minded clusters" has had two related effects. First, when we live among and interact largely with people who think and see the world as we do, we create an echo chamber that reverberates with only our own preferences. Bishop elaborates: "We now live in a giant feedback loop, hearing our own thoughts about what's right and wrong bounced back to us by the television shows we watch, the newspapers and books we read, the blogs we visit online, the sermons we hear, and the neighborhoods we live in."[12] This continuous cycle of confirming our own beliefs leads people to "become more extreme in their thinking."[13] We see this effect in the red state/blue state polarization of politics and in the confrontational "us versus them" animus that pervades talk media, Internet communications, and even news programming.

The second significant effect of conflating the pursuit of understanding with agreement, acquiescence, or conformity is that it generates disparagement of those who live elsewhere and believe differently. During national election cycles, this denigration has found voice in denigrating phrases, such as "San Francisco Values."[14] In this example, the city of

San Francisco became a metaphor for public policies opposed by the Republican Party, in the way that "Hicksville" operates more generically for regions considered very conservative. More to the point, both of these terms reveal the "segregation by way of life" in the United States. The consequences, declares Bishop, are "pockets of like-minded citizens that have become so ideologically inbred that we don't know, can't understand, and can barely conceive of 'those people' who live just a few miles away."[15]

In effect, there is an increasing tendency among people in the United States to "understand" only those with whom they already agree and to demonize those with whom they differ. Communication patterns during the last thirty years have intensified the trend, but the concern that understanding others' views conveys agreement or acquiescence is not new. This idea also functions as a defense or coping mechanism to deal with the unfamiliar or unwanted. If we believe that understanding differences opens the door to condoning ideas or values we find objectionable, then we are justified in "standing outside and observing." We may take comfort in being right inside our like-minded communities and close the door to different perspectives.

Sorting ourselves into like-minded communities replaces the struggle to control outcomes or to win arguments. We shift our efforts to maintaining conformity with those who think as we do. Our search for others who are "like-minded" can have other negative consequences. We may submerge self-interest not to the common good but to *shared norms*. Robert J. Samuelson warns about the dangers of conformity for democracy:

> What Arthur Schlesinger Jr. called "the vital center" is being slowly disenfranchised. Party "bases" become more important than their numbers justify. Passionate partisans dislike compromise and consensus. They want to demolish the other side. Whether from left or right, the danger is a tyranny of true believers.[16]

Misunderstanding Number Three: Understanding Differences Increases the Risk of Being Wrong

Equating the pursuit of understanding with signaling agreement or uncertainty leads to a third concern: that *understanding differences increases the risk of being "wrong"* and becoming a "loser" in the argument culture. Admitting an error is always difficult, but acknowledging fallibility becomes even more challenging when we are emotionally attached to a particular perspective. The human tendency to want to be right and to "save face" grows even more intense when situated in a culture that declares "victory" when proving others wrong. This adversarial opposition inhibits people from learning new things—because of the fear of being wrong. As Thomas W. Martin points out, it also prevents us from learning from our mistakes:

Many commentators have rightly implored us to make certain that young people encounter the "thrill" of discovery. While this is undeniably desirable, it is arguably even more crucial that they experience the agony (if only on a modest scale) of having a pet hypothesis demolished by facts.[17]

Martin emphasizes the importance of teaching students to learn from mistakes because it instills the value of scientific knowledge over the all-too-human desire to verify preconceptions or to privilege personal accomplishment. He also is concerned about the cultural assumption that being wrong is the same as being weak:

> Several current presidential candidates have insisted that they oppose the scientific account of earth's natural history as a matter of principle. In the present cultural climate, altering one's beliefs in response to anything (facts included) is considered a sign of weakness. Students must be convinced that changing one's mind in light of evidence is not weakness: Changing one's mind is the essence of intellectual growth.[18]

The argument culture's concern that understanding different perspectives increases the risk of being wrong devalues the important lesson of learning from our mistakes. It also imposes a negative connotation on accountability. Helen Thomas, a White House correspondent who covered ten presidential administrations, describes the impact that the fear of being wrong has on our presidents' willingness to be accountable for their decisions:

> I have learned a lot about presidents, and one thing is sure. None will ever admit there is a change in policy. The world can change, but they always insist that they are on the same course, steering steadily. . . . It's also tough to admit a mistake. [President] Johnson in particular would never admit a change even if it was a 180-degree turn. It's point of pride and perhaps a president's belief in his own infallibility. Perhaps it is a feeling that changing one's mind is a weakness.[19]

Within the argument culture, the negative associations of seeking to understand as a risk or as a weakness promote the value of being right and saving face over the virtues of learning, humility, courage, building community, and social responsibility. Combined with undesirable pressures to conform or anxieties over authority, these misunderstandings generate serious consequences.

Within a culture of engagement, people are encouraged to develop the courage to subject their ideas to scrutiny and to question authority. Some people worry, however, that efforts such as these to restore the importance of understanding are creating new difficulties. One of the most salient is the subject of the next misunderstanding.

Misunderstanding Number Four: Listening to Understand Endorses Entrenched Forms of Relativism

One of the most compelling concerns regarding the engagement culture's call to pursue mutual understanding is the belief that *understanding endorses an entrenched form of relativism*—the abandonment of standards, guidelines, principles, and other reliable pathways to knowledge and truth. This perspective holds that encouraging people to gain mutual understanding supports the belief that all ideas and perspectives are equally valid.

Relativism takes different forms. One is the belief that whatever an individual believes is true and valid for that person—and therefore not subject to scrutiny. "I'm okay, you're okay" is a popular manifestation of this form of relativism. *Individual relativism*, as this orientation is called, appears highly tolerant and open to a multiplicity of worldviews. In this sense, it would appear to fit well within a culture of engagement. At the same time, however, entrenched forms of individual relativism rest on the assumption that people are infallible and that their ideas need not be subjected to the scrutiny of others.

Contrary to these assumptions, the dialogic culture of engagement and ethic of interdependence rest on a recognition of each person's fallibility. Openness to the scrutiny of others' views is a hallmark of this perspective. The culture of engagement's recognition of human fallibility, embrace of thinking critically, call for humility, and courage to subject our ideas to reasoned deliberation directly challenge the philosophical underpinnings of individual relativism.

A second form of relativism is called *conventional relativism* by some and *cultural relativism* by others. This perspective holds that one's cultural "home" or primary affinity group provides a legitimate and valid basis for grounding one's beliefs. Religious communities are especially well-known agents for propagation of core beliefs such as these. Cultural relativists hold the view that subjecting people's "core group" beliefs to this kind of outside scrutiny is not only inappropriate but a violation of the members' basic human rights. This perspective offers important protections to minority groups around the globe. In today's complex, globally interdependent environments, such rights are especially vulnerable, and cultural relativism's protections are therefore potentially invaluable.

At the same time, however, entrenched forms of cultural relativism rest on assumptions of group infallibility, and they encourage people to act on group beliefs without subjecting the ideas to critical thinking and other forms of scrutiny. Terrible tragedies have been associated with adoption of this perspective. Consider, for example, the profound harms associated with the 9/11 terrorist attacks. The people perpetrating these acts were convinced of the validity of their groups' views. They sacrificed their own lives, and those of countless innocent others, convinced that the group to which they belonged was "right" in its convictions regarding how best to address global injustices.

While entrenched forms of cultural relativism support this potentially catastrophic approach to decision making, the culture of dialogic engagement recognizes that no individual or group is infallible. This recognition within an ethic of interdependence calls for humility and the courage required to subject our beliefs—even those associated with our close affinity-group identities—to the scrutiny of others.

Contrary to entrenched forms of relativism, this orientation to decision making recognizes that the human family within today's globally interdependent world shares many needs and interests. In such an environment, what happens to one of us affects the quality of life for us all. As we have seen, this inevitable connection compels consideration of interdependent principles, such as the Golden Rule. Later in the book, as we explore the process of discernment, we will feature a number of related grounding principles and guidelines for sound decision making. These and related resources within the culture of engagement provide critical antidotes for the dangers inherent in unfettered relativism.

Within the context of the argument culture and adversarial individualism, however, the dispute over the merits of diversity and more moderate forms of relativism often takes the shape of a zero-sum power struggle. It finds its expression in the "culture wars" over whose values and norms will be established as the standard for inquiry, knowledge, and truth.

Similarly, this struggle takes place within the array of political and religious views that self-identify as "fundamentalist." Their disputes over who is "absolutely correct" also come into to conflict with those who describe themselves as "tolerant" for their willingness to see merit in different belief systems.

Yet, as we have seen, successful deliberative inquiry depends upon a willingness and ability to understand and engage different systems of belief. Ironically, *the risks of acting out of mistaken beliefs, false perceptions, and misunderstandings are heightened significantly when we shut off the possibility of meaningful engagement with others' perspectives.*

In sum, rather than heighten the risk of succumbing to entrenched forms of relativism, pursuit of mutual understanding within a culture of engagement enables decision makers to subject available information and ideas to close scrutiny. Through open inquiry, critical thinking, dialogic engagement, and reasoned deliberation, people within and across cultural boundaries equip themselves and the broader community with the tools needed to make the best possible decision in any given situation.

The four concerns outlined above are outgrowths, in part, of the argument culture's focus on *controlling the outcome* of a disagreement. Efforts to control and to "win" promote a competitive opposition—a situation in which comprehension is subverted and replaced with judging, blaming, and defending differences.

As we have seen, the four common misconceptions regarding the nature and purposes of understanding discourage its pursuit, creating feelings poignantly described in the following: "To be lonely is to be among people who do not know what you mean."[20] Listening well offers a vital antidote to this condition. However, more is required.

Earlier explorations of meaningful engagement with others revealed that this process is contingent in part upon where and how we are situated. Similarly, our efforts to make meaning together in pursuits of mutual understanding and sound decision making are influenced significantly by the *interpretive frames* each of us brings to the occasion. *Awareness of the factors influencing development of interpretive frames is a vital stepping stone to pursuit of understanding.*

Interpretive Frames

Social scientists have long recognized that no two people experience the same tree, plant, or person, let alone event, in exactly the same way. Criminologists understand, for example, that witnesses at a crime scene cannot be expected to provide exactly the same account of the event. One person may focus on the person perpetrating the crime, another on the victims. One pays close attention to the getaway car, another to the bank teller lying on the floor. And even when two people attend closely to a single feature of the event, they provide their own distinctive accounts of what they witnessed.

This phenomenon is especially evident within families. Kate and Myra, for example, are twins who have grown up together and are rarely apart. And yet, their accounts of childhood experiences are often markedly different. Kate "remembers," for example, that she and Myra had *limited freedom* to explore the outside world throughout their youth. Myra, in contrast, "remembers" the two of them *electing* not to explore the outside world. When Kate and Myra discuss their experiences, they are often struck by these and other substantively different interpretations of the "same" events.

These differences reflect the distinctive interpretive frames individuals and groups bring to the meaning-making process. In chapter 4, we learned that meaning-making is a social process shaped through language. When we use the term *interpretive frame*, we have in mind the constellation of factors giving shape to each individual's or group's distinctive way of *taking in* and *making meaning* of experiences, artifacts, and encounters. In the introductory exploration below, we will provide brief overviews of several factors helping to shape people's unique filters, including dispositional traits, cultural influences, and social location, among others.

As we will see, although each of us encounters the world through our own distinctive lens, we are not isolated in how we make meaning.

As with every facet of the human condition, meaning-making is an inherently relational, interdependent process. On the one hand, the size, shape, and number of readily available frames are shaped in part by the society in which we live and in part by our "hard wiring." On the other hand, each of us utilizes, builds upon, and sometimes consciously selects frames that "fit" our sensibilities. The variety of frames is influenced by a number of factors that we will introduce and explain, beginning with dispositional traits.

Dispositions and Moral Maps

One of the many factors influencing how each individual takes in the world is his or her unique personality. The term *disposition* refers to an individual's *general orientation toward all forms of experience—including relationships, interactions, and encounters with others and with the natural world.* Although each individual's disposition is unique, it is possible (and even helpful) to identify broad classes of disposition.

For example, some people tend to be bold, while others tend to be more careful. Some tend to be shy, while others are more outgoing. Some people tend to be highly emotional in response to challenges, while others are more reserved. Some tend to be aggressive, while others tend to be passive. These are only a few of the many dispositional traits and tendencies distinguishing people from one another.

As with other forms of diversity, however, dispositional traits are complex, fluid, and often hidden. Sometimes people who appear to be reserved in response to difficult circumstances are actually experiencing tumultuous, unexpressed internal emotion. People who appear to be extroverts are sometimes much more shy than they appear on the surface. Often, people who appear arrogant are masking deep fears and insecurities.

Dispositional traits evolve over time as people develop intellectually, emotionally, spiritually, and physically. Personal experiences often help to shape dispositional traits, as do education and other forms of exposure. Understanding the fluid nature of these traits can help people develop greater capacities to read their own and others' responses to circumstances and to interpret meanings more accurately.

Jonathan Haidt has made important discoveries regarding the nature and sources of several core dispositional traits.[21] Of special interest, for example, are his efforts—in partnership with researchers across disciplinary and cultural boundaries—to uncover possible links between this facet of the human condition and people's orientation toward moral decision making.

Haidt and his colleagues have discovered, in particular, that people who self-identify as social and political liberals tend to rate high on openness to experience. In general, he notes, these people tend to crave novelty, variety, new ideas, and change. In contrast, people who self-identify as social and political conservatives tend to crave familiarity. As a rule, they value security and dependability over other interests.

Haidt has identified five sources of intuition and emotion governing people's *moral maps*, or how they develop as moral beings: (1) approaches to issues of harm and care, (2) questions of fairness and reciprocity, (3) the importance of in-group loyalty, (4) considerations of authority and respect, and (5) issues of purity and sanctity. While nearly all people tend to take seriously the importance of harm and care and of fairness and reciprocity in their moral mapping, liberals tend to privilege these categories. Conservatives, in contrast, recognize the importance of these categories but are more inclined to privilege in-group loyalty, authority and respect, and purity and sanctity when these conflict with the first two categories of concern.

Haidt's extensive research has led him to conclude that conservative and liberal orientations both offer potentially invaluable insights. He notes, for example, the importance of conservative insights regarding difficulties associated with establishing and maintaining order, and the corresponding potential harms associated with its breakdown. Similarly, he observes the importance of liberal insights regarding the importance of recognizing the grave harms associated with uncritical acquiescence to authority and traditional hierarchical arrangements.

Steven Pinker's extensive work in this area has enabled him to contribute related insights. He has identified, for example, a distinctive part of human psychology associated with a phenomenon he calls *moralization.* This psychological state has several hallmarks. The first is that *the rules it invokes are felt to be universal.* The second is that *people feel that those who commit immoral acts deserve to be punished.* Pinker goes on to observe that within the United States, "much of our recent social history, including the culture wars between liberals and conservatives, consists of the moralization or amoralization of particular kinds of behavior."[22] On the one hand, for example, many people who self-identify as social liberals "moralize" about behaviors they perceive as affecting others' well-being. Rather than viewing a particular behavior such as smoking as a poor choice because of the risk to one's health, the behavior is moralized into harming others through second-hand smoke. Increasingly, smokers throughout the nation find themselves shunned by otherwise "tolerant" liberals. On the other hand, people who self-identify as social conservatives believe that morality itself is under assault because of amoralizing many behaviors. Once widely recognized as immoral, many behaviors—divorce, illegitimacy, marijuana use, and homosexuality, for example—are now regarded as lifestyle choices rather than moral failings.[23]

Haidt notes that while genetics can influence moral inclinations, traits are not innate. Rather, they are "organized in advance of experience."[24] Most people are born with the *capacity to step outside of their given moral matrix*. People who are able to make this move, he adds, are especially well equipped to contribute to humanity's quest for reasoned, just, and wise decision making.

Among the first steps toward achieving this goal, suggests Haidt, are to gain an understanding of who we are and to cultivate the *moral humility required to step outside our moral matrix in the collaborative pursuit of truth.* In this way, self-identified conservatives and liberals alike are able to benefit from the assets associated with partiality without falling prey to adversarial partisanship.

This is especially important in helping us to understand and responsibly address problems in today's complex, globally interdependent world. For our moral sense, as Pinker reminds us, "is as vulnerable to illusions as the other senses." Sometimes, for example, we confuse "morality per se with purity, status, and conformity." At other times, we "reframe practical problems as moral crusades and thus see their solution as punitive aggression." Still other times, our moral sense "imposes taboos that make certain ideas indiscussible." And often, our moral intuitions incline us to always put ourselves "on the side of the angels." "Wise people," Pinker adds, "have long reflected on how we can be blinded by our own sanctity."[25] Developing the habit of exploring the nature and roots of our unique moral vision helps to mitigate this obstacle to informed and reasoned deliberative inquiry.

Other Types of Influence

Apart from hardwiring, a number of other variables shape our dispositions, moral maps, and related traits. Each person's unique combination of genetic material and experiences create that person's capacity and inclination to perceive the world and all that she or he encounters. Similarly, our perceptions are influenced by the values and beliefs associated with our different cultural affiliations.

Many patterns of response are associated directly with cultural backgrounds. *The Week* magazine reports findings from studies, for example, suggesting that "Westerners and Asians literally see the world differently." In one study "American and Japanese volunteers were shown underwater scenes and asked to describe what they saw. The Americans tended to stress the brightest or most rapidly moving objects, such as trout swimming. The Japanese were more likely to say that they saw a stream, or that the water was green." These and related differences were said to be attributable, at least in part, to more general differences in cultural orientation. In the words of one researcher, "Harmony is a central idea in East Asian philosophy, and so there is more emphasis on how things relate to the whole." In contrast, in the West, "life is about achieving goals" and greater value is placed on "putting objects in categories." Researcher Kyle Cave of the University of Massachusetts is cited in the article as concluding that the way that we see and explore the world may well depend, to a significant degree, on our cultural origins.[26]

In today's increasingly complex and often heated political climate, other forms of cultural influence play significant roles in shaping interpretive lenses as well. In July 2010, for example, the French Assembly voted overwhelmingly in support of a bill banning anyone from wearing a veil covering his or her face in public. Someone growing up in an environment in which covering one's face is viewed as a sign of reverence and humility for a deity would likely respond with sadness—and perhaps even anger and fear—at this affront to their form of spiritual expression. In contrast, a person growing up in a feminist environment with secular values in which covering one's face is viewed as a sign of submission to patriarchy may be likely to respond with relief to this legislative attempt to protect secular and feminist values and ideals. Learning to recognize these differences, and their roots, can prove invaluable to people grappling with complex issues.

More broadly, all facets of our personal identity often play significant roles in how we experience events. This combination of our identities, status, and experience forms a *standpoint*—a particular position that connects who we are with our ways of knowing, being, and valuing. For example, someone who self-identifies as a white, bisexual, able-bodied, middle aged, financially stable, well-educated, spiritually pluralistic, committed partner, emotionally secure, Central Coast Californian will be influenced by all of these (and other) complex dimensions of her social location. Any and all of these aspects of identity have the potential to affect the individual's understanding of what she hears, reads, views, and experiences.

Numerous factors—from dispositional traits, moral maps, cultural influences, and social location, to a myriad of other influences on personal and communal identity—inform how we take in the world. These and related factors profoundly affect the quality of the processes required for sound deliberation. Principal among these are deliberative framing processes, the subject of the following chapter.

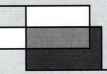

SECTION THREE

Deliberation

8

Deliberative Framing and Belief Systems

Thus far, we have explored attentive listening, pursuits of understanding, and other forms of deliberative inquiry as pathways to human flourishing in today's globally interdependent world. We have recognized *partiality* as an inevitable and, when recognized, often valuable feature of deliberative inquiry and engagement, and we have learned the importance of distinguishing partiality from its avoidable and potentially destructive counterpart, *partisanship*. As we have seen, the ability to recognize the former while avoiding the latter is key to meaningful engagement across differences.

Throughout the two opening sections, we explored some of the obstacles adversarial individualism poses to dialogue and deliberation. We learned, for example, how participation in the argument culture often fosters feelings of vulnerability, insecurity, and defensiveness which, in turn, motivate people to become entrenched in their positions. Rather than "risk" being wrong within an argumentative environment, people confronted with evidence that their beliefs are potentially mistaken are motivated to cling to their misconceptions, sometimes with even greater conviction. As we have seen, such an environment threatens the very fabric of our efforts to pursue mutual understanding, knowledge, and truth. In place of deliberative inquiry, the argument culture threatens to foster partisan framing designed to *control outcomes* rather than to *mutually pursue informed and wise decision making*.

Given the reality of our interdependence, and the nature of this moment in history, humanity's destiny may well rest to a significant degree upon our shared recognition of the need to change course from a culture of argument to a culture of engagement. As we learned in the previous chapter, seeking to understand is a hallmark of this transformation. We concluded our discussion by recognizing the importance of gaining insights into how each of us takes in, makes sense of, and interprets any given situation, experience, and interaction. To foster such awareness, we introduced a diversity of factors influencing individual and group interpretive frames.

In this chapter, we build on this foundation by turning our attention to the processes involved in understanding and interpreting deliberative contexts. As we will see, working together in shared pursuit of responsible deliberative framing is an important pathway to deliberation.

Introduction

The chapters in section 2 of this volume revealed that dialogic communication is a process of interaction involving reflection, responsiveness, and sincere, mutual inquiry. Dialogue enables people to reach across differences in pursuit of meaningful connection. When successful, dialogic interactions provide opportunities for such people to know and understand one another.

The introduction to deliberative inquiry in chapter 3 revealed that deliberation has a different, though intimately related, underlying purpose. The art of deliberation involves working together in a spirit of critical inquiry with a common quest for wise and accepted decision making. *Making a wise choice* is the outcome uniquely associated with *successful deliberation*.

Whether in private, civic, or public arenas, individuals and communities may be said to be *deliberative* when they *seek to tap available resources in pursuit of the most informed and wise decision possible in any given context*. Dialogic skills and sensibilities equip people with tools critical to fulfillment of this goal. People who successfully employ dialogic skills are receptive to others' insights and create conditions enabling them to engage constructively across their differences.

In ideal circumstances, dialogue enables people to work together to identify and frame issues and to collaborate in seeking viable alternative options. In real-world deliberative contexts, however, decision makers invariably confront constraints. Among other things, time and resource constraints limit opportunities for unfettered inquiry. In the face of such realities, being able to frame the context collaboratively significantly enhances the promise of sound deliberation.

For insights into this phenomenon within public spheres, it is helpful to turn to the landmark study by Amy Gutmann and Dennis Thompson about deliberation in nations and states aspiring to fulfill democratic ideals. "Deliberative democracy asks citizens and officials to justify public policy by giving reasons that can be accepted by those who are bound by it. This disposition to seek mutually justifiable reasons expresses the core of the process of deliberation."[1]

Gutmann and Thompson go on to identify three principles—*reciprocity, publicity, and accountability*—at the heart of successful public deliberations. *Reciprocity* is tied directly to the recognition that policies framed within such contexts are mutually binding. Given this reality, "citizens should aspire to a kind of political reasoning that is *mutually justifiable.*"[2] Importantly, this condition does not entail agreement. Many factors, including "scarcity of resources, limited generosity, incompatible values, and incomplete understanding," among others, often prevent deliberative partners from reaching consensus. However, reciprocity does require sincere pursuit of "fair terms of cooperation."[3]

Extending the principle of reciprocity, Gutmann and Thompson devised standards for citizens dealing with deliberative disagreement.

> The principles of accommodation are based on a value that lies at the core of reciprocity and deliberation in a democracy—mutual respect.... It requires a favorable attitude toward, and constructive interaction with, the persons with whom one disagrees. It consists in an excellence of character that permits democracy to flourish in the face of fundamental moral disagreement. It is the character of individuals who are morally committed, self-reflective about their commitments, discerning of the difference between respectable and merely tolerable differences of opinion, and open to the possibility of changing their minds or modifying their positions at some time in the future if they confront unanswerable objections to their present point of view.[4]

In short, reciprocity as a condition for public deliberation is met most fully when deliberative partners are equipped with the dialogic and deliberative skills and sensibilities explored throughout this volume.

The second principle for successful public deliberation, *publicity*, demands that officials and citizens make public the "information necessary to assess" the reasons given in support of their political actions.[5] Gutmann and Thompson are careful to observe that this principle is complex, especially in the face of legitimate demands for privacy and even secrecy. In general, however, publicity holds *strong presumptive weight* in its favor. We will explore the implications of this presumption more fully in the next chapter.

Accountability, the third principle, is rooted in the fact that "each is accountable to all" within deliberative forums.[6] This foundational principle is intimately aligned with the ethic of interdependence. Importantly, as Gutmann and Thompson note, accountability in this sense does not require acquiescence to the demands of populism, thereby avoiding the risk of placing undue weight on public opinion. Nor does accountability require alignment of decisions with the demands of one's constituency at the expense of the common good. Finally, accountability is not restricted to elitist constructs of reasoning and recognizes the important roles of passion and emotion in deliberative processes.

The demand for accountability, however, does entail effectively anticipating (to the extent possible) and responsibly considering the needs and interests of all potential stakeholders in any given deliberative context. Accountability in this sense reaches beyond consideration of the needs and interests of those vested with power and includes the voiceless. Deliberative accountability requires identifying creative options and discerning the likely consequences of each to all potential stakeholder individuals and communities. Skillful and responsible deliberative framing helps to insure fulfillment of these and related basic guidelines for sound deliberation.

Deliberative Framing

Mauro Baristone, a political sociologist at Milan University, provides a concise overview of scholarly findings regarding deliberative framing, informing us that it involves communication processes of structuring the context of meaning in which a deliberation is held.[7] Deliberative framing reflects participants' *understanding of the deliberative context*, including *how they identify and interpret relevant issues* and *how they discern and assess available options*.

Within an interdependent world, everyone benefits when decision makers are able to work together to understand what is at stake in a given deliberative context. Who are the stakeholders? What are their interests and concerns? What options are available? What are the likely consequences of these options, short and long term? *Responsible deliberative frames* reflect as *clear*, *representative*, and *comprehensive* an understanding of these and related elements of the deliberative context as time and resources permit.

In the previous chapter, we identified a myriad of factors shaping each individual's unique interpretive lens. Given the inevitability of partiality, the individual informed only by his or her own interpretive lens will be ill equipped to provide a comprehensive deliberative frame. Through dialogue and other forms of skillful deliberative inquiry, however, decision makers working together in pursuit of wise decision making are positioned to transcend these limits. Together, they have the potential to enrich their own and each other's understanding of the context, from gaining greater clarity regarding the nature of the relevant issues and related stakeholder interests to creatively discerning and competently assessing available options.

Issues

Issues are among the most important elements of deliberative frames. When we make reference to *central issues*, we have in mind *significant points in dispute* within any given deliberative context that *must be addressed to meet minimal standards of sound deliberative inquiry*. As we will see from the following discussion, the way in which issues are framed profoundly affects the nature and quality of deliberative processes.

Baristone notes, for example, that a deliberative frame suggests "that an issue or information should be understood, read, or judged in some terms rather than in others, according to a given perspective." Studies of framing, he observes further, consistently reveal that frames "generally tend to organize the discussion, and hence the collective decision-making or preference formation process."[8]

Communication scholars Stephen Bloch-Schulman and Spoma Jovanovic analyzed this phenomenon in university classrooms. They observed, for example, that the framing of economic issues in many mainstream business schools within the United States privileges laissez-faire capitalist economic frameworks, shielding fundamental questions from scholarly inquiry. Within this framework, educators are encouraged to train "students to be corporate managers intent on maximizing profit as a moral necessity."[9] Discussions in such contexts often focus primarily on how managers can most efficiently overcome obstacles to profitability and otherwise develop strategies for maximizing profits.

This narrow framing does not meet minimal standards of deliberative inquiry. Economists disagree sharply, for example, regarding the consequences of laissez-faire capitalist economic frameworks on human flourishing. Among the approaches to economics not considered in such a narrow framing are systems incorporating forms of economic regulation designed to avoid the hazards of monopolies, unfettered greed, corruption, fraud, social inequities, poverty, environmental perils, and other threats to people's security and prosperity. One of the key central issues in this context, then, is which economic system is most likely to foster people's well-being. Identifying and addressing this central issue would help enrich participants' understanding of what is at stake and of the options available.

Stakeholders

Gaining insight into what is at stake in any given deliberative context requires, among other things, identification of *stakeholders*. When we use this term, we have in mind all those potentially affected by the outcome of the deliberative process.

Primary stakeholders are those with the most at stake. In some cases, impacts on these stakeholders' interests and values are direct; in other instances, they are indirect. Impacts may be short or long term as well. Either way, primary stakeholders have a significant vested interest in the deliberative context. *Secondary stakeholders* are also potentially affected, though less significantly. Because identifying and responsively addressing their concerns is an important element of sound decision making, responsible deliberative framing requires representation of each of these groups' interests, values, and related concerns as accurately and fairly as possible.

Dialogue and other forms of deliberative inquiry provide critical resources for this process. Consider, for instance, the following scenario.

Jennifer, Rosa, Julia, and Rupert have been commissioned by the state to help frame abortion policy deliberations for the upcoming legislative session. Included in the assignment is representation of central issues, key stakeholders, stakeholder interests and values, and available options.

Jennifer and Rosa are pro-life advocates who believe passionately that life begins at conception. From their perspective, the primary stakeholders in abortion policy deliberations are the babies whose lives are at stake. In the absence of consultation with others, they have defined the central issue in abortion policy deliberations as whether the state should permit mothers to kill their babies.

Pro-choice advocates Julia and Rupert come to the deliberative context with a different orientation. They believe that life begins at viability, rather than at conception. From their perspective, laws preventing or restricting women's access to abortion before viability are devastatingly, and needlessly, coercive. They see women whose physical, emotional, and economic well-being are at stake as the primary stakeholders in this context. Before consulting those who disagree with them, they have framed the central issue in these terms: Should the state be permitted to control women's bodies?

If left unchecked, these partisan deliberative frames would potentially compromise the quality of the deliberative process. We learned in chapter 3, for example, that sound deliberative inquiry rests on thoughtful determination of the information and insights needed to make an informed and wise decision. Rosa and Jennifer's *assumption* that life begins at conception masks deliberative questions at the heart of controversy in abortion policy deliberations. Julia and Rupert's *assumption* that life begins at viability similarly compromises deliberative inquiry. These advocates' frames suffer from a fallacy common to adversarial deliberative framing. Known as *begging the question*, this fallacy is marked by a failure to recognize and address one or more central issues.

As noted earlier, sound deliberations require, at a minimum, that participants frame issues as inclusively, fairly, clearly, and comprehensively as possible. Identification of the following elements are essential in every deliberative context: Who are the stakeholders? What are their concerns? What are the available options? What are the likely short- and long-term consequences of each of these options? Where can we turn for the most reliable insights and information on each of these issues? On what grounds might thoughtful, informed, and caring people disagree on each of these issues?

Working together to address these foundational questions, Jennifer, Julia, Rosa, and Rupert would quickly discover that their narrow deliberative frames do not meet minimal standards for sound deliberative inquiry. Through dialogue and other forms of deliberative inquiry, these advocates would have the opportunity to replace their partisan frames with more inclusive representations of the primary stakeholders and more accurate and comprehensive articulations of the formative issues. The enriched understanding of the deliberative context gained from these processes would create conditions for creatively discerning the available options to respond to all key stakeholder concerns.

Within the argument culture, people representing different constituencies, backgrounds, or beliefs are often encouraged to manipulate deliberative framing to their advantage. Yet as we've seen in the case above, this approach would severely compromise the prospect of successful deliberation. The case below illustrates further.

Senators Horn and Chase have been charged with drafting immigration reform legislation. Senator Horn's orientation to immigration reform features concern for social justice. He believes strongly that existing immigration policies exacerbate inequities between people born into lives of privilege and those born into lives of poverty and other forms of deprivation. From his perspective, the central issue is how legislation can help to level the playing field. Senator Chase, on the other hand, approaches immigration policy with a strong commitment to maintaining the security of her constituents. From her perspective, the central issue in this deliberative context is how immigration reform can help to insure citizens' safety.

Within the argument culture, these legislators would be urged to do whatever is required to insure that their primary concerns dominate the deliberative framing processes. Each would be urged, for example, to formulate the central issue in terms privileging the stakeholder interests and values most important to them. If necessary, Senators Horn and Chase might even be encouraged to *manipulate* representations of the central issue to help insure a "favorable" outcome.

Under these circumstances, both senators would employ narrow visions in searching for solutions. Senator Horn, for example, would likely entertain only those options that would enhance equal access to opportunities for social mobility, particularly for historically marginalized groups. Senator Chase, on the other hand, would likely endorse only options that insure the security and safety of constituents in her district. Neither would be inclined to consider the other's concerns as central to the deliberative process. Nor would they be likely to collaborate with one another to frame the central issue in more expansive and inclusive terms.

Legislators adopting an interdependent approach to deliberative framing, in contrast, would recognize the importance of moving beyond their narrow frames to a broader understanding of the deliberative context. They would be encouraged to listen receptively to one another's perspectives and to seek the resources required to frame the issues as inclusively, accurately, and comprehensively as possible.

In adopting this approach, the legislators would not abandon their primary commitments. In the case at hand, for example, Senator Horn would continue to provide passionate support for pursuit of social justice, and Senator Chase would continue to argue passionately for the need to protect her constituents' safety. Each would do their best to insure inclusion of their constituents' particular concerns throughout the deliberative framing and decision-making processes. Working together to frame the issues as comprehensively as possible, these advocates would foster conditions required to meet the basic standards of reciprocity, accountability, and publicity.

In part, these outcomes would be met by working together to discern subordinate issues. When we use this term, we are referring to the underlying issues that must be identified and addressed in order to meet minimal standards of sound deliberative inquiry. The exploration of facts, values, and value hierarchies in chapter 3 offers a window into this part of the framing process. Learning to discern underlying contested facts, values, and value hierarchies is key to responsible deliberative framing.

In the immigration policy deliberation context explored above, for example, dialogue would enable Senators Horn and Chase to discover that some of the grounding beliefs they each bring to the table are *shared*, while others are *contested*. Senator Horn disputes, for example, Senator Chase's grounding belief that providing amnesty for undocumented immigrants would gravely compromise her constituents' security. Discovering this disagreement of fact enables the legislators to pose the following deliberative question as an issue: What impact would amnesty for undocumented immigrants have on the security of people living within Senator Chase's district? Framing the question in this way enables the legislators to use deliberative inquiry to assess the verifiability of Senator Chase's assumption. Working together to uncover and frame this important issue could reveal common ground as well. The legislators could discover, for example, that they both value security. They could discover further that they share commitments to justice and fairness.

If deliberative inquiry affirmed Senator Chase's belief that amnesty risks imperiling people's security, the principles of accountability and reciprocity would compel inclusion of this risk in the deliberative frame. Similarly, if deliberative inquiry supported Senator Horn's belief that denying amnesty potentially violates basic principles of fairness and justice, conditions for responsible framing would compel inclusion of this risk in the deliberative frame.

As we learned in chapters 3 and 7, however, these findings alone would not be adequate to insure responsible deliberative inquiry and framing conducive to sound decision making. Competing value hierarchies accompanied by conflicting beliefs create potentially significant obstacles to success. Responsible deliberative framing requires participants to try to discover the elusive roots of these potential barriers to sound deliberation.

Toward this end, the next discussion provides overviews of belief systems often at the heart of seemingly intransigent differences. Try to identify your orientation and analyze the roles that your ways of seeing, knowing, and valuing play in influencing how you frame the relevant issues and available options.

Belief Systems

The term *belief system* refers to the *constellation of beliefs* influencing how individuals and groups *take in* and *make meaning* of events, information, ideas, interactions, and other forms of experience. Anthropologists, sociologists, economists, cultural theorists, rhetorical scholars, psychologists, and philosophers have long established the importance of belief systems to consciousness; their work reveals that systems of belief serve as powerful interpretive frames, significantly influencing how individuals and groups take in the world, interpret experiences, frame issues, identify and assess options, and ultimately choose to act in any given context.

To a large degree, belief systems regarding the nature of the material world profoundly affect how those adhering to them interpret and understand issues related to the environment. Exploring the question of ownership offers an informative window into at least three different belief systems informing people's deliberative frames.

Communion, Stewardship, and Dominion Belief Systems

Consider the question, "who owns the clouds?" For many people living in the United States today, such a question may seem bewildering. How, they might ask, can one *own* a cloud? And yet, related questions regarding who has the right to seed clouds in order to stimulate rain (especially during prolonged periods of drought) pose significant challenges to principalities within and between states. This move to claim clouds as belonging to one or another group is not surprising when considered in light of related beliefs firmly established in the United States and gaining currency in other parts of the world. These beliefs are part of a system of ideas related to land, plant, and animal ownership.

When we unpack the idea of one person or group of persons owning land—of owning a piece of the earth—we can more easily recognize the roots of this belief system. Historically, many groups of people found the idea of owning pieces of the earth unintelligible. When asked to sell their land to Europeans seeking to settle in parts of the continent now called North America, for example, many of the native peoples living in this part of the world responded with bewilderment. They had lived in harmony with the land, deeply respectful of and grateful for its harvest. Animals and plants were sacred. From these peoples' perspective, the natural world they inhabited was not theirs to sell, no matter how long they had lived there. For purposes of this exploration, we will refer to this orientation—that all life is sacred, and that nature and humans are intimately connected—as the *communion orientation*.

A different belief system holds that humankind and the rest of the natural world are separate, a part of a hierarchy with humankind at the top and all other life-forms underneath. Many who embrace this perspective believe that nature is a gift from a deity or deities to the human family. Others share the hierarchical view of humanity's relationship to nature, but do so outside of a religious or spiritual framework. Among those who view nature and humankind as separate from one another (that is, not in spiritual or material union with one another), there are two different belief systems.

One of these is the *stewardship orientation*. This perspective views humankind and the rest of the natural world as separate. Humanity has naturally endowed power and authority over nature. However, with this power comes the moral obligation to take care of the natural world. This view differs from the communion orientation significantly in that stewardship implies *separation, power, and authority (rather than union and equality)*. At the same time, however, the stewardship orientation has much in common with the communion orientation. Both include the natural world—plants, nonhuman animals, land, and seas—within the moral domain. Both of these perspectives hold that humanity has moral responsibilities beyond self-interest.

A third belief system differs sharply from both of these orientations. Often referred to as the *dominion orientation*, this point of view sees nature as an *alien force*, one that must be *conquered* in the service of humanity. Those subscribing to this orientation pursue methods of inquiry and intervention designed to equip humanity with the tools needed to *control nature*.

These three orientations to nature—communion, stewardship, and dominion—play instrumental roles in shaping how individuals and groups understand and confront environmental issues. Beatrice, Joan, and Carl's differences regarding how best to approach a landscaping plan proposed for the condominium complex in which they live offers an example.

Joan recently purchased a condominium in the complex and has volunteered to serve as the chair of the landscaping committee. Carl has lived in the complex for many years but does not serve on the board. Beatrice has lived in the complex for nine years and would welcome the opportunity to participate in board deliberations. As a renter, however, she is permitted to express her views to members but is not eligible for board membership.

Joan is disturbed by what she sees as the uncontrolled wildness of the complex's natural environment. She would like to see a more polished look, with human-made mulch and a manicured gardening scheme. She has found a landscaping architect with special skills in developing such a controlled environment. Included in the architect's plan is removal of most of the current plant life in the complex and an orderly introduction of carefully selected flora and fauna. To protect this new landscaping scheme, the board would need to hire an exterminator to rid the complex of squirrels, gophers, and other creatures. Although not detrimental to the current vegetation, the animals could threaten the new, polished look.

Beatrice has a long-established communal relationship with the trees, plants, and animals existing within the complex. She routinely feeds the birds and squirrels, and she cherishes the richly abundant diversity of plant life surrounding the residence. She is horrified at the prospect of the destruction of life required in order to realize Joan's vision.

Carl, on the other hand, has mixed feelings about the new landscaping proposal. He shares Joan's enthusiasm for the prospect of a more orderly, manicured environment. At the same time, however, he believes strongly that the board should dedicate itself to finding humane ways to remove the animals. He has proposed handling existing trees and plants as sensitively as possible.

These three residents approach the deliberative context with fundamentally different frames. Representing a communion perspective, Beatrice views the trees, plants, and animals as stakeholders whose interests should be taken seriously in the deliberative process. Representing a dominion perspective, Joan does not view plants and animals as stakeholders. From her perspective, they are valuable only insofar as they serve human interests. And representing a stewardship perspective, Carl shares Joan's view that human interests should be privileged. However, he rejects her view that no consideration is due the current animals and plants. From his perspective, the board has a responsibility to insure that actions taken minimize the suffering of plant and animal life to the extent possible.

As these three residents seek to engage with the board and with one another, it will be important for them to understand and recognize the roots of their own and each other's perspectives. Similarly, as the board members frame the issues and identify and assess the soundness of available options, their abilities to recognize and consider each of the three advocates' underlying belief systems will prove critical to development of a comprehensive frame.

In later chapters, we will delve more deeply into what is required for sound deliberative judgment in such difficult cases. At a minimum, however, it is important to recognize the role deliberative partnerships have in helping participants transcend the limits of their individual interpretive frames.

Differences between communion, stewardship, and dominion orientations toward the natural world mirror differences in framing other contentious areas of deliberation. Family life issues are particularly salient.

Just as people's presuppositions regarding humanity's foundational relationship with the earth and other life-forms inform how they frame environmental issues, people's basic assumptions regarding the nature and purposes of family form the basis of their approach to framing family-life issues. Individuals' orientations to family are central, for example, to how they frame issues related to same-sex marriage, abortion, sex education, parental rights and authority, character education, women's rights, gender norms, or governmental support for child care.

Belief Systems Related to Family Life

Societal expectations often play significant roles in shaping foundational beliefs regarding the place of gender in every aspect of life. The term *norm* is used to encapsulate expectations and guidelines for behavior. In relation to gender, for example, traditional expectations and guidelines for men and for women have differed significantly over time and across cultural contexts. For centuries, men in many parts of the world were expected to provide leadership, security, and safety for their families and for the broader community. Women were expected to provide nurturance, love, care, and support for children and for their spouses. These expectations were considered "normal," a product of the "natural" differences between men and women. The resulting norms were seen as helping to provide a strong infrastructure for families and communities. Such arrangements provided both men and women the benefit of readily apparent guidelines for behavior. Among other things, this clarity helped to avoid confusion. And in many cases, clearly delineated gender norms such as these helped to mitigate conflicts regarding each person's authority and responsibilities.

In the United States, many factors have undermined the stability of these gender norms. Today, for example, only a relatively small percentage of two-parent families are "headed" by a single wage earner. The distribution of labor in many households is also considerably more fluid and complex than in the past. As a result of these and related changes, long-standing assumptions have been shattered. In such a context, evolving belief systems are playing increasingly important roles in shaping family life.

Traditional Family Models

Those who embrace a *traditional family model* support predetermined, clear delineations of responsibility and authority. From this perspective, the term *family* refers exclusively to relationships of blood or marriage. A traditional family consists of a monogamous, heterosexual, married couple and children and their relations (either by blood or marriage). Everyone in the family is expected to adhere to preestablished gender norms.

Within the nuclear family unit, the father has the authority and responsibility to establish rules for the household. He is expected to be reasonable, fair, just, loving, and firm. The mother has the authority and responsibility to manage the household, with the understanding that the father will serve as primary disciplinarian when (or if) needed. The father and mother are a "team," working collaboratively to support each other, their children, and the family unit as a whole. The distribution of labor is predetermined, based on traditional gender norms. Boys and girls have different expectations based on traditional gender norms as well. Young boys learn to develop masculine qualities and fulfill male responsibilities, while young girls are groomed for motherhood and spousal nurturance.

Partnership Family Models

Partnership family models differ significantly from the traditional model summarized above. *Family* is defined by *relationships* rather than by *gender*. Two or more people who devote themselves to one another may form a family unit. Close friendships may fall under the rubric of family, depending on the nature and quality of the friends' commitments to one another. Among nuclear-partnership family arrangements are groupings of two women with or without children, two men with or without children, or a man and woman with or without children. This perspective views authority and responsibilities as aligning with individuals' abilities, interests, and strengths.

In a partnership household with a mother, father, and two young children, for example, the parents deliberate to determine how best to meet everyone's needs. If the mother is an especially skilled attorney and the father is especially nurturing by nature, the parents may decide that the mother will be the wage earner, while the father will stay home with the children. Similarly, if a boy child appears to enjoy nurturing activities, he will be encouraged to develop this set of interests. And if a girl child appears to enjoy sports activities, she will be encouraged to develop skills in this area. No predetermined set of norms based on gender is used to govern how the collaborative family household is run or how the children are raised.

Importantly, both the traditional and the partnership family models embrace a shared set of guidelines for raising children. Among these are common ground regarding the importance of providing loving, caring, safe, secure, and nurturing environments for children. Similarly, both belief systems recognize the importance of avoiding violence and deception. Both systems value kindness and generosity, and both recognize the importance of fostering conditions for peace and harmony.

Despite this common ground, however, significant differences inform this deliberative context. Children raised in partnership households, for example, tend to have different experiences and expectations from those whose parents subscribe to a traditional family orientation.

Similarly, couples informed by these diverse frames are expected to relate differently to one another and to others.[10]

For example, as a young boy, Gregory expressed interest in playing with dolls. He avoided participation in sports and other traditionally masculine activities. Had he been born into a traditional family, he would likely have been strongly discouraged from playing with his favorite toys and instead encouraged to develop more male-appropriate interests. His parents might have sought counseling or other forms of intervention to assist Gregory in conforming to traditional gender norms. His traditional parents would have been likely to view such intervention as key to his well-being, as well as to his ability to contribute meaningfully to society. Raised in a partnership home environment, however, Gregory encountered support for his native interests and abilities. His parents did not see a need to seek counseling or intervention. Instead, they believed that freeing Gregory from the constraints of traditional gender norms would be the most likely pathway to his finding happiness and living a good life.

It is easy to imagine how people embracing these highly diverse models of family life would struggle when attempting to frame the issues at the heart of deliberations regarding same-sex marriage, character education, or how schools should introduce children to such concepts as duty, honor, and responsibility. Decision makers in each of these models would likely approach the deliberative framing process with narrow orientations; they might have difficulty transcending their orientations to view a wider range of available options. Insight into relationships between belief systems and deliberative framing, however, could pave the way for collaborative deliberative framing and sound deliberation.

Internal Conflicts

In some cases, individuals' core identities cross between two or more potentially incompatible belief systems. In a 2011 *New York Times Magazine* essay titled "Living the Good Lie," reporter Mimi Swartz offers a compelling example of this phenomenon. Her essay focuses on the extraordinary difficulties facing gay and lesbian people whose devoted affiliation with a fundamentalist religious sect proscribes their pursuits of intimate same-sex relations.[11]

Until recently, the American Psychological Association offered little if any guidance for how to counsel clients facing this dilemma. In the words of one therapist, "We're supposed to support religious beliefs and to support sexual orientation. But there was nothing I knew of that says what to do when they conflict."[12]

Noting that people such as nuns and priests have long prioritized "their religion over their sexuality," the APA's report on the subject recognizes that for some people, religious identity trumps sexual orientation.[13] According to Douglas Haldeman, a specialist in this area, this holds true for some Evangelical Christians struggling to reconcile their faith with their sexual orientation. "In the case of such clients," he writes, "abandoning the church meant abandoning the entire belief system by which they defined themselves."[14]

When framing and confronting issues in such contexts, decision makers will inevitably face deeply challenging obstacles. Specialists in this area note that, at the end of the day, people faced with dilemmas of this kind find themselves forced to decide how to prioritize their core values. Therapist Warren Throckmorton counsels clients in such circumstances to develop a life lived "through the values that matter most" to them.[15] Gaining clarity regarding the roots and nature of the conflict is an important starting point for personal decision making in such contexts.

When framing issues related to family life, the roots of our own and others' orientations are often relatively easy to recognize in the face of disagreement. In some deliberative contexts, however, the most foundational differences are also the most elusive. This is especially evident in contexts involving diverse *philosophies of life*.

Belief Systems Regarding the Nature and Purpose of Life

What is the purpose of life? Why are we here? What constitutes a *good life*? These are a few of the questions at the heart of different philosophies of life. A number of assumptions about the human condition, and related narratives, govern how individuals and communities frame issues within related deliberative contexts. Some people believe, for example, that everything in life happens for a reason. Others believe that events are random. Some believe that most people are basically good; others believe that most people are essentially bad; and still others see features of both good and bad in each person.

We saw glimpses of these differences in the opening chapters. The argument culture's orientation is rooted in a narrative about a dog-eat-dog environment in which pursuit of self-interest is one's only reliable choice. In such a world, engagement across differences is seen as potentially hazardous, something to be avoided when possible. While other chapters have questioned the reliability of this narrative in today's globally interdependent world, it remains important to recognize the tenacity with which the argument culture's individualist adversarial narrative continues to capture the imaginations of many people.

Differences in foundational beliefs regarding other facets of life are equally important. For example, some believe that people have free will to determine their destiny. Others believe that each person's path on the earthly plane is predestined by higher powers. Still others believe that genetics, biochemistry, and institutional power relations completely constrain individual choice—meaning that free will is a myth. These differences in turn drive master narratives that govern how individuals and groups frame issues and options in a diversity of deliberative contexts.

As with beliefs about the human condition, there are many different beliefs about the purposes of life. Some believe that after working to discover their native intelligences, talents, gifts, and passions, people should pursue these potentialities to their fullest. In contrast, others believe that the purpose of each life is to be dutiful to family and community, to obey communal norms, and to contribute as fully as possible to communal harmony. Still others believe that each person's purpose is to serve the will of the Creator, divined through Revelation or Scripture. Yet others believe that there is no such thing as a purpose for each life; people construct their destinies in relation to what they have been given by virtue of their birth and social location.

Recognizing our own and others' foundational assumptions is essential to efforts to work together in pursuit of accurate and comprehensive deliberative framing. Imagine, for example, the obstacles to working together in pursuit of common purpose when people falsely assume others share their foundational beliefs regarding what counts as success in any given situation. To illustrate, consider the influence of belief systems in deliberative framing processes within the context of education.

Belief Systems Regarding the Nature and Purposes of Education

What are the primary purposes of a K–12 education in the United States? What about college education? Whose interests and values should educational institutions serve? Given the huge investments communities, families, and individuals make to help insure access to education, how should educational institutions insure "successful" fulfillment of the purposes for which they were created?

Sharon believes, for example, that the primary purpose of a K–12 education is to transmit the knowledge, values, value hierarchies, and belief systems of the dominant culture. Helping each individual assimilate into a homogenous value and belief system helps sustain a sense of communal harmony, helps to insure the society's success, and fosters a sense of achievement for all.

Dan disagrees strongly with this philosophy and believes that the primary purpose of a K–12 education is to help each individual discover his or her native intelligences, gifts, abilities, and interests to her or his fullest potential.

Masha's philosophy of K–12 education shares Dan's premise that education should help individuals discover their native strengths and tap these potentials as fully as possible. However, she promotes a civic engagement philosophy of education. From her viewpoint, children should be equipped with the knowledge, skills, and abilities required to make reasoned, just, and informed decisions. Preparing students for a good life entails fostering a sense of connection with others, critical thinking and related communication skills, and commitment to the pursuits of truth, justice, peace, and wisdom.

While Sharon, Dan, and Masha's philosophies of education share much common ground, they offer different lenses for assessing the strengths and limits, successes and failures of each school district's approach to K–12 education. As policy makers responsible for deciding the future of school funding, these decision makers have an obligation to frame the issues and available options as responsibly as possible. Recognizing how their own and others' belief systems inform their deliberative framing processes is a critical pathway to fulfillment of this responsibility.

Belief Systems Regarding Textual Interpretation

Thus far, we've explored belief systems related to concrete deliberative contexts. Belief systems regarding textual interpretation are instrumental to the ability of deliberative framing to bridge a diversity of contexts. As you review the summary below, see if you can identify your perspective on how to interpret texts and the implications of this philosophy for your deliberative framing processes.

Philosophies of Interpreting Texts

One school of literary analysis argues that accurate interpretation of a text depends on understanding the historical moment when the text was crafted. Another suggests, in contrast, that we can best interpret a work through a careful reading. The text itself includes an implied authorial voice, offering us clues into the work's "true" meaning. From this standpoint, the text's meaning evolves as humanity itself changes; as readers from varying generations take in the text, the work will reveal evolving truths.

Within the context of jurisprudence in the United States, philosophies of textual interpretation such as these play important roles in shaping the outcome of judicial deliberations. Conflicts between *strict constructionist* and *loose constructionist* approaches to textual interpretation are especially significant.

Strict constructionists suggest that our interpretations of legal texts should rely on information regarding what the authors had in mind at the time they wrote the constitutional clause or legislative bill in question. Since those who crafted the U.S. Constitution made no provision for recognizing a right to privacy, for example, strict constructionists do not believe courts should use the Constitution as a basis for enacting such a right. From their perspective, using the Constitution to introduce a right to privacy is an act of *judicial activism*.

In contrast, *loose constructionists* view the Constitution as a living text to be interpreted within the context of changing times. People's rights to use contraceptives, for example, fall under this rubric. Although the First and Fourteenth Amendments make no specific mention either of the right to privacy or of contraceptives *per se*, the underlying intent found in these clauses—when understood within the context of today's evolving social fabric—provide grounding for protection of people's rights in these areas.

Similarly contentious differences in textual interpretation underlie debates regarding prohibitions against various kinds of discrimination. For example, loose constructionists read the Fourteenth Amendment provision prohibiting the state from denying "any person within its jurisdiction the equal protection of the laws" as protecting against all forms of *arbitrary* discrimination, as defined within the social context of the day.

In legal circles, the term *arbitrary* refers to an absence of good reasons to justify one's actions. In the case of disputes regarding the legitimacy of various kinds of discrimination, the concept of arbitrariness is especially important. At one time, for example, preventing women from voting or owning property was considered reasonable. In some parts of the world, discrimination of this kind continues to be supported by the weight of the law.

Similarly, until recently, discrimination against homosexuals on the basis of their sexual orientation had been considered reasonable in many parts of the world. In some nations today, however, such discrimination is considered arbitrary and unlawful. For example, in the Netherlands, Argentina, Norway, Spain, Belgium, and South Africa, among other nations, the government is forbidden from preventing same-sex couples to marry. Homosexuals in these countries cannot be denied employment, housing, or civil liberties of any kind based on their affectional orientation. All discrimination against homosexuals is considered arbitrary in these nations. Yet, in other parts of the world, discrimination against homosexuals continues to be viewed as legitimate and reasonable, as least by those in power. Gay rights activists in Russia are routinely refused the right to assemble "on the grounds that other people find it offensive."[16] A few nations even go so far as to "have the death penalty for homosexuality," while still others "make same-sex relationships punishable by imprisonment."[17]

Within the United States, there is much controversy regarding the legitimacy of such forms of discrimination. In some states, legislators have passed laws protecting the rights of people who self-identify as gay, lesbian, bisexual, or transgendered to employment, housing, and basic civil liberties. Other states, however, continue to permit discrimination based on an individual's sexual orientation in employment, housing, adoption, taxation, marriage, access to benefits, and other areas. In many of these states, the government itself uses sexual orientation as a criterion for determining individuals' eligibility for certain kinds of employment, access to benefits, and other rights.

Strict constructionists do not view evolving standards on these issues as relevant to constitutional interpretation. Because sexual orientation is not mentioned in the Constitution, duly elected state and federal officials may discriminate on this basis should they elect to do so. In contrast, loose constructionists believe that the Fourteenth Amendment was intended to incorporate a flexible and evolving understanding of its protections. Society's understanding of what counts as legitimate or reasonable discrimination evolves; so must our application of the Fourteenth Amendment's equal protection and due process.

Related to these diverse approaches to textual interpretation are other overarching interpretive frames. These core belief systems are often especially compelling sources of differences in framing deliberative contexts. As we will see, differences within and across religious contexts provide particularly salient examples.

Overarching Lenses within and across Belief Systems

When we speak of *overarching lenses,* we have in mind particularly salient frames through which we understand and assess experiences, points of view, issues, and available options. Among these is the belief system underpinning the approach to communication and deliberation introduced throughout this book.

The *argument culture* approaches communication and deliberation differently than the *culture of engagement.* The differences are grounded in overarching interpretive frames. For example, within the argument culture, disagreement is understood as a challenge to overcome. Listening is recognized as a tool to assist communicators in gaining and retaining control or dominance. The primary concern for people within the argument culture is to attend to their own interests. Communication is a means to an instrumental end; strategic communication is a sign of strength. Listening to understand is a virtue only insofar as it furthers the listener's strategic goals. The abilities to dominate and control are viewed as virtues. Reasonableness is an illusion; responsiveness to the interests of others is a sign of weakness. Only instrumental rationality prevails.

In contrast, within a culture of engagement, deliberative partnerships are not only possible, but vital. Communication is seen as a resource for fostering meaningful relationships and for facilitating sound decision making across contexts. Interdependence is recognized as an inescapable material reality. As a result, individuals and communities are mutually accountable. Preserving individual rights is critical, as is recognizing each person's social responsibility. Kindness, generosity, humility, and moral courage are viewed as virtues.

Beyond these diverse cultures of communication are related over-arching interpretive lenses at the root of many of the world's most entrenched conflicts. Judeo-Christian and Muslim religious traditions offer particularly salient examples. As the discussion below reveals, these frames are instrumental to differences in deliberative framing.

People who self-identify as *fundamentalist* or *orthodox* Christians, Jews, or Muslims share some foundational interpretive lenses. Although these groups follow different traditions, they approach *many social issues from within compatible frameworks.* For example, most fundamentalists or orthodox followers within these diverse faiths share commitments to preserving traditional family values. Strict separations between men and women are important to nearly all those who share this framework. Similarly, men and women's roles are clearly defined and play critical roles in family life and children's education. Prohibitions against homosexual relations of any kind, abortion, and sexual relationships outside of marriage are strong.

Most people who self-identify as *reform* Christians, Jews, or Muslims, in contrast, support women's rights, favor laws preventing discrimination against homosexuals, and embrace partnership family life models. In general, these groups tend to reject calls to restore traditional gender norms and support the ideal of helping each child develop his or her native gifts independently of links to their gender.

Differences of perspective between fundamentalist and reform Christians in some areas of inquiry are greater than differences between Christians and Muslims. A similar pattern shapes differences between fundamentalist and reform Muslims. Often conflicts internal to the faith tradition are greater in some areas of inquiry than differences between followers of different faiths. *Overarching interpretive frames* sometimes surpass *religious doctrines* in shaping deliberative framing processes. In complex contexts such as these, recognizing the roots of differences can contribute valuably to people's abilities to work together in pursuit of responsible deliberative framing.

Conclusion

As we have seen throughout this chapter, the quality of our deliberative framing processes profoundly affects the quality of deliberations. Learning to identify and represent issues, stakeholders, and available options as fairly, accurately, and comprehensively as possible is a critical pathway to skillful deliberative inquiry and sound deliberation.

Belief systems and related interpretive frames significantly influence how each of us define, understand, and respond to the deliberative contexts we encounter. Recognizing our own and others' belief systems equips us to transcend the limits of our interpretive frames in shared pursuit of responsible deliberative framing. Adopting this approach enables us to tap the benefits of partiality without succumbing to the disabling hazards of partisanship.

Steven Pinker admonishes us to take careful note of this feature of human psychology and to learn about ourselves and others in the process. He observes that these insights will help us recognize that

> even when our adversaries' agenda is most baffling, they may not be amoral psychopaths but in the throes of a moral mind-set that appears to them to be every bit as mandatory and universal as ours does to us. . . . In any conflict in which a meeting of the minds is not completely hopeless, a recognition that the other guy is acting from moral rather than venal reasons can be a first patch of common ground. One side can acknowledge the other's concern for community or stability or fairness or dignity, even while arguing that some other value should trump it in that instance.[18]

Pinker's observations underscore the importance of forging deliberative partnerships, working together to frame issues, and identifying options as creatively and responsibly as possible. Only through such partnerships can we hope to meet the compelling demands of this historic moment.

As we will discover in the remaining chapters, however, fulfillment of this goal requires even more than the skills of dialogue and deliberative inquiry discussed in this volume thus far. Discernment, the subject of the next chapter, is among the important additional skill sets required for responsible deliberative framing and sound deliberation.

9

Discernment

We learned in the previous chapter that sound deliberative framing of issues is marked by fair, inclusive, and comprehensive representation of all stakeholder interests, values, and related concerns. Decision makers informed by a broadly inclusive understanding of an issue are well positioned to identify, skillfully frame, and carefully consider viable alternative options in shared pursuit of sound decision making.

Thus far, we've explored the roles skillful dialogic communication and other forms of deliberative inquiry play in helping to insure fulfillment of these criteria for responsible deliberative framing. The previous chapter focused on the critical role that discernment of our own and others' belief systems plays in fostering responsible deliberative framing. This is only one of the vital ways discernment serves the art of deliberation.

Introduction

When we speak of *discernment*, we have in mind *the critical thinking and reflective processes involved in unmasking, understanding, and assessing the relative merits of our own and others' grounding assumptions and beliefs in any given situation.* Through discernment, we are able to take the steps required to uncover and assess points of convergence. Discernment further enables us to deepen our awareness of what is at stake for all concerned and to assess the strengths and limits of our own and others' views—equipping us for more informed, considered, and wise assessments of available options than would otherwise be possible. There are several different types of discernment, each instrumental to the quality of our deliberative framing and deliberation processes. We begin with an introduction to *introspective discernment*.

Introspective Discernment

An extension of the reflective processes explored in previous chapters, *introspective discernment* is the art of *discovering, understanding, and meaningfully assessing the relative merits of our grounding beliefs and assumptions.* Our overview of interpretive frames in chapters 7 and 8 revealed multiple factors influencing meaning-making processes. As we have seen, for example, each of us comes "hardwired" with a moral map and dispositional traits as starting points for taking in the world. Our discussions of moral maps revealed, for example, patterns of difference between "liberal" and "conservative" responses to experience and encounters. These differences often play a significant role in shaping how individuals and groups take in issues, encounters, and experiences.

Researchers have found that these and other inclinations, while ingrained to some degree, are nevertheless subject to evolution. Most people have the potential to move in and out of their original positions, especially when exposed to different ways of being, knowing, and valuing. Steven Pinker illustrates this belief by quoting Chekhov: "Man will become better when you show him what he is like."[1] Development of the ability to recognize the grounds of our own and others' interpretive frames significantly strengthens capacities for working together in pursuit of sound deliberative framing and inquiry.

In earlier discussions we have learned how dialogues with those who disagree potentially enrich our capacities to transcend our limited visions, enabling us to make more informed decisions. Fulfillment of this potential depends on our willingness and capacity to attend carefully to our personal responses when faced with disagreement. In our discussion of attentive listening we learned, for example, how paying close attention to our reactions when listening enables us to discover insights about ourselves. In part, this is because our reactions often express our innermost feelings and thoughts. Actors are especially familiar with this phenomenon. In response to a particularly outstanding performance by a male colleague, for example, award-winning actor Robert Duvall observed: "He's really in touch with himself."[2]

Tapping the well of insight and information available through reflection requires us to pay close attention to how we react, especially in the face of intense disagreement. As you listen to others' voices, what language and perspectives give rise to feelings of fear, despair, or frustration for you? What forms of discourse and points of view appear to help you feel a sense of safety and security? Under what circumstances are you inclined to want to escape from others' efforts to engage with you? Under what circumstances do you find yourself responding defensively? What words, ideas, expressions of value, types of proposals ignite your anger? What language, ideas, and appeals appear to inspire your enthusiasm? Attentive listening and self-reflection provide a means for *unmasking,* for shedding light on our often hidden impulses, our emotional makeup, our evolving moral map, dispositional traits, motivations, and related guiding frames. In turn, this process of shedding light on what drives our responses significantly enhances the potential for successful engagement of difference, particularly when in pursuit of informed decision making.

Impact of the Performance Culture

Recent research suggests that the introspection may be facing unanticipated obstacles in today's externally driven social media environment. *New York Times Magazine* commentator Peggy Orenstein writes about the impact of social media use on people's engagement in reflection. She notes that the expansion of social media such as Second Life, Facebook, MySpace, and Twitter has changed both how we spend our time and how we construct our identity. She cites the work of Sherry Turkle, whose book *Alone Together* discusses how the self is now externally manufactured for other's consumption and approval rather than internally developed.[3]

This phenomenon has led to users becoming increasingly grounded in and driven by *performance*. While this outward-reaching approach to communication would appear to enhance the potential for connection with others, "the risk of the performance culture, of the packaged self, is that it erodes the very relationships it purports to create, and alienates us from our own humanity." Among the many consequences of this shift are emphases on "self-promotion" at the expense of "self-awareness." Orenstein goes on to ask," when every thought is externalized, what becomes of insight? When we reflexively post each feeling, what becomes of reflection?"[4]

The argument culture reinforces the emphasis on self-promotion at the expense of self-awareness. When being right and winning are privileged over listening and connecting with those who disagree, for example, individuals readily embrace media applications helping them to communicate strategically. It is easy to see how the strategic use of communication (whether electronic or face-to-face) for such purposes is unlikely to foster meaningful engagement in pursuit of deliberative partnerships.

Strategic uses of information within the argument culture similarly exacerbate our innate tendencies to confirmation bias. Alluding to this phenomenon, Journalist Joe Keohane reminds us that we often twist facts to fit our preconceived notions or turn to demonstrably unreliable information to reinforce our beliefs. And when confronted with evidence in conflict with our most firmly held beliefs, we often entrench ourselves even more deeply in our mistaken beliefs. Keohane goes on to observe that "this effect is only heightened by the information glut, which offers—alongside an unprecedented amount of good information—endless rumors, misinformation, and questionable variations on the truth. In other words, it's never been easier for people to be wrong, and at the same time feel more certain that they're right."[5]

Fortunately, as we have seen throughout this book, *we are not bound by the argument culture's norms.* Introspective discernment enables us to transcend the anxieties we sometimes experience when exposed to evidence that conflicts with our beliefs. Rather than become entrenched, we are able to open ourselves to the possibilities made available through engagement with the perspectives of others. Learning to recognize when our communication practices are likely to compromise our own and others' abilities to hear and be heard and to understand and be understood, we can replace our responses with more constructive forms of engagement.

Similarly, dialogic communication and honest self-reflection enable us to deepen our understanding of *how we take in the world and why*. These processes, in turn, equip us to begin the critical process of *assessing* our grounding beliefs and values with a clearer lens, *rather than promoting them uncritically*. Discernment is likely to prove more important than ever for the fulfillment of communication's constructive potential in an increasingly externalized social media environment.

The following highly publicized case involving Shirley Sherrod illustrates this phenomenon. Sherrod's youthful experiences as part of a community routinely subjected to racial prejudice and social injustice had been instrumental in hardening her to the suffering of anyone she perceived as affiliated with her community's oppressors. Thus, when a white farmer came to her for help in her role as an employee in the United States Department of Agriculture (USDA) in 1986, she was initially reluctant to assist him.

During a presentation at a meeting of the NAACP in 2010, Sherrod spoke openly about this experience. She went on to observe how reflection opened her heart to the farmer's plight, enabling her to transcend her prejudice against whites in rural Georgia. This in turn led her to introspective discernment, assessing the merits of her grounding assumptions and recognizing the limits they placed on her. After realizing the flaws in her grounding beliefs, she reconsidered her position and did all that she could to provide the requested aid, grateful for the opportunity to serve responsibly in her USDA staff role.

Sherrod shared this story of her 1986 experience of transcendence with the NAACP in 2010 in the hope of inspiring others to rise above the limits of their own hardened, narrow visions. Unfortunately, however, a blogger placed a video clip on the Web showing only the portion of Sherrod's speech in which she revealed her initial reluctance to assist the farmer because of race. Taken out of context, the video clip appeared to expose a black USDA official subjecting a white farmer to injustice on the basis of his race. The blogger concealed the rest of the video, thus creating a false impression.

Within a short time, Sherrod was the object of scorn and contempt from high-level officials across the political spectrum. NAACP leaders renounced her ostensibly racist action, as did pundits from politically conservative quarters. She was fired from her position at the USDA and roundly reprimanded for abuse of her position.

After a video revealing the *complete context* of Sherrod's presentation was released to the public, she received apologies from her employer as well as from the NAACP leadership. The blogger responsible for publishing the misleading video clip did not provide a public apology, but many others recanted their criticisms of her.

The irony of this turn of events was not lost on Sherrod or others fully informed of the circumstances. Recognizing the important lessons inherent in the incident, President Obama offered the following counsel: "Rather than jump to conclusions . . . we should try to examine what's in our hearts."[6] The president's admonition underscores the rich potential for insights available to us in moments of intense disagreement. Self-reflection and introspective discernment provides invaluable tools for mining such circumstances.

Discernment and Critical Self-Awareness

Self-reflection and introspective discernment also enable us to enrich our understanding regarding how orientations toward an issue or circumstance are informed by standpoint. In earlier explorations we learned, for example, that abilities to recognize our own standpoint and commitments, and their impact on others in dialogue, derive from a willingness to practice critical self-awareness. Developing an unflinching understanding of intersections between our personal perspectives, our social identities, and how others perceive us significantly enhances the potential for fruitful engagement across differences.

Discernment and critical self-awareness mutually reinforce the potential inherent in such deep probing. When we ask ourselves how and to what extent our reactions are products of our identity, background, social status, and position, we foster conditions for meaningful connection. Similarly, when we open ourselves to authentic discovery of how others' standpoints intersect with our own, as well as how they help to inform others' responses to us, we deepen the possibilities. Finally, when we apply the critical thinking skills introduced in our discussion of deliberative inquiry to assessments of the relative merits of our grounding assumptions, we create the possibility of collaborating in pursuit of responsible, responsive decision making.

In Sherrod's case, for example, her standpoint as a member of a historically oppressed black community in rural Georgia was instrumental to her initial inclination not to assist the white farmer in need, as she herself recognized. Her thoughtful self-reflection, moral imagination, critical self-awareness, and introspective discernment enabled her to transcend the limits of her interpretive lens, helping her to move toward the goal of balanced partiality explored in previous chapters. Through a dedicated commitment to fairness, Sherrod was able to assess her initial response, revise her thinking, and ultimately, do the right thing.

Sociologist Troy Duster has researched standpoint's role in decision making across cultures extensively. Among his findings are that elites tend to be "threatened by insurgent and populist calls for social change because such changes constitute a possible redistribution of wealth and privilege that have been assumed as established rights and entitlements."[7] He goes on to observe that, "as a general phenomenon, elites of every society come to believe that their status, their high position in the social hierarchy, is both natural and just."[8]

Many other studies underscore the importance of Duster's observations. Sociologists, economists, and political scientists have found, for example, that within the United States a person's racial identity is a significant factor in predicting the individual's wealth. Lani Guinier and Gerald Torres found that this reality is the result of historical discrimination as well as an infrastructure mitigating equitable access in every major institutional context, from education, to banking, to housing, to employment, to media representations, to health care.[9]

When people situated in the upper levels of a social hierarchy *uncritically assume* that their status is deserved or that less-privileged others have equal access to opportunities on a "level playing field," their uncritical acceptance of these assumptions poses major obstacles to understanding racial, ethnic, gender, and socioeconomic differences. Research has found that the playing field encountered by large numbers of people around the globe is far from level; "access to resources, institutional structures, dominant norms, and the discourses supporting each are skewed sharply in favor of the privileged few at the expense of the many."[10]

Utilizing our capacity for discernment, it is not difficult to understand how someone born into a position of extreme poverty and other forms of socioeconomic disadvantage might respond during an encounter with a person born into a life of privilege, especially if the latter appears to have little understanding of the many real-world obstacles to social and economic mobility in today's marketplace. Given the profound and growing disparities between haves and have-nots, recognition of standpoint's influence in shaping an individual's interpretive frame is an especially important prerequisite for connection.

Consider the following example. Amir and Jasmine met at a local Muslim Youth Center in Detroit and became fast friends. They thoroughly enjoyed opportunities to play chess, read the Quran, study history, and volunteer at the local food pantry together. When they sought to engage one another in a discussion of the nation's health-care crisis, however, they discovered very different and seemingly incompatible perspectives.

As the only son of parents from a long line of wealthy entrepreneurs, Amir was unfamiliar with the struggles Jasmine's impoverished single mother confronted when seeking access to health care for her three children. In conversations regarding the health-care debate, Amir's father routinely expressed contempt and disdain for congressional efforts to "force" the public into a single-payer health insurance program. His father believed strongly that parents should take personal responsibility for securing health care for their children. From his perspective, redistributing wealth through governmental programs such as Medicare would gravely imperil the economic order, violate fundamental rights to property, and otherwise compromise people's cherished and God-given freedom from the government.

As a loyal son who greatly respected his father's wisdom, Amir accepted the patriarch's orientation without reflection. Thus, when Jasmine expressed passionate support for a mandated single-payer governmental health-care reform plan, Amir was appalled. He could not imagine how such a seemingly intelligent and thoughtful person could support socialism and spared no words in expressing his deep concerns.

Jasmine, in turn, was stunned at what she perceived as Amir's failure to understand the hardships that people in marginalized positions face as they struggle to secure health care for their loved ones. She found herself overwhelmed by feelings of outrage in response to Amir's words. Through reflection, Jasmine would have had the opportunity to uncover and meaningfully assess some of the roots of her feelings. She might have been able to identify, for example, that her strongly held values of fairness and caring were the source of her outraged reaction to Amir's lack of awareness of the many structural safeguards supporting his privileged status. Had she been able to attend to the source of her feelings, she might have avoided her angry retort of "how could you possibly be so coldhearted, Amir?" She could have devised a response that was true to her convictions without being personally insulting. She could convey that she feels outraged because she believes deeply in a society that cares for the health and well-being of everyone and that a for-profit health-care system is unfair because it prioritizes making money over caring for people. She also might have been able to ask Amir questions about his own thoughts and feelings, possibly leading to his seeing potential contradictions in his standpoint. For example, what happens when responsible parents who can afford health coverage for their children are denied because the insurance company cites a "preexisting condition" or deems a medical treatment recommended by a doctor as "experimental"?

Similarly, self-reflection and introspective discernment would have afforded Amir the opportunity to learn a great deal about the roots, nature, strengths, and limits of his response. Among other things, he might have discovered that he had been taught to fear change and that his uncritical acceptance of his father's perspective on social and political issues did not meet the basic tests of deliberative inquiry and critical thinking. Although critical thinking might well have led him to share his father's conclusions, Amir's lack of reflection and discernment prevented him from being able to make this assessment and to have confidence in his position. Most importantly for our purposes, thoughtful integration of reflection and discernment would have heightened Amir's ability to hear and be heard across the ideological divides created by his and Jasmine's diverse socioeconomic backgrounds.

In the end, as we have emphasized throughout this book, no amount of self-reflection and introspective discernment would enable individuals such as Amir and Jasmine to escape fully from the inherent limits of their partiality. However, through receptive and honest engagement with one another—coupled with recognition of the role that their standpoints play in shaping their perspectives—they have the potential to come away with *broadened visions*, enabling them to *transcend the limits of their otherwise singular orientation*.

Paving the Way for Deliberative Partnerships

We noted earlier that when we use the term *discernment*, we have in mind *the critical thinking and reflective processes involved in unmasking, understanding, and assessing the relative merits of our own and others' grounding assumptions and beliefs in any given situation*. These include not only the processes involved in uncovering and assessing the relative merits of our own systems of value and belief but also those at play for our deliberative partners. Through discernment, we are able to heighten understanding of the roots of our differences, as well as to discover and assess often hidden points of convergence.

Within the argument culture, seeking mutual understanding and common ground is often discouraged. Absorbed by protecting what we construe as our self-interest in the heat of conflict within an adversarial environment, it is easy to miss the values and interests we share with others. Integrating reflection and discernment offers us the potential to move beyond the anxieties, insecurities, and reflexive responses cultivated by adversarial individualism. In the discussion below, we show how special forms of discernment help pave the way for sound deliberation.

Efforts at cross-cultural communication sometimes fail because participants have difficulty discovering common ground. Similarly, failed attempts to reach across ideological and other divides are sometimes direct products of people's inabilities to recognize potential sources of communion with one another.

Among the many traits attracting Amir and Jasmine to one another was their shared desire to be of service. Working together at the local food pantry, Amir and Jasmine experienced a sense of affinity with one another and with the pantry's clientele. As both recognized, love for and service to one's neighbors was among the core values found in the Holy

Book to which they are both committed. Through their participation in a weekly Quran reading group, Amir and Jasmine came to cherish these and related lessons, strengthening their personal resolves to pursue lives of service. Other values Amir and Jasmine have shared during conversations include deep love of family and country, personal integrity, the value of hard work, and the importance of freedom.

The process of discernment would have helped Amir and Jasmine discover common ground during their discussion of health-care policy issues, aiding them in understanding and refining the issues dividing them. They might have discovered, for example, that they share grounding goals, such as protecting individuals from governmental tyranny or from other forms of excessive intervention, as well as fostering the well-being of all within the community. This process of discernment would have enabled them to make sense of their differences and perhaps to transcend them in shared pursuit of sound deliberative judgment. Amir and Jasmine might have been able to arrive at *foundational deliberative questions*, such as: How can we best protect everyone's freedom from governmental tyranny and preserve the nation's distinctive freedoms, while insuring the well-being of all members of the community? What options are available to balance these core values and interests? And what criteria might we develop together to assess the strengths and limits of these options as pathways for viable health-care reform?

Amir and Jasmine's lost opportunity in many ways parallels the ongoing partisan health-care debates in the United States. Most people across the political spectrum within the United States polity, for example, share a deep and abiding commitment to freedom. Yet partisans from diverse political orientations in the charged health-care reform debates have difficulty transcending their standpoints to pursue shared starting points. Proponents of a single-payer health-care plan are often portrayed by partisan opponents as socialists seeking to rob people of their freedom. Conversely, opponents of such a plan are routinely portrayed as uncaring, greedy oligarchs determined to maintain inequitable relations of power dividing society's haves and have-nots.

A dedicated effort to hear and to be heard, to understand and to be understood might well foster mutual recognition of shared commitments to freedom, thereby enabling participants to discover a constructive starting point for dialogue and deliberation. Through collaborative deliberative inquiry and discernment, policy makers have the potential to explore creative alternatives designed to address diverse stakeholders' needs, values, interests, and concerns responsibly.

Identifying common ground in this way does not, however, necessarily provide clarity about the *degree, natures, sources, or type of agreement* surrounding it. Most deliberative contexts, for example, are influenced significantly by a specific type of common ground known as *presumption*.

Discernment enables us to uncover, assess, and give variable weights to these starting points for deliberation.

Presumptions

When we speak of *presumption,* we have in mind *grounding beliefs and values granted without argument* by decision makers in specific contexts. Some presumptions reflect decision makers' grounding assumptions regarding *the way things are.* These are known as *factual presumptions,* ordinarily expressed as *descriptive* statements. Decision makers across boundaries grant the presumption, for example, that all people are mortal. Anyone wishing to contest this starting point for decision making has a *burden of proof.* By this we mean that *people engaged in deliberation who wish to override the authority vested in the presumption that all people are mortal are required to provide compelling evidence to the contrary.*

Value presumptions also commonly appear as starting points for dialogue and deliberation. As noted in our exploration of belief systems, values are *beliefs (or judgments) about what is right and wrong, good and bad, more or less important, and so on.* Ordinarily, then, value presumptions are expressed as *prescriptions,* reflecting their focus on *how things should be.* For example, decision makers across most deliberative contexts grant the *presumption* that, *when possible, people should be treated fairly.* Anyone wishing to dispute this grounding value presumption has a strong *burden of proof.*

Apart from differences between factual and value presumptions are other categories of relevance to the discernment process. In particular, presumptions are divided into three overarching types: *technical, ideal conventional,* and *real conventional.* The discussion below begins with an overview of the first type and moves from there to an exploration of two variations of the second. As we will see, discerning, assessing, and giving differential weights to these forms of presumption are important starting points for deliberation.

Technical presumptions are imposed on decision makers. Usually, this form of presumption takes the form of a governing rule, often with corresponding procedural guidelines. The most well-known form of *technical presumption* within the United States is the provision that defendants in criminal trials are to be *presumed innocent unless proven guilty beyond a reasonable doubt.* Numerous rules and procedures have been created to clarify and apply this presumptive starting point for trial.

In reality, of course, some jurors and judges do not actually presume the defendant's innocence at the beginning of a trial. Media coverage of cases, for example, sometimes encourages whole groups of potential jurors to doubt the defendant's innocence before the trial begins. The imposition of a *technical presumption of innocence* is intended to help ensure that even jurors who come to the forum with a bias against a defendant will nevertheless recognize their obligation to find verifiable proof of the defendant's guilt, beyond a reasonable doubt, before rendering a guilty verdict. If there is evidence that jurors have not used the presumption of innocence in their decision making, this finding provides appellate courts just cause to override the jury's decision. In short, technical presumption in this context is designed to help prevent miscarriages of justice.

Within competitive debate circles, technical presumptions function differently. In these contexts, teams calling for change from the *status quo*, or *the way things are*, have the *burden to prove that change is needed*. They must establish that there are significant, inherent problems with the *status quo* that call for adoption of an affirmative plan of action.

In contrast to their technical counterparts, *conventional presumptions* are not imposed from the outside. In this sense, they are more malleable. Conventional presumptions include *grounding beliefs and values accepted without argument by specific groups of decision makers*. Included are the factual and value presumptions alluded to in our opening exploration. As noted there, anyone within the group who wishes to argue against one of these beliefs or values has the *burden to prove* that the grounding assumption is false (or that the relevant counterclaim is true).

> The concept of presumption suggests the momentum of the decision makers. Which way are they leaning? Where do they seem inclined to go if no counterargument intervenes?[11]

Importantly, however, conventional presumptions are *not equal* in terms of their *legitimate* authority. Sometimes, for example, the grounding presumptions accepted by a group are *real* in the sense that they are guiding decision making *in actuality*—but not *ideal* in the sense that they have *legitimacy*. Discernment plays a critical role in helping to avoid such potentially harmful circumstances.

This phenomenon is especially characteristic of the groupthink contexts discussed in our exploration of deliberative inquiry. Recall, for example, how in an effort to remain cohesive or to reflect in-group loyalty, groups sometimes rally around an idea or perspective even in the face of compelling evidence to the contrary. As we have learned, clinging to a group's prevailing beliefs in the absence of legitimate ground—and especially in the face of compelling contrary evidence—often proves devastating to other stakeholders.

While accepting less than ideal conventional presumptions can prove harmful, so too can circumstances in which conventional presumptions in a given context are *ideal but not real*. *Ideal* presumptions have the *weight of relevant authority* or some other legitimate basis to justify their role in determining the outcome of decision making. In some contexts, however, these ideal grounding beliefs and values do not always hold presumptive status for actual decision makers. Consider, for example, the ideal value presumption that people ought to be treated fairly whenever possible.

Sometimes, this presumption is not shared *in reality* by all decision makers within a given context. Under these circumstances, the presumption may be said to be ideal but not real.

An especially important example relates to a conventional presumption at the heart of meaningful engagement across differences. As we have seen throughout the previous chapters, *truthfulness* has *strong ideal presumptive authority*. Within the field of applied ethics, this presumption is called the *principle of veracity*. According to the principle, deception *can be morally justified* in some special circumstances; however, *truthfulness has inherent moral presumption in its favor*.

In *Lying: Moral Choice in Public and Private Life*, renowned ethicist Sissela Bok offers an overview of why truthfulness long has been, and should continue to be, vested with strong presumptive authority.[12] She begins by acknowledging that truthfulness by itself does not in any way assure accuracy or truth. Truth and truthfulness, she observes, are quite different. After all, people can—and often do—honestly convey inaccurate or otherwise false information or ideas. Quite simply, people are fallible!

At the same time, however, *intentional* deception inevitably risks compromising pursuits of truth, knowledge, and understanding. Even when in the service of noble purposes, deception risks undermining decision-making processes. This is especially evident in public policy contexts. When the public is deceived by their elected representatives or by the media, the very basis of democratic governance is imperiled. Bok adds that deception in interpersonal contexts can be equally destructive—compromising trust, undermining mutual respect, and ultimately jeopardizing the very foundations of the relationship.

Apart from the relatively apparent risks outlined above are harms to the deceivers themselves. Bok reminds us that every act of deception compromises the individual's character, often with potentially devastating consequences, particularly over time. "These inherent risks—threats to trust, respect, sound decision making, the broader community's well-being, and personal integrity—are but a few of the inevitable dangers associated with deception within and across communication contexts."[13]

It is not difficult to understand why and how truthfulness has earned its authoritative status as an *ideal presumption* in relational communication. Yet as Bok has observed, individuals who choose to deceive others often *overestimate the benefits and underestimate the harms of their decision*. Focusing primarily on their own good intentions, deceivers often persuade themselves that their actions are morally justified. In this sense, deception is often fueled by self-deception. The presumption in favor of truthfulness is, therefore, often more ideal than real for decision makers.

Michael Walzer explains that "competition for political power puts people under great pressure—to shout lies at public meetings, to make promises they can't keep, to take money from shady characters, to compromise principles that shouldn't be compromised." Walzer goes on to observe that many players seeking to enhance the bottom line in the competitive economic marketplace similarly engage in endless self-deception regarding what is "necessary" to achieve their goals. Often, for example, they persuade themselves that lying, cheating, and other forms of corruption are morally justified. In the process, he adds, they corrode their moral character.[14]

During the course of an investigation of a large food group owner's business practices, for example, federal agents revealed that the executive responded to a colleague's concerns regarding the company's mislabeling of products by saying: "We have always manipulated inventory and will continue to. We will lie to anyone outside the circle, but not to each other." According to government documents, the business owner was shocked to discover concerns regarding his routine use of deception.[15]

This sensibility is found often within the argument culture. People embroiled in high-stakes contests in politics and economics are often persuaded that deception in service to their purposes is justified. Even in less adversarial relational environments, the argument culture's focus on instrumentalism encourages use of deception to achieve one's goal. This is especially evident in the case of so-called paternalistic lies, in which deception is used to "protect" the deceived.

However, as Bok reminds us, truthfulness is critical even (and perhaps especially) in such contexts. As we have seen throughout the previous chapters, constructive engagement, relational integrity, sound deliberation, mutual trust, and respect all depend on honesty.

Presumption and Four Types of Discernment

Four types of discernment help remove the breach between the ideal and real status of the principle of veracity and to determine whether, in any specific set of circumstances, deception can be justified.

The first mirrors self-reflection practices and related forms of introspective discernment. Before choosing to deceive, we check in with our conscience by asking questions, such as: Does the use of deception *feel* warranted by the circumstances? What are my true intentions? Is my primary goal in this case the pursuit of justice, fairness, care, loving-kindness, or another laudable end? Or are my true intentions to spare myself possible complications, to make myself look good, to seek revenge, to gain power over vulnerable others, or for purposes of self-aggrandizement, or other less noble ends? What *overall state of heart and mind* governs my inclination to deceive in this case? If at any point in this process we discern that our intentions are not as honorable as we might have imagined, or if our conscience concludes that deception is not morally justified in the case at hand, we need reflect no further. We have not met the burden of proof required to override the presumption in support of truthfulness.

Suppose, however, that our conscience is clear. We are confident of the purity and nobility of our motives and intuitively sense that the deception is justified. Although this is an important (and necessary) form of discernment, it is not by itself enough to justify the use of deception. Often, for example, our intuitions are subject to the narrow vision of our interpretive frames. Without the aid of further discernment, our conscience alone is not an adequate guide. To address this phenomenon, the burden of proof supporting truthfulness requires *three additional types of discernment*.

The second type of discernment involves exploring available options. Given the inherent and often significant harms associated with deception, *finding a viable truthful alternative* is necessarily a more desirable pathway. To illustrate, consider the case of a caring oncologist confronting a patient whose tests suggest a diagnosis of untreatable, fourth-stage lung cancer. Through extensive research and her own observations, Dr. Lee has come to learn that patients with this particular form of cancer tend to live longer, and suffer less, when they are unaware of the seriousness of their condition.

With this in mind, Dr. Lee considers telling Ari that the results of his tests offer him more hope than the medical evidence suggests. Checking in with her conscience—the veracity principle's first form of self-reflection and introspective discernment—Dr. Lee feels no qualms. She has the best of intentions, wanting only the best for Ari. When she moves to the second type of discernment, however, she uncovers an alternative to deception; she could introduce Ari to research revealing the powers of positive thinking, meditation, and related forms of healing. Letting Ari know of her honest diagnosis, while sharing these findings, enables Dr. Lee to provide Ari genuine grounds for hopefulness without violating his trust, showing him disrespect, or undermining his autonomy. Through this form of discernment, Dr. Lee has avoided succumbing to a *false dilemma*. She has found a viable alternative between deception on the one hand and hurting Ari with the "brutal truth" on the other.

In this example, only two steps were needed to apply the principle of veracity responsibly. While the first appeared to support deception, the second revealed that a viable alternative to lying was available. Suppose, however, that Dr. Lee's consultations with Ari's family and counselor revealed his inability to take advantage of alternative forms of healing. And suppose further that learning of Dr. Lee's honest diagnosis would likely do Ari grave harm, even beyond his medical condition. In such a situation, Dr. Lee's decision would have been considerably more difficult. Engaging the second type of discernment might even have led her to conclude that no viable options were available.

When decision makers reach such a point in the deliberative process, there is another type of discernment—consultation with peers (either real or imagined). If peers are available, direct dialogue with them is ideal. However, when talking with them is not an option, imagining their perspective is a possibility. Because Dr. Lee does not have an opportunity to consult with her peers, she would need to ask herself: "If my peers were aware of all the relevant facts, would they be likely to support deceiving Ari?"

If, as a result of this process Dr. Lee concludes that her peers would not support deception, then she need go no further; she would need to be honest with her patient, doing her best to find a caring, loving means for conveying the truth. However, if Dr. Lee's pursuit of peer counsel reveals that they would be likely to authorize deception in this case, the principle of veracity provides Dr. Lee one final test. Because peers tend to privilege one's own self-interests over others, the principle requires moving beyond one's inner circle in pursuit of a responsible decision. Having consulted one's conscience, sought viable truthful alternatives, and checked in with real or imagined peers, the principle of veracity requires decision makers to meet the *test of publicity*.

This fourth, and final, type of discernment calls for a *shifting of perspective*, with a focus on the *values and interests of the person being deceived*. In the case at hand, would Ari himself want to be deceived? And how would people who share Ari's values and interests—as well as members of the broader community—be likely to view the case? If they were familiar with all of the facts in the case, would they be likely to support deceiving Ari? While members of Ari's family have beseeched Dr. Lee to lie, is their assessment of Ari's emotional state reliable? Are they able to give voice to Ari's point of view? The test of publicity requires Dr. Lee to consider these types of difficult reflective questions.

It is important to remember that each case involving discernment to determine whether deception can be justified is unique; every situation requires attention to the particular details of the moment. *No general rule can be applied uniformly*. The four types of discernment embedded in the principle of veracity offer decision makers invaluable resources to guide their deliberations in each unique situation. Other processes are useful for assessing and applying cross-cultural conventional presumptions within real-world contexts.

Discernment and Cross-Cultural Conventional Presumptions

Throughout the book, we have discussed the importance and value of acknowledging, understanding, and valuing the rich diversity of perspectives associated with the world's many racial, ethnic, cultural, religious, sexual, gender, economic and social class groupings. In his insightful book, *Ethnic Ethics*,[16] Anthony Cortese sheds additional light on the importance of recognizing that people from diverse cultures hold significantly different sets of fundamental beliefs and values. As he observes, ethical deliberations within these diverse cultural boundaries are bound by different sets of conventional presumptions.

While there are numerous cultural variations in values, there are also fundamental similarities. Earlier chapters have highlighted, for example, various iterations of the Golden Rule—a cross-cultural conventional presumption that provides a compelling foundation for deliberation across contexts. Steven Pinker, whose work we explored in earlier chapters, observes that most people generally believe that "it's bad to harm others and good to help them."[17] Most people share a basic respect for life, an abhorrence of cold-blooded murder, the belief that fairness is important, and so on. We learned in our exploration of diverse belief systems, for example, that even people who disagree about hotly contested family-life issues nevertheless share many values in common with one another. Most people value stability, security, well-being for all, a safe and nurturing environment for children, warm and caring relationships, and a loving home environment.

This sharing of ideal conventional presumptions across diverse cultures was evidenced dramatically when Nobel Peace Prize laureates from around the world convened for an international peace conference at the University of Virginia. During the conference, Archbishop Desmond Tutu of South Africa and former Costa Rican president Oscar Arias Sanchez joined Tibet's spiritual leader, the Dalai Lama. These respected international leaders, representing diverse religious, ethnic, and cultural perspectives, agreed on several fundamental values.

The Dalai Lama referred, for example, to "basic human values" and "good qualities of human nature." He spoke eloquently of the human potential for gentleness, compassion, and care. Similarly, President Arias Sanchez spoke of the "need for a new ethics." To resounding applause and support from his fellow Nobel Prize winners, he suggested: "there is a need for more compassion, for more generosity, more tolerance, and certainly for more love."

For nearly three decades, Western writers such as Sissela Bok, Clifford Christians, Deni Elliot, Cornel West, and Richard Johannesen, among many others, have called for recognition of similar underlying values and ethical commitments.[18] Their studies of cross-cultural values reveal common commitments to truthfulness, empathy, compassion, caring for self and others, respect, equity, fairness, solidarity with others—particularly those who are vulnerable—attentive and realistic love, commitment to human dignity, and loving kindness.

In December 1948, the international community adopted a Universal Declaration of Human Rights embodying several of these cross-cultural values. The preamble of this remarkable document—reaffirmed by the General Assembly of the United Nations during a fifty-year anniversary celebration in December 1998—recognizes the "inherent dignity" and "the equal and inalienable rights of all members of the human family." According to the preamble, these form the foundation of "freedom, justice, and peace in the world." Article 1 of the Declaration notes further that all human beings "are endowed with reason and conscience and should act towards one another in a spirit of brotherhood."

The presumptions listed above are relevant for relationships between strangers or those who do not share a particular intimacy or closeness. Other cross-cultural presumptions relate to more intimate relationships. Consider, for example, the presumption that intimate friends are trustworthy. This widely held conventional presumption significantly influences perceptions about the quality of relationships. In most cultures people know the difficult burden of proof that comes with trying to persuade someone that his or her friend is not trustworthy. Most people know too that satisfying this burden often leads to a painful shift of presumption. This shift usually undermines and often destroys the quality of the relationship.

These cross-cultural values and the emotions associated with them carry the weight of conventional presumptions across boundaries. In most contexts, advocates whose social, political, or moral arguments appeal to love, compassion, respect, care for self and others, tolerance, human dignity, fairness, equity, and social justice carry strong presumptive weight. Conversely, people whose arguments appeal to hatred, prejudice, intolerance, and injustice bear a strong burden of proof, regardless of cultural context.

The importance of conventional presumptions such as these is especially evident in group decision making. Consider, for example, situations in which members of a group are deadlocked on an issue. Bioethics committees considering the fate of a patient whose life is sustained by a mechanical support system often confront "double" presumptions. They accept the long-standing presumption that the medical practitioner's first responsibility is to "do no harm" they further accept the presumption that "not prolonging life does harm." Taken together, these presumptions often lead an otherwise deadlocked committee to lean in favor of maintaining the patient's life-support system. Someone wishing to move the committee in the opposite direction has the burden to overcome this double presumption.

The four types of discernment embedded in the principle of veracity are applicable in nearly every context engaged by cross-cultural presumptions. For example, when contemplating whether violating the injunction to fairness is morally justified in any given context, applying the four forms of reflection will prove critical. Does our conscience support the unfairness in the case at hand? Are viable alternatives available? How would our peers advise us? And, upon shifting perspectives, how would we assess the situation?

Sometimes the core values associated with cross-cultural presumptions offer clear and compelling counsel for how to act in a given situation, as illustrated by the decision made by Shirley Sherrod discussed at the beginning of the chapter. Following deep self-reflection and intro-spective discernment, Sherrod was able to do the right thing. Discerning the relative merit of fair and just exercise of her responsibilities over her initial inclination to let her prejudices rule was difficult in the sense that all transformative moments can be. On a higher level, however, Sherrod's decision was not complex; few would challenge her conclusion that being fair was the right thing to do.

Often, however, discerning the right—or even the wisest or most ethical—path is not so easy. Dr. Lee's decision revealed, for example, the complexities of making a decision when core values conflict. In Dr. Lee's case, reflection opened the door to finding creative alternatives. When we find ourselves bereft of viable options, however, the path may not be so clear. Under these circumstances, we must turn to discernment pro-cesses for help assessing the relative merits of competing values.

Earlier in this chapter, for example, we mentioned the involvement of a large food company in serious ethics and law violations. The com-pany president routinely adopted a policy of mislabeling company prod-ucts, many of which were sold to public schools. In their efforts to establish a case against the company president, federal agents relied heavily on the assistance of a company vice president. A man of dignity and honor, he greatly valued truthfulness, fairness, and care for the broader community's well-being. At the same time, however, he also placed a high value on loyalty to the company and on his family's eco-nomic stability, which his testimony against his employer could put at risk. The informant had to decide which of his values would prevail. In the end, he chose the path of a "whistle-blower," risking both the wrath of the company leadership and devastating consequences to his family's economic stability. This would have been a difficult choice for anyone but was especially so for someone with such a strong commitment to com-pany loyalty and to his family's well-being.

As we discovered in our exploration of value hierarchies in a previous chapter, nearly all conflicting approaches to decision making—whether internal or between people, individuals or groups—call upon us to make hard choices of this kind. Recall, for example, the dilemma facing Edward as he sought to reconcile his devout evangelical Christian faith with his love for James. Similarly, consider the challenges governments confront when in the face of terrorist threats they must choose between individuals' rights to privacy and the need for security. As we have learned throughout our explorations, disagreements and internal conflicts are often not so much about core values *per se* but rather about how they should be inter-preted and which should be privileged in any given situation.

In the cases above, the value hierarchies framing decision makers' perspectives are readily apparent. Sometimes, however, shifts in order-ings of value are *relatively hidden from view, yet profound in their impact.* Under such circumstances, discernment plays a particularly important role. As a representative example, consider the many contexts in which technological advancements have served to reshape value hierarchies, often without detection.

Discernment and Shifting Value Hierarchies

University of Westminster School of Law Professor Radha D'Souza has observed, for example, that in this historical moment "economy and technology" often dictate "human purpose instead of the other way around."[19] Research reveals further that "the *machine* advances its cause without consideration of humane values; *techne* serves itself."[20]

Among the consequences of technology's growing dominance in the human landscape is a demonstrable shift toward the privileging of *efficiency* over other values. Consider, for example, that in the last century war machines have resulted in more civilian deaths than in all of recorded human history. Despite international efforts to institutionalize rules of engagement strongly admonishing against civilian casualties, the machine's "efficiency" continues to prevail.

In the field of medicine, pursuits of efficiency through technological intervention increasingly trump other historically cherished values as well. As a humanist, scientist, and clinician Stanford University Medical School Professor Abraham Verghese offers valuable insights into this shift in value hierarchy. He notes, for example, that patient-physician visits consist "of one individual coming to another and confessing to them things they wouldn't tell their spouse, their preacher, their rabbi, and then even more incredibly, disrobing and allowing touch, which in any other context would be assault."[21] Increasingly, physicians shortchange patients by not being attentive or by inputting shared comments into the computer while the patient is talking. As a result, the physician risks destroying the opportunity for transformation inherent in the patient-physician bond.

Verghese goes on to observe the irony inherent in this shifting value hierarchy. Reliance on technology, he notes, often undermines the very core of medical practice. When efficiency trumps more humane values—such as care, compassion, empathy, trust, respect, and intimacy—errors of judgment and "inefficient" treatments often follow. Recent studies reveal, for example, that a physician's tone of voice, words of comfort, and other forms of connection "trigger biological reactions" directly correlated with healing. When physicians rely on machines, their capacities to foster healing are often diminished. Further, through their respectful and caring engagements with patients, physicians gain access to information and insight not available through their use of machines. Through a well-trained and sensitive touch, for example, physicians can discern sources and forms of discomfort often critical to an accurate diagnosis.[22] In these ways, the human being offers levels of efficiency not possible through the use of a machine.

The examples above reveal that value hierarchies change along with societal conditions, creating the need for ongoing discernment. What is appropriate, true, or right in one situation may prove inadequate, inappropriate, or wrong in another. In an interview after the publication of her book *(Not) Keeping Up with Our Parents*, Nan Mooney commented on debates regarding governmental support for housing, child care, health care, and retirement, noting that the issues are far more than financial. This is a "moral issue about the shifting values of a country where a staggering number of people cannot manage to get by."[23]

As the United States and other nations continue to cope with growing gaps between those who experience economic security and material well-being and those struggling each day for survival, sound policy making will depend more than ever on lawmakers' abilities to recognize and responsibly address the values and interests at stake in their deliberations.

Discernment and Context

Developing sound deliberative partnerships requires discerning points of controversy and convergence, identifying their roots, and critically assessing their relative merits. Cross-cultural presumptions about truthfulness, fairness, compassion, and care are especially important in guiding deliberative processes. In today's globally interdependent world, deliberative partners will need to take special care to consider these starting points for responsible and responsive decision making.

We've also seen the importance of standpoint, particularly as we consider the needs and interests of those most vulnerable in any given context. The cross-cultural presumptions explored in this chapter provide important safeguards. People in marginalized positions, for example, often derive particular benefits in truthful relations where they are treated fairly and with compassion. This is especially true for the voiceless. Children, wildlife, people outside of the mainstream, and many others whose well-being rests on the outcomes of decision making by others are often unrepresented in deliberative contexts.

In contrast, some types of conventional presumption pose potential obstacles to sound deliberations. In some contexts, for example, decision makers' prevailing beliefs or the long-standing rules of a system may be said to have a *conservative bias*, placing disabling obstacles in the path of justice. History reveals many instances in which such biases have prevented society from recognizing the wisdom of enlightened calls for change. Consider, for example, the once widely held conventional presumption in favor of slavery. Consider too the long-standing technical and conventional presumption that rape victims were somehow responsible for their assailants' brutal attacks.

Today we recognize the serious flaws in the reasoning that led to widespread acceptance of these conventional presumptions. However, it is not so easy for us to see whether currently accepted presumptions are equally vulnerable to widely held biases. We may one day decide, for example, that the presumptions which now favor maintaining life support for the terminally ill fail to serve the interests they were designed to serve. Perhaps one day bioethics committees will require that someone who wishes to maintain life support in such a case must satisfy a burden to prove the wisdom of this practice.

Presumptions regarding the rights of same-sex couples illustrate further. During the Clinton administration in the 1990s, the federal legislative branch in the United States adopted the Defense of Marriage Act, prohibiting legal recognition of same-sex couples' unions. The following decade, however, led to a number of rulings indicating that the Constitution prohibits discrimination against same-sex couples. In November 2008, for example, voters in California passed Proposition 8, an initiative banning marriage between two men or two women. Yet two years later, Federal District Court Judge Vaughn Walker ruled that Proposition 8 violated same-sex couples' constitutional rights. During this same period, several other state legislatures enacted laws protecting same-sex couples' rights to equal treatment, in some cases through legally sanctioned civil unions and in others through marriage. These and related events reveal that conventional presumptions in this area are in the process of being redefined.

In the area of animal welfare, activists believe that the widely held technical and conventional presumptions favoring factory-farming methods, hunting, animal experimentation, and other common uses of animals will one day be replaced with presumptions favoring stronger consideration of animal, as well as human, welfare. California's landslide 2008 vote in favor of protecting factory-farmed chickens' welfare and the 2012 ban on the sale of goose liver produced through means deemed cruel are seen by many as support for this movement. Future generations may well view current practices in the use of animals as barbaric. On the other hand, some regard this perspective as radical and without substance. The evolving nature of presumptions in the cases outlined above mirror the shifts in dominant value hierarchies explored in this and previous chapters. It will be fascinating to see which presumptions and value hierarchies will prevail in the years ahead.

Attentive listening, reflection, dialogic communication and discernment provide deliberative partners with tools needed to *recognize, understand,* and *critically question* these and other prevailing systems of belief. Discernment processes in particular help deliberative partners to assess the validity and wisdom of their technical and conventional presumptions. In this and related ways, these processes offer means for evaluating and reevaluating the *status of claims.* Should a claim have presumption in its favor? Should someone who wants to defend the claim have a burden to prove its acceptability? To what degree? In what contexts? Why?

Philosopher Robert Pinto goes so far as to suggest that it would be "enormously fruitful" to view arguments and other forms of engagement across difference as "attempts to confer on their conclusions the status of a presumption—or, what is to say the same thing, to shift the burden of proof to those who would dispute them."[24] Even if we do not go so far as to view all engagements in these terms, we can share Pinto's belief that presumption is an important element of dialogue and deliberation. As we begin embracing deliberative argumentation in real situations, we should not underestimate the importance of understanding, recognizing, acknowledging, and critically assessing the role that presumption plays in fostering sound deliberation.

Equipped with the knowledge and skills required for discernment, deliberative partners are prepared to pursue deliberative argumentation, the next critical step toward fulfillment of communication's constructive potential.

Deliberative Argumentation

Previous chapters have explored the many influences helping to shape how people frame the deliberative contexts they encounter. As we have seen, each of us takes in the world through an inherently partial lens. Recognizing how and why we disagree provides a pathway for reaching across our individual interpretive frames in pursuit of enriched understanding of issues, stakeholder interests, values, concerns, and available options. Discernment processes help to create the conditions required to assess the reliability of our own and others' assumptions and beliefs.

In this chapter, we build on these capacities by focusing attention on *intersections between argumentation, discernment, deliberation, and decision making*. This exploration takes us full circle from our starting point by *reconceptualizing argumentation*.

Introduction

Throughout this volume, we've revealed how and why arguments are often experienced as *combative interactions* within the adversarial individualist framework. Arguments of this kind are often associated with "fighting" in the judge-blame-defend cycle of communication endemic to the argument culture.

Delores Williams, a theologian, recalls the ways in which she learned to associate this type of argument with violence:

> Every time we used the word *(argument)* in class, I remembered two women in my neighborhood. When I was very young, these two women got into arguments with their husbands, and I saw their husbands beat them unmercifully in the street. Mrs. Johnson (a fictitious name) argued with her husband on the corner and killed him. On Saturday night, oppressed, depressed black men, enraged at the system, met at the tavern on Sixteenth and Walnut streets. Every Saturday night some of the men would get into arguments and somebody would get killed. My grandparents told us over and over again that if

the white police ever stopped us for anything, we were not to argue. We were to do whatever they said because if we argued the police might kill us. In fact, we were to be as silent as possible in our encounter with white policemen because anything we said might be mistaken for argument. This was one of the survival strategies that we were taught. The word, idea, and fact of *argument* in the community challenged the collective and cooperative efforts black community leaders (often women) exerted to hold us together as a people.[1]

When argumentative discourse is practiced as combative interaction or otherwise associated with verbal, emotional, or physical violence, it is understandable that many people either avoid it or learn how to best each other through its use. And yet, throughout millennia within the East and West, a substantively different form of argumentation has been recognized as a critical resource for decision making. In Ancient China, Greece, Persia, and Rome, for example, the skillful practice of argumentation was widely recognized as critical to deliberations in contexts such as law, medicine, and policy making. As the remainder of this chapter will reveal, *deliberative argumentation* framed within an interdependent model of communication continues to offer promise as a vital resource in these and other practical contexts. When we speak of *deliberative argumentation,* we have in mind *reasoned discourse* that represents the culmination of advocates' deliberative inquiry, discernment, reflection, creative imagination, and related critical thinking processes.

Deliberative Argumentation, Decision Making, and Deliberation

James Klumpp reminds us how dialogic communication, deliberative inquiry, and reflection contribute to decision making. Through "the variety of observation that comes from different eyes focused on a given moment, the variety of interests that make our choices responsive to the values, wishes, and desires of others," through the "testing of ideas, the challenging of faith, the exploration of alternatives," and related processes, we are able to pursue "the power to make decisions with others."[2] Klumpp distinguishes decision making and deliberation by noting that the latter "emphasizes the concluding of the process in choice."[3] In short, decisions are the "achievements" of the choices generated by deliberations. After we deliberate, we have the information necessary to make a decision and move toward action. In this sense, decisions are actions in the making.

In these and related ways, inquiry, communication, reflection, decision making, and deliberation go hand in hand. When we exercise responsible and responsive communication, we create conditions for deliberative choice making. And when this process is successful, we are equipped to arrive at the best decision possible in a given situation.

Psychology professors Irving Janis and Leon Mann have conducted extensive research on sound decision making. They have identified the following seven especially important steps required to make well-informed and wise decisions:[4]

1. Canvassing alternative courses of action
2. Surveying the full range of objectives and the values implicated by the choice
3. Examining consequences of each alternative
4. Searching for new relevant information
5. Assimilating new information
6. Reexamining consequences of each alternative
7. Making detailed provisions for implementing or executing the chosen course of action

Janis and Mann note that failure to fulfill any of these steps "constitutes a defect in the decision-making process. The more defects, the more likely the decision maker will undergo unanticipated setbacks and experience post-decisional regret."[5]

Dialogic communication, deliberative inquiry, discernment skills, and deliberative argumentation provide critical tools for the decision-making process. The dialogic and deliberative spirit and skills explored in earlier chapters, for example, enable people from diverse backgrounds and perspectives to "take in" the wide diversity of perspectives available. Discernment processes in turn equip decision makers to critically assess their own and others' views.

The moral courage and humility associated with dialogic communication, deliberative inquiry, and introspective discernment further motivate and enable people to reach across their differences in pursuit of information and insights. Similarly, through empathic and compassionate regard and a keen sense of human interdependence, deliberative partners are open to examining potential consequences for proposed alternatives and motivated to search collaboratively for additional information.

Deliberative Partnerships

In earlier chapters, we noted that people form deliberative partnerships when they want to hear and to be heard, to understand and be understood, and when they seek to work together in pursuit of the information and insights needed to make the best possible assessment or decision in any given context. Clusters of deliberative partners in turn form deliberative communities.

Deliberative partnerships serve decision-making processes across contexts. From interpersonal to group deliberations, personal to professional decision making, familial to communal contexts, the formation of deliberative partnerships contributes invaluably to the quality of deliberative processes. Among other things, deliberative partnerships expose points of agreement and disagreement, introduce participants to alternative perspectives, and expose underlying assumptions.

As a result, participants can better evaluate their personal views, identify and assess their options, and reason well across their differences. As each probes more deeply into the reasons behind their differing points of view, deliberative partners determine the underlying sources of disagreement. And through their constructive exchanges, they learn the "roots" of their thinking. These discoveries afford deliberative partners the opportunity to probe the origins of their beliefs and to engage in critical self-assessment. The example below offers a concrete illustration of how a deliberative partnership within an interpersonal communication context fosters sound personal decision making in these and related ways. As you read the example, notice the alignment between this process and the criteria outlined in Janis and Mann's overview of sound decision making.

Gorge and Juanita find themselves disagreeing about whether Gorge's eleven-year-old daughter, Laura, should be permitted unsupervised access to the Internet. Gorge believes that children Laura's age should not have "independent" access to Internet communication devices. Juanita believes children of this age should be allowed at least one hour a day of "unsupervised" Internet exploration.

Both Gorge and Juanita have a stake in making the best decision possible. Gorge is Laura's father, and Juanita is Laura's grandmother. Juanita would like Laura to spend a week at her house. Gorge would like Laura to stay with her grandmother as well, but he is concerned that Laura be "protected" from potentially "dangerous" Internet sources. Gorge and Juanita begin their argumentative exchange by acknowledging that both are primarily concerned with what is best for Laura. Through their deliberative partnership, Gorge and Juanita exchange their reasons for their beliefs. Respectful of one another and determined to collaborate in pursuit of the best decision possible, Juanita and Gorge want to tap their collective wisdom.

Juanita begins their deliberative exchange by pointing to a scientific website suggesting that providing children relative autonomy at an early age enhances their moral and cognitive development. Juanita adds her own sense that the ability to determine their own destinies gives preteens a sense of independence and helps prepare them for future decision making. She also argues that providing unsupervised access to Internet resources demonstrates respect and trust, thereby strengthening relational bonds at a critical point in Laura's development.

Gorge listens attentively and openly to Juanita's reasoning. As he begins his response, he notes that he shares Juanita's beliefs regarding children's early need for autonomy. However, his research into child development has led him to conclude that preteens are not yet capable of discerning more or less harmful Internet resources. He identifies two websites and a peer-reviewed text providing research findings in support of this assessment. Gorge notes his agreement with Juanita's view that preteens have some measures of discernment, but he adds that the force of this skill set is often overridden by preteens' vulnerability to exploitation by corrupt adults. Finally, Gorge cites the testimony of psychologists who believe that parental supervision of preteens' Internet activities helps them feel secure in an otherwise chaotic world. Security at an early age, argues Gorge, helps young people to gain the foundation they need to adapt to the many difficult situations they will encounter in their later years.

Gorge and Juanita's deliberative partnership serves their decision making by: (1) identifying points of agreement and disagreement; (2) introducing each of them to alternative perspectives; and (3) exposing their own and each other's underlying assumptions. As a result, both Juanita and Gorge are now more able to evaluate their views.

As each probes more deeply into the reasons behind their differing points of view, Gorge and Juanita determine that their stated reasons do not account for the *intensity of their disagreement.* Through more deliberative exchanges, they learn that their respective parents have influenced their thinking. This discovery affords Juanita and Gorge the opportunity to probe the origins of their beliefs.

Juanita recalls, for example, that she lived in a closely knit, extended family atmosphere where nearly every decision other than reading and television viewing was imposed on the children. Because of the restrictions in other areas, the autonomy granted to choose media outlets without supervision was valued highly. Gorge recalls that his father's career as a traveling musician resulted in feelings of chaos and irregularity. Gorge's father did what he could to help Gorge and his sisters suffer minimally from the family's frequent moves. Among other things, the children had a rigorously supervised bedtime schedule. They were not permitted to watch television and had only supervised exposure to music and print materials. The security of imposed supervision contrasted with the other disruptions they experienced and provided a comfort level in contrast to the many uncertainties in their lives.

Juanita and Gorge's deliberative partnership has enabled them to critically assess the available information, to reassess available options, and to reflect upon the values underlying each pathway available to them. Through careful reflection, they have been able to assess whether the circumstances leading each of them to their opening points of view apply to Laura's situation. Through further exploration, they conclude that Laura generally experiences more overall autonomy than children in Juanita's family and experiences less chaos than members of Gorge's family circle. These insights enable Juanita and Gorge to think critically about the "roots" of their perspectives and to assess the applicability of their ideas to the current context.

After weighing all of the available information and insights, Gorge and Juanita determine that Laura's circumstances differ substantively from their own. This realization enables them to reassess the available options and to arrive at a creative solution. Together, they conclude that Laura's interests would best be served by utilizing available "parental screening" tools for all electronic devices in Juanita's household. With this stipulation, Gorge "authorizes" Juanita to provide Laura one hour of "unsupervised" use of the household's "secured" electronic devices. Although Juanita would have preferred more latitude than this outcome affords her, she concludes that Gorge's proposal is reasonable. She is not completely happy with the decision but is persuaded that the deliberative process has led to a fair and responsible decision reflecting Laura's best interests.

Through their deliberative partnership, Gorge and Juanita have been able to discover some of the foundations of their beliefs and to assess the applicability of their findings to the context at hand. Through deliberative inquiry, listening, dialogue, discernment, and deliberative argumentation, each was able to articulate and assess the best reasons for and against their respective views. As a result of their deliberative exchange, Gorge and Juanita were able to make a decision they both deem wise given all of the available information. Perhaps most importantly, deliberative argumentation has enabled Gorge and Juanita to achieve their ultimate shared goal of serving Laura's interests to the best of their abilities. During the final stages of decision making, deliberative partners such as Gorge and Juanita have opportunities to consider new information and insights and to reexamine their assessments of the likely consequences of alternative proposals.

Richard Fulkerson suggests that instead of thinking of people with whom we disagree as adversaries, we should regard them as *partners*. Dialectical partnerships allow communicators to pursue "mutually enlightening understanding."[6] Participants in deliberative argumentation recognize that their views can only be enlightened by as comprehensive and receptive an exchange as is possible. They learn to view those who disagree with them as *deliberative partners* capable of enlightening them.

Deliberative Argumentation's Distinctive Features

In earlier chapters, we offered the following definition of *dialogue: A process of communicating with others—a sincere and mutual exchange involving inquiry, reflection, and responsiveness.* We showed how and why this form of communication is especially well suited to foster abilities to hear and be heard, to understand and be understood. Deliberative partners skillfully engaged in argumentation meet these conditions. Deliberative argumentation as a form of interaction is also defined by the elements assigned to other forms of dialogic communication (see the graphic differentiating dialogue from competitive debate in chapter 4). Recall, for example, that unlike competitive debate, all forms of dialogic communication assume fallibility, seek balanced partiality, and investigate differing views. Dialogue fosters deliberative inquiry and is collaborative, with two or more sides working together in pursuit of shared understanding. People engaged in dialogue listen to learn and understand and to reflect critically—integrating facts, feelings, values, interests, and beliefs to discern meaning.

Unlike other forms of dialogic communication, however, deliberative argumentation features *reasoned interaction*, is *tailored for presentation to an audience*, and *comes to closure when participants are equipped to make informed and wise decisions*. In support of the latter important feature of this distinctive form of dialogic communication, deliberative argumentation *represents the culmination of the processes* discussed so far—inquiry and deliberative framing, critical and creative thinking, discernment and other forms of reflection, and responsiveness.

The next chapter focuses on advocacy's place within an interdependent communication framework. For now, however, it is important to recognize that deliberative argumentation is a special kind of dialogic communication, representing advocates' perspectives as effectively as possible. The discussion below introduces key elements of deliberative argumentation, beginning with reasonableness.

Elements of Argumentation

Reasonableness

In defining deliberative argumentation as *reasoned interaction*, we have aligned this form of dialogic communication with the ancient art of practical reasoning. One of the most important elements of this form of interaction—and in some senses its essence—is *reasonableness*, a difficult construct to define. It is somewhat similar to Supreme Court Justice Potter Stewart's declaration that he would not attempt further definitions of pornography but he knew it when he saw it.

One important aspect of reasonableness is logic. As we have learned previously, however, emotions play vital roles in practical reasoning as well. Argumentation in service to deliberation involves a delicate balance between logic and critical emotions. Supreme Court Justice William J. Brennan was heralded by many as a decision maker who successfully integrated these two elements of practical reasoning. Shortly after Justice Brennan's death in July 1997, Justice David Souter described him as "a man who loves." With tears in his eyes, Justice Souter added, "the Brennan mind, which held a share of the judicial power of the United States, has met its match in the Brennan heart. And in their perfect match lies the secret of the greatness of our friend."[7]

Technological advances have helped to underscore the importance of balancing emotion and logic in practical contexts. Consider, for example, the important roles played by empathy and compassion in bioethical decision making. Without these critical emotions, decisions regarding such complex issues as when and how to use technology in the beginning and end stages of human life would be bereft of a resource vital to just and wise decision making.

Similarly, jurists in criminal cases must analyze mitigating circumstances. To do so, they draw on their experiences and shared sense of humanity to make the best decision possible. It is difficult to imagine how a machine, devoid of the ability to feel *empathy, love, or compassion*, would be able to provide a comparably nuanced decision.

As discussed in previous chapters, a *well-developed moral imagination* is critical to sound deliberation as well. Cultivating empathy, compassion, and respect for others has always been important but may prove even more so as we evaluate and moderate the consequences of technological advancements.

Jonathon Haidt's research underscores the important role that the moral imagination plays in transcending narrow vision in pursuit of reasoned deliberation. When arguing political or moral issues, we often shift into combat mode, where our "righteous mind" is wedded to a moral matrix. It is difficult, under these circumstances, to use argumentation for any purpose other than to win or to hold our ground in the face of disagreement. Through moral imagination, however, we can overcome this obstacle to balanced partiality and reasonableness.

Haidt discusses the communicative practices of Dale Carnegie, author of *How to Win Friends and Influence People*. He describes Carnegie as:

> a brilliant moral psychologist who grasped one of the deepest truths about conflict. He used a quotation from Henry Ford to express it: "If there is any one secret of success it lies in the ability to get the other person's point of view and see things from their angle as well as your own."[8]

Haidt goes on to observe that if you can truly see a moral or political issue from the other's perspective, you create the potential for receptiveness on your part as well as your interlocutor's. "Empathy is an antidote to righteousness, although it's very difficult to empathize across a moral divide."[9]

Haidt's insights regarding the value and importance of empathy in moral deliberations are echoed by philosopher Martha Nussbaum in *Upheavals of Thought: The Intelligence of Emotions*. Drawing on scholarship from many fields (including psychology, philosophy, literary studies, and rhetorical theory), Nussbaum provides compelling support for a view of emotions as "essential elements of human intelligence." Nussbaum's comprehensive analysis reveals the vital roles emotional discernment and well-being play in deliberations aimed at supporting human flourishing.[10] Nussbaum's work offers critical insights regarding emotion's role in helping people sense how the world relates to one's goals and projects.[11] Emotions are also instrumental in establishing and assessing value hierarchies.

Like all other aspects of reasoning and evaluative processes, *emotions are more or less justifiable within any given context*. Previous chapters, for example, have provided examples when appeals to fear were neither justified nor reasonable. History is replete with examples of how such appeals have profoundly compromised the quality of deliberations with grave consequences to the human family. However, fear is sometimes not only reasonable and justified but also a vital resource for sound decision making.

Unlike fear, empathy, love, and compassion routinely serve deliberations in pursuit of human flourishing. Nussbaum notes that societies need compassionate judges and jurors.[12] Appeals to these emotions have presumptive weight for the jury. In some contexts, however, overreliance on or inappropriate use of these emotions potentially compromises sound deliberations.[13]

To summarize, skillful deliberative argumentation integrates logic, justifiable emotion, and moral imagination, among other features of reasonableness. Importantly, however, reasonableness as a construct and norm differs substantively from rationality. The discussion below provides an overview of key differences between these norms.

Distinguishing Rationality from Reasonableness

Within Western analytic schools of philosophy, the premise that certainty of an argument's conclusion was a requirement for validity held sway for many years. In their groundbreaking volume, *The New Rhetoric: A Treatise on Argumentation*, Chaim Perelman and Lucie Olbrechts-Tyteca challenged this view.[14]

Relying on insights from Aristotle and other ancient rhetorical theorists, these and other new rhetorical theorists offered an alternative framing of the place of reason in deliberative contexts. They noted that Aristotle was careful to distinguish different types of reasoning. In practical fields such as law and medicine, for example, Aristotle recognized that it is never possible to make decisions based on certainty. Here, decision makers are called upon to assess the limits and strengths of arguments within the domain of *the probable*. Decisions in such practical contexts are subject to *reasonableness standards integrating emotions, intuitions, facts, values, critical thinking, related discernment processes, and logic*.

In short, reasonableness as a key element of deliberative argumentation differs substantively from the Western analytic construct of rationality. While the latter orientation views self-evidence and certainty as defining characteristics of validity, deliberative argumentation turns to practical standards of reason integrating logic, imagination, and emotion for evaluating the relative merits of arguments.

We will provide further insight into the nature and substance of practical standards of reason in chapter 12. The important lesson for the moment, however, is the recognition that reasonableness is neither a product of, nor aligned with, the formal logician's framework for defining and assessing rationality. Importantly, a profoundly different understanding of rationality prevails in many circles outside the field of philosophy. Unlike the Western philosophical analytic view explored above, this perspective makes no effort to align rationality with either reason or formal logic.

Within the individualist adversarial framework, rationality as a construct is aligned with instrumentalism. Individuals acting to preserve their self-interest are enacting *instrumental rationality*. Conversely, acting against one's personal interests is considered irrational. Instrumental rationality of this kind is considered a hallmark of skillful, effective, and successful argumentation within the individualist adversarial framework of argument.

Using all available means to persuade others to adopt one's perspective or to act in accordance with one's wishes exemplifies instrumental rationality. Consider, for example, the exchange below between *New York Times Magazine* reporter Deborah Solomon and prominent political strategist Frank Luntz. In the midst of the nation's 2009 deliberations regarding how best to address the nation's health-care crisis, Luntz sent a 28-page memo titled, "The Language of Health Care" to congressional Republicans.

In her interview, Solomon asked Luntz about his counsel to "speak about health-care reform in ominous phrases."[15] In particular, she asked Luntz about his suggestion that Republicans refer to President Obama's health-care proposal as a "Washington takeover." In framing her question, Solomon noted that this representation of the president's plan did not appear to reflect what was actually at issue in the health-care debate. In her words, the health-care reform proposal seeks to enable "everyone to be able to choose between their old, private health insurance plan and an all-new, public health insurance option."

In effect, Solomon's questions invited Luntz to consider how his apparent misrepresentation of the issues might affect the quality of the deliberative process in this critically important decision-making context. In his response to Solomon's concerns, Luntz observed simply, "I'm not a policy person. I'm a language person."

As Solomon continued probing, Luntz offered further glimpses into his philosophy of communication:

> **Solomon:** You have devised many phrases to help sell Republican policies to the public. Like "energy exploration" instead of "drilling for oil" in the Arctic. What are some of your other coinages?
>
> **Luntz:** It's "death tax" instead of "estate tax" or "inheritance tax." It's "opportunity scholarships" instead of "vouchers." It's "electronic intercepts" rather than "eavesdropping."

This exchange concisely illustrates the instrumentalist approach at the heart of adversarial individualism. This orientation enables, and in some contexts even encourages, *segregating communicative choices from their implications to deliberative processes.* More generally, instrumentalism of this kind rests on the assumption that the *ends justify the means.* Gaining strategic advantage for one's cause justifies the means required to achieve one's outcome.

Given the dominance of the adversarial individualist argument culture, it is not surprising to discover that many people have learned to adopt this approach to argumentation. Cognitive scientists Hugo Mercier and Dan Sperber, cited in Haidt's work, have concluded from their review of research on "motivated reasoning (in social psychology) and on the biases and errors of reasoning (in cognitive psychology), for example, that "skilled arguers . . . are not after the truth but after arguments supporting their views."[16]

Importantly, because deliberative argumentation represents the culmination of advocates' dialogic and deliberative processes, *deliberative partners seek to support their views through their arguments.* Unlike their adversarial counterparts, however, these advocates share a mutual commitment to pursue knowledge and truth in service to sound deliberation. In support of this framework, instrumental rationality is recognized as a potentially debilitating obstacle to wise decision making. The ability to recognize differences between reasonableness as a norm on the one hand and instrumental rationality on the other helps deliberative partners to *both* support their views *and* pursue the truth, avoiding the false dilemma associated with the kind of advocacy Mercier and Sperber have identified.

Within an interdependent communication framework such as this, the rationale for combative interaction subsides, and the need for learning about different perspectives and for building relationships takes precedence. Reasonableness replaces both formal and instrumental rationality as a guideline. This approach to argumentation creates conditions for fulfillment of the three principles of sound deliberation explored earlier in this volume. *Reciprocity, publicity, and accountability* minimally require mutual commitments to pursuits of knowledge, truth, and justifiability.

This orientation toward argumentation stresses that *how* we do things—in this case, the process of arguing—necessarily shapes what we are capable of doing. Gandhi's principle that *the means are the ends in the making* lies at the heart of deliberative argumentation.

Nelson Mandela's personal encounters with profound injustice position him well to assess the efficacy of this principle. As a skilled orator and advocate, Mandela often encountered opportunities to exploit people's anger and fears and to otherwise compromise the integrity of communication processes in order to prevail. Recognizing that hatred begets hatred, that fear promotes tyranny, and that deception fosters mistrust, Mandela steadfastly embraced truthful, noncoercive means of communication.

Following years of imprisonment and suffering, Mandela rose to the highest position of leadership in his nation. At his presidential inauguration Mandela declared that "out of the experience of an extraordinary human disaster that lasted too long, must be born a society of which all humanity will be proud."[17] In his words, "to be free is not merely to cast off one's chains, but to live in a way that respects and enhances the freedom of others."[18] According to this great leader, South Africa's triumph over hatred and terror must be understood as a "common victory for justice, for peace, for human dignity."[19]

Mandela's steadfast commitment to truth and truthfulness, to relational accountability and mutual responsibility, were reflected in his approach to engagement across difference. Like so many other respected guardians of humanity's quests for peace and justice, this Nobel Prize winner's approach to communication reflects his recognition that "the means are the ends in the making."

Rhetorical Context

Thus far, we have observed that argumentation differs from other forms of dialogic communication in its emphasis on reasonableness. The rhetorical contexts within which deliberative arguments are situated also distinguish this from other types of dialogic interactions. When we speak of *rhetorical context*, we have in mind the *audience, purpose, and occasion* situating communicative acts.

There are many different kinds of audiences, including some groupings that are generalized and others that are more specialized. *General* audiences include people with differing levels of expertise. Examples include audiences at boards of supervisor meetings, viewers taking in a State of the Union Address, or audiences attending a roundtable forum. In each of these contexts, audiences often include people equipped with significantly different levels of insight, information, and background knowledge on the subject matter at hand.

Specialized audiences, in contrast, usually share discourse and expertise with one another. When famed physicist Steven Hawking narrates programs for public television, for example, he seeks to share his thoughts, insights, and ideas with a generalized audience. In more specialized settings, however, he addresses his thoughts to fellow physicists who share language and expertise with him and with one another. Similarly, when lawyers prepare arguments for juries, they tend to conceptualize the jury as a generalized audience. In contrast, when preparing arguments for the United States Supreme Court, lawyers anticipate a more specialized audience. Supreme Court justices share specific language, expertise, and a set of expectations that differ from those of the general population. Lawyers who are assigned to present cases to this group do so with this level of specialization in mind.

Representative of all rhetorical artifacts, the occasion, audience, and purpose of an advocate's argumentative presentation inform how the advocate's specific arguments are most effectively framed. For example, an argument framed for a general audience will, of necessity, need to be framed using different language and appeals than one targeted for a more specialized audience. In this sense, responsiveness to audience and occasion are critically important for success in deliberative argumentation just as they are for adversarial arguments.

At the same time, however, the *grounding purpose* of deliberative argumentation across contexts is fostering reasoned and wise deliberation. The standard for effective deliberative argumentation differs from the standard of success for argumentation within the adversarial individualist model. Whereas adversarial communication valorizes solitary victors, deliberative argumentation succeeds when we are able to build deliberative community across differences. When we are able to understand and be understood, to hear and be heard, to share information and insights, to question together and probe with one another, we become equipped to tackle the complex issues of the day.[20] When deliberative argumentation is able to contribute to reasoned and wise decision-making processes, advocates have fulfilled their primary purpose.

While an audience may be specialized or general in nature, they may also be relatively *informed* or *uninformed*. Additionally, audience members' *critical thinking and related discernment skills may be more or less developed*. As a result, audience members may have varying degrees of skillfulness at making critical and informed judgments. Among the important pathways to successful communication in deliberative contexts, therefore, is sensitivity and responsiveness to audience. This is true for all of the key elements of argumentation discussed below.

Claims

Among the most basic of the other elements that make up deliberative arguments are *claims*. When we use the term *claim* we have in mind *any statement, either implied or openly stated*. As noted in previous chapters, there are various types of claims, each with its own domain for verification and support. Claims of fact, for example, convey beliefs about the material world and human condition subject to empirical verifiability. Claims of value, in contrast, convey beliefs about what is right, good, wrong, bad, and so on, subject to moral and ethical assessment.

Claims of all kind can serve either as premises or as conclusions of arguments. When we use the term *premise*, we have in mind *any claim provided in support of the conclusion*. Discernment is required to ascertain whether a given claim may be verified as a fact or assessed as a judgment of value or aesthetics, and whether the claim is meant to serve as a premise or a conclusion. These are critical starting points for effective argumentation.

Issues and Common Ground

Issues are also key elements of deliberative argumentation. As we learned in our discussion of deliberative framing, *issues* arise whenever there are *clashes between two or more claims*. Careful framing of issues is important to both deliberative argumentation and to skillful adversarial argumentation.

Effective deliberative argumentation taps *points of agreement*. Among other things, common ground provides beginning points for argumentation. Without such starting points, argumentation in service to advocacy and deliberation is not possible. Often in the course of argumentation, sets of issues and common ground change as a result of interaction. As we learned in our exploration of presumption and burden of proof in chapter 9, identifying a claim as generally accepted by a group of decision makers does not necessarily provide clarity about the *degree or type of agreement* surrounding it. Some beliefs are shared more strongly than others. Some have a kind of societal privilege earned over time. Others result from careful discussion.

In some instances, shared beliefs are held so strongly that they serve as *presumptions*, creating a *burden of proof* for those who wish to challenge them. The ability to discern levels of agreement and disagreement is an important element of argumentation. Responsibly and skillfully addressing the conventional, technical, and cross-cultural *presumptions* discussed in chapter 9 is especially critical to successful deliberative argumentation. Advocates who meet the *burdens of proof* associated with these presumptions provide valuable resources for audiences seeking to make informed and wise decisions.

Definitions of terms also serve as important elements of deliberative argumentation. In some instances, definitions are either obvious or quickly shared. However, *definitions of terms often become issues*. Consider, for example, uses of terms such as "freedom," "security," "fairness," "justice," and "rights." These are only a few examples of words that often play instrumental roles in framing moral and political argumentative contexts. Recognizing the ambiguity or vagueness of these terms, and the importance of clarifying how the terms are being used, is an important pathway to addressing issues through argumentation.

Equally important is the search for information and insights. Chapter 3 provides overviews of pathways for securing and assessing the fruitfulness of available resources. Recall, however, that advocates prepare deliberative arguments after they have completed the earlier processes of deliberative inquiry, discernment, and deliberation. As a result, the exploratory spirit associated with early deliberative inquiry processes shift in important ways as advocates work to develop their arguments. In particular, rather than look for information and insights to *form* a view, advocates at this stage search for *evidence in support* of their claims.

Types of Support

There are many types of support available for the development of deliberative arguments. Among these, specific instances, such as examples and illustrations provided in narrative format, often help to lend presence to a problem or point of view.

Consider, for example, the power of "making present" in the story that unfolds in the *Diary of Anne Frank*. Statistical accounts of the horrors of the Holocaust rarely evoke a sense of strong presence and connection. In contrast, there are few people not moved by the compelling story of tragedy experienced by Anne Frank, a young, sensitive, vulnerable girl hiding with her family in an Amsterdam attic during the German occupation of Holland.

While examples such as these can prove compelling, heavy reliance on them can defeat the purposes of either deliberative or adversarial argumentation. Examples and illustrations can be overcome by *counterexamples* and illustrations. Even carefully developed illustrations are vulnerable to refutation. To serve as effective support, examples need to be representative and sufficient in number.

Thus far, we've included only "real" examples in our exploration of this form of evidence. When real examples are not available, *hypothetical* examples can be used to support controversial claims. This form of evidence is potentially compelling in part because the author is able to control all of the example's details. When the details match readers' or listeners' conceptions of reality, the example conveys, clarifies, or supports a point. However, when the hypothetical example does not reliably match readers' or listeners' conceptions of the world, its value is diminished. In such a situation, what was once a source of its power becomes a weakness.

Statistics also provide potentially valuable sources of support. As we learned in chapter 3, statistics are numerical compilations of specific instances. Statistical evidence may include raw numerical data or data that have been tabulated and evaluated. To facilitate argumentation, statistical data need to satisfy at least the following basic criteria: They should come from *reliable sources*; rely on *valid measurements*; be *current*; and be *representative*.

Another type of evidentiary support is *testimony*. In most cases, testimonial evidence is used to give greater credibility to a claim. There are two types of testimony: *testimony of fact* and *testimony of opinion*. In a criminal trial, witnesses are often asked to give testimony of fact. Was the defendant at the scene of the crime? Did the witness see the defendant use the stick to hurt the child? Testimony of opinion is also often used in criminal proceedings. For example, psychiatrists are often asked to provide their opinion of whether a defendant was criminally sane at the time a crime was committed.

These uses of testimony help provide substantive evidence to support an advocate's claim. But as noted in the exploration of deliberative inquiry in chapter 3, the value of testimonial evidence is directly tied to the witness's *credibility*. How believable is the witness? How reliable is the witness's testimony? The widespread use of testimony in advertisements illustrates this point. Consider the actor who plays a doctor on a popular daytime television series. When this actor testifies that he favors one brand of aspirin over another, he lacks credibility with critical viewers. Unfortunately, some less critical viewers might attribute to the "doctor" (clad in professional medical clothing) a kind of medical expertise. This example illustrates the importance of carefully assessing a testimonial source's credibility.

Inferences

Once support for potentially contested claims has been acquired, advocates are ready to move to the next element of argumentation, known as inference making. *Inferences* move audiences from what is known, or believed to be true, to what is not known, or not believed to be true. There are many forms of inference, each with potential strengths and limitations to argumentation.

Formal logicians—specialists who study inference structures—are primarily interested in what is often referred to as *demonstrative* forms of inference. A demonstrative argument form is valid if and only if it is not possible for the conclusion of the argument to be false when all the premises are true. This approach to validity assessment is usually referred to as *formal validity*. Importantly, as noted earlier, argumentation by its nature always occurs in the realm of the *probable*. If we were able to demonstrate our conclusions with certainty, there would be no need for argumentation. As a result, argumentation inevitably falls outside of logicians' criteria for formal validity.

Forms of Argument

There are many different types of *nondemonstrative* forms of inference available to advocates as they develop their arguments. Among these, *arguments by comparison* are especially helpful for conveying, explaining, and supporting claims. Arguments by *analogy, metaphor, simile,* and *example* are four commonly used types of arguments by comparison.

Analogies use terms from four different spheres. The inferential pattern for argument by analogy is: A is to B as C is to D. Arguments by *metaphor* and *simile* have much in common with arguments by analogy. All three types of argument rely on comparisons between objects in two different spheres (or categories). However, unlike analogies, metaphors and similes compare only one set of objects, in two different spheres. The inferential forms in these two types of argument are: Metaphor: A *is* B; Simile: A *is like* B.

Metaphors can be used to enlighten, educate, move to action, or any combination of these. A popular metaphor used to help socialize people, for example, is to urge them to "build bridges, rather than walls." Teachers might use the following extended metaphor, attributed to Aristotle, to inspire children to learn: "Learning is an ornament in prosperity; a refuge in adversity; and a provision in old age." To help people understand the importance of considering public consequences of their actions, moralists have been known to say, "No person is an island." And many parents teach their children that they will "reap what they sow."

Metaphors often are designed to persuade. A popular way to get funding and support for a cause is to refer to it as a "war against" something most people fear, dislike, or oppose. The "war against poverty," "war against drugs," "war against inflation," "war against disease," and "war against pollution" are but a few examples. Use of the war metaphor might seem, on the surface, to simply invite interest in a cause, or to gain support for it, or to emphasize its importance. But when we consider the perceptual framework encouraged by adoption of the war metaphor, we see the importance of carefully assessing its appropriateness and validity.

Consider, for example, the war on drugs metaphor. Use of the term "war" might encourage readers and listeners to support killing people who are on the "wrong" side of the battleground. "War" connotes circumstances that justify suspending ordinary boundaries of conduct. During war, countries often suspend such rights as the right to privacy, free expression, and a fair trial. Use of the war metaphor in the context of the drug problem in the United States has the potential, then, to influence the public's assessments of policies about the situation.

Thus, as with all comparative argumentative forms, metaphors may serve valuable purposes to decision makers, teachers, and advocates. However, metaphors need to be presented with great care, sensitivity, and wisdom—and received with discernment.

Like metaphors, the selection of a simile can influence interpretations of the topic. Although care is therefore required in the use of similes, the term "like" helps discernment processes by making evident the fact that a comparison or association is being made.

Fostering Sound Deliberative Argumentation

Earlier we noted that the success of deliberative arguments depends in large measure on responsiveness to the specific rhetorical context. The more audiences develop their critical thinking, creativity, moral imagination, and related discernment skills, the more sophisticated the argumentation available to them may be. In this important sense, the careful development of an audience's critical thinking and discernment skills significantly improves the speaker's or writer's possibility for using deliberative argumentation meaningfully. This is likely what John Stuart Mill had in mind when writing:

> The greatest orator, save one, of antiquity, has left it on record that he always studied his adversary's case with as great, if not still greater, intensity than even his own. What Cicero practiced as the means of

forensic success requires to be imitated by all who study any subject in order to arrive at the truth. He who knows only his own side of the case knows little of that. His reasons may be good, and no one may have been able to refute them. But if he is equally unable to refute the reasons on the opposite side, if he does not so much as know what they are, he has no ground for preferring either opinion.

So essential is this discipline to a real understanding of moral and human subjects that, if opponents of all-important truths do not exist, it is indispensable to imagine them and supply them with the strongest arguments which the most skillful devil's advocate can conjure up.[21]

Learning to subject ideas and arguments to the strictest scrutiny in this way is a key element of skillful deliberative argumentation. As Mill pointed out, however, an ideal audience that can provide skillful refutation for one's arguments is often unavailable. Under these circumstances, we must create this ideal in our own minds. Dialogic communication with a deliberative community—particularly with people whose experiences, backgrounds, interests, and perspectives differ from our own—provides direct input into the process of conceiving such an audience. Introspective discernment and reflective processes such as those outlined in chapter 9 are also helpful.

Procedural Norms

Many scholars interested in the functioning of deliberative democracy have proposed procedures designed to guide constructive interactions in pursuit of sound decisions. Traditionally, the following procedural norms have been associated with democratic deliberative processes:

1. The inclusion of everyone affected by a decision
2. Substantial political equality including equal opportunities to participate in deliberation
3. Equality in methods of decision making and in determining the agenda
4. Free and open exchange of information and reasons sufficient to require an understanding of both the issue in question and the opinions of others[22]

Although *ideal*, the conditions recommended by these procedural norms are not often realized. In practice, it is not always possible to include everyone affected by a given decision in the full deliberation process, nor do circumstances always permit exchanges of ideas and information sufficient for deep understanding of issues and of multiple views. Under some circumstances, representative forms of deliberation are required. At other times we are required to make immediate decisions with little benefit of others' input. Under these circumstances, concepts such as reciprocity and equity become especially important features of judicious deliberation. Thus, although participants are often not able to fully realize the ideals associated with democratic procedural norms, sincere and competent efforts to incorporate the principles of *equity, publicity, accountability,* and *reciprocity* explored in earlier chapters are vital to participation in deliberative community.

Pragmatic and logistical concerns are not the only reasons why idealized deliberative communities are rarely obtained. As we have discussed throughout the previous chapters, ideological commitments to competitiveness, individualism, and winning also compromise interdependent decision making. We have had little difficulty seeing how, when participants are motivated primarily by the desire to win or to further only their own immediate self-interests, realization of an ideal deliberative community is nearly impossible.

However, even when participants seek to suspend their own self-interests for a greater good, hierarchical ideologies are sometimes so normative and pervasive that they may undermine such shared efforts. When practiced within the hierarchical ideological contexts of the kind outlined in previous chapters, even the sincerest efforts at reciprocal exchange may inadvertently reproduce adversarial interactions or unilateral decision-making processes. Vigilance, receptivity, openness, humility, reciprocity, responsiveness, and related dialogic sensibilities and skills help prevent this and related obstacles to deliberative argumentation.

Courage

To transform rivals into deliberative partners, however, we must be willing to take risks. Unlike the dangers of combative interactions, the risk entailed in deliberative argumentation "is not that you may lose but rather that you may change."[23] Given this critical feature of constructive engagement, we cannot overstate the important place of courage in pursuing deliberative argumentation.

Initially, the fear of change prevents many people from arguing constructively with one another. Yet, as Parker Palmer reminds us, "To learn is to face transformation."[24] And though many of us explicitly value the growth that comes from learning, we may hesitate "to enter into relationships requiring us to respond as well as initiate, to give as well as take."[25]

Even model international change agents, such as Aung San Suu Kyi— leader of the democracy movement in Burma, opponent of its military dictatorship, and recipient of the Nobel Peace Prize—acknowledge that such preparation is challenging, because it involves facing one's fears. Suu Kyi explains,

> I don't think that anyone is totally fearless in this life. I myself am not entirely without fear. I think perhaps we should talk in terms of courage rather than fearlessness. Freedom from fear means that you don't let fear dominate you. It does not mean that you don't know fear. It does not mean lack of knowledge of fear. It means that you are not controlled by it. I often say to our people that, even if you are afraid,

you must have the ability to do what you know is right. That is overcoming fear. That is freedom from fear. It's not that you do not know
fear. You do know fear, but you are not going to let it shackle you.[26]

A willingness to face change through the development of moral courage enables individuals to form deliberative partnerships and communities. The same is true in reverse. The development of deliberative
partnerships depends on courageous individuals committed to productive change through constructive means. Under these interdependent
conditions, deliberative communities flourish, and the best decisions for
collective well-being are made possible.

As we learned in our earlier discussions of dialogic communication, the
willingness to change in the context of argumentation often depends on the
win-win context. Developing this supportive environment asks much of us.
It asks that we generate enough political will and moral courage in order to
find strength in our mutual vulnerability. In short, we must learn to *trust in
the process*. We can be skeptical of trusting particular people or promises,
but we rely on the process because "trust is the outcome of successful
problem solving."[27] This apparent leap of faith is ostensibly so uncommon
in the United States today that one of the most frequently asked questions
about deliberative argumentation is, "What happens when other people
don't cooperate?" In chapter 5, we mentioned Reverend Martin Luther
King, Jr.'s advice to his brother: "Somebody got to have some sense on this
highway."[28] By emphasizing *personal dignity and relational integrity, responsiveness and reason*, a constructive approach to argument enables us to tap the
strengths of our diversity. Reverend King addressed what needs to happen
for individuals to engage in meaningful interactions: "Somewhere somebody must have a little sense, and that's the strong person."[29]

Critical Consciousness

This redefinition of strength through interdependence, vulnerability,
and shared risk taking bears further exploration, particularly in the context of power imbalances. The civil rights context for Dr. King's story
allows us to understand his message as a call for nonviolent action in the
face of violent repression. Similarly, Gloria Anzaldúa urges us to challenge injustice by going beyond the necessary first step of opposition. In
her essay, *"La Conciencia de la mestiza:* Towards a New Consciousness,"
she explains why we need to move beyond opposition, beyond the
boundaries of pro and con:

> It is not enough to stand on the opposite river bank, shouting ques-
> tions, challenging patriarchal, white conventions. . . . All reaction is
> limited by, and dependent on, what it is reacting against. Because the
> counterstance stems from a problem with authority—outer as well as
> inner—it's a step towards liberation from cultural domination. *But it
> is not a way of life.* At some point, on our way to a new consciousness,

we will have to leave the opposite bank, the split between two mortal combatants somehow healed so that we are on both shores at once, and, at once, see through serpent and eagle eyes.[30]

Deliberative argumentation facilitates this change in consciousness, enabling us to recognize necessary oppositions and to innovate constructive alternatives. Cornel West describes this critical consciousness as "a desirable way of being in the world because it does, in fact, give you a sense of meaning and purpose. It gives you a sense of camaraderie, connectedness, and relatedness."[31]

Critical consciousness allows us to recognize the benefits of deliberative argumentation as well as its risks and rationales. Minnie Bruce Pratt articulates three gains associated with critical consciousness and constructive change. She writes, "One gain for me [is that] I learn a way of looking at the world that is more accurate, complex, multilayered, multidimensional, more truthful."[32] Now able to "understand myself in relation to folks different from me," Pratt says that she can "follow my need to loosen the constrictions of fear, [to] be a break in the cycle of fear and attack. When I can do this, that is a second gain."[33] Here Pratt combines an awareness of interdependence with "having a little sense" as described by Dr. King. Last, Pratt is able to use her new insights toward participating differently in community settings. Now she can "break through the shell around me, a coming through into a new place, where, with understanding and change, the loneliness won't be necessary. And when this happens, I feel a third gain."[34]

As we have discovered throughout our explorations thus far, new ways of knowing, relating, and community building are inherent features of argumentation within deliberative communities. Anyone can argue both ethically and effectively when they apply an ethic of interdependence and *value their relationships as much as they do their convictions*. Stanley Deetz and William J. White concur, writing that "relational responsibility moves us from "doing no harm" to work at reciprocal good; fortuitously, in interdependent systems, supporting the good of the other leads to self-benefit."[35] Former mayor of Salinas and California Assemblywoman Anna Caballero also emphasizes the need to recognize our interdependence and to proactively cultivate communicative alternatives. In a city council meeting addressing violence prevention, Caballero urged her audience to consider that they were "not looking at violence reduction, but the cultivation of peace."[36]

As a mode of communication, deliberative argumentation respects our interdependent relationships by *prioritizing sensitivity, responsiveness, and accountability* between communicators and audiences. Such priorities are very practical, for they simultaneously provide the most conducive conditions for evaluating our ideas. In this way, deliberative argumentation is one method helping us to build moral communities that are needed to make informed, reasonable, and fair decisions. As Amy Gutmann and Dennis Thompson note, "Through the give-and-take of argument, citizens and their accountable representatives can learn from one another, come to recognize their individual and collective mistakes, and develop new views and policies that are more widely justifiable."[37]

As we draw this exploration to a close, it will be helpful to review a few key reciprocal strategies for the formation of deliberative communities.

1. In order to foster development of deliberative communities, look first to build on the contributions of others. When necessary, offer criticism and opposing perspectives as a means of refocusing deliberation on the common goal.

2. To ensure inclusiveness, verify that people can "successfully initiate deliberation, introduce new themes into public debate, and influence the outcome."[38] Create a space to risk change by asking "what if?" apart from making a decision or acting on the conclusion.

3. Share all the information available to you, even with those who advocate views at odds with your own.

4. Listen empathically to gain deep understanding of others' perspectives and experiences.

5. Finally, as revealed in our earlier discussions of ethical and effective dialogue, give and receive feedback, listen attentively, check in on the communication and deliberation processes, and determine accountability.

The quality of our deliberative communities depends on these and the related dialogic and deliberative sensibilities, knowledge, skills, and values explored throughout the book. Entering into deliberative partnerships calls on us to embrace and enact a willingness and capacity to take in others' perspectives with nondefensive self-awareness; ability to present deeply held beliefs with a dedicated commitment to fairness; empathic communication skills; personal accountability; care for self and others; integrity; honesty; a mutual commitment to securing the best assessment of the facts, issues, and circumstances; and shared commitment to forming partnerships in pursuit of the most reasonable, responsive decision possible.

When proposing such a model of communication and deliberation, legal scholar and educator Lani Guinier was once asked by an audience member, "How do you explain a cooperative style of decision making in a competitive culture?" Professor Guinier responded, "I think the best explanation is to model it."[39] The next chapter will focus on developing an approach to advocacy that responds directly to Guinier's sage counsel. Helping to reunite reason and communication, this approach promises to foster critical pathways for understanding and resolving the complex issues confronting humanity in our ever-changing world.

11

Advocacy

The previous chapter featured argumentation as a primary resource for advocates seeking to contribute to sound deliberation processes. Many scholars and activists, however, question this approach. They perceive advocacy as incompatible with dialogue and deliberation because advocates require unhindered expression to debate competitively, so that the better argument will win. If reasoned argument proves insufficient, advocates rely on a combative repertoire of confrontation, strategy, and pressure to advance their causes.[1]

From this standpoint, dialogue's relational concerns and deliberation's mutual consideration for action become burdens to advocacy. Advocacy enjoys a traditional status. Foundations for this approach can be a sincere belief in adversarialism as a truth-seeking process or a passionate desire to change perceived wrongs or, in some cases, an advocate's sense of entitlement if accustomed to getting his or her own way. Whatever reason inspires advocates to engage competitively and combatively, the goal is the same: "to get something done in the world."[2]

As we learned in the previous chapter however, committed advocates must consider how the means become the ends in the making. Adversarial communication on behalf of particular ideas or actions not only shapes what can be done but also affects the community's capacity to enact agreed-upon goals. The interdependent principle—the quality of communication affects the quality of the community and the ability to act together in common purpose—also applies to advocates. In this chapter, we turn to how committed and conscientious advocates can practice in the argument culture. In particular, we will discuss the ways in which a deliberative approach helps to transform central concerns about principled advocacy: its practical realities, relationship to power and accountability, and its communicative necessities.

Practical Realities

The limits on advocacy within the argument culture are readily apparent. We have seen, for example, how winning can become even more important than being right about the facts or judicious about the issues. We've learned as well how adversarial communication habits—such as judgment, blame, and defensiveness—negatively affect interpersonal interactions and civic life. No matter how urgent the need, the argument culture's "pervasive warlike atmosphere" compels us to approach "just about anything we need to accomplish, as if it were a fight."[3] Under these circumstances, efforts to work together in pursuit of common purpose face extraordinary obstacles.

The argument culture pressures advocates to wield verbal fisticuffs against others in order to succeed. A senatorial candidate in 2012 asserted: "We are at that point where one side or the other has to win this argument. One side or the other will dominate." The interviewer asked the aspiring politician about his approach to governance. He replied, "I hope to build a conservative majority in the United States Senate so bipartisanship becomes Democrats joining Republicans." When the interviewer pointed out that the candidate's definition of bipartisanship was actually the opposite of compromise, he declared, "Well, it is the definition of political effectiveness."[4]

Even though "my way or the highway" advocacy often appeals to a polarized electorate frustrated over gridlock, its actual practice dispels the merits of this approach. This point was illustrated recently by the acrimonious political debate over whether to raise the United States' debt ceiling. During the summer of 2011, the nation risked national default—jeopardizing its ability to pay its debts to creditors around the globe—and sent international financial markets reeling. Although the crisis was averted at the last moment, the political fiasco undermined the government's credibility and led to the nation's first ever credit rating downgrade. Condemnation for the unproductive and protracted confrontation was widespread.

The international critique crossed political divides and national interests. A leading conservative news outlet in Germany, for example, deplored the weeks-long spectacle and criticized U.S. politicians for their intransigence: "[T]here are few signs of self-doubt or self-awareness in the U.S." where negotiations "are only successful if the enemy is defeated. Compromise, they feel, is a sign of weakness and cowardice." A state-owned Chinese newspaper concurred: "Given the United States' status as the world's largest economy . . . such political brinksmanship in Washington is dangerously irresponsible." The French media simply concluded that U.S. politicians had become a "laughingstock."[5]

Within the United States, nearly every political commentator and, in fact, many politicians denounced the debt ceiling debate as a "debacle."

The partisan conflict undermined credibility and confidence in Washington and carried a heavy price tag for an already struggling economy. The delay in raising the debt ceiling cost the nation an extra $1.3 billion in borrowing costs[6] and the protracted bickering nearly "wrecked the [nation's economic] recovery," as consumer confidence fell more steeply during the debate than it had during the 2008 recession. Alarmed by these findings, one political analyst publicly pleaded, "Let's never, ever do anything like this again, please."[7]

Most significant was the first-ever downgrade of the United States' credit rating. Standard and Poor's, a credit rating agency, explained their decision by pointing directly to the debt ceiling debate. "The political brinkmanship of recent months highlights what we see as America's governance and policy making becoming less stable, *less effective*, and less predictable than what we previously believed."[8] In unvarnished terms, winner-take-all advocacy played an instrumental role in the country losing its sterling reputation and status.

The debt ceiling debacle dramatically displayed the real-world limitations and consequences of adversarial advocacy. And yet, many continue to adhere to the tenet that advocates need to exercise power over others in order to be effective. This belief aligns with the worldview that human nature is predominantly competitive and confrontational and that reality is shaped by a struggle to survive amidst scarce resources, both material and social. If others are treacherous and cruel, we must act accordingly. As Charles Hauss writes, "Thinking this way also leads us to expect that intense conflict can only have a zero-sum or win-lose outcome. Since our enemy's interests are at odds with our own, we assume that anything it does to pursue or defend those interests will somehow be detrimental to ours. Disagreement becomes dangerous."[9]

Given the argument culture's dominance, it often appears as if we must fight for our side and win or suffer the decisions made by others. As we have demonstrated throughout this book, this conclusion rests on ideological presumptions about human nature and reality that are inaccurate. Philosophical and scientific advances regarding human nature and reality[10] provide compelling evidence that challenges the Hobbesian narrative about the "survival of the fittest" in a "dog-eat-dog" world. The studies reveal the reality of interdependence and humanity's long-standing reliance on cooperation and compassion to promote flourishing societies.

These empirical truths have many thoughtful activists and engaged scholars reconsidering the practical realities of advocacy. Van Jones (discussed in chapter 5 as an example of someone who practices self-reflection) has been vocal about his own transformation. After acknowledging that he had been a practitioner of the politics of confrontation and outrage for most of his life, he said he finally realized that those behaviors simply multiplied enemies. Activists who concentrate on showing how other people are wrong have produced "a logjam of accusation and blame on all sides of American politics . . . it's time for some of us to give up the addiction to being righteous, being victims, and having the right to be mad at somebody."[11] Jones changed his adversarial behaviors. In 2009, *Time Magazine* recognized him as one of the world's most influential people for his Green Jobs Initiative, which integrates environmental justice and economic opportunity.[12] His new approach to advocacy reflects his insight that "what we need is less investment in the fight *against* and more energy in the fight *for*."[13]

Sharon Welch cautions that the challenge for activists is to develop an effective practice that moves beyond critique and opposition. "We know how to create forms of public witness that denounce what is wrong—demonstrations, boycotts, sit-ins. What is harder, however, is finding the means of providing energizing and compelling public support for what *may* be right."[14]

Van Jones and Sharon Welch represent a growing awareness that meaningful success is elusive for those who practice adversarial individualism. When advocates establish sides, create oppositions, and fight for their views, they sometimes achieve their immediate goals. But they regularly fail to build bridges with the opposition, thus undercutting lasting progress. All advocates require support and cooperation to implement their goals successfully and to sustain them over time. Nelson Mandela clearly identified the challenge. "It is a relatively simple proposition to keep a movement together when you are fighting against a common enemy. But creating a policy when that enemy is across the negotiating table is another matter altogether."[15]

Despite our differences and disagreements, we must rely on one another to act together in common purpose. These practical realities highlight the necessity for contemporary advocates to develop the skills of a deliberative advocate—*the ability to maintain principled convictions, build durable coalitions, and communicate constructively for change.* To hone this balance, deliberative advocates may take concrete steps, many of which have been described throughout this book. First and foremost, advocates must *choose how to exercise power.*

Advocacy and Power

Charles Hauss notes that the conventional definition of power is "my ability to get you to do something *you otherwise wouldn't do*."[16] Typically, advocates employ the instrumentalist view, which authorizes them to use whatever means are available in order to be successful. Accordingly, partisans rarely concern themselves with questions about how to exercise power but only consider which actions might be taken to utilize it most effectively. Such an uncritical stance, however, leaves advocates vulnerable to the well-known risks inherent in conventional power.

Significantly, the conventional exercise of power produces unreliable results. Even if an advocate's goals appear to be met, this win-loss approach typically generates the next conflict. Professor Paul Collier's research on postconflict recovery in war-torn nations documents this effect. The conventional approach to restoring security, he explains, is to hold elections in order to produce a legitimate and accountable government. This is a necessary step in establishing democratic governance. However, within strife-ridden contexts, "What an election produces is a winner and a loser. And the loser is unreconciled."[17] The central issue, Collier maintains, is that electoral competitions determine who acquires power, but it is the democratic process of checks and balances that determines how power is used.[18] Without the latter, an unfettered competitive struggle continues. Those who "lost" will seek to reassert their position and those who "won" will aim to prevail yet again. Within a decade, Collier reports, forty percent of all postconflict situations had reverted back to conflict.[19] It's difficult to be truly effective when the cycle of conflict is continuous in this way.

The continuous cycle of conflict that ultimately undermines an advocate's objectives is not the only risk inherent in the use of conventional power. Because this approach privileges one side's views and promotes the unilateral pursuit of those interests, advocates can become callous to the perspectives and interests of others. This relational indifference obstructs the possibility of a reality check on one's own views, permitting them to become more extreme. It also allows unilateral action that increases the likelihood of unanticipated consequences, prompting surprise (as in "I didn't see that one coming") and criticism of one's actions ("They just don't get it").

Perhaps most importantly, conventional approaches to power essentially insure that advocates will treat others in ways they would not wish to be treated themselves. While proponents may characterize their use of influence and persuasion as productive resources, audiences often experience the strategies as manipulative and even deceptive. If unchecked by consideration for others, partisans may be willing to open the door to threats or actual use of force or violence—relying on such coercive tactics to maintain their dominance.

An overreliance on adversarial ideologies in pursuit of self-interest can result in callous disregard for others. This is a formula for corruption as well as for creating and escalating conflicts. Lord Acton summarized this risk succinctly with his famous dictum, "Absolute power corrupts absolutely." Human history is rife with examples of this phenomenon, from fallen emperors to crony capitalists to spouse batterers. Inevitably, their pursuit of *power over others* eventually becomes the source of their own undoing.[20]

In this book, dialogue and deliberation have been presented as important methods of communication to remedy such ideological extremism and its attendant abuses of power. Dialogue was introduced to promote reciprocal understanding and to address basic human needs to belong, to be known and to matter. Deliberation combines reasoning with dialogic skills and sensibilities—including empathy, compassion, and critical reflection—so that decision makers can generate workable solutions for all concerned. Together, dialogue and deliberation offer a communicative framework that incorporates relational concerns and mutual consideration—in short, a solid foundation for advocates aspiring to be *ethical and effective.*

So how might committed and conscientious advocates exercise power? Forceful responses, no doubt, will be required at times to secure a just outcome, but these limitations should be imposed with ample concern for the effects on self and others.[21] Moreover, the vast majority of everyday conflicts do not require physical, legal, or militaristic constraints; many can be addressed without resorting to any use of conventional power. But to be effective—even when force is necessary—*advocates need to exercise power with regard for individual interests and social responsibilities.*

Advocates who exercise power with regard for individual interests and social responsibility utilize the communicative skills and sensibilities described throughout the previous chapters. They make a sincere effort to understand relevant views and to reflect deeply on their own. From this critical awareness, advocates take positions and propose specific actions in order to make the best decision possible for everyone affected by the issue. In the midst of conflicts and controversies, such advocates certainly "speak truth to power" in order to critique and challenge an unjust status quo. To be accountable to themselves and others, they also endeavor to "use power truthfully."[22]

Advocates and Accountability

Although these two expressions—"speak truth to power" and "use power truthfully"—both emphasize accountability, the former adage has taken on an "in your face," bumper-sticker quality that tends to stray far afield from its origins. This well-known call to action was first issued in 1955, during the height of the cold war. The American Friends Service Committee (Quakers) had been seeking ways to move toward international peace and to ease tensions between democratic and communist governments. They dedicated years of study and published a series of pamphlets to promote these goals. Their search was guided by two fundamental questions that remain relevant today: "Is there a method for dealing with conflict which does not involve us in the betrayal of our own beliefs, either through acquiescence to our opponent's will or through resorting to evil means to resist him?" and "Is there a way to meet that which threatens us, without relying on our ability to cause pain to the human being who embodies the threat?"[23]

They answered in the affirmative, by urging peace advocates to "speak truth to power." Contemporary activists, however, typically observe only the first of three senses of power articulated by the committee. According to the Quakers, one method for dealing with the cold war conflict was to speak directly to "those who hold high places in our national life and bear the terrible responsibility of making decisions for war or peace."[24] Current usage privileges this approach of confronting power elites. At its best, this principle empowers truth-telling practices, such as witnessing, whistle-blowing, and various types of direct action.[25]

But the American Friends Service Committee did not stop there. They also called on advocates to tell the truth to the American people, believing that democratic values and expectations set limits on authority. To know how to exercise these limits democratically, the Quakers appealed to advocates to tell the truth about the "idea of Power itself, and its impact on Twentieth Century life."[26] Speaking truth to power, therefore, was aimed not only at distant elites and authorities but also at the citizens and residents of the United States to raise consciousness and encourage collective action.

In its fullest sense, speaking truth to power is a mode of advocacy that expresses time-honored ideals. During the cold war, *advocates who maintained principled convictions and behaved accountably* would have been described as a "straight shooter." More contemporary usage might observe, "She was straight-up when she offered another way of seeing the problem." But confidence in each other's veracity has been damaged by life in the argument culture. It's difficult to trust others in a "what's in it for me" environment. Public confidence in our institutions has diminished as well. The most recent Gallup Poll in the United States found public trust in banks, public schools, organized religion, and television news at record lows, with confidence in Congress ranking dead last.[27]

Today, the phrase, "using power truthfully," rekindles confidence in advocates' accountability. Like its cold war predecessor, this approach encourages advocates to express principled convictions regarding self and others. In theory, then, a "straight-up" advocate respects others and uses reason, dialogic skills, and measured approaches to influence and persuasion in an effort to do the right thing. But what does this approach to "using power truthfully" look like in practice in the twenty-first century? How does this method guide advocates in balancing individual interests and social responsibilities within the argument culture? Sharon Welch offers advocates a caveat and some guidelines.

Principled advocates must learn from the mistakes of the conventional approach to power. So often, its righteous certainty, relational indifference, and short-sighted, narrowly considered actions create more problems than any win-loss calculus can offset. The tough-love lesson in this, according to Welch, is that *all advocates are vulnerable to these failures.*

In our zeal to accomplish our goals, she explains, the "attraction of power overrides critical judgment."[28]

In an earlier chapter, we described the ease with which people can deceive themselves into justifying "immoral, corrupt, shortsighted, and self-serving actions."[29] Such wrongdoing is motivated, ironically, to bolster a positive self-image or public reputation as much as it is to avoid harm or to produce benefit for one's cause.[30] But no matter the motivation, every advocate must grapple with conventional power's allure that the ends can justify the means. In the words of the renowned union leader César Chavez, "A lot depends on how power is used." Well-intentioned, passionate advocates sometimes persuade themselves to pursue shortcuts for the cause; good people can and do make bad choices about power.

Practicing accountability in the expression of one's interests and in the pursuit of one's goals offers an antidote to instrumentalism's seductive call. When we use the term "instrumentalism," we have in mind communicative choices that privilege ends over means. It is easy to understand why advocates would find instrumentalism so seductive, especially if they are convinced of the righteousness of their causes. Recognition of accountability's importance helps to mitigate this orientation.

Earlier chapters have explored accountability's central role in responsive dialogue and sound deliberation. Philosopher Margaret Urban Walker offers insights of particular relevance to responsible advocacy. To be accountable, means "to be required to give an account of yourself and to have to settle accounts with others through admission, elaboration, explanation, justification, excuse, amends, and assurances concerning what you have done."[31]

Advocates who take these insights to heart and humbly accept human fallibilities are poised to use power truthfully, even within the argument culture. Sharon Welch offers advocates a set of basic guidelines for assessing the truthfulness of strategies:

1. Their actual effects in the lives of people
2. Their openness to further critique and hence modification
3. Their resiliency in the face of both critique and unintended consequences.[32]

These criteria offer advocates opportunities to be responsive to the actual effects of their decisions. The first point evaluates people's real experiences, rather than judging effects based on ideological expectations or desired outcomes. The second and third criteria encourage responsibility by inviting advocates to be open to critique and additional alternatives and to be resilient enough to act.

In 2012, the *New York Times* published two opinion articles by advocates who implicitly applied these criteria to their own activism. Both remained committed to their original convictions but had reconsidered their methods for accomplishing their goals. As the overview below reveals, these two articles, written from divergent political views, align with the practice of using power truthfully.

David Blankenhorn is an outspoken advocate for "traditional marriage." He has published a book on the topic and made national news by testifying on behalf of California's controversial Proposition 8, a ballot initiative banning same-sex marriage. In his opinion piece, Blankenhorn reaffirmed his belief in marriage as a heterosexual union designed to produce and care for children. Gay marriage, he asserted, cannot fulfill this purpose. "I have written these things in my book and said them in my testimony, and I believe them today. I am not recanting any of it."[33]

This committed advocate, however, did change his mind about his strategy for protecting the institution of marriage. His explanation for the change parallels the criteria for using power truthfully. "I don't believe that opposite-sex and same-sex relationships are the same, but I do believe with growing numbers of Americans that the time for denigrating and stigmatizing same-sex relationships is over." The opposition to same-sex marriage was creating harmful effects in people's lives, he observed, by treating gay and lesbian couples and their children unfairly.

Blankenhorn also employed the second set of criteria: critique and modification. He had hoped that the same-sex marriage debate would encourage Americans to recommit to the institution but found that he and other advocates had failed in that goal. "With each passing year, we see higher and higher levels of unwed childbearing, nonmarital cohabitation, and family fragmentation among heterosexuals." Dismayed by these results, Blankenhorn modified his approach to protecting marriage. He shifted from fighting *against* toward fighting *for.* "My intention is to try something new." A willingness to take action in response to critique and unanticipated consequences demonstrates resilience. Instead of fighting gay marriage, Blankenhorn proposes to "build new coalitions bringing together gays who want to strengthen marriage with straight people who want to do the same." As a committed advocate, David Blankenhorn used power truthfully. His change in strategy ends his unintended contribution to the harmful "anti-gay animus" in the marriage debate. It also creates the possibility, he hopes, to reinvigorate a societal commitment to marriage as a family institution. "Will this strategy work?" he asks. "I don't know. But I hope to find out."[34]

Predictably and understandably, Blankenhorn's change in strategy had its detractors, some saying that he had both gone too far and others that he had not gone far enough.[35] The point here is not to evaluate the merits of the issue. The advocate's explanation, accepted at face value, demonstrates the practice of using power truthfully, for he was true to his convictions and accountable for their effects.

Steve Almond, a former adjunct professor at Boston College, wrote the second opinion piece. He resigned his faculty position in 2006 to protest the school's selection of then secretary of state Condoleeza Rice as commencement speaker. In an open letter to the college president, published by the *Boston Globe*, Almond made the case that the secretary of state had been deceitful and lied repeatedly to justify a misguided foreign policy. "I cannot, in good conscience, exhort my students to pursue truth and knowledge, then accept a paycheck from an institution that displays such flagrant disregard for both."[36] Like Blankenhorn, Almond did not change his mind about his original conviction. But he did reassess his methods for advocating his view.

After his resignation letter went viral, Almond received numerous invitations to appear on cable television. He accepted an offer to interview with Sean Hannity, an outspoken supporter of the Bush administration in which Secretary Rice served. Almond was excited about the prospect of confronting Hannity. He was disappointed, however, that he was given little time to voice his objecting to Rice, spending most of the three minutes sparring verbally with Hannity. "Not what I'd envisioned, but I managed to outlast his bullying and even launch a few zingers before my mike was cut. I was immensely pleased with myself, and I happily accepted kudos from my fellow lefties."[37]

Almond later characterized the episode as somewhat less heroic. "I hadn't spoken truth to power or caused anyone to reassess Secretary Rice's record. I merely provided a few minutes of gladiatorial stimulation for Fox News. In seeking to assert my moral superiority, I enabled Hannity." With this reassessment, a committed partisan acknowledged the disappointing effects of his activism: it merely produced a pyrrhic victory for ideologues on both sides.

Almond takes himself to task for this failure, critiquing his complicity in the argument culture. "Too often we serve as willing accomplices to this escalation and to the resulting degradation of our civic discourse." His critical reevaluation led him to conclude that his advocacy and partisan media habits were ineffective, for they were confined to "a closed system of scorn and self-congratulation." He admitted that he had regarded all conservatives as extremists rather than as a diverse spectrum of citizens who shared many of the same values, anxieties, and goals. He used the example of the audience at a Republican presidential debate cheering for capital punishment. He said his reaction was to write them off as sadists, rather than accepting them as citizens seeking a means of keeping communities safe. He warned that the most insidious effect of such labeling has been the erosion of our more generous instincts.

Steve Almond has not changed his views about the issues, but he has decided to modify how he promotes them. In part, the desire to change derives from the negative effects cynical partisanship has had on him. He is dismayed by his willingness to find convenient scapegoats for complex issues and to use political partisanship "as an acceptable form of bigotry." But even more significant than the personal effects are the public ones—pressing problems remain unresolved. Therefore, this committed advocate has decided to work with people willing to engage in genuine dialogue to breach the artificially inflated partisan divide.[38]

Almond's proposal to ignore demagogues to deprive the argument culture of attention and energy drew contentious objections.[39] It's a debatable strategy, but he is seeking a resilient and realistic response to cynical partisanship. He suggests that advocates should define themselves "not by who we hate but by what we can do to strengthen our communities and country."[40] Both David Blankenhorn and Steve Almond demonstrate that one can exercise power truthfully and accountably. By so doing, they underscore the interdependent principle that one's methods not only affect what can be done in the world; they also shape one's character and relationship to community.

As these examples illustrate, approaching power through an interdependent ethical framework provides openings for advocates to meet the moment *both* responsibly *and* effectively. To illustrate further, consider how conceptualizing the art of advocacy within an interdependent framework contributes to fulfillment of this goal. As the discussion below reveals, this method of response is among the most valuable resources available to advocates in support of their quests. Within the argument culture's adversarial individualist framework, however, this tool is often used in ways that compromise deliberative processes.

An Interdependent Approach to Refutation

When we use the term *refutation*, we have in mind *responses to opposing arguments or perspectives*. In the traditional competitive model, refutation is thought of by most advocates as "the process of meeting and overcoming the arguments of your opponent."[41] The adversarial mind-set of the conventional power paradigm comes through even more starkly in the argument culture's definition: "refuting an opposing view means to attack it in order to weaken, invalidate, or make it less credible to a reader."[42] It is easy to see the limits of this approach in fostering dialogue, attentive and nondefensive listening, self-awareness, understanding, responsiveness, creativity, discernment, or other qualities key to sound deliberation.

Within the interdependent framework, advocates recognize these limits and reframe refutation as *an opportunity to exercise power with others*. As we learned from the exploration of deliberative argumentation in chapter 10, advocates from this perspective recognize the value of listening receptively to and meaningfully connecting with those who disagree—pro and con, for and against. Such a stance helps both advocates and their audiences to think through issues as allies, sincerely asking "what if?" and "have you considered this?" or "how is that an acceptable consequence?" John A. Williams describes the benefit of this practice:

> The great merit of hearing a convinced and articulate expression of a
> point of view you disagree with is the possibility of sharpening and

strengthening your own attitudes. The most effective argument for any case will incorporate and give full consideration to the best available counterevidence against that case.[43]

In this regard, refutation within a mutual power paradigm is reconceptualized as an advocacy strategy that enables deliberative partners to gain insight through diversity and disagreement. From this viewpoint, refutation affords advocates and their audiences opportunities to communicate critical comprehension of issues while remaining in touch with the humanity in ourselves and in those with whom we disagree. Pema Chödrön explains how the power associated with refutation can be exercised critically and with care:

> Whether it's yourself, your lover, your boss, your children, your local Scrooge, or the political situation, it's more daring and real not to shut anyone out of your heart and not to make the other into an enemy. If you begin to live like this, you'll find that you actually can't make things completely right or completely wrong anymore, because it's a lot more slippery and playful than that. Everything is paradoxical, everything is always shifting and changing, and there are as many different takes on any given situation as there are people involved. Trying to find absolute rights and wrongs is a trick we play on ourselves to get secure and comfortable.[44]

When refutation is a critical and compassionate act of reflection rather than an effort to be exclusively right and to exercise power over others, it can become a means of engaging perspectives seriously and respectfully. In this way, advocates and other members of deliberative communities may use refutation to sift and sort through varying perceptions of what is real, what is needed, what is ethical, and what is effective. Refutation, then, *allows us to critically engage but not to claim absolute certainty or to achieve unilateral closure.* Maria Lugones elaborates:

> We must understand others' places and our own interest in them. A group putting forth its own interests is not good enough. We must work for the understanding necessary to be able to put forth a perspectival account of others' needs that is not violent (discounting, devaluing, radically distorting) but rests on communication across cultural, situational, and other "group" differences. . . . To take such political action, you must be willing to adopt an epistemic attitude of being comfortable with uncertainty, moving in and out of places where you do not know what is going to happen.[45]

This seemingly paradoxical ability to refute and yet remain open to further input enables us to engage critically without polarizing the community. Williams describes this capacity as being "convinced and also tentative—a difficult combination and one we need to consider seriously."[46] This persistent effort to balance one's convictions with one's relationships transforms refutation from a haughty competition over right and wrong to an endeavor where we rely on one another for truthfulness in our efforts to make the best decision possible.

To illustrate, consider the following example involving advocates representing opposing perspectives on the right to die. Following extensive deliberative inquiry, thoughtful discernment, and reflection, Reina and Raul have drawn fundamentally different conclusions regarding the efficacy and morality of affording people the right to die. Reina believes passionately that people should have the right to end their own lives under special circumstances, while Raul disagrees strongly. He urges fellow citizens to vote against right-to-die policy proposals.

Whether presenting written or oral arguments, advocates can make ethical and effective use of several approaches to refutation in pursuit of their goals.[47] One option is *direct refutation*, or a *point-by-point* response to arguments opposing the legislation. Another is to *question the credibility of sources* used by the policy's opponents. A third is to invite the audience to take an *even if* stance. Yet another is to offer *additional support* for a particular perspective. Whatever approach advocates elect to use, they will be *most effective* in being heard and understood to the degree that they *anticipate and thoughtfully address concerns* regarding their positions.

Reina has learned through dialogic interaction with Raul, for example, that one of the primary reasons some people oppose the legislation is their concern that poor people would be under pressure to end their lives because they or their families could not afford end-of-life care. To address this important concern, Reina could introduce research about the demographics of terminally ill patients in Oregon who availed themselves of the right to die between 1997 (when the law was implemented) through 2011. Contrary to expectations, the majority of patients choosing to end their own lives were white, well-educated and financially comfortable.[48] Throughout this time frame, there was no evidence that anyone who chose this pathway experienced pressure associated with affordability of care.

In his refutation, Raul might acknowledge that this is an important finding but add that it fails to address a more fundamental concern. He could state that the American Medical Association opposes right-to-die legislation in part because prescribing drugs to end life is antithetical to the role of doctors as healers. To underscore this concern, Raul might reference the words of Vice President of the Physicians for Compassionate Care Education Foundation Dr. Kenneth Stevens: "I didn't go into medicine to kill people."[49]

In response, Reina might begin by acknowledging the AMA's concerns but could invite listeners to consider the views of physicians who understand their professional organization's reasoning yet do not share the group's conclusion. She might turn, for example, to the testimony of physicians in Oregon who supported that state's right-to-die legislation.

As she prepares a rebuttal to Raul's case against the legislation, Reina has an additional approach available to her: *supportive refutation*.

This approach calls for thoughtful development of arguments to support her case in light of Raul's refutation of it. She might, for example, call upon the personal experience of Dr. Richard Wesley, a pulmonologist and critical care physician whose experience with the disabling and terminal effects of Lou Gehrig's disease qualify him for a right to die under the legislation in his home state of Washington. Dr. Wesley's personal testimony offers Reina potentially compelling supportive refutation: "I don't know if I'll use the medication to end my life, but I do know that it is my life, it is my death, and it should be my choice."[50] Or perhaps Reina will elect to present other forms of support for the belief system and moral matrix at the heart of her orientation to the topic.

In this example, both Raul and Reina are arguing passionately on behalf of their perspectives regarding the efficacy and morality of right-to-die legislation. Neither, however, has presented a specific proposal detailing precisely how their policy preferences would be implemented. If either had provided such a proposal, the other could have offered a *counterproposal.* This approach to refutation allows advocates to concede premises that lead to an opposing advocate's call for a general policy change, while rejecting the specific plan provided to implement the policy.

Whatever approach Reina and Raul eventually adopt in presenting their cases, they will need to remind themselves continually that the *effectiveness of their presentations depends in large measure on their sensitivity and responsiveness to the deliberative community's beliefs, values, and interests.* Throughout any written or oral presentation, *Reina and Raul must ask themselves how an audience that does not share their views on the topic might respond to the arguments they are presenting to them.* This audience orientation will significantly increase the chances that their perspectives will be considered thoughtfully during the deliberative process.

By recognizing and addressing both their common ground and the most salient issues of conflict between them, these advocates offer their audiences critical insights. For example, acknowledging that they are both committed to patients' autonomy as well as to the reduction of suffering to the extent possible enables them and their audiences to resist the temptation to demonize one another. By emphasizing that they both value life and that they share a commitment to protect those who are vulnerable from others' greed and oppression, these advocates help their audiences to identify and address the most relevant issues in this deliberative context. Similarly, helping their audiences understand that neither of them wishes to compromise the integrity of physicians' commitment to healing nor to support legislation vulnerable to abuse also helps audiences to make informed and wise decisions.

As this example reveals, exposure to advocates' effectively framed, impassioned arguments provides audiences with potentially invaluable insights. By adopting an interdependent approach to refutation, advocates are able to sustain their commitments, represent their cases with passion, and help to insure that they are heard and understood in the process. The explorations above offer windows into the process by which committed and conscientious advocates can reach audiences effectively without sacrificing their loyalties or responsibilities. Rather than succumb to temptations to demonize opposing views or to control the outcome of deliberations through adversarial communication strategies, these advocates utilized dialogic communication skills to enable their audiences to hear and understand their perspectives. They have done everything possible to present compelling arguments in support of their perspectives without compromising their integrity.

Advocates can fulfill their goals while also applying the Golden Rule at the heart of interdependent communicative ethics. In adopting their interdependent approach to speaking truth to power and to using power truthfully, for example, Blankenhorn and Almond included their "adversaries" in their *moral communities*. Similarly, despite their profound differences of perspective on an issue of great importance to each of them, Raul and Reina recognized one another as members of the moral community. For help defining this important concept, we turn to philosopher Judith Boss.

> The moral community is composed of all those beings that have moral worth or value in themselves. Because members of the moral community have moral value, they deserve the protection of the community, and they deserve to be treated with respect and dignity.[51]

Including those with opposing viewpoints within our moral community is a hallmark of responsible advocacy.

Advocacy, Power Imbalances, and Moral Discernment

In some circumstances, however, the promise of successful deliberative advocacy is compromised by profound power inequities or other compelling factors outside the control of one or another advocate. History is replete with examples of social justice activists encountering intransigence by those perpetrating acts of oppression or other forms of injustice. Under extreme circumstances, severe abuses of power sometimes compel the use of force.

In response to such exigencies, advocates have a number of available options. The civil rights movement in the United States during the 1960s provides a compelling example. In the face of entrenched resistance to their cause, civil rights activists resorted to acts of civil disobedience when all other pathways to change proved ineffective. Within the movement, some individuals and groups urged more extreme measures, including demonization of adversaries and even violence.

Advocates confronting such circumstances face difficult moral choices, requiring deeply thoughtful consideration. Archon Fung, cofounder of the Transparency Policy Project, offers valuable counsel to deliberative activists seeking to pursue moral discernment when confronted with unequal resources, status, and other forms of privilege that inevitably "upset the communicative equality" required for deliberation.[52] Fortunately, when advocates are faced with these or other "unfavorable conditions such as economic inequality, cultural difference, or the absence of a reciprocal willingness to engage in the practice of deliberation," they are not without resources to guide their deliberations on how best to respond.[53]

Principles of Deliberative Activism

Fung recognizes that "sometimes, forces more compelling than the better argument are necessary to establish fair and inclusive deliberation or conditions that support such deliberation."[54] Like the principle of veracity introduced in chapter 9, Fung's principles of deliberative activism address issues at the heart of communicative ethics.

The first guideline applies to all interactions inside and outside the context of deliberative activism. The *principle of fidelity* requires *faithfulness to one's promises and commitments*. Fidelity is widely recognized as integral in developing and sustaining meaningful relationships. As a guideline for ethical communication, the centrality of reciprocity means that being faithful to one's commitments involves the reciprocal of expecting others to be faithful as well.

Within the specific context of deliberative activism, the principle of fidelity focuses on two related commitments. The first relates to deliberative activists' commitment to advancing *deliberative* decision making. Mindful that the world is fraught with imperfections that often compromise the possibility of fair and balanced deliberation, responsible activists often face difficult choices. The principle of fidelity in the context of deliberative activism requires advocates to give *strong presumption to pursuing as deliberative a method as possible* under difficult circumstances. Fung notes that deliberative activists are committed to the integrity of the liberal society in which they live. The second fidelity-related commitment requires deliberative activists to favor approaches that are likely to achieve "incremental improvement in a deliberative direction" rather than result in "institutional rupture."[55]

Fung's second principle of deliberative action is what he terms the *principle of charity*.

> Though political waters in liberal democracies are filled with sharks, the principle of charity requires the deliberative activist to act as if his would-be interlocutors are willing to engage in good faith deliberations, until they prove themselves unwilling to comply with the norm of reciprocity.[56]

The *principle of exhaustion* requires deliberative activists to avoid using non-deliberative methods unless and until all reasonable and fair efforts to "institute fair, open, and inclusive deliberations fail."[57]

The fourth and final principle is the *principle of proportionality*. This principle applies to circumstances in which deliberative activists find themselves bereft of deliberative means to address the power imbalances, inequities, arbitrariness, or other impenetrable obstacles to fair, just, informed, and reasoned deliberation. Under these profoundly difficult circumstances, the principle requires deliberative advocates to choose means proportional to "the extent to which political adversaries and opponents reject the procedural norms of deliberation and the substantive values that ground it."[58]

The Principle of Non-Harm

Overarching these and all other principles governing responsible advocacy is the *principle of non-harm*. This transcendent guideline emphasizes the interdependent values introduced throughout this volume. The principle encompasses truthful, caring, thoughtful, responsive, kind, respectful, and compassionate communication in interactions. Conversely, deceptive, cruel, insensitive, demonizing, coercive, and manipulative communication is considered morally suspect. Use of these or other inherently harmful forms of interaction requires meeting a very strong burden of proof.

Civility, understood as a means of communicating respectful regard for one another, holds presumptive status under the principle of non-harm. As noted in the exploration of the nature, role, strengths, and limits of civility in chapter 4, this norm does not require advocates to be "nice" or "polite," or to avoid "upsetting" people who are uncomfortable engaging in disagreements. Clearly, deliberative activists adopting the four principles introduced by Fung must often engage people who would prefer to avoid discussions. Indeed, as we have learned throughout this volume, communicating respectful regard often *requires* individuals to confront disagreements, *even when doing so potentially causes discomfort*.

Contributing meaningfully to just and informed deliberation also requires activists to pursue their efforts even, and often especially, when those in power have called upon them to cease. So long as activists remain committed to communicating respectful regard in the face of such circumstances, their efforts fall well within in the bounds of civility. When deliberative activists face situations in which the powerful are unwilling to deliberate, Fung observes that they may need to employ strategies to alter the balance of power including "persuasion, public shame," or means for "altering the balance of power."[59] Though often causing deep discomfort, these approaches are not inherently at odds with the call to civility, particularly when adopted with commitments to mutual regard.

At the same time, however, *choosing when and how to pursue one's cause* is a critical issue for advocates and deliberative activists seeking faithfulness to the principle of non-harm. For example, although intimidation or other forms of incivility are morally suspect, communication strategies violating this norm are nevertheless sometimes warranted by special circumstances. Applying the four types of discernment outlined in chapter 9 enables advocates and deliberative activists to determine when and how such breaches of civility are justified under the principle of non-harm.

In particular, recall that the first step in discerning whether otherwise morally suspect forms of interaction are justified in any given circumstance is to look for viable alternatives. In applying the principle of non-harm, advocates seeking to discern whether demonizing, verbally attacking, or otherwise moving outside the bounds of civility is morally justified in any given context must first make every effort to pursue viable alternatives. *If there is a feasible way to use communication's constructive potential successfully without breaching interdependent ethical norms, the principle of non-harm requires adoption of the responsible alternative.*

In the context of deliberative activism, this step mirrors Fung's principle of exhaustion. Only after pursuing all available alternatives are activists justified in using nondeliberative methods. If no viable alternative options are available, the principle of exhaustion for deliberative activists in particular and the principle of non-harm more broadly require advocates to look to their conscience. However, just as those who deceive often underestimate the harms and overestimate the benefits of their dishonesty, social justice advocates and deliberative activists are also vulnerable to the seductive influences of believing that their cause is so just that they can use any means to advance it.

For help insuring that they do not fall prey to instrumentalism, advocates and activists have available the two additional types of moral discernment outlined in chapter 9. The first involves asking how their peers would counsel them if informed of all of the circumstances. As we learned in chapter 9, however, peers tend to privilege their own self-interests over others. Given this inevitable bias, moral discernment requires moving beyond one's inner circle in pursuit of a responsible decision. They can also apply the *test of publicity*, which requires advocates and deliberative activists to use their moral imaginations to shift perspective and to focus on the values and interests of the person or persons likely to be harmed as a result of their decision to breach interdependent ethical norms. Holding themselves fully accountable for the likely short- and long-term consequences of their choice, advocates are asked to consider whether fully informed members of the deliberative community would be persuaded that their choice is justified in the given context. Importantly, as we learned in chapter 9, each case is unique; every situation requires attention to the particular details of the moment. In this sense, no general rule can be applied uniformly in the assessment of whether or how aggressive adversarial communication strategies are justified.

Advocates and Communication

Advocates who remain true to their principled convictions and exercise power within the bounds of the principles articulated above are better able to build the durable coalitions necessary for meaningful success. Meeting the moment responsibly requires not only that advocates and activists communicate productively *within* conflict in the ways outlined above but also *about* conflict as well.

Communicating productively about conflicts calls for discernment and responsibility in framing disagreements. Recall the discussion in chapter 2 about the three metaphor families that structure how people perceive events and possible responses. Conflicts can be framed as competitive, cooperative, and connection metaphors. Pamela Morgan recommends considering whether an issue is "a matter of adjusting competing claims (competition), or of voluntary association (cooperation), or of interdependent necessity (connection)."[60]

The choice of metaphors points to specific options. Conflicts described through competition metaphors are understood as a situation in which only entity will achieve its goal.[61] Advocates should be aware that competition metaphors, which are the most frequently used in the argument culture, typically invoke a "struggle to impose one's definition of reality upon the other. Thus, the question is also whose description of reality is taken seriously, and even acted upon."[62] Competition metaphors, which heighten the perception that there must be winners and losers, intensify the possibility that disagreement will become dangerous.

Unlike the competitive metaphor, cooperation metaphors structure perceptions and responses such that the parties work together to achieve a goal."[63] Teamwork and family are examples of cooperation metaphors. Advocates should be mindful of one caveat. Cooperative metaphors tend to minimize power differentials. For example, describing a corporation as a "family" may structure cooperation, but it also obfuscates the power inherent in different roles and responsibilities in the organization. Cooperative metaphors that recognize power differentials include mediation, alliances, and partnerships.

The third metaphor group, connection, emphasizes interdependence: the whole is more than the sum of its parts, and all parts are essential to the goal. Choosing this metaphor to talk about conflict conveys a sense of equality. Morgan notes: "All of the subparts . . . are equally important to the stability or functioning of the system. Remove one part, and the system fails: it comes apart, or it stops working."[64] Ecosystems, bodies, and even machines can communicate integral connections in a conflict.

As noted in previous chapters, advocates must consider not only the metaphors they employ as descriptors but also the conceptual frames they apply to the issues. Will Friedman, a deliberative democracy theorist and practitioner, advises: "framing refers to how information and messages—such as media stories, political arguments and policy positions—are defined, constructed, and presented in order to have certain impacts rather than others."[65] As discussed in chapter 10, framing also has the potential to represent issues fairly or to skew perceptions about points of disagreement.

The way an issue is framed has an impact "on the capacity and willingness of diverse groups of individuals to engage in productive dialogue and deliberation about complex issues."[66] Advocates who wish to ensure that their course of action reflects the best choices possible to foster lasting change need to refrain from the partisanship inherent in "spin." Any short-term advantages gained selectively presenting the facts for a favorable interpretation are more than offset by the potential for diminished trust. Advocates and deliberative activists who use influence and persuasion to manipulate jeopardize their audience's attention and engagement. Deliberative democracy theorists affirm that the legitimacy of any decision rests on the extent to which those subject to the outcome of the decision have the opportunity and capacity to contribute to deliberation about that decision[67] and that the decision-making process has fulfilled the related conditions of publicity, accountability, and reciprocity.

When framed within an interdependent ethic, advocacy is a critical resource for communities seeking to make well-informed, just, and wise decisions. Responsiveness and responsibility in framing and addressing differences are not only compelling ethical mandates but are also critical to advocates' abilities to be heard and understood. Development of the dialogic and deliberative skills and sensibilities outlined throughout this book prepares advocates and deliberative activists to present passionate appeals in support of their perspectives and causes. Advocates and activists across the political spectrum who use their skills to meet the conditions for successful and responsible deliberative advocacy offer the promise of contributing immeasurably to deliberative processes.

Realizing this promise requires one final set of knowledge, skills, and sensibilities. When confronted with advocates' presentations, audiences need to be able to evaluate the strengths and limits of the arguments. These capacities are vital to the fulfillment of communication's constructive potential, particularly in the complex deliberative contexts confronting humanity in today's world. The final chapter provides an overview of guidelines and resources available to address this critical need.

Evaluating Deliberative Arguments

As we've learned throughout this volume, there are no universal, airtight rules or guidelines for crafting effective deliberative arguments. The particular character of the deliberative partners involved plus the myriad other variables influencing the specific historical, deliberative, and rhetorical contexts interact to affect any presentation. Communication habits and procedures that prove constructive and valid in one sphere are not necessarily so in another. Similarly, the evaluation of arguments, the subject of this chapter, must be able to adapt to the most varied circumstances, audiences, and occasions. Recognizing context variability and fluidity does not, however, leave us without standards for evaluating the *deliberative quality* of arguments across contexts.

James Bohman reminds us that procedural guidelines alone provide inadequate resources for addressing disagreements involving people from widely diverse backgrounds. Neither misunderstandings borne of divergent interpretive frames nor seemingly intransigent disagreements rooted in incompatible belief systems can be addressed meaningfully through appeals to procedure alone. Bohman argues for deliberation based on dialogue. He notes, for example, that "democracy is justified to the extent that it makes possible the public use of common practical reason."[1] Bohman warns about the limits of external standards of justification in today's richly diverse social and political deliberative contexts.[2] His caveat reminds us of the important role *context* plays in *applying deliberative principles and related guidelines*. This is especially apparent in assessing *reasonableness*.

Assessing Reasonableness

Throughout this volume we have underscored the importance of reasonableness to dialogic engagement, deliberative inquiry, and discernment. Chapter 10 highlighted the critical role reasonableness plays in skillful deliberative argumentation. To review briefly, reasonableness differs substantively from instrumental and formal constructs of rationality. On the one hand, instrumental rationality privileges self-interest at the expense of accountability, publicity, and reciprocity. On the other hand, formal rationality associates validity with self-evidence and certainty, thereby limiting the possibilities for practical arguments and compromising efforts to foster sound deliberations in such practical contexts as law, medicine, and public policy.

In contrast, reasonableness integrates emotions, intuitions, facts, values, critical thinking, and logic. Deliberative approaches to inquiry, critical self-reflection, discernment, dialogical skills and sensibilities, and responsible advocacy help deliberative partners *tap the benefits of partiality without succumbing to the hazards of partisanship*. Reasonableness is at the heart of these endeavors. We've explored how deliberative partners are able to foster and maintain a sense of fairness to develop trust. Shared commitments to fairness and mutual experiences of trust, in turn, are critical to maintaining the conditions required for deliberative partners to engage openly, experience reciprocity, risk publicity, and pursue accountability.

Given the centrality of reasonableness to sound deliberation, evaluation of arguments for their deliberative value must assess this element carefully. The exploration of reasonableness in chapter 10 revealed, however that reasonableness is difficult to define. Fortunately, the studies of informal logic and argumentation theory in the fields of rhetoric and philosophy provide valuable resources for evaluating the reasonableness of arguments.

Informal Logical Analysis[3]

Scholarship in informal logic and argumentation theory provide resources for *logical analysis* within *practical domains*. These general assessment guidelines enable us to assess the *degree to which inference(s), or moves between supporting reasons and a conclusion, are reasonable* as opposed to formally valid. Among the best known and most widely adopted of these general guidelines are *internal consistency* and the *avoidance of reasoning fallacies*.

Internal Consistency and Reasonableness

Commitments to consistency, fairness, and the rule of law are compelling foundations for deliberation within contexts aspiring to fulfill democratic ideals. They help to a*void either real or imagined experiences of arbitrariness*. Except when used to convey an irony or a paradox, *internally inconsistent arguments fail to offer a meaningful position*. To illustrate, consider an advocate who opens a presentation by suggesting that abortion involves the taking of an innocent life but who concludes by suggesting that legalizing abortion does not risk infringing human rights. Without an explanation for this apparent inconsistency, deliberative partners listening to the presentation are left without meaningful counsel for deliberation.

Logicians have developed a number of schema for identifying and analyzing apparent inconsistencies. These include differentiations between contradictions, contraries, and other forms of inconsistency. While these are invaluable resources for specialized forms of analytic argumentative contexts, most of the deliberative contexts people encounter call for more nuanced resources such as those explored throughout this volume. Consider, for instance, intentional uses of an oxymoron. Combining contradictory terms such as "jumbo shrimp," "act natural" or "clear as mud," constructs figures of speech that provide effective and memorable communication.

Similarly, as we've learned throughout our explorations, words in ordinary or natural language often have more than one possible meaning. As a result, what may appear to be an inconsistency in a specific context may simply be a set of statements employing the same word but connoting different meanings. For example, if an otherwise reasonable person says, "When Suzie and Andy dance, they are not both dancing," or "They live in the same world, yet they do not live in the same world," deliberative partners should look carefully for a meaningful interpretation to eliminate the apparent incoherence. Was the person using poetic license—combining two seemingly inconsistent statements—for a dramatic impact?

As we learned in our explorations of attentive listening, making sincere efforts to understand each other requires that we try to make sense of what we each of us is seeking to convey. Empathic listening and deliberative inquiries enable deliberative partners to seek mutual understanding. When a logical analysis of a deliberative partner's arguments reveals apparent internal inconsistencies, it is important to determine as fully as possible whether the inconsistencies are inadvertent or otherwise unintended—in other words, are they, in fact, instances of logical incompatibility?

Evaluation of deliberative arguments requires more than just a review of the argument's internal consistency. Deliberative partners listening and reading attentively focus not only on explicit statements made but also on shared assumptions in statements assumed, inferred, and implied. Assessment of consistency similarly requires consideration of statements *implied as well as presented*.

Such analyses reveal that deliberative partners seldom *explicitly* make inconsistent claims. Yet even skilled and experienced advocates sometimes *provide arguments that lead to conclusions that are inconsistent with shared assumptions*. Hamid's argument regarding the morality of using animals for psychological experimentation illustrates. Hamid rests his argument on three premises:

Premise 1: Whatever enriches our understanding of suffering and leads to its alleviation is morally justified.

Premise 2: Psychological experimentation on human prototypes enriches our understanding of suffering and leads to its alleviation.

Premise 3: Nonhuman animals capable of suffering pain, stress, and anxiety are human prototypes.

From these premises, Hamid concludes that psychological experimentation on sentient creatures is morally justified. So far, the argument is not vulnerable to a charge of internal inconsistency.

Suppose, however, that in the course of discussion, Hamid grants the following three assumptions:

Assumption 1: The success of psychological experimentation often depends on the intentional infliction of stress or pain on, or the induction of anxiety in, lab animals capable of experiencing such feelings.

Assumption 2: Researchers know that laboratory animals suffer when they experience stress, pain, or anxiety.

Assumption 3: All intentional infliction of suffering is morally reprehensible.

In granting these assumptions, Hamid acknowledged that some types of psychological experimentation on laboratory animals involve the intentional infliction of suffering; he thus must confront an inconsistency. Assumption 3 holds that all intentional infliction of suffering is morally reprehensible, yet premise 1 implies that experimentation on laboratory animals is morally justified. Recognizing that such experimentation intentionally inflicts suffering, Hamid's own standard compels him to conclude that such experimentation is morally reprehensible.

Within the argument culture, advocates for animal rights would be encouraged to seize the moment, to reveal the inconsistency in Hamid's argument, and to "call him on it." In a culture of engagement, in contrast, deliberative partners would invite Hamid to reconcile the apparent inconsistency in his argument. Whether in the argument culture or in a culture of engagement, Hamid's challenge would be to *reconcile his position on animal experimentation with the shared set of assumptions*. In a culture of engagement, the deliberative partners would share the common goal of *gaining insight* in pursuit of the wisest decision possible.

Apart from the limits of ambiguity, the challenges of misunderstanding, and the importance of discernment explored thus far, analysis of consistency within a culture of engagement also requires *sensitivity to the complex, dynamic nature of moral and political deliberations*. Consider, for example, the extraordinarily challenging circumstances confronting a fundamentalist Christian mother of a pregnant 11-year-old rape victim whose continued pregnancy gravely threatens her well-being. Somehow the mother must reconcile her convictions regarding abortion with her obligations to protect her child's well-being.

In cases such as these, we are compelled to turn to our *value hierarchies* for resolution. Relying on a simple understanding of consistency, the mother could not reconcile the inconsistency. When understood within the more *nuanced context of deliberative exercise of good judgment*, however, the mother's challenge would be to provide a thoughtful *justification* for her decision regarding whether to support or deny her daughter's request for an abortion.

In discussing internal inconsistency, we have noted the importance of looking for an explanation that would overcome the problem. The presumption of reasonableness is equally useful when confronting an apparent inconsistency between a normally reasonable person's claim and some other justified belief. Bethtina and William's exchange about legislating morality illustrates this point. Bethtina's assertion, "You can't legislate morality," proved to be inconsistent with beliefs that she and William share. Rather than simply rejecting the claim due to this apparent inconsistency, however, William sought an explanation for it.

In the course of their conversation, Bethtina and William agreed that marriage and divorce laws are examples of moral legislation. Bethtina conceded further that laws protecting animals and children from abuse, laws against stealing, laws protecting the environment, laws against fraud, and so on are also attempts to legislate morality. After some discussion, Bethtina concluded that most laws in some sense probably legislate morality. She acknowledged further that these laws have often prevented immoral acts. She recalled, for instance, a man who would have cheated on his taxes had he not feared legal retribution. Despite these acknowledgments, however, Bethtina maintained her overarching thesis: "You can't legislate morality," she repeated. But this time she clarified her meaning by adding, "No law can change what is in a person's heart."

William suddenly understood what Bethtina had in mind when she made her original claim. For many English language speakers, the term "morality" involves action at least as much as it does thoughts. For example, a person who thinks about prostitution, but never acts on those thoughts, is not usually viewed as behaving immorally; immorality, for many people, involves at least some conduct.

Because of their dialogic exchange, William now understands that Bethtina's statement was meant to refer only to moral thoughts. Although her statement seemed to imply that legislation could have no impact on moral conduct, Bethtina's use of the term "morality" was meant to encompass only moral consciousness. By presuming Bethtina's reasonableness, William was able to ascertain the intention of Bethtina's statement.

The resulting discussion clarified for Bethtina the common usage of the term "morality" and helped William consider the possibility of an

interesting idea: that laws have little power to influence moral consciousness. Bethtina and William will now be able to meaningfully consider
this controversial and provocative concept. For them, the presumption of
reasonableness was productive.

In sum, analysis of a deliberative argument's internal consistency
requires more than just a review of what an advocate says or writes.
Statements implied by the advocate's arguments, shared assumptions,
and empathic reading and listening also provide important material for
the analysis of consistency. Internal consistency offers an important
guideline for assessing the reasonableness of arguments. In this sense,
consistency has a strong presumption in its favor whenever deliberative partners convene together in pursuit of wise and just decision making.

Fallacies of Reasoning

Beyond inconsistencies, arguments are often vulnerable to other *fallacies of reasoning*. Evaluating arguments deliberatively requires careful
assessment of the degree to which advocates have been able to avoid
these obstacles to deliberation. The overview below introduces a few of
the most common reasoning fallacies.

Straw argument—providing weak representations of opposing views—is
among the most common fallacies of reasoning. Within the argument
culture, this is a widely used tactic often designed to mislead audiences.
Even within a culture of engagement, however, advocates are sometimes
vulnerable to *straw argumentation*.

Luis believes strongly that public funding of day-care centers is ill
advised. In a public presentation, he suggests that the primary reason
some people support public funding of day-care centers is that such funding will create badly needed jobs for day-care workers and administrators.
Advocates for such funding are quick to respond, however, that although
they view the creation of jobs as a valuable outcome of public support for
day care, this is not among their most compelling reasons for proposing
such a policy. Based on their research, they have concluded that families
with access to publicly funded day-care centers are significantly more
likely to contribute to the community's well-being in a number of important ways. Principal among these are reduced crime rates, higher standards of living, stable families, and children enriched intellectually and
physically, and otherwise well equipped for success in school and beyond.
Their studies suggest further that public funding of day-care centers
would ultimately save taxpayers countless dollars by helping single welfare mothers get and retain jobs and by giving children (who might otherwise end up needing medical care or becoming juvenile delinquents)
the care and attention they need to become productive, healthy citizens.

Luis's straw argument—providing a false representation of day-care
funding supporters' views—fails to consider these more compelling arguments. To contribute meaningfully to deliberation on the subject, Luis

will need to carefully consider the reasons articulated above. If after careful reflection, Luis determines that there are better ways to achieve the goals described above, he will be significantly better equipped to contribute to the public's consideration of the issues. *Counterintuitively, representing and directly addressing the most compelling reasons available to those who disagree with his position enhances the deliberative value of the presentation as well as helping Luis enhance the effectiveness of his arguments.* As this example illustrates, avoidance of the straw argument fallacy is important to anyone seeking to contribute meaningfully to deliberation. Similarly, making sure that advocates have avoided straw arguments is important to the deliberative evaluation of arguments.

Another common fallacy of reasoning that often poses obstacles to deliberation is referred to as *begging the question* (discussed briefly in chapter 8). This fallacy occurs when advocates *avoid the relevant issue.* In the following brief dialogue, Josie begs the question:

> **Johanna:** The United States should enhance its commitment to providing adequate medical care for the homeless.
>
> **Josie:** Russia has more homeless people than the United States does.

In her response, Josie has failed to address the central issues implicit in Johanna's claim. Not only does this approach fail to contribute meaningfully to the deliberative process but begging the question actually *diverts attention from the central issues,* thereby posing potentially significant obstacles to deliberation on the subject.

Related to begging the question is *circularity.* This fallacy has aroused considerable debate among argumentation theorists, but all agree that arguments are circular when *unsupported assertions or assumptions are used to advance controversial claims.* The following argument for mandatory seat belt laws provides a typical example of circularity:

> Mandatory seat belt laws should be passed immediately because they are needed. Society needs to have laws that require people to wear seat belts, even if they do not want to wear them. Therefore, we should adopt mandatory seat belt laws.

In this example, the advocate claims that we need mandatory seat belt laws because we need them! "Radical" circularity of this kind fails to contribute meaningfully to deliberation. Philosopher Monroe Beardsley notes, however, that "the most deceptive circular arguments are rather long ones; circularity is easiest to conceal when the distance between the premise and conclusion is great."[4] Within the argument culture, this is a common strategy. However, even sincere advocates dedicated to deliberative inquiry sometimes miss the circularity of their arguments.

Kacey has prepared an argument in favor of legalizing adult access to recreational drugs. Kacey wrote the following paragraph in a sincere effort to articulate her position:

Legalizing adult access to recreational drugs in this country will save money, energy, time, and many lives. It is understandable that people want to stop drug use. After all, the drug problem in this country is significant. There are literally thousands of lives lost to the ravages of drug addiction. Each day, more and more children fall prey to the drug dealer's seductive tactics. Because so many young people feel vulnerable, confused, and alone in today's complex world, it's not surprising that they are such easy targets for the dealer's campaign. It's sad too to see how many upwardly mobile people in our culture find themselves turning to drugs to escape the pain of their lonely, empty lives. Legalizing adult access to recreational drugs will address this problem. It will save time, energy, money, and many lives.

Kacey was surprised when a careful reader informed her that her paragraph failed to provide support for her conclusion. Kacey's insightful critic showed her that she had presented no support to show that legalization would result in saving time, money, and lives. Because Kacey approached the topic with humility and balanced partiality, she was receptive to the critic's observations, and she quickly understood that the circular reasoning used in her paragraph failed to provide reliable assistance to readers who wished to determine whether we should legalize adult access to recreational drugs. As a result, the critic's comments afforded Kacey the opportunity to develop a new, less circular argument.

Circularity of some kind is *rarely possible to escape fully* in many deliberations, especially when the issues are complex. Deliberative partners often face time constraints in addition to an urgent need to move toward decision making. Under such circumstances, it is difficult to craft fully developed philosophical grounding for each and every underlying assumption and claim. The standard of reasonableness in "real-world" contexts requires, at a minimum, *identifying and providing support for contested claims and avoidance of "radical" circularity* (represented in Kacey's argument). At best, the standard calls for *the fullest explication and support possible in given circumstances.* The tools associated with deliberative inquiry and discernment explored in earlier chapters provide important resources both for helping deliberative partners avoid the extreme cases of circularity and to assess the seriousness of circular arguments they encounter through exchanges with advocates.

Non-Sequitur Reasoning

Overarching the particular types of reasoning fallacies discussed above is a broad, all-encompassing category called *non-sequitur* reasoning. The Latin expression *non sequitur* means *does not follow.* Advocates employ the *non-sequitur* fallacy whenever the claims they advance do not logically follow from the premises and evidence they provide in support of their claims. Even if we accept the premises and the evidence provided in these arguments, we would still not be obliged to accept the conclusion. The example below illustrates how this fallacy works:

Caring for the elderly is very costly. Furthermore, every dollar expended on caring for the elderly limits by a dollar the amount of money available for other important enterprises, such as educating the young. Therefore, we should stop caring for the elderly.

It is easy to see how it would be possible to accept the premises in the argument above without granting the conclusion. *Non-sequitur* reasoning has the potential to seriously compromise sound deliberation. Imagine, for instance, the devastating nature of policies resting on the "reasoning" advanced in this example.

Other forms of *non-sequitur reasoning* further illustrate why we must look carefully for these potential obstacles to deliberation when evaluating deliberative arguments. The *appeal to popular prejudice* offers a particularly compelling example. Typically, the advocate employing this fallacy claims that because most people believe a claim to be true, it is true. Advertisements for products and political candidates, as well as social commentaries, often appeal to popular prejudice:

Example 1: This computer monitor is our best seller. Therefore, you should buy this model.

Example 2: The majority of the public believes he is guilty despite the jury's ruling to the contrary. Therefore, he is guilty.

Example 3: The majority believes capital punishment is the best way to punish murderers. Therefore, capital punishment should remain legal in the United States.

Example 4: Most people in this country waste water. Therefore, it is morally acceptable for me to waste water.

Example 5: Most people get married. Therefore, you should get married.

In each of these examples, popular opinion provides the *sole justification* given to support the conclusion. Example 1 represents a type of appeal that is frequently found in the marketplace. How often have you been told that you should purchase a particular product simply because it is popular? Yet what does its popularity have to do with whether the product best meets your individual needs?

Examples 2 and 3 are also representative of a prevalent use of popular prejudice. How often have you heard people justify their beliefs on the grounds that others agree with them? Yet history provides countless examples of the harms resulting from uninformed adherence to unjustified popular opinion. Popular support of slavery, child and other domestic abuse, witch burning, and cockfighting are but a few examples of harmful popular prejudices. Deliberative evaluation requires that we carefully scrutinize arguments that rely heavily on this type of reasoning. Example 4 represents a widely used version of the appeal to popular prejudice. How often have you heard people defending behavior they know is unacceptable on the grounds that others also engage in it? It takes little reflection to see how dangerous this type of reasoning can be for deliberative processes.

Example 5 also represents a widely used type of appeal to popular prejudice. Acceptance of this type of appeal can lead people to behave against their better judgment, or interests, or both. Consider the example given above. Even if 99 percent of the world gets married, what does this have to do with whether marriage best meets your individual needs? How much should your decision rely on the fact that other people have found this a suitable or valuable course of action? Furthermore, what does the simple fact that many people get married tell us about whether getting married fulfilled these people's needs? In this, as in other contexts, the appeal to popular prejudice is by itself an inadequate basis for reasoned decision making.

Related to appeals to popular prejudice is the *appeal to tradition*. Essentially, the advocate argues that a *practice is moral or a belief is correct because it conforms with tradition*: "Women have always had primary responsibility for domestic duties; therefore, men should not be expected to take responsibility for housework and child care." This appeal fails to take into account what we have learned through discernment about the need to consider the changing nature of conditions facing people during any given moment. As we've seen, for example, socioeconomic changes, scientific discoveries, demographic shifts, technological advancements, and countless other changes create circumstances that often require reconsideration of traditional views and practices.

As our discussions of shifting value hierarchies and the fluid nature of presumption have revealed as well, traditions do not, *by their mere existence*, necessarily merit acceptance. Many states within the union maintained a tradition of slavery in the United States that has since been exposed for its ruthlessness and immorality. Similarly, the white South African government maintained a long tradition of apartheid. The fact that this practice was traditional in no way established its merit. Argument by tradition plays a significant role in many public deliberations across the globe. Although such arguments may be appropriate as supplements to other reasons, argumentation that relies exclusively on this appeal falls seriously short of the guidelines for deliberative argumentation.

As with other guidelines for evaluating deliberative arguments, determining the applicability of the appeal to tradition is complex. For example, some communities around the globe continue to subscribe to traditions that those outside the community view as conflicting with basic human rights. Controversies surrounding forced clitoridectomy in some communities illustrate the complexity. Highly publicized cases of women seeking asylum in the West in order to avoid the ceremonial practice have heightened conflicts between those who subscribe to the view that the community's tradition should take precedence and those who believe that the tradition violates the basic rights of an individual. The example below illustrates further.

Less complicated to assess, but equally important to discern, is the *ad hominem* fallacy. Used often as a strategy for undermining opposition within the argument culture, this fallacy involves *attacking the person rather than his or her ideas.* During the course of partisan congressional rankling over budget negotiations in 2011, for example, advocates on either side of the aisle often leveled attacks on each other's motives and characters. These *ad hominem* attacks not only failed to contribute to deliberation on the issues so critical to the nation's well-being but they also actually undermined deliberative processes.

Another fallacy of reasoning that compromises deliberations is *oversimplification.* Speakers and writers commit this fallacy when they *overlook potentially relevant considerations.* Two of the more common forms of oversimplification are *false dilemma* and *oppositional thinking.*

False dilemmas oversimplify by posing *arbitrarily limited options.* Corky's argument for abusing nonhuman animals employs this fallacy. In support of his approach to animal training for films, Corky has argued that the only options available to him are either to chain and beat his horses or to lose his effectiveness as an animal trainer. Discerning evaluation reveals, however, that this argument fails to consider a third option, namely, making use of the many gentle but highly effective methods of animal training developed by experts during the past twenty years. Adoption of this third option would prevent animal cruelty while helping Corky do his job effectively. Ignoring this important option jeopardizes Corky's decision making on this topic.

False dilemma is perhaps *one of the most common fallacies in everyday thinking.* So often we imagine that we must choose between two unappealing alternatives when there are other, more constructive options open to us. Jacob and Joseph's decision-making pattern is representative. Buddies throughout middle school, they went to the corner store with just enough money to buy one pint of their favorite ice cream. They approached the ice cream bin enthusiastically, relishing the prospect of their purchase. They soon discovered, however, that they each had a different flavor in mind. One of them wanted chocolate and the other vanilla, so they quarreled. Jacob's response was to say, "Fine, well then, let's just not get any ice cream at all!" Falling prey to the false dilemma fallacy, they left the store rather than consider alternatives such as buying two pints of a less expensive brand, taking turns (this time one flavor, next time the other), or getting Neapolitan (and finding a friend who wants strawberry).

Creativity is a vital resource for avoiding false dilemmas. Had Jacob and Joseph creatively considered the alternatives available to them, they would both have enjoyed the pleasures of sharing ice cream with their best buddy. While youthfulness and inadequate training were no doubt at play in Jacob and Joseph's failure to imagine other possibilities, public communicators within the argument culture sometimes deliberately use false dilemma to achieve personal objectives.

Some politicians have been known to employ false dilemma in this way. Either we must raise taxes, they might say, or we must cut back on subsidizing medical care for the poor. This argument fails to consider other plausible alternatives, such as cutting back on other domestic or military programs, pursuing taxpayers who are delinquent in their payments to the Internal Revenue Service, redistributing tax dollars, eliminating waste in federal spending, and so on. Without public consideration of these and other alternatives, the nation is vulnerable to policy making that has potentially negative or even harmful consequences.

Another form of non-sequitur reasoning is *hasty generalization. Generalizations that are unwarranted by the support provided on their behalf* are considered hasty generalizations. Wendell claims, for example, that women prefer married life to single life. He bases this claim on his interviews with seven women over a period of ten years in Eugene, Oregon. Clearly, his generalized conclusion is unwarranted given his small (and possibly biased) sample.

Hasty generalizations often result from small and biased personal samples. Carlos concludes from his exposure to three untrained dogs that all dogs are poorly behaved. Levi meets two quiet cousins and concludes that all the cousins in that family must be quiet. Because we live in such a complex world, it is tempting to make this type of inference. If we have been exposed to only two Baptists and both were introverted, the inclination to assume that all Baptists are introverted is understandable. As we've seen throughout this volume, however, avoiding hasty generalizations of this kind in interpersonal relations, governmental policy judgments, and business deliberations is critical to human flourishing. It is therefore important for critics to identify any instances of this fallacy during their evaluations of deliberative arguments.

Another common form of faulty reasoning that poses significant obstacles to deliberation is the fallacy of *post hoc, ergo propter hoc,* or "*after the fact, therefore because of the fact.*" This form of non-sequitur reasoning *assumes that because one event occurred prior to another, the one was caused by the other.* Historically, many tragic errors of judgment have been associated with this fallacy. Consider, for example, the false convictions resulting from inferences based solely on the proximity of events. Inferences in daily life are also vulnerable to this common fallacy. Consider the following example.

Carole: I've finally found a way to cure my eczema.

John: Really? That's great! What's the cure?

Carole: Vitamin D. I started taking it last week, and my eczema has disappeared.

Carole's self-diagnosis and treatment plan rests entirely on her observation that adding Vitamin D to her daily vitamin regimen coincided with her skin's healing. Without further evidence of a causal link between these events, however, Carole's inference is not justified. There are numerous factors implicated in eczema, many of which may well be at play in Carole's case. Because she has fallen prey to the seductions of the *post hoc* fallacy, however, Carole will be unlikely to gain insight into these myriad factors, thereby making herself vulnerable to the problem in the future. In this, as well as in countless other contexts, the *post hoc ergo proctor hoc* fallacy has compromised the quality of deliberation.

We can better assess the reasonableness of advocates' arguments if we use the tools of logical analysis to assess the internal consistency of arguments and if we work to recognize fallacies of reasoning.

Emotions and Reasonableness

As we've learned throughout this volume, *reasonableness* requires *both logic and emotion*. Evaluating arguments therefore requires attentiveness to the deliberative value of a given argument's emotional appeals.

Assessing the Deliberative Value of Emotional Appeals

Emotions play key roles in constructive engagements, deliberative inquiry, discernment, and deliberative argumentation. Drawing on Aristotle's insights, Bernard Yack observes that decisions about future action are inevitably informed by an integration of intellect, emotion, and reason. He goes on to observe the critical role emotion plays in informing what he identifies as the "live reason" at the heart of sound deliberative judgments.[5]

Within the argument culture, advocates are trained to use appeals to emotion strategically. As noted in earlier chapters, appeals to fear are especially prevalent—and often highly effective—means for manipulating audiences. Historically, as we've seen, such appeals have been linked to decisions with profoundly tragic consequences. Accordingly, President Franklin Delano Roosevelt during his first inaugural address admonished the public that in the face of the nation's crisis, "the only thing we have to fear is fear itself."

As noted in chapter 9, *presumption and burden of proof* play key roles in sound deliberative judgments. Given the powerful sway of fear—especially in the face of real or perceived vulnerability—appeals to this emotion have the potential to pose significant obstacles to deliberative judgments. In light of this phenomenon, advocates employing appeals to fear face a substantial burden of proof to justify their choice. Strict scrutiny may, in some cases, determine that the strategy is reasonable in some deliberative contexts.

Recognizing the complexity of the issues related to the debt crisis confronting the nation in Spring 2011, as well as the public's apparent relative apathy on the subject, Senator John Warner made impassioned appeals to fear. He cautioned, for example, that failure to raise the debt limit would have dire, long-term consequences to the nation's economic well-being, international standing, security, and abilities to provide global leadership in the pursuit of human rights. Without apology, Warner used concrete examples—aligned closely with the audience's personal stakes—to arouse the public's deep concerns.[6]

In his presentation Warner provided compelling support for his impassioned pleas, grounded in reliable forms of justification. Following Warner's remarks, former Democratic Senator Evan Bayh commended his Republican colleague for underscoring the gravity of the debt crisis. Joining in Warner's appeals to fear regarding the nation's security and economic well-being, Bayh passionately admonished the audience to take careful heed of the debt crisis debate and its consequences.[7]

Bayh and Warner's remarks were part of a program titled: "Can Civility Be Returned in Governing Our Nation?" Although they represented two distinctly different economic and governance worldviews, Bayh and Warner shared a commitment to fostering reasoned deliberations on subjects of importance to the nation's well-being. Reflecting this shared commitment, the senators' appeals to fear were supported by compelling evidence and were balanced with other forms of argument. In short, their appeals to fear were reasonable and grounded, and they otherwise met the rigorous burden of proof faced by advocates who employ such appeals. Often, however, advocates' appeals to fear fall short of meeting the test of reasonableness.

Appeals to anger are related to appeals to fear. As we learned in earlier explorations, *anger* has the potential to contribute valuably to dialogic communication and deliberative inquiry. This is particularly true in the face of grave injustice. Under these circumstances, appeals eliciting anger potentially meet the requirements of strict scrutiny. As we've seen, however, this potentially volatile emotion also often compromises our abilities to live and reason well together. Within the argument culture, appeals to anger are used strategically, often with negative consequences. In recognition of this phenomenon, appeals to anger within an interdependent ethic face a burden of proof comparable to that for appeals to fear. Evaluating appeals to anger for their deliberative value requires critics to review and tap the insights offered throughout our analyses of this emotion's relationship to reasonableness. Only through this high level of scrutiny can we be confident that advocates' appeals to anger have met the burden of proof associated with them.

Appeals to *hatred* face an even stricter standard. On the one hand, much like fear and anger, hatred in the face of grave injustices is not only understandable but potentially important, especially when the injustice or other form of abuse is perpetrated against vulnerable individuals and communities. And yet, history is replete with the horrors borne of unfettered hatred. Importantly, unlike fear and anger, appeals to this emotion seldom foster constructive engagement and reasoned deliberation. Within a culture of engagement—guided by an ethic of interdependence—appeals to hatred must meet the strictest standards of evaluation.

Emotional Intelligence and Deliberative Assessments

Thus far, our focus has been on evaluating the deliberative value of emotions known for their volatility and potential harms. Appeals to these emotions, as we have seen, face a significant burden of proof. In contrast, appeals to *positive* emotions are recognized for their potential in fostering sound deliberations. Appeals to emotions such as love, compassion, empathy, and related dialogic sensibilities have presumption in their favor. Importantly, however, as noted in chapter 10, appeals to these emotions are not immune to problems. Arguments relying too heavily upon—or providing irrational appeals to—one or more of these emotions at the expense of reasonableness can compromise the quality of deliberations.

Martha Nussbaum's work on the intelligence of emotions assists us in discerning the strengths of, and problems with, deliberative advocates' emotional appeals. Nussbaum counsels that development of emotional intelligence is key to fostering deliberative abilities and that attentiveness to the development of "emotional well-being" fosters "our reasoning capacity as political creatures."[8]

As we learned in chapter 10, Nussbaum provides compelling support for her assertion that "emotions, like other beliefs, can be true or false" and are appropriately assessed as "justified or unjustified, reasonable or unreasonable."[9] Her research further reveals the intimate links between individuals' emotions and their capacities "for setting priorities and making decisions."[10]

> Compassion is not 'irrational' in the sense of 'impulsive' or 'lacking thought.' Nor in central cases, is it normally irrational in the sense of being based on bad thought, as the Stoics charged. On the other hand, it is admittedly fallible and easily led astray; so we need to ask how we could avail ourselves of its best, rather than its worst, possibilities.[11]

Nussbaum's comments underscore the importance of evaluating the strengths and weaknesses of appeals to compassion and related positive emotions within any given context.

One of Nussbaum's important observations is that "human beings experience emotions in ways that are shaped both by individual history and by social norms."[12] Tapping extensive research on cultural and individual variability, she cautions against generalizations that fail to take full account of the often significant differences between individuals and communities. However, she also advises that core emotions such as "fear, love, anger, and grief" are experienced across cultural boundaries.[13] She concludes this facet of her exploration by noting that "all human emotions are in part about the past, and bear the traces of a history that is at once commonly human, socially constructed, and idiosyncratic."[14]

Nussbaum states that no matter how perfect the institution, we need the sound deliberation of compassionate individuals to contribute political insights. "Political systems are human, and they are only good if they are alive in a human way."[15] She illustrates the point by stating that even a fully just society needs compassionate judges and jurors. Such capacities are more salient than ever in today's challenging political environments. Dialogic sensibilities are critical to sound deliberative argument and should be recognized when evaluating the deliberative value of arguments.

Critical Self-Reflexivity, Emotions, and Deliberative Assessments of Arguments

As discussed in previous chapters, the term *standpoint* refers to the identities, roles, or status occupied by a communicator in any given context. Although a standpoint does not necessarily determine a person's position on an issue, it often influences how an individual interprets a controversial topic. Sensitivity to social and political dynamics is an especially important element for establishing credibility and rapport with deliberative partners. Overlooking or dismissing the impact of standpoint may create tensions and spur discord or animosity within a deliberative community.

Kitty and Aubrey work for a local AIDS prevention project to fulfill part of their service-learning requirement in their undergraduate degree programs. The AIDS prevention project's administrators have called an organizational meeting to consider whether to initiate a needle exchange program. At the meeting, Kitty, a social work student, argues passionately on behalf of providing clean needles to people who inject illegal drugs in order to prevent the transmission of Hepatitis C and AIDS. She also sees the needle exchange program as a means of referring people to drug treatment centers. "We could save these people's lives," she argues. Aubrey, a psychology student, supports Kitty's public health concerns, but she feels conflicted over supplying needles to drug addicts. "People should be responsible for their own behavior," she states. "They chose to use drugs, and they can choose not to share needles." Moreover, Aubrey is concerned that a needle exchange program conveys the message that illegal drug use is being condoned or at least tolerated.

Peter, the sponsor of the needle exchange proposal and a former drug user, discounts both students' remarks, believing that they are applying textbook theories to populations of people whom they don't know. He appeals to other activists in the meeting to support the needle exchange program as an act of civil disobedience against unjust prescription and paraphernalia laws. Aubrey objects immediately, disclosing that her younger brother died as a result of a drug overdose; Kitty reasserts the significance of her field's research findings and the importance of rehabilitating addicts.

This argument develops in a series of clashes between various and overlapping standpoints as well as the potential credibility of college students, a former drug user, a family member, and activists. What is more relevant: theoretical knowledge, life experiences, or activist commitments? Critical self-reflexivity about the influence and impact of these standpoints occurs as people who disagree exercise a balanced partiality and self-awareness.

As discussed in earlier chapters, dialogic skills and related sensibilities help decision makers prevent becoming caught up in their own or other people's self-interests and emotional states. Critical self-reflexivity does not prevent bias or strong emotional reactions; rather, it helps us recognize these responses and either prevent or account for their impact on our deliberative processes.

Assessing Responsiveness

As we've seen throughout this volume, responsiveness is a highly complex phenomenon incorporating dialogic skills and sensibilities as well as key elements of discernment. Evaluating deliberative arguments requires careful attentiveness to whether advocates are responsive. Our previous explorations have revealed that advocates demonstrate responsiveness to a large degree by attending thoughtfully to others' claims, views, interests, values, and perspectives. Anticipating and thoughtfully addressing the potential concerns of others demonstrates respect for deliberative partners, helps to develop and maintain meaningful relationships, and otherwise contributes valuably to deliberations. Conversely, failure to anticipate and thoughtfully address dissenting views not only compromises the deliberative value of arguments but also often disrupts constructive engagements by creating the impression of disregard or even contempt.

Evaluating responsiveness calls, above all, for careful review of the degree to which an advocate avoids making uncontested claims without support as well as how he or she anticipates, sensitively articulates, and thoughtfully addresses dissenting views. This evaluative process requires critics to imagine how those who disagree with the advocate might respond to every feature of a presentation—from an advocate's narrative accounts, uses of metaphor, and emotional appeals, to the forms of support used in defense of the advocate's potentially contested claims. In each of these steps, critics seeking to assess responsiveness are required to use perspectival thinking and narrative imagination, as well as to assess the advocate's responsiveness to the levels of presumption framing the deliberative context.

Thus far, our discussion of argument evaluation has revealed how assessing the complex interplays of logic, emotion, standpoint, critical self-reflexivity, and responsiveness contribute to evaluations of arguments' deliberative value. Earlier in this volume, we discussed the importance of assessing the *relevance, credibility and reliability of sources*, as well as discerning the deliberative value of evidence advocates use to support their claims and inferences. As we've seen, use of evidence in the context of deliberative argumentation is complex, nuanced, and varies depending on the context.

Fallacies of Evidence

One common fallacy of evidence is the *repeated assertion* fallacy. An author or speaker commits this fallacy whenever he or she relies on repetition to provide support for an unwarranted claim. Within the argument culture, this fallacy is particularly prevalent in political communication. Political advocates who lack support for their claims sometimes hope that if these claims are repeated frequently, people will begin to accept them. Critical listeners and readers realize that an unsupported claim remains unwarranted regardless of how many times it is repeated. Many advertisements also rely on the effectiveness of repetition. The audience is repeatedly told that a particular product performs better than its competitors. Without thinking, some members of the audience begin to accept the manufacturer's claim. Critical thinkers can avoid falling prey to this type of manipulation by recognizing the fallacy underlying it.

The *unreliable source* fallacy also requires critical thinking and discernment. This fallacy occurs when arguers use sources that are likely either to be particularly biased or to lack credibility in the given context. Often, as we learned in our exploration of this phenomenon in chapter 9, a reliable source in one context may not be reliable in another.

Consider the example from chapter 3 about the relevance and expertise of Chief Justice Roberts advising policy makers on capital punishment. If the question were whether capital punishment laws violate the U.S. Constitution, Chief Justice would be a reliable source. If the question is whether capital punishment in fact deters crime, a social scientist or an expert criminologist specializing in criminal deterrence would have greater reliability. Similarly, a victim of a violent crime might be a reliable source on the question of who committed that crime, but he or she is likely to be seriously biased on the question of what punishment the perpetrator of the crime should receive.

Two related common fallacies of evidence are the *non-representative and insufficient instance* fallacy. Only data that provide reasonably accurate reflections of reality and that offer generalizable instances facilitate good reasoning. Instances that are either not representative or insufficient to be generalizable create distorted justifications for points of view and hence jeopardize the quality of the reasoning process. Work by a social scientist illustrates. He hoped to argue that there is more sex-role stereotypic behavior on television programming for children than on adult programming. To support his claim, the scientist compared sex-role stereotyping on three adult programs to sex-role stereotyping on three children's programs. Further research reveals, however, that there are more than fifty adult programs and more than thirty-five children's programs available. Results from a sample that includes only three adult and three children's programs would not adequately support the scholar's generalization. Without either a significantly larger sample or a strong argument to support the special representational quality of his small sample, the scientist's study would fail to meet basic standards of validity.

Among the most general fallacies of evidence is the *invalid statistical measure* fallacy. Biased and atypical samples, misleading graphs, and nonrepresentative averages are among the many sources of invalid statistical measures. For example, a poll following a televised presidential debate that cost the respondent fifty cents would primarily measure the opinions of people who could afford the calls. It is easy to see how well-funded supporters of a debate participant could use this opportunity to register as many votes as possible in favor of their candidate. Given these and other validity problems, such polls do not accurately reflect public reaction to the debates.

In evaluating statistical data, it is important to distinguish different uses of the data. *How the data are used often determines the deliberative value of the evidence.* Consider, for example, a survey accompanied by a questionnaire with a partisan account of American defense policy. Under these circumstances, it is clear that the researchers are promoting a partisan agenda rather than pursuing sound forms of inquiry. In examples such as these the survey results would not accurately reflect the general public's beliefs on the topic in question. Use of such a survey as evidence of public sentiment would be fallacious.

While the example above qualifies as a politically motivated strategic campaign, other researchers and those who publish their findings may also fall prey to evidentiary fallacies. In 2012, for example, the *Chronicle of Philanthropy* published research findings regarding the giving habits of populations within different regions across the United States. According to Associated Press news accounts, the researchers found that people in "less religious states give less to charity." The study identifies Utah as "the most generous state." Reportedly, the "Northeast, with lower religious participation is the least generous to charities, with the six New England states filling the last six slots among the 50 states."[16]

It is easy to imagine how audiences reading these AP reports might draw inferences linking generosity to religiosity. Alan Wolfe observes, however, that the published findings reflect patterns of giving that include followers' donations to their synagogues, mosques, churches, and other places of worship but fail to reflect broader, secular forms of giving. He points out that people in less religious states give based on need rather than religious affiliation. They are more willing to pay higher taxes so the government can provide benefits to those in need. According to Wolfe, many people in predominately secular regions "view the tax money they're paying not as something that's forced upon them, but as a recognition that they belong with everyone else, that they're citizens in the common good."[17]

Although Wolfe strongly encourages readers to question how the report's findings have been framed, he is careful not to draw broad inferences from his observations. And despite his concerns regarding methodological issues with the design of the study and potential "misuses" of its findings, Wolfe carefully avoids maligning the motives either of the study's research team or of those who published its findings. As a deliberative critic, Wolfe recognizes that vulnerability to evidentiary fallacies is not limited to instrumentalist argumentation. Humanity's inherent fallibility means that even advocates passionately committed to constructive engagements are subject to error.

In closing, as we review the resources available for evaluating the deliberative value of advocates' presentations—from criteria for evaluating emotional appeals and standards for assessing reasonableness, to evidentiary guidelines—it is important to emphasize the *context-specific application* of any analysis. Responsible and effective evaluation requires attentiveness to the *particular audience, purpose, and occasion* framing the *rhetorical context,* as well as to the numerous factors shaping the *specific deliberative context.*

Like dialogue, discernment, deliberative framing, and advocacy, evaluating the deliberative value of arguments is a deeply complex, often challenging, but vitally important process. Without a spirit of exploration, empathy, a commitment to fairness, attentive listening, reading, critical thinking skills, and self-awareness, for example, critics risk compromising rather than facilitating deliberative processes. Applying evaluative resources with humility, care, sensitivity, responsiveness, and balanced partiality enables critics to help fulfill communication's constructive potential.

As we've seen throughout this volume, confronting the obstacles facing anyone seeking to engage disagreement and other forms of difference constructively is not a path for the fainthearted. Courage is required every step of way, from subjecting our assumptions, values, and beliefs to others' scrutiny, to risking change. Yet the way is marked with support and encouragement as well. As Noelle McAfee notes, engaging together in substantive deliberations helps participants experience *"inter-esse,* a way of being *between and with others."*[18] Successful deliberative processes help participants aim "for a choice that reflects a considered, public judgment on the issue."[19] And as Jonathon Haidt observes, "wisdom" is the gift that "comes out of a group of people well constituted who have faith and trust in each other."[20]

With so much at stake—from the quality of our relationships and communities, to the destiny of our planet—this moment compels each of us to consider whether and how we will choose to participate in pursuit of the gift of wisdom and engagement. We invite you to join us in this quest, trusting that your decision will enable you to experience the fulfillment of living and doing well.

Lexicon of Key Terms

Accountability: anticipating and responsibly addressing the needs and interests of potential stakeholders in a given deliberative context; accounting for the likely consequences of one's decisions and actions; being answerable to others; providing public justification for decisions and actions responsive to the needs and interests of stakeholders; holding oneself to account for one's decisions and actions; justifying actions in moral terms.

Adversarial individualism: a framework grounded on the belief in a "dog-eat-dog" world in which rational individuals privilege self interest at all costs.

Assumptions: beliefs held to be true without the need for argument or supporting evidence.

Balanced partiality: demonstrated recognition of one's standpoint and commitments, accounting for their potential impact on a dialogue with a caring dedication to fairness.

Belief system: the constellation of assumptions, values, beliefs, and emotions at the root of an individual or group's perspective on controversial issues.

Burden of proof: the rhetorical and deliberative burdens associated with seeking to advance a claim or inference at odds with one or more presumptions in any given context.

Civility: a means of communicating respectful regard for one another; a resource for empowering people to become allies in common pursuit of mutual recognition; respectful regard for human dignity.

Cognitive development: Development of an individual's intellectual, logical, critical thinking, reasoning, and related abilities.

Collaborative communication: the process of interacting with others in shared pursuit of common goals, such as reasoned, wise, and just decision making; communication used to pursue mutually fulfilling relationships.

Common ground: shared assumptions, beliefs, interests, perceptions, values, value hierarchies, or emotional responses.

Compassion: a form of considerate responsiveness; connecting intimately with another's suffering; taking in, understanding, and experiencing another's sorrow, grief, loss, anguish, loneliness, anger, pain, or other form of suffering; experiencing someone else's suffering as one's own.

249

Critical self-awareness: an unflinching understanding of the intersection between an individual's personal perspectives, social identity and location, and how others perceive him or her.

Cynicism: the absence of hope in humanity's potential to transcend destructive forces such as greed, corruption, and hypocrisy in any given circumstance; the view that attempts to reach out across differences in mutual pursuit of understanding, knowledge, truth, or justice are hopelessly naïve and foolhardy; a common substitute for critical thinking; privileging negativity over deliberative inquiry, dialogue, discernment, or deliberation.

Deliberation: the processes used in efforts to make informed, just, and wise decisions in any given context; within public sectors, deliberation evokes a spirit of balancing or weighing and thoughtfully considering a matter in consultation with others.

Deliberative argumentation: reasoned interaction tailored for presentation to an audience in support of sound deliberation; discourse reflecting the culmination of an advocate's deliberative inquiry, discernment, reflection, creativity, narrative and moral imagination, and related critical thinking processes.

Deliberative community: the multiplicity of stakeholders and stakeholder allies—representing diverse and sometimes conflicting interests, beliefs, and values—collaborating across their differences in pursuit of an informed, just, and wise decision.

Deliberative framing: the communication processes used to structure the context of meaning or the interpretive framework in which a deliberation is held; a reflection of participants' understandings of the deliberative context, including how they identify and interpret relevant issues, stakeholders, and available options.

Deliberative inquiry: an exploratory approach to inquiry involving the following related steps: engaging disagreement, deliberative questioning, gathering, and appraising relevant information and insights, critical thinking, and discernment.

Deliberative partners: individuals working together in mutual pursuit of the best decision possible in a given context.

Deliberative questions: reflecting a spirit of exploration, this type of question is framed to elicit insights and information directly relevant to understanding and responsibly addressing relevant issues.

Dialogue: a process of communicating with others; a sincere and mutual exchange involving inquiry, reflection, and responsiveness; interactions *with* one another, rather than *to*, *at*, or *for* others.

Dialogic sensibilities: attitudes, emotions, dispositions, and values required for skillful dialogic interaction.

Discernment: critical thinking and reflective processes involved in unmasking, understanding, and assessing the relative merits of our own and others' grounding assumptions and beliefs.

Diversity: Multiple forms of variability found in nature and society. Human diversity encompasses variability of many forms. These include, but are not limited to, differences in identity, interests, values, beliefs, belief systems, character and disposition, desires, forms of intelligence, perceptual frames, physical characteristics, genetic traits, political sensibilities, passions, moral development, cognitive development, emotional development, aesthetic sensibilities, age, race, religion, ethnicity, education, sex, gender, affectional orientation, and experiences.

Empathy: a means of sincere inquiry; taking deep interest in another's experience, connecting emotionally with another person, and participating in another's experience on his or her own terms.

Epistemology: the study of knowledge and belief.

Ethics: the study and justification of values and of behavioral guidelines; frameworks and resources for recognizing and assessing more or less justified decisions and actions in any given situation.

Formal rationality: associating argumentative validity and reason with certainty and self-evidence.

Instrumental rationality: acting in accordance with one's self interest; privileging ends over means.

Interdependence: a network of relationships where each affects the other in ever widening circles, and in which survival and well-being depend on interconnectedness and reciprocity.

Issue: a point of controversy or disagreement.

Norms: guidelines for disposition, character, communication, and behavior.

Partiality: an orientation to an issue or experience influenced by one's standpoint and commitments; the product of an individual's interpretive lens; communication reflecting one's orientation to an issue or experience.

Partisanship: communication aimed at manipulating audiences or otherwise controlling outcomes in pursuit of one's ends.

Perceptual framework: the lens through which an individual or group perceives experiences, events, information, and ideas.

Perspective: how an individual or group views or relates to relationships, events, circumstances, experiences, ideas, and issues.

Presumption: grounding beliefs and values granted without argument by decision makers in specific contexts.

Publicity: Making public the information necessary to assess deliberations, decisions, and actions.

Reasonableness: a key element of sound deliberative arguments and deliberation integrating emotions, intuitions, facts, values, critical thinking, related discernment process, and logic; a vital antidote to arbitrariness; the heart of sound deliberative argumentation.

Reciprocity: fulfillment of the principle of mutual justifiability; sincere pursuit of fairness; mutual accommodation; treating others as one would wish to be treated.

Responsiveness: taking in and reflecting back the values, needs, interests, and perspectives of another person on his or her own terms; anticipating, fairly representing, and thoughtfully addressing potential stakeholders' values, needs, interests, perspectives, and concerns.

Rhetorical context: The audience, purpose, and occasion situating a communicative act.

Shifting perspectives: imagining circumstances from others' perspectives; standing back and assessing potential consequences of one's actions or decisions from others' points of view; taking full measure of circumstances with others' interests and values at the center; actively pursuing deep insight into what it is like to be in another's place.

Stakeholders: all those potentially affected by the outcome of a deliberative process.

Standpoint: the identities, roles, and status an individual occupies at any given time.

Values: deeply held beliefs or judgments about what is right and wrong, good and bad, just and unjust, wise and unwise, and more or less important.

Value Hierarchy: an individual or group's ordering of values.

Veracity: truthfulness in purpose and means.

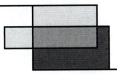

Endnotes

Introduction

[1] James A. Macklin, Jr., *Community over Chaos: An Ecological Perspective on Communication Ethics* (Tuscaloosa and London: The University of Alabama, 1997), p. 2.

[2] Jonathon Haidt, *The Righteous Mind: Why Good People Are Divided by Politics and Religion,* (New York: Pantheon Books, 2012).

[3] Michael Scherer, "Blue Truths, Red Truths," *Time*, October 15, 2012, pp. 24–30.

[4] Ibid., p. 27.

Chapter 1

[1] Deborah Tannen, *The Argument Culture: Moving from Debate to Dialogue* (New York: Random House, 1998).

[2] Ibid., p. 3.

[3] Kristen Renwick Monroe, *The Hand of Compassion: Portraits of Moral Choice during the Holocaust* (Princeton, NJ: Princeton University Press, 2004), p. 222.

[4] Jeffrey B. Rubin, "Hang Up the Gloves: You Landed a Few Good Jabs and Scored the Final Knockout Point. But Did You Really Win Your Last Argument, or Did You Just KO Your Relationship?" *Oprah Magazine*, August 1, 2004, p. 122.

[5] Dennis A. Lynch, Diana George, and Marilyn M. Cooper, "Moments of Argument: Agonistic Inquiry and Confrontational Cooperation." *College Composition and Communication*, 48.1 (February 1997): 65.

[6] Gordon Fellman, *Rambo and the Dalai Lama: The Compulsion to Win and Its Threat to Human Survival* (Albany: State University of New York Press, 1998), p. 44.

[7] Abe Silvers and Ian I. Mitroff, "Parties' Worldviews Limit Real Answers to Problems," *San Francisco Chronicle*, March 14, 2010, p. E8.

[8] "Scott McClellan's Confession," *Wall Street Journal*, May 28, 2008, http://online.wsj.com/article/SB121198457525625977.html?KEYWORDS=scott+mcclellans+confession. For an overview of the controversy surrounding McClellan's critique of Washington's "permanent campaign culture," see, for example, Richard Drew, "Traitor or Truthteller?" May 31, 2008, at http://www.newsweek.com/id/139573

[9] Evan Bayh, "Why I'm Leaving the Senate," February 20, 2010, *New York Times*, http://www.nytimes.com/2010/02/21/opinion/21bayh.html

[10] Daniel Boorstin, cited in Roger Rosenblatt, "The Rugged Individual Rides Again," *Time Magazine*, October 15, 1984, http://www.time.com/time/magazine/article/0,9171,923739,00.htm

[11] Ibid.

[12] President Herbert Hoover, "Rugged Individualism Speech," October 22, 1928, http://www.digitalhistory.uh.edu/disp_textbook.cfm?smtID=3&psid=1334

[13] Joannie Fischer, "Those Rugged Individuals," *U.S. News & World Report*, June 28, 2004, http://www.usnews.com/usnews/news/articles/040628/28self.htm

[14] Kenneth Gergen, *An Invitation to Social Construction*, 2nd ed. (Thousand Oaks, CA: Sage Publications, 2009), p. 86.

[15] Margaret J. Wheatley, *Turning to One Another: Simple Conversations to Restore Hope to the Future* (San Francisco: Berrett-Koehler, 2009), p. 28.

[16] Martha L. McCoy and Patrick L. Scully, "Deliberative Dialogue to Expand Civic Engagement: What Kind of Talk Does Democracy Need?" *National Civic Review*, 91.2 (2002): 117.

[17] Rosenblatt, "The Rugged Individual Rides Again."

Chapter 2

[1] "Ban Stresses Need for Tolerance and Civility Amidst Increasing Polarization," United Nations News Centre, September 10, 2010, http://www.un.org/apps/news/story.asp

[2] Jay Walljasper, "The Victory of the Commons," *Yes Magazine*, October 27, 2009, http://www.yesmagazine.org/new-economy/the-victory-of-the-commons

[3] Vernon L. Smith, "Governing the Commons," *Forbes*, October 12, 2009, http://www.forbes.com/2009/10/12/elinor-ostrom-commons-nobel-economics-opinions-contributors-vernon-l-smith.html

[4] Scott London, "Book Review," review of *Governing the Commons* by Elinor Ostrom, 1998, http://www.scottlondon.com/reviews/ostrom.html

[5] Emphasis added. Fran Korten, "Elinor Ostrom Wins Nobel for Common(s) Sense," *Yes Magazine*, February 26, 2010, http://www.yesmagazine.org/issues/america-the-remix/elinor-ostrom-wins-nobel-for-common-s-sense. Garrett Hardin has since clarified his theory to represent the "tragedy of the unmanaged commons." See Walljasper, "The Victory of the Commons."

[6] Ibid. See also Elinor Ostrom, "8 Keys to a Successful Commons," *Yes Magazine*, February 26, 2010, http://www.yesmagazine.org/issues/america-the-remix/8-keys-to-a-successful-commons

[7] http://www.buzzaboutbees.net/honeybees.html

[8] Doug Schultz (Producer/Writer), *Silence of the Bees*, Nature, 2007, http://www.pbs.org/wnet/nature/episodes/silence-of-the-bees/video-full-episode/251/

[9] For Native American beliefs, see "Shared Beliefs in the Golden Rule (a.k.a. Ethic of Reciprocity)," http://www.religioustolerance.org/reciexce.htm; for the South African philosophy of Ubuntu, see B. J. de Klerk, "Nelson Mandela and Desmond Tutu: Living Icons of Reconciliation," *The Ecumenical Review*, 55.4 (2003): 322–334; Alexandre Dumas, *The Three Musketeers* (Oxford, NY: Oxford University Press, 1998).

[10] For these and other expressions of the concept of interdependence, see "Shared Beliefs in the Golden Rule."

[11] Parliament of the World's Religions, "Declaration Toward a Global Ethic," September 4, 1993, Chicago, IL, http://www.parliamentofreligions.org/_includes/FCKcontent/File/TowardsAGlobalEthic.pdf

[12] Charles Hauss, *Beyond Confrontation: Transforming the New World Order* (Westport, CT: Praeger, 1996), p. 6, emphasis added.

[13] Peter Dizikes, "The Meaning of the Butterfly," *The Boston Globe*, June 8, 2008, http://www.boston.com/bostonglobe/ideas/articles/2008/06/08/the_meaning_of_the_butterfly/?page=2

[14] "Earth Day: The History of a Movement," http://www.earthday.org/earth-day-history-movement

[15] "World Environment Day 2010," United Nations Environment Programme, http://www.unep.org/wed/

[16] "Think Globally, Act Locally," http://en.wikipedia.org/wiki/Think_Globally,_Act_Locally

[17] Sean Cleary, conference remarks [video], "Taking Interdependence Seriously Part 2/10," June 24, 2009, http://www.youtube.com/watch?v=wLHRYnxZoIU

[18] Benjamin Barber, conference remarks [video], "Taking Interdependence Seriously Part 4/10," June 24, 2009, http://www.youtube.com/watch?v=q_ITz7NM7TA

[19] Ibid.

[20] Gordon Brown, "Foreign Policy in an Interdependent World," April 18, 2008, speech presented at the John F. Kennedy Library, Boston, MA, http://www.jfklibrary.org/About-Us/News-and-Press/Press-Releases/~/media/assets/Foundation/Special%20Events/SE_2008_doc_01.pdf

[21] Ibid.

[22] Ibid.

[23] Joseph Farah, "The Meaning of 'Interdependence,'" World Net Daily, May 8, 2008, http://www.wnd.com/2008/05/63630/

[24] Phyllis Schlafly, "Brown's Global Ideals Threaten U.S. Sovereignty," April 28, 2008, http://townhall.com/columnists/phyllisschlafly/2008/04/28/browns_global_ideals_threaten_us_sovereignty

[25] John F. Kennedy, "Address at Independence Hall," July 4, 1962, speech presented at Independence Hall, Philadelphia, PA, http://www.jfklibrary.org/Research/Ready-Reference/JFK-Speeches/Address-at-Independence-Hall-July-4-1962.aspx

[26] Lani Guinier and Gerald Torres, The Miner's Canary: Enlisting Race, Resisting Power, Transforming Democracy (Cambridge, MA: Harvard University Press, 2002), p. 118.

[27] "Tennessee Family's Home Burns to the Ground as Firefighters Stand and Watch," October 5, 2010, http://abcnews.go.com/US/tennessee-familys-home-burns-ground-firefighters-stand-watch/comments?type=story&id=11806407

[28] International Association of Fire Fighters, "Fire Fighters Condemn South Fulton's Decision to Let Home Burn," October 5, 2010, http://www.iaff.org/Comm/PDFs/SouthFulton.pdf

[29] Adam Cohen, "Should Tennessee Firemen Have Let the House Burn?" Time Magazine, October 13, 2010, http://www.time.com/time/nation/article/0,8599,2025342,00.html

[30] Michael Laris, "Should Firefighters Have Let the House Burn?" Seattle Times, October 16, 2010, http://seattletimes.nwsource.com/html/nationworld/2013182015_fees17.html

[31] "Enron: The Smartest Guys in the Room" (Los Angeles: Magnolia Home Entertainment, 2005).

[32] Dr. Dean Robb, "Building Entrepreneurial Enterprises: Lessons from AT&T and Enron," 2004, http://www.barrettwells.co.uk/Entrepreneurial%20Enterprises-ATT-n-Enron4.pd

[33] "Enron."

[34] Ibid.

[35] Ibid.

[36] Simon Romero and Riva D. Atlas, "WorldCom's Collapse: The Overview; WorldCom Files for Bankruptcy; Largest U.S. Case," New York Times, July 22, 2002, http://www.nytimes.com/2002/07/22/us/worldcom-s-collapse-the-overview-worldcom-files-for-bankruptcy-largest-us-case.html

[37] "Financial Crisis of 2007–2008," Wikipedia, http://en.wikipedia.org/wiki/Financial_crisis_of_2007%E2%80%932010

[38] Sam Mamudi, "Lehman Folds with Record $613 Billion Debt," Marketwatch, September 15, 2008, http://www.marketwatch.com/story/lehman-folds-with-record-613-billion-debt?siteid=rss

[39] Gael O'Brien, "Lehman Brothers' Perfect Storm: Where Ethical Lapses Met Bad Judgment," This Week in Ethics, April 20, 2010, http://theweekinethics.wordpress.com/2010/03/18/lehman-brothers%E2%80%99-perfect-storm-where-ethical-lapses-met-bad-judgment/; Stephen Gandel, "Lehmann Examiner Finds Fraud, Probably," Curious Capitalist Blog, Time

Magazine, March 12, 2010, http://curiouscapitalist.blogs.time.com/2010/03/12/lehman-examiner-finds-fraud-possibly/

[40] Andrew Sheng, Chief Advisor, China Banking Regulatory Commission, quoted in Charles Ferguson, transcript for "Inside Job," September 2010, http://www.sonyclassics.com/awards-information/insidejob_screenplay.pdf.

[41] Thomas B. Edsall, "Surveys: Americans Grip to Individualism in Economic Storm," April 17, 2009, *Huffington Post*, http://www.huffingtonpost.com/2009/03/17/surveys-americans-grip-to_n_175618.html

[42] Ibid.

[43] Palash R. Gosh, "Income Gap between Rich and Poor at Record High," *International Business Times*, September 29, 2010, http://www.ibtimes.co.in/art/services/print.php?articleid=66809

[44] Edsall, "Surveys."

[45] Dr. Ralph de la Torre, "The Values that Shape the Health Care Debate," *Bloomberg Business Week*, April 23, 2010, http://www.businessweek.com/managing/content/apr2010/ca20100422_198383.htm

[46] Joannie Fischer, "Those Rugged Individuals," *U.S. News & World Report*, June 28, 2004, http://www.usnews.com/usnews/news/articles/040628/28self.htm

[47] Ira Chaleff, "Congress Needs to Avoid Metaphor," *Monterey Herald*, June 6, 2011, p. A-10

[48] David Korten, "We Are Hard-Wired to Care and Connect," *Yes Magazine*, October 2008, p. 51.

[49] Thomas Hobbes, *The Leviathan* (1651), http://oregonstate.edu/instruct/phl302/texts/hobbes/leviathan-c.html

[50] Korten, "We Are Hard-Wired," p. 49.

[51] Ibid.

[52] Ibid.

[53] Dachner Keltner, "The Compassionate Instinct," in D. Keltner, J. Marsh, and J. A. Smith (Eds.), *The Compassionate Instinct* (New York: W.W. Norton, 2010), p. 11.

[54] Elizabeth W. Dunn, Lara B. Aknin, and Michael I. Norton, "Spending Money on Others Promotes Happiness," *Science*, 319.5870 (March 2008): 1687–1688.

[55] Ibid., pp. 49–50.

[56] Frans de Waal, *The Age of Empathy: Nature's Lessons for a Kinder Society* (New York: Harmony Books, 2009), p. 11.

[57] Keltner, "The Compassionate Instinct," p. 15.

[58] Daniel Cohen, "Argument Is War . . . and War Is Hell: Philosophy, Education, and Metaphors for Argumentation," *Informal Logic*, 17.2 (1995): 178. The war-metaphor observation is attributed originally to George Lakoff and Mark Johnson's *Metaphors We Live By* (Chicago: University of Chicago, 1980).

[59] Deborah Tannen, *The Argument Culture: Moving from Debate to Dialogue* (New York: Random House, 1998), p. 3.

[60] Ronald D. Gordon, "Beyond the Failures of Western Communication Theory," *Journal of Multicultural Discourses*, 2.2 (2007): 100.

[61] Pamela Morgan with Susan Bales, "Competition, Cooperation, and Connection: How These Metaphors Affect Child Advocacy," *Frameworks Institute: Changing the Public Conversation about Social Problems*, http://www.frameworksinstitute.org/ezine11.html

[62] Ibid.

[63] Ibid.

[64] James R. Brockman, *The Violence of Love: Oscar Romero* (Farmington, PA: Plough Publishing House, 1998), p. 29.

[65] Sharon D. Welch, *Sweet Dreams in America: Making Ethics and Spirituality Work* (New York: Routledge, 1999), p. 84.

Chapter 3

[1] David Matthews, "Foreword," in Derek W. M. Barker, Noelle McAfee, and David W. McIvor (Eds.), *Democratizing Deliberation: A Political Anthology* (Dayton, OH: Kettering Foundation Press, 2012), p. viii.

[2] Ibid.

[3] See, for example, Haidt's discussion of why "our in-house press secretary automatically justifies everything" in Jonathon Haidt, *The Righteous Mind: Why Good People Are Divided by Politics and Religion* (New York, Pantheon Press, 2012), pp. 78–80.

[4] Ronald C. Arnett, *Communication and Community: Implications of Martin Buber's Dialogue*, (Carbondale: Southern Illinois University Press, 1986), p. 97.

[5] Amy Gutmann and Dennis Thompson, *Democracy and Disagreement: Why Moral Conflict Cannot Be Avoided in Politics and What Should Be Done about It* (Cambridge: Harvard University Press, 1996), p. 1.

[6] Ibid., p. 2.

[7] Barack Obama, *The Audacity of Hope* (New York: Crown Publishers, 2006), p. 48.

[8] Peter James Spielmann, "Researchers Battle Over War Dead," *Monterey Herald*, July 13, 2009, pp. A1 and A11.

[9] Ibid.

[10] Darrel Huff, *How to Lie with Statistics* (New York: W.W. Norton, 1954).

[11] From Karyn C. Rybacki and Donald J. Rybacki, *Advocacy and Opposition: An Introduction to Argumentation* (Englewood Cliffs, NJ: Prentice-Hall, 1986), pp. 150–151.

[12] Edward D'Angelo, *The Teaching of Critical Thinking* (Amsterdam: B.R. Gruner, 1971), p. 7.

[13] John Chafee, *Thinking Critically*, 2nd ed. (Boston: Houghton Mifflin, 1988), p. 1.

[14] Sut Jhally (Producer), *bell hooks: Cultural Critical and Transformation* (video) (Media Education Foundation, Northampton, MA, 1997).

[15] Trudy Govier, *Social Trust and Human Communities* (Montreal and Kingston: McGill-Queens, 1997), p. 244. For an extended discussion of cynicism, see chapter 11, "Cynicism, Pessimism, Optimism, and Hope," pp. 237–257.

[16] Martha C. Nussbaum, *Cultivating Humanity: A Classical Defense of Reform in Liberal Education* (Cambridge: Harvard University, 1997), p. 38.

[17] President Barack Obama, remarks presented in Cairo, June 4, 2009, http://www.whitehouse.gov/the-press-office/remarks-president-cairo-university-6-04-09

[18] Kate Miller Heidtke, "Caught in the Crowd," *Song of the Day*, May 10, 2010, NPR music, http://www.npr.org/templates/story/story.php?storyId=126556535

[19] Irving I. Janis, *Groupthink*, 2nd ed. (Boston: Houghton Mifflin, 1982), pp. 14–47.

[20] Ibid., p. 2.

[21] "The Defense Secretary Who Was Undone by Vietnam," *The Week*, Obituaries, July 17, 2009, p. 43.

[22] Janis, *Groupthink*, p. 197.

Chapter 4

[1] The phrase "bowling alone" has come to signify community breakdown in the United States, made popular by Robert Putnam's best-selling book, *Bowling Alone: The Collapse and Revival of American Community* (New York: Simon and Schuster, 2000), http://bowlingalone.com/

[2] Jesse Washington, "Rodney King Death: 'Can We All Get Along?' Plea Measures His Lasting Meaning," *Huffington Post*, June 17, 2012, http://www.huffingtonpost.com/2012/06/17/rodney-king-death-can-we-all-get-along_n_1604450.html; see also Rodney King, "L.A. Riots 1992: Rodney King Speaks," http://www.youtube.com/watch?v=tgiR04ey7-M

[3] Robert Wright, *Nonzero: The Logic of Human Destiny* (New York: Vintage, 2000), p. 98.

⁴ Joshua Wolf Shenk, "What Makes Us Happy?" *The Atlantic*, June 2009, http://www.theatlantic.com/magazine/archive/2009/06/what-makes-us-happy/7439/1/

⁵ Sharon Begley, "Why Money Doesn't Buy Happiness," *Newsweek*, October 15, 2007, http://www.newsweek.com/2007/10/14/why-money-doesn-t-buy-happiness.html

⁶ John Donne, *Meditation XVII*, cited online at http://isu.indstate.edu/ilnprof/ENG451/ISLAND/text.html

⁷ Michael P. Nichols, cited in Kathleen M. Hunzer, "Lessons from the Public Sphere: Listening, Adversity, and Learning," *The International Journal of Listening*, 22 (2008): 97.

⁸ See, for example, Kirsten Powers, "Rush Limbaugh Isn't the Only Media Misogynist," *The Daily Beast.com*, March 4, 2012, http://www.thedailybeast.com/articles/2012/03/04/rush-limbaugh-s-apology-liberal-men-need-to-follow-suit.html

⁹ J. Peder Zane, "The Lost Art of Empathy," *The Daily Caller*, April 10, 2012, http://dailycaller.com/2012/04/10/the-lost-art-of-empathy/

¹⁰ Dara Chadwick, "To Hell with That: Why Being 'Ladylike' Can Be Bad for Your Body Image," *Psychology Today*, July 25, 2011, http://www.psychologytoday.com/blog/youd-be-so-pretty-if/201107/hell-why-being-ladylike-can-be-bad-your-body-image

¹¹ John E. McIntyre, "Getting Uppity," *The Baltimore Sun*, December 1, 2011, http://weblogs.baltimoresun.com/news/mcintyre/blog/2011/12/getting_uppity.html

¹² Nina M. Lozano-Reich and Dana L. Cloud, "The Uncivil Tongue: Invitational Rhetoric and the Problem of Inequality," *Western Journal of Communication*, 73.2 (April–June 2009): 223.

¹³ A. C. Grayling, "The Last Word on Civility," *The Guardian*, April 14, 2000, http://www.guardian.co.uk/books/2000/apr/15/books.guardianreview7

¹⁴ Shankar Vedantam, "Social Isolation Growing in U.S., Study Says," *Washington Post*, June 23, 2006, http://www.washingtonpost.com/wp-dyn/content/article/2006/06/22/AR2006062201763_pf.html

¹⁵ Lynn Smith-Lovin, cited in ibid.

¹⁶ "69 Percent of Americans Shut Their Wallets Due to Incivility, According to New Weber Shandwick Survey," June 21, 2011, http://www.webershandwick.com/Default.aspx/AboutUs/PressReleases/2011/69PercentofAmericansShutTheirWalletsDuetoIncivilityAccordingtoNewWeberShandwickSurvey

¹⁷ Megan J. Laverty, "Communication and Civility," in Deborah S. Mower and Wade S. Robison (Eds.), *Civility in Politics and Education* (New York: Routledge, 2012), p. 65.

¹⁸ Kay Whitlock, "Our Enemies, Ourselves: Why Anti-Violence Movement Must Replace the Dualism of 'Us and Them' with an Ethic of Interdependence," in Elizabeth J. Castelli and Janet R. Jakobsen (Eds.), *Interventions: Activists and Academics Respond to Violence* (New York: Palgrave Macmillan, 2004), p. 211.

¹⁹ Robert A. Bode, "Mahatma Gandhi's Theory of Nonviolent Communication," paper presented at the Annual Meeting of the Western States Communication Association, Portland, OR, February 1995.

²⁰ Michael Bader, "How We Can Inspire People to Care about Social Change and Feel Good about Themselves in the Process," *Alternet*, August 2, 2011, www.alternet.org/story/151868

²¹ Kenneth L. Smith and Ira G. Zepp, Jr., "Martin Luther King's Vision of the Beloved Community," *Christian Century*, April 3, 1974, pp. 361–363, reprinted online at http://www.religion-online.org/showarticle.asp?title=1603

²² A. C. Grayling, "The Last Word on Civility."

²³ We take up the concept of understanding—and all the attendant misunderstandings surrounding it—in a later chapter.

²⁴ C. W. Nevius, "Little Bird Coffeehouse Dispute Gets Settled," *San Francisco Chronicle*, March 22, 2011, p. C1, emphasis added.

²⁵ A number of graphs contrasting dialogue and debate are available online and in press. Three representative examples which informed the enclosed table include A. Diaz and S. Hiroshi Gilchrist, "Dialogue on Campus: An Overview of Promising Practices," *Journal of Public Deliberation*, 6.1 (2010): 2–3, http://services.bepress.com/jpd/vol6/iss1/art9/; O. Escobar, "The Dialogic Turn: Dialogue for Deliberation," *In-Spire Journal of Law, Politics*

and Societies, 4.1 (2009): 55, http://www.in-spire.org/archive/vol4-no2/Escobar42.pdf; and "The Difference between Debate and Dialogue," in *One America Dialogue Guide: The President's Initiative on Race*, n.d., http://clinton3.nara.gov/Initiatives/OneAmerica/a2.html. Notably, most graphs depict debate as inevitably adversarial. In our explorations of the genre, we've offered a cooperative approach to debate featuring the knowledge, skills, sensibilities, and purposes associated with dialogic communication. For details, see J. M. Makau and D. L. Marty, *Cooperative Argumentation: A Model of Deliberative Community* (Long Grove, IL: Waveland Press, 2001).

26 The concept, *balanced partiality*, will be explained in later chapters. The phrase comes from Quaker mediator Mike Yarrow. See John A. McConnell, *Mindful Mediation: A Handbook for Buddhist Peacemakers* (Bangkok: Buddhist Research Institute and Mahachula Buddhist University, 1995), p. 246.

27 Robyn Penman, *Reconstructing Communicating: Looking to a Future* (Mahwah, NJ: Lawrence Erlbaum Associates, 2000), p. 5.

28 W. Barnett Pearce and Kimberly A. Pearce, "Taking a Communication Perspective on Dialogue," in R. Anderson, L. Baxter, and K. N. Cissna (Eds.), *Dialogue—Theorizing Difference in Communication Studies* (Thousand Oaks, CA: Sage Publications, 2004), p. 45.

29 Public Conversations Project, "Talking with the Enemy," *Boston Globe*, January 28, 2001, http://pubpages.unh.edu/~jds/BostonGlobe.htm; see also http://www.publicconversations.org/

30 Kenneth J. Gergen, *An Invitation to Social Construction* (London: Sage Publications, 1999), p. 155.

31 Ibid.

32 Ibid., pp.155–156.

33 Renato Rosaldo, *Culture and Truth: The Remaking of Social Analysis* (Boston: Beacon Books, 1993), p. 19.

34 Sharon Ellison, *Don't Be So Defensive: Taking the War Out of Our Words with Powerful, Non-Defensive Communication* (Kansas City, MO: Andrews McMeel Publishing, 1998), p. 15. Emphasis in the original.

35 Ronald D. Gordon, "The Difference between Feeling Defensive and Feeling Understood," *The Journal of Business Communication*, 25.1 (1988): 62.

36 Frances S. Chen, Julia A. Minson, and Zakary L. Tormala, "Tell Me More: The Effects of Expressed Interest on Receptiveness during Dialog," *Journal of Experimental Social Psychology*, 46 (2010): 850.

37 William Blake, "Auguries of Innocence," in David V. Erdman (Ed.), *The Complete Poetry and Prose of William Blake* (Berkeley: University of California Press, 1982), p. 490.

38 The concept of *interpretive framing* is explained in later chapters.

39 "Amish Forgive, Pray and Mourn," *CBS News*, October 4, 2006, http://www.cbsnews.com/stories/2006/10/04/national/main2059816.shtml

40 Trudy Govier, *Social Trust and Human Communities* (Montreal: McGill-Queen's University Press, 1997), p. 61.

41 Leonard Swidler, "Seven Stages of Deep Dialogue," *The Dialogue Institute*, http://institute.jesdialogue.org/resources/tools/sevenstages/

42 Bob Abernethy, "Amish Forgiveness: An Interview with Stephen Nolt," *Religion and Ethics Newsweekly*, September 21, 2007, http://www.pbs.org/wnet/religionandethics/episodes/september-21-2007/amish-forgiveness/4295/

43 Kristen Renwick Monroe, *The Hand of Compassion: Portraits of Moral Choice during the Holocaust* (Princeton, NJ: Princeton University Press, 2004), p. 222.

44 Parker J. Palmer, *To Know as We Are Known: Education as a Spiritual Journey* (New York: HarperCollins, 1983), p. 40.

45 Ibid.

46 Michel Martin, "Urban Violence on the Rise: An Interview with Gary Fields and Tio Hardiman," *National Public Radio*, May 8, 2008, http://www.npr.org/templates/story/story.php?storyId=90272826. Emphasis added.

47 "Riding Along with CeaseFire's 'Violence Interrupters,'" *CBS Chicago*, June 2, 2011, http://chicago.cbslocal.com/2011/06/02/the-ceasefire-method-defuse-tension-before-violence/

48 Mat Edelson, "Murder, Interrupted. Can an Innovative Anti-Violence Program Rewrite the Code of the Streets?" *Urbanite*, May 1, 2008, http://www.urbanitebaltimore.com/baltimore/murder-interrupted/

49 "CeaseFire: The Campaign to Stop the Shooting," *The Chicago Project for Violence Prevention*, http://www.ceasefirechicago.org/cpvp.shtml; Nancy Ritter, "CeaseFire: A Public Health Approach to Reduce Shootings and Killings," *National Institute of Justice Journal*, 264 (November 2009), http://killingseasonchicago2010.blogspot.com/2010/08/ceasefire-campaign-to-stop-shooting.html; Josh Gryniewicz, "CeaseFire in Iraq—The Social Innovation Kind," *Insight on Conflict*, March 30, 2011, http://www.insightonconflict.org/2011/03/ceasefire-in-iraq/

50 "Talking with a Purpose: When Dialogue Is Not Just Talk," *Communication for Social Change Consortium*, n.d., http://www.communicationforsocialchange.org/mazi-articles.php?id=268

51 "Iran and Switzerland Hold the 3rd Conference on Interfaith Dialogue," *Ahlul Bayt News Agency*, January 8, 2008, http://www.abna.ir/

52 Katherine Cramer Walsh, *Talking about Race: Community Dialogues and the Politics of Difference* (Chicago and London: University of Chicago Press, 2007), p. 49.

53 Robert C. Solomon and Fernando Flores, *Building Trust in Business, Politics, Relationships, and Life* (New York: Oxford University Press, 2001), p. 99. Emphasis in the original.

54 Audre Lorde, *Sister/Outsider: Essays and Speeches* (Trumansburg, NY: The Crossing Press, 1984), p. 115. Lorde actually said that "we have no patterns for relating across our human differences as equals," but, as this book has demonstrated, many scholars and activists have been developing theories, models, and practices to remedy this lack.

55 Mark DeMoss, "Don't Expect Civility," *Politico*, January 17, 2011, http://www.politico.com/news/stories/0111/47677.html

56 Ibid. The three politicians who signed the civility pledge were Senator Joseph Lieberman (I-CT), Rep. Frank Wolf (R-VA), and Rep. Sue Myrick (R-NC).

57 Ibid., emphasis added.

58 Mark DeMoss, "Open Letter to Sen. Lieberman, Rep. Wolf, and Rep. Myrick," January 3, 2011, http://www.demossnews.com/resources/civility_project.pdf. Emphasis added.

59 Mark DeMoss, "Don't Expect Civility."

60 Taffy Brodesser-Akner, "I Can't Believe My Best Friend Is a Republican," *Salon*, April 5, 2011, http://www.salon.com/2011/04/06/my_best_friend_is_a_republican/

61 Matthew Cochrane, "Help! My Best Friend Is a Liberal Democrat!" Conservative 21: Using Conservative Principles to Solve 21st Century Problems, July 21, 2011, http://www.conservative21.net/displayart.cfm?docid=4873

62 Elizabeth Lesser, "Take 'The Other' to Lunch," talk given at *TED: Ideas Worth Spreading*, January 2011, http://www.ted.com/talks/elizabeth_lesser_take_the_other_to_lunch.html

63 Dana Bash, "Mikulski Makes History While Creating 'Zone of Civility' for Senate Women," *CNN*, March 17, 2012, http://www.cnn.com/2012/03/16/politics/mikulski-history/index.html

64 Sam Stein, "Podesta: Obama-Bush Relationship 'Collegial and Cooperative,'" *Huffington Post*, November 11, 2008, http://www.huffingtonpost.com/2008/11/11/podesta-obama-bush-relati_n_143061.html

65 Cal Thomas, "Rachel Maddow and My Lesson in Civility," *The Baltimore Sun*, February 18, 2012, http://articles.baltimoresun.com/2012-02-18/news/bal-rachel-maddow-and-my-lesson-in-civility-20120216_1_apology-contraception-red-meat

66 Ibid.

67 Ibid., emphasis added.

68 Rachel Maddow, transcript, "The Rachel Maddow Show for Monday, March 5, 2012," http://www.msnbc.msn.com/id/46642619/ns/msnbc_tv-rachel_maddow_show/t/rachel-maddow-show-monday-march/#.T4nyCdnGjcY

[69] James Lawrence, "The Cal Thomas-Rachel Maddow Pow-Wow," *The Democrat and Chronicle.com*, March 8, 2012, http://blogs.democratandchronicle.com/editorial/

[70] Thomas W. Benson, "The Rhetoric of Civility: Power, Authenticity, and Democracy," *Journal of Contemporary Rhetoric*, 1.1, (2011): 23, http://contemporaryrhetoric.com/articles/benson1_3.pdf

[71] Ronald C. Arnett and Pat Arneson, *Dialogic Civility in a Cynical Age: Community, Hope, and Interpersonal Relationships* (Albany: State University of New York Press, 1999); Susan Herbst, *Rude Democracy: Civility and Incivility in American Politics* (Philadelphia: Temple University Press, 2010); Rod L. Troester and Cathy Sargent Mester, *Civility in Business and Professional Communication* (New York: Peter Lang Publishing, 2007).

[72] Cheshire Calhoun, "The Virtue of Civility," *Philosophy and Public Affairs*, 29.3 (2000): 260, emphasis added.

[73] Ismael Garcia, *Dignidad: Ethics Through Hispanic Eyes* (Nashville, TN: Abingdon Press, 1997), p. 67.

[74] Trudy Govier, *Dilemmas of Trust* (Montreal: McGill-Queen's University Press, 1998), p. 106.

[75] Robert B. Lousen, *Morality and Moral Theory: A Reappraisal and Reaffirmation* (New York: Oxford University Press, 1992), p. 25.

[76] Richard L. Johannesen, *Ethics in Human Communication*, 6th ed. (Long Grove, IL: Waveland Press, 2008), p. 56

[77] Ibid., p. 52.

[78] bell hooks and Cornel West, *Breaking Bread: Insurgent Black Intellectual Life* (Boston: South End Press, 1991), p. 5.

[79] Ibid.

[80] Sara Lawrence-Lightfoot, *Respect: An Exploration* (Reading, MA: Perseus, 1999), p. 9.

[81] Ibid., pp. 9–10.

[82] Ryan Lizza, "Biden's Brief: Obama Picked His Running Mate to Help Him Govern," *The New Yorker*, October 20, 2008, http://www.newyorker.com/reporting/2008/10/20/081020fa_fact_lizza

[83] Congressional Power Rankings 2008, http://www.congress.org/congressorg/power_rankings/overall.tt. Senator Biden was ranked 19th overall in senatorial effectiveness, based on criteria including position, influence, and legislation. When it came to passing legislation, which depends on the ability to work with colleagues for support and votes, Senator Biden ranked 5th.

[84] Samantha Pergadia, "Ginsburg: Mutual Respect Unites Nine," *The Daily Princetonian*, October 24, 2008, http://www.dailyprincetonian.com/2008/10/24/21918

[85] Marguerite La Caze, "Seeing Oneself through the Eyes of the Other: Asymmetrical Reciprocity and Self-respect," *Hypatia*, 23.3 (2008): 121.

[86] Ibid., pp. 121–122.

[87] Megan Laverty, "Communication and Civility," p. 67.

[88] "The Universal Declaration of Human Rights" was adopted by the United Nations General Assembly in 1948, emphasis added. http://www.un.org/en/documents/udhr/

Chapter 5

[1] Michael E. Ross, "Oh Lord, Kumbaya: How an Innocent Campfire Song Got Warped by the Cynicism of Our Times," *The Root*, October 13, 2008, http://www.theroot.com/views/oh-lord-kumbaya

[2] The term *critical self-reflection* connotes an interdependent sense of self, rather than rugged individualism. This meaning adheres in all usages including critical self-reflection, self-reflection, and simply, reflection.

[3] W. Barnett Pearce and Kimberley A. Pearce, cited in N. J. Heidlebaugh, "Invention and Public Dialogue: Lessons from Rhetorical Theories," *Communication Theory*, 18 (2008): 30.

[4] Professor Lynne Cameron distinguishes between self-focused and other-focused empathy. "The former," she says, "requires me to understand how I would feel in the other's situation—to walk in someone else's shoes—while the latter seeks to understand how it is to be in the other's situation." See Cameron's comments in "New Approaches to Conflict Transformation: Trust, Empathy and Dialogue," a Workshop Report, David Davies Memorial Institute of International Studies, Department of International Politics, Aberystyth University, June 23–24, 2010.

[5] Toni Suzuki Laidlaw, David M. Kaufman, Joan Sargeant, Heather McLeod, Kim Blake, and David Simpson, "What Makes a Physician an Exemplary Communicator with Patients?" *Patient Education and Counseling*, 68.2 (2007): 153–160. Emphasis added.

[6] Ibid.

[7] The term "non-judgmental" is used often to describe the basis for compassionate communication. Below, we use the phrase "suspending judgment" to more precisely describe the actual process of setting aside the inevitable reactions that occur during dialogue. However, both terms appear in the interdisciplinary literature on compassion and communication and, ultimately, describe the same communication dynamic.

[8] Laidlaw, et al., "What Makes a Physician an Exemplary Communicator?"

[9] Ibid.

[10] Peter R. Lichstein, "The Medical Interview," in H. K. Walker, W. D. Hall, and J. W. Hurst (Eds.), *Clinical Methods: The History, Physical and Laboratory Examinations*, 3rd ed. (Boston: Butterworths, 1990), http://www.ncbi.nlm.nih.gov/books/NBK349/

[11] Laidlaw, et al., "What Makes a Physician an Exemplary Communicator?" Emphasis added. For corresponding research on nurses' communication skills, see Anne Lene Sorenson, "Developing Personal Competence in Nursing Students through International Clinical Practice: With Emphasis on Communication and Empathy," *Journal of Intercultural Communication*, 19 (2009).

[12] "Obama Nominates Sonia Sotomayor to Supreme Court," May 26, 2009, http://www.cnn.com/2009/POLITICS/05/26/supreme.court/

[13] Peter Slevin, "Obama Makes Empathy a Requirement for the Court," *Washington Post*, May 13, 2009, http://www.washingtonpost.com/wp-dyn/content/article/2009/05/12/AR2009051203515.html

[14] Rich Lowry, "A Bad Day for Impartiality," *National Review Online*, May 26, 2009, http://article.nationalreview.com/?q=MzBhMjVjYTcyNjU0ZmU1NzVhMjM0YWE5ZTdkYmY1ODM=

[15] Slevin, "Obama Makes Empathy a Requirement for the Court."

[16] Karl Rove, "'Empathy Is Code for Judicial Activism," *The Wall Street Journal*, May 28, 2009, http://www.rove.com/articles/156

[17] Slevin, "Obama Makes Empathy a Requirement for the Court."

[18] Ellen Goodman, "What's So Bad about Empathy?" *Boston Globe*, May 22, 2009, www.boston.com/bostonglobe/editorial_opinion/oped/articles/2009/05/22/whats_so_bad_about_empathy/

[19] Eric Liu, respondent to "What Is It about the Word Empathy?" *Politico: The Arena*, May 22, 2009, http://www.politico.com/arena/archive/newspoliticosupremecourtempathy.html, emphasis in the original.

[20] Kent Greenfield, "The Supreme Court, Empathy, and the Science of Decision Making," *Huffington Post*, May 25, 2009, http://www.huffingtonpost.com/kent-greenfield/the-supreme-court-empathy_b_206604.html

[21] Dan Froomkin, "The Empathy War," *Washington Post*, May 13, 2009, http://voices.washingtonpost.com/white-house-watch/2009/05/the_empathy_war/pf.html

[22] The interdisciplinary literature on perspective taking is extensive and problematizes the understanding of empathy as "walking a mile in someone else's shoes."

[23] Douglas W. Kmiec, "The Case for Empathy: Why a Much Maligned Value Is a Crucial Qualification for the Supreme Court," *The National Catholic Weekly*, May 11, 2009, www.americamagazine.org/content/article.cfm?article_id=11649

[24] Lynne Henderson, "Legality and Empathy," *Michigan Law Review*, 85 (June 1987): 1576–1577, emphasis added.

[25] Ibid., p. 1576. On the definition of empathy, Henderson states that there are "three basic phenomena captured by the word: (1) feeling the emotion of another; (2) understanding the experience or situation of another, both affectively and cognitively, often achieved by imagining oneself to be in the position of the other; and (3) action brought about by experiencing the distress of another (hence the confusion of empathy with sympathy and compassion). The first two forms are ways of knowing, the third forms a catalyst for action."

[26] Cameron, "New Approaches to Conflict Transformation.

[27] Daniel Goleman, "On Compassion," *TED: Ideas Worth Spreading*, March 2007, http://www.ted.com/talks/daniel_goleman_on_compassion.html

[28] Charles Derber, *The Pursuit of Attention: Power and Ego in Everyday Life* (New York: Oxford University Press, 2000), p. 27. For an in-depth explanation of supportive, nondefensive assertions and questions, see Sharon Ellison, *Don't Be So Defensive: Taking the War Out of Our Words with Powerful, Non-Defensive Communication* (Kansas City, MO: Andrews McMeel Publishing, 1998).

[29] Roger Fisher and Daniel Shapiro, *Beyond Reason: Using Emotions as You Negotiate* (New York: Penguin, 2005), p. 29.

[30] Sara H. Konrath, Edward H. O'Brien, and Courtney Hsing, "Changes in Dispositional Empathy in American College Students Over Time: A Meta-Analysis," *Personality and Social Psychology Review*, 15 (May 2011): 180–198.

[31] Pamela Paul, "As for Empathy, The Haves Have Not," *New York Times*, December 30, 2010, http://www.nytimes.com/2011/01/02/fashion/02studied.html?_r=0; Maia Szalavitz, "The Rich Are Different: More Money, Less Empathy," *Time Magazine*, November 24, 2010, http://healthland.time.com/2010/11/24/the-rich-are-different-more-money-less-empathy/

[32] Joan Silk, "Fellow Feeling—Review of *The Age of Empathy: Nature's Lessons for a Kinder Society* by Frans de Waal," *American Scientist*, May 23, 2010, http://www.powells.com/review/2010_05_23.html

[33] Urie Bronfenbrenner, cited in Sheldon H. Berman, "The Bridge to Civility: Empathy, Ethics and Service," *The School Administrator* (May 1998), http://www.aasa.org/SchoolAdministratorArticle.aspx?id=15272

[34] Jim A. Kuypers, Megan Hitchner, James Irwin, and Alexander Wilson, "Compassionate Conservatism: The Rhetorical Reconstruction of Conservative Rhetoric," *American Communication Journal*, 6 (Summer 2003), http://ac-journal.org/journal/vol6/iss4/iss4/articles/kuypers.htm

[35] President George W. Bush, "The President's Radio Address to the Nation," June 28, 2008, http://georgewbush-whitehouse.archives.gov/rss/radioaddress.xml

[36] Rachel Naomi Remen, "Helping, Fixing or Serving?" *Shambhala Sun*, September 1999, p. 25.

[37] Ibid.

[38] Ibid.

[39] Ibid.

[40] Diana L. Rehling, "Compassionate Listening: A Framework for Listening to the Seriously Ill," *International Journal of Listening*, 22.1 (2008): 84–85.

[41] Ibid., p. 85.

[42] Ibid.

[43] Marshall B. Rosenberg, *Nonviolent Communication: A Language of Life*, 2nd ed. (Encinitas, CA: Puddle Dancer Press, 2003), pp. 92–93. Some modifications were made to Rosenberg's list.

[44] Rehling, "Compassionate Listening," p. 86.

[45] Ibid., p. 88.

[46] See chapter 9 for an in-depth exploration of discernment.

[47] Martha Nussbaum, cited in Lisbeth Lipari, "Listening Otherwise: The Voice of Ethics," *International Journal of Listening*, 23.1 (2009): 50.

[48] Lipari, "Listening Otherwise," p. 50.

[49] Pema Chodron, *Start Where You Are: A Guide to Compassionate Living* (Boston: Shambhala, 2001), pp. 5–6.

[50] Sharon Salzberg, *The Force of Kindness* (Boulder, CO: Sounds True, 2005), pp. 54–55.

[51] Katherine I. Miller, "Compassionate Communication in the Workplace: Exploring Processes of Noticing, Connecting, and Responding," *Journal of Applied Communication Research*, 35.3 (August 2007): 225.

[52] Theodore Roethke, "Lines Upon Leaving a Sanitarium," in *The Collected Poems of Theodore Roethke* (New York: Anchor, 1975), p. 249.

[53] Carol Parker Terhune, "'Can We Talk?' Using Critical Self-Reflection and Dialogue to Build Diversity and Change Organizational Culture in Nursing Schools," *Journal of Cultural Diversity*, 13.3 (Fall 2006): 144.

[54] Public Conversations Project, "Talking with the Enemy," *Boston Globe*, January 28, 2001.

[55] Rosenberg, *Nonviolent Communication*, p. 142.

[56] David Stein, "Teaching Critical Reflection," Myths and Realities 7, 2000, http://www.calpro-online.org/eric/textonly/docgen.asp?tbl=mr&ID=98

[57] Michelle Maise, "The Need for Dialogue." In Guy Burgess and Heidi Burgess (Eds.), *Beyond Intractability*. Conflict Research Consortium (Boulder: University of Colorado, 2003), http://www.beyondintractability.org/essay/dialogue/

[58] Stephen Brookfield, "Critically Reflective Teaching," talk given at J. Sargeant Reynolds Community College, April 19, 2001, http://vccslitonline.cc.va.us/mrcte/brookfield.htm

[59] Kristin Neff, "Why Self-Compassion Trumps Self-Esteem," Greater Good: The Science of a Meaningful Life, May 27, 2011, http://greatergood.berkeley.edu/article/item/try_selfcompassion/

[60] Van Jones, "A License to Be Human: An Interview with Laird Thompson," *Orion Magazine*, May/June 2006, http://vanjones.net/

[61] Ibid.

[62] Jack R. Gibb, "Defensive Communication," *Journal of Communication*, 11 (1961): 141.

[63] Ellison, *Don't Be So Defensive*, p. 16.

[64] Khaleel Mohammed, "The Art of Heeding," *Journal of Ecumenical Studies*, 43.2 (Spring 2008): 75–97. As noted above, dialogic participants will differ in their assessments of each other's behavior. What is rude to one may be direct communication to another.

[65] Indra Nooyi, "The Best Advice I Ever Got," April 30, 2008, http://money.cnn.com/galleries/2008/fortune/0804/gallery.bestadvice.fortune/7.html

[66] Ibid.

[67] A. C. Grayling, "The Last Word on Civility," *The Guardian*, April 14, 2000, http://www.guardian.co.uk/books/2000/apr/15/books.guardianreview7

[68] Megan Laverty, "Civility, Tact and the Joy of Communication," *Philosophy of Education*, 2009, p. 235, http://ojs.ed.uiuc.edu/index.php/pes/article/view/2706/1036

[69] Ibid., emphasis added.

[70] Gibb, "Defensive Communication," p. 147.

[71] Jon Katz, *Izzy and Lenore: Two Dogs, an Unexpected Journey, and Me* (New York: Villard, 2008), p. 38.

[72] Ibid.

[73] Gibb, "Defensive Communication," pp. 38–39. In his explanation, Gibb's terminology comingles language set out earlier to distinguish empathy and compassion. Not only are the definitions of empathy and compassion often conflated, these communication capacities do work in concert to support dialogic goals.

[74] Joanna Macy, *Despair and Personal Power in the Nuclear Age* (Philadelphia: New Society, 1983), pp. 44–45.

[75] Julian Portilla, "An Interview with Julia Chaitin: To Reflect and Trust," 2003, http://beyondintractability.colorado.edu/audio/10188/

[76] Sissela Bok, *Lying: Moral Choice in Public and Private Life* (New York: Vintage, 1999), p. 31.

[77] Mohammed, "The Art of Heeding."

[78] William B. Irvine, *A Guide to the Good Life: The Ancient Art of Stoic Joy* (New York: Oxford University Press, 2008), pp. 136–137.

[79] Ibid.

[80] Ibid.

[81] Martin Luther King, Jr. "Loving Your Enemies," Montgomery, AL, November 17, 1957, http://www.ipoet.com/ARCHIVE/BEYOND/King-Jr/Loving-Your-Enemies.html

[82] Sharon D. Welch, *Sweet Dreams in America: Making Ethics and Spirituality Work* (New York: Routledge, 1999), p. 46.

[83] Henri J. M. Nouwen, Donald P. McNeill, and Douglas A. Morrison, *Compassion: A Reflection on the Christian Life* (New York: Doubleday, 1983), p. 124.

[84] Susan Van Haitsma, "Peace Is Not the Absence of Conflict; It Is a Way Through It," *Austin American-Statesman*, September 21, 2008, reprinted at https://www.commondreams.org/view/2008/09/21-5

[85] Ronald C. Arnett, *Dwell in Peace: Applying Nonviolence to Everyday Relationships* (Elgin, IL: Brethren Press, 1980), p. 124.

[86] The Confucian concept of *jen* is described by Dacher Keltner in the first chapter of his book, *Born to Be Good*, excerpted in the *New York Times*, January 19, 2009, www.nytimes.com/2009/01/19/books/chapters/chapter-born-to-be-good.html. See also Wendi L. Gardner and Elizabeth A. Seeley, "Confucius, Jen, and the Benevolent Use of Power," in A. Y. Lee-Chai and J. A. Bargh (Eds.), *The Use and Abuse of Power: Multiple Perspectives on the Causes of Corruption* (Philadelphia: Psychology Press, 2002), pp. 263–280.

[87] Leonard Felder, "In Your Face, Mussar Style," *Tikkun*, 23.2 (March–April 2008), http://www.tikkun.org/article.php/Felder-In-your-face

[88] Ibid.

[89] Ibid.

[90] Nouwen, et al., *Compassion*, p. 125.

[91] Qi Wang, Deborah Cai, and Edward Fink, "A Typology of Conflict Avoidance," paper presented at the annual meeting of the International Association of Conflict Management, 2007, http://papers.ssrn.com/sol3/papers.cfm?abstract_id=1066821

[92] Ibid., p. 16.

[93] Audre Lorde, "The Uses of Anger: Women Responding to Racism," in *Sister Outsider: Essays and Speeches* (Trumansburg, NY: Crossing Press, 1984), p. 127.

[94] Jean Baker Miller and Janet L. Surrey, "Rethinking Women's Anger: The Personal and the Global" in Judith V. Jordan (Ed.), *Women's Growth in Diversity: More Writings from the Stone Center* (New York: Guilford, 1997), p. 202.

[95] Salzberg, *The Force of Kindness*, p. 5.

[96] "Is Ken Salazar Too Nice?" Editorial, *New York Times*, January 2, 2009, http://www.nytimes.com/2009/01/02/opinion/02fri1.html

[97] Ronald D. Gordon, "The Difference between Feeling Defensive and Feeling Understood," *The Journal of Business Communication*, 25.1 (Winter 1988): 53–64.

[98] Ibid., p. 53, emphasis in the original.

[99] Li Xiaojiang, cited in Marguerite Waller and Sylvia Marcos, (Eds.), *Dialogue and Difference: Feminisms Challenge Globalization* (New York: Palgrave MacMillan, 2005), p. 46.

Chapter 6

[1] *The View*, July 18, 2008, http://www.huffingtonpost.com/2008/07/17/whoopi-and-elisabeth-spar_n_113316.html

[2] Cenk Uygur, "Elizabeth Hasselbeck and Whoopi Goldberg Have Emotional Race Discussion," July 19, 2008, http://news.aol.com/newsbloggers/2008/07/19/elizabeth-hasselbeck-and-whoopi-goldberg-have-emotional-race-dis/

[3] Ibid.

4 Sharon D. Welch, *Sweet Dreams in America: Making Ethics and Spirituality Work* (New York: Routledge, 1999), p. 84.

5 Public Conversation Project, cited in Kathleen M. Hunzer, "Lessons from the Public Sphere: Listening, Adversity, and Learning," *The International Journal of Listening*, 22, (2008): 93.

6 Rachel Naomi Remen, *Kitchen Table Wisdom: Stories That Heal* (New York: Riverhead Books, 1996), p. 143.

7 Sara Lawrence-Lightfoot, *Respect: An Exploration* (Reading, MA: Perseus Books, 1999), p. 143.

8 John A. McConnell, *Mindful Mediation: A Handbook for Buddhist Peacemakers* (Bangkok: Buddhist Research Institute and Mahachula Buddhist University, 1995), p. 228.

9 "Enemies of Open-Minded Listening" (section 4.2 in Listening Actively with an Open Mind), http://talkworks.wikidot.com/listening-actively. The list has been modified to describe reactions, rather than listening styles.

10 Mike Allen and David S. Broder, "Bush's Leadership Style: Decisive or Simplistic?" *Washington Post*, August 30, 2004, p. A1.

11 Charles Hauss, *Beyond Confrontation: Transforming the New World Order* (Westport, CT: Praeger, 1996), p. 6, emphasis added.

12 Debra Worthington, "Exploring the Relationship between Listening Style and Need for Cognition," *The International Journal of Listening*, 22 (2008): 46–58.

13 Ibid., p. 47.

14 Ibid.

15 Ibid., p. 48.

16 Ibid.

17 Christian Kiewitz, James B. Weaver III, Hans-Bernd Brosius, and Gabriel Weimann, "Cultural Differences in Listening Style Preferences: A Comparison of Young Adults in Germany, Israel and the United States," *International Journal of Public Opinion Research*, 9.3, (1997): 233–247.

18 Debra Worthington, "Exploring Jurors' Listening Process: The Effect of Listening Style Preference on Juror Decision Making," *The International Journal of Listening*, 15 (2001): 20–29.

19 Lisbeth Lipari, "Listening Otherwise: The Voice of Ethics," p. 55, *The International Journal of Listening*, 23 (2009): 44–59.

20 Ibid., p. 56.

21 Steve Heilig, "Why Can't We Be Good?: Overcoming Obstacles to Our Higher Ideals—A Conversation with Jacob Needleman," June 2, 2007, http://www.dailygood.org/view.php?sid=25, italicized emphasis added.

Chapter 7

1 Dalai Lama, "Questions and Answers," http://www.dalailama.com/biography/questions-and-answers

2 Queen Rania Al Abdullah, "My Message of Cross-Cultural Understanding," October 22, 2007, http://www.huffingtonpost.com/rania-al-abdullah/my-message-of-crosscultu_b_69473.html

3 Thich Nhat Hanh, *The Heart of Understanding* (Berkeley, CA: Parallax, 1988), p. 11.

4 British Broadcasting Company, "Religion and Ethics—Thich Nhat Hanh," April 4, 2006, http://www.bbc.co.uk/religion/religions/buddhism/people/thichnhathanh.shtml

5 Thich Nhat Hanh, *Being Peace* (Berkeley, CA: Parallax, 1987), p. 95.

6 John McCain, "Remarks by John McCain to the Los Angeles World Affairs Council," March 26, 2008, http://thinkprogress.org/politics/2008/03/26/20858/embargoed-mccains-speech-to-the-los-angeles-world-affairs-council/

7 Star Parker, "Senator McCain, It's Getting Dark on that 'City on the Hill,'" *Monterey Herald*, March 30, 2008, p. 8.

8 Bill Bishop, *The Big Sort: Why the Clustering of Like-Minded America Is Tearing Us Apart* (Boston and New York: Houghton Mifflin, 2008), p. 39.

[9] Ibid., p. 13.

[10] Kirk Nielson, "Views, Reviews, and Interviews," *Miller-McCune Reports*, January–February 2010, p. 82.

[11] Ibid.

[12] Ibid., p. 39.

[13] Ibid., p. 6.

[14] Joe Garofoli, "Three Dirty Words: San Francisco Values," November 3, 2006, *San Francisco Chronicle*, p. A1.

[15] Bishop, *The Big Sort*, p. 40.

[16] Robert J. Samuelson, "Political Perils of a 'Big Sort'?" *Washington Post*, August 6, 2008, p. A17.

[17] Thomas W. Martin, "Scientific Literacy and the Habit of Discourse," September 21, 2007, http://seedmagazine.com/content/article/scientific_literacy_and_the_habit_of_discourse/

[18] Ibid.

[19] Helen Thomas, *Thanks for the Memories, Mr. President* (New York: Lisa Drew/Scribner, 2002), p. 78.

[20] Herder's quote cited in Terrance Keenan, *St. Nadie in Winter: Zen Encounters with Loneliness* (Boston: Journey Editions, 2001), p. 21.

[21] See Jonathan Haidt, *The Righteous Mind: Why Good People Are Divided by Politics and Religion* (New York: Pantheon, 2012), and "The Moral Roots of Liberals and Conservatives," posted September 2008, www.ted.com/speakers/jonathan_haidt.html

[22] Steven Pinker, "The Moral Instinct," *The New York Times Magazine*, January 13, 2008, http://www.nytimes.com/2008/01/13/magazine/13Psychology-t.html?pagewanted=all&_r=0

[23] Ibid.

[24] Haidt, *The Righteous Mind*, p. 131

[25] Pinker, "The Moral Instinct."

[26] "The Yin and Yang of Seeing," *The Week*, September 16, 2005, p. 22.

Chapter 8

[1] Amy Gutmann and Dennis Thompson, *Democracy and Disagreement: Why Moral Conflict Cannot Be Avoided in Politics, and What Should Be Done About It* (Cambridge, MA: The Belknap Press of Harvard University, 1996), p. 56.

[2] Ibid., p. 57.

[3] Ibid.

[4] Ibid., pp. 79–80. The authors go on to explore some other key elements of moral accommodation including *civic integrity* and *civic magnanimity*. Time constraints prevent us from doing justice to these constructs. However, we encourage readers to turn directly to pp. 78–94 of Gutmann and Thompson's book for further insights.

[5] For a detailed exploration of this principle, see pp. 95–127 of Gutmann and Thompson.

[6] Ibid., p. 128.

[7] Mauro Baristione, "Framing a Deliberation, Deliberative Democracy, and the Challenge of Framing Processes, *Journal of Public Deliberation*, 8.1 (2012): 3.

[8] Ibid., p. 6.

[9] Stephen Bloch-Schulman and Spoma Jovanovic, "Who's Afraid of Politics? On the Need to Teach Political Engagement," *Journal of Higher Education, Outreach, and Engagement*, 14.1, (2010): 91.

[10] Linguist George Lakoff's research suggests that these systems of belief regarding family life correlate to broader political ideologies. See, for example, *Moral Politics: How Liberals and Conservatives Think*, 2nd ed. (Chicago: University of Chicago, 2002). Many other scholars have written extensively about different systems of belief regarding family life. For particularly illuminating explorations, see Riane Eisler's *The Chalice and the Blade* (San Francisco: Harper and Collins, 1988) and *The Power of Partnership* (Novato, CA: New World Library, 2002).

11 Mimi Swartz, "Living the Good Lie: Should Therapists Help God-Fearing Gay People Stay in the Closet?" *The New York Times Magazine*, June 19, 2011, p. 57.

12 Ibid.

13 Ibid.

14 Ibid., p. 33.

15 Ibid., p. 34.

16 "Russian Police Detain Gay Activists," Associated Press, *Monterey Herald*, June 26, 2011, p. A5.

17 John F. Burns, "Cast Out, but at the Center of the Storm," *New York Times*, August 3, 2008, Wk. p. 3.

18 Steven Pinker, "The Moral Instinct," *The New York Times Magazine*, January 13, 2008, http://www.nytimes.com/2008/01/13/magazine/13Psychology-t.html?pagewanted=all&_r=0

Chapter 9

1 Steven Pinker, "The Moral Instinct," *The New York Times Magazine*, January 13, 2008, http://www.nytimes.com/2008/01/13/magazine/13Psychology-t.html?pagewanted=all&_r=0

2 Jake Coyle, "Duvall Lets Characters Come to Him," *Monterey Herald*, July 25, 2010, p. C7.

3 Peggy Orenstein, "I Tweet, Therefore I Am: Are Twitter Posts an Expression of Who We Are—Or Are They Changing Who We Are?" *New York Times Magazine*, August 1, 2010, pp. 11–12.

4 Ibid.

5 Joe Keohane, "How Facts Backfire," http://www.boston.com/bostonglobe/ideas/articles/2010/07/11/how_facts_backfire/

6 Lonnae O'Neal Parker and Michael D. Shear, "Ousted USDA Official Vows to Sue Blogger," *Monterey County Herald*, July 30, 2010, p. A3.

7 Troy Duster, "The Long Path to Higher Education for African Americans," *Thought and Action*, 25 (Fall 2009): 109.

8 Ibid., p. 106.

9 Lani Guinier and Gerald Torres, *The Miner's Canary: Enlisting Race, Resisting Power, Transforming Democracy* (Cambridge: Harvard University Press, 2002).

10 Josina Makau, "Response and Conclusion: A Vision of Applied Ethics for Communication Studies," in Steven May, Debashish Munshi, and George Cheney (Eds.), *ICA Handbook of Communication Ethics* (New York: Routledge Press, 2011). Columbia sociology professor Shamus Khan notes that, like the social locations of their wealthy counterparts, the socioeconomic positions of a large majority of the poor are "most often bound to a history not of their own choosing or responsibility." He admonishes people of privilege to acknowledge the structural inequities at the heart of differences across socioeconomic lines and urges shared recognition that "there is a commonweal that we all have a responsibility to improve." Shamus Khan, "The New Elites," *The New York Times*, July 8, 2012, Week in Review, p. 6.

11 Richard D. Reike and Malcolm O. Sillars, *Argumentation and the Decision Making Process*, 2nd. ed. (Glenview, IL: Scott Foresman, 1984), p. 153.

12 Sissela Bok, *Lying: Moral Choice in Public and Private Life* (New York: Vintage Books, 1989).

13 Josina Makau, "Ethical and Unethical Communication," in William Eadie (Ed.), *21st Century Communication: A Reference Handbook*, vol. I (Thousand Oaks, CA: Sage Publications, 2009), p. 438.

14 "Does the Free Market Corrode Moral Character?" *New York Times*, November 16, 2008, Wk., p. 9. Walzer's comments are cited as part of a Templeton Fund Project exploring diverse responses to the question in the title.

15 Larry Parsons, "Feds Defend Evidence in Salyer Case," *Monterey Herald*, August 12, 2010, p. A19.

[16] Anthony Cortese, *Ethnic Ethics* (Albany: State University of New York Press, 1990).

[17] Pinker, "The Moral Instinct."

[18] See, for example, Deni Elliot, "Universal Values and Moral Development Theories," in Clifford Christians and Michael Traber (Eds.), *Communication Ethics and Universal Values* (Thousand Oaks, CA: Sage Publications, 1998), pp. 68–86; Richard Johannesen, "Communication Ethics: Centrality, Trends, and Controversies," 1997, National Communication Association Conference, Chicago, IL; Richard Johannesen, Kathleen Valde, and Karen Whedbee, *Ethics in Human Communication*, 6th ed. (Long Grove, IL: Waveland Press, 2008); Sissela Bok, *Common Values* (Columbia: University of Missouri, 1995); Dalai Lama, *Ethics for the New Millennium* (New York: Riverhead Books, 1999); and Cornel West, *Race Matters* (New York: Vintage, 1994).

[19] Radha D'Souza, "International Legal Frameworks, Trade and Communication Networks," in Steven May, Debashish Munshi, and George Cheney (Eds.), *ICA Handbook of Communication Ethics* (New York: Routledge Press, 2011), p. 485.

[20] Makau, "Response and Conclusion," p. 495.

[21] "Doctor Stresses Intuition of Touch, Not Technology," *PBS News Hour*, July 29, 2010, www.pbs.org/newshour/bb/health/july-dec10/healing_07-29.html

[22] Ibid.

[23] Nan Mooney, "Are Gen X-ers Falling Behind?" *U.S. News & World Report*, July 7/July 14, 2008, p. 16, http://money.usnews.com/money/personal-finance/articles/2008/06/25/are-gen-x-ers-falling-behind

[24] Robert C. Pinto, *Argument, Inference, and Dialectic: Collected Papers on Informal Logic* (Dordrecht, Netherlands: Kluwer Publications, 2001), p. 17.

Chapter 10

[1] Delores S. Williams, "Womanist/Feminist Dialogue: Problems and Possibilities," *Journal of Feminist Studies in Religion*, 9.1–2, (Spring–Fall 1999): 69–70.

[2] Citations are taken from James F. Klumpp, "Deliberation, Debate, and Decision Making," in William F. Eadie (Ed.), *21st Century Communication: A Reference Handbook* (Thousand Oaks, CA: Sage Publications, 2009), p. 202.

[3] Ibid., p. 203.

[4] Irving L. Janis and Leon Mann, *Decision Making* (New York: Free Press, 1979), p. 11.

[5] Ibid., p. 13.

[6] Richard Fulkerson, "Transcending Our Conception of Argument in Light of Feminist Critiques," *Argumentation and Advocacy*, 32 (Spring 1996): 211–212. For an insightful introduction to relevant issues, see also Catherine Helen Palczewski, "Argumentation and Feminisms: An Introduction," *Argumentation and Advocacy*, 32 (Spring 1996): 161–169.

[7] Sandy Banisky and Joe Mathews, "Brennan, a Lion of Liberalism, Dead at 91," *The Sun*, July 25, 1997, p. 16A.

[8] Jonathon Haidt, *The Righteous Mind: Why Good People Are Divided by Politics and Religion* (New York: Pantheon, 2012), p. 49, citing Dale Carnegie, *How to Win Friends and Influence People*, rev. ed. (New York: Pocket Books, 1981/1936), p. 37.

[9] Haidt, *The Righteous Mind*, p. 49.

[10] Martha Nussbaum, *Upheavals of Thought: The Intelligence of Emotions* (Cambridge, MA: Cambridge University Press, 2001).

[11] Ibid., p. 117.

[12] Ibid., p. 404.

[13] Ibid., p. 441.

[14] Chaim Perelman and Lucie Olbrechts-Tyteca, *The New Rhetoric: A Treatise on Argumentation* (Notre Dame, IN: University of Notre Dame Press, 1969).

[15] Interview with Deborah Solomon, "Wordsmith: Questions for Frank Luntz," *New York Times Magazine*, May 24, 2009, p. 17.

16 H. Mercer and D. Sperber, "Why Do Humans Reason? Arguments for an Argumentative Theory," *Behavioral and Brain Sciences*, 34 (2011): 5 (cited in Haidt, *The Righteous Mind*, p. 89). In his introduction to Mercer and Sperber's findings, Haidt writes, "Anyone who values truth should stop worshipping reason. We all need to take a cold hard look at the evidence and see reasoning for what it is." As a moral psychologist, Haidt's focus here is on description rather than on prescription. Our research corresponds with his findings regarding the dearth of reasonableness in public discourse within the dominant argument culture. We are proposing, however, that reconceptualization of argumentation coupled with a recognition of differences between formal rationality and reasonableness create legitimate grounds for the hope that Haidt and we share regarding pathways for more constructive engagements and responsible and responsive deliberations in today's globally interdependent world.

17 Nelson Rolihlahla Mandela, *The Long Walk to Freedom* (New York: Little, Brown and Company, 1994), p. 620.

18 Ibid., pp. 624–625.

19 Ibid., p. 620.

20 For a thoughtful exploration of this phenomenon, see James Bohman, *Public Deliberation: Pluralism, Complexity, and Democracy* (Cambridge, MA: MIT Press, 1996), p. 33.

21 John Stuart Mill, *On Liberty* (1859), reprint (Indianapolis: Bobbs-Merrill, 1956), pp. 45–46.

22 Bohman, *Public Deliberation*, p. 16.

23 Dennis A. Lynch, Diana George, and Marilyn M. Cooper, "Moments of Argument: Agonistic Inquiry and Confrontational Cooperation," *College Composition and Communication*, 48.1 (February 1997): 80.

24 Parker Palmer, *To Know as We Are Known: Education as a Spiritual Journey* (New York: HarperCollins, 1983), p. 40.

25 Ibid.

26 Judith A. White, "Leadership through Compassion and Understanding: An Interview with Aung San Suu Kyi," *Journal of Management Inquiry*, 7.4 (December 1998): 291.

27 Charles Hauss, *Beyond Confrontation: Transforming the New World Order* (Westport, CT: Praeger, 1996), p. 142.

28 Reverend Martin Luther King, Jr., "Loving Your Enemies," in Clayborne Carson and Peter Holloran (Eds.), *A Knock at Midnight: Inspiration from the Great Sermons of Reverend Martin Luther King, Jr.* (New York: Warner, 1996), p. 50.

29 Ibid.

30 Gloria Anzaldúa, *Borderlands/La Frontera* (San Francisco: Aunt Lute, 1987), p. 78.

31 Cornel West with Vitka Eisen and Mary Kenyatta, "Cornel West on Heterosexism and Transformation: An Interview," *Harvard Educational Review*, 66.2 (Summer 1996): 363.

32 Minnie Bruce Pratt, *Rebellion: Essays 1980–1991* (Ithaca, NY: Firebrand, 1991), p. 33.

33 Ibid., p. 35.

34 Ibid., p. 36.

35 Stanley Deetz and William J. White, "Relational Responsibility or Dialogic Ethics?" in S. McNamee and K. J. Gergen (Eds.), *Relational Responsibility: Resources for Sustainable Dialogue* (Thousand Oaks, CA: Sage Publications, 1999), pp. 114–115.

36 Kevin Howe, "City Council Considers Ways to Cultivate Peace," *Monterey County Herald*, August 11, 1999, pp. B1 and B3.

37 Amy Gutmann and Dennis Thompson, *Democracy and Disagreement: Why Moral Conflict Cannot Be Avoided in Politics and What Should Be Done about It* (Cambridge: Harvard University Press, 1996), p. 43.

38 Bohman, *Public Deliberation*, p. 124.

39 Sut Jhally (Producer), *Democracy in a Different Voice with Lani Guinier* (video) (Media Education Foundation, Northampton, MA, 1995).

Chapter 11

[1] Stephen D'Arcy, "Deliberative Democracy, Direct Action and Animal Advocacy," *Journal for Critical Animal Studies*, 5.2 (2007): 1, http://www.criticalanimalstudies.org/wp-content/uploads/2009/09/Deliberative-Democracy-Direct-Action-and-Animal-Advocacy.pdf

[2] This quotation illustrates the discussion of the primary function of argumentation in the last chapter, drawn from Dennis A. Lynch, Diana George, and Marilyn M. Cooper's "Moments of Argument: Agonistic Inquiry and Confrontation Cooperation," *College Composition and Communication*, 48.1 (February 1997): 65.

[3] Deborah Tannen, *The Argument Culture: Moving from Debate to Dialogue* (New York: Random House, 1998), p. 3.

[4] Jonathan Miller, "Mourdock: Compromise Is Democrats Agreeing with Republicans," *National Journal*, May 9, 2012, www.nationaljournal.com/congress/mourdock-compromise-is-democrats-agreeing-with-republicans-20120509

[5] Ken Sofer, "World Reacts to Debt Ceiling Debacle: 'Irresponsible,' 'Worst Kind of Absurd Theatrics,' U.S. Politicians a 'Laughing Stock,'" July 29, 2011, http://thinkprogress.org/security/2011/07/29/283703/world-reacts-to-debt-ceiling-debacle-irresponsible-worst-kind-of-absurd-theatrics-u-s-politicians-a-laughing-stock/

[6] United States Government Accountability Office, *Report to the Congress: Debt Limit—Analysis of 2011–2012 Actions Taken and Effect of Delayed Increase on Borrowing Costs*, July 2012, GAO 12-701, http://www.gao.gov/assets/600/592832.pdf

[7] David Frum, "2011's Debt Ceiling Debacle," *The Daily Beast*, May 29, 2012, http://www.thedailybeast.com/articles/2012/05/29/debt-ceiling.html

[8] Jim Puzzanghera, "S&P Downgrades US Credit Rating," *Los Angeles Times*, August 6, 2011, http://articles.latimes.com/2011/aug/06/business/la-fi-us-debt-downgrade-20110806, emphasis added.

[9] Charles Hauss, *Beyond Confrontation: Transforming the New World Order* (Westport, CT and London: Praeger, 1996), p. 101.

[10] Dachner Keltner, *The Compassionate Instinct: The Science of Human Goodness* (New York: W.W. Norton, 2010); Elinor Ostrom, *Governing the Commons: The Evolution of Institutions for Collective Action* (Cambridge, MA: Cambridge University Press, 1990).

[11] Sarah van Gelder and Van Jones, "Van Jones: Beyond the Politics of Confrontation," *Yes Magazine*, Spring 2009, http://www.yesmagazine.org/issues/food-for-everyone/van-jones-beyond-the-politics-of-confrontation. Emphasis in the original.

[12] Leonardo Dicaprio, "Van Jones—Heroes & Icons" *Time Magazine*, April 30, 2009, http://www.time.com/time/specials/packages/article/0,28804,1894410_1894289_1894360,00.html

[13] Van Jones, "It Is Time to Change from Fighting against Something to Fighting for Something," *Alternet*, November 7, 2008, http://current.com/community/89501959_it-is-time-to-change-from-fighting-against-something-to-fighting-for-something.htm

[14] Sharon D. Welch, "The Machiavellian Dilemma," *Tikkun Magazine*, May/June 2010, http://www.tikkun.org/nextgen/the-machiavellian-dilemma, emphasis in the original.

[15] Nelson Mandela, cited in Welch, "The Machiavellian Dilemma."

[16] Hauss, *Beyond Confrontation*, p. 101.

[17] Paul Collier, "New Rules for Rebuilding a Broken Nation," *Ted Talks*, June 2009, http://www.ted.com/talks/paul_collier_s_new_rules_for_rebuilding_a_broken_nation.html

[18] Paul Collier, "Four Ways to Help the 'Bottom Billion,'" *Ted Talks*, March 2008, http://www.ted.com/talks/paul_collier_shares_4_ways_to_help_the_bottom_billion.html

[19] Paul Collier, "New Rules."

[20] For a recent tragic example see, Chris Dufresne, "When Power Corrupts: Penn State Struggles with Tarnished Legacy," *Christian Science Monitor*, July 29, 2012, http://www.csmonitor.com/USA/Latest-News-Wires/2012/0729/When-power-corrupts-Penn-State-struggles-with-tarnished-legacy

[21] Archon Fung, "Deliberation before the Revolution: Toward an Ethics of Deliberative Democracy in an Unjust World," *Political Theory*, 33.3 (June 2005): 397–419.

[22] American Friends Service Committee, "Speak Truth to Power: A Quaker Alternative to Violence," March 2, 1955, http://www.quaker.org/sttp.html; Sharon D. Welch, *Sweet Dreams in America: Making Ethics and Spirituality Work* (New York and London: Routledge, 1999), p. 34.

[23] American Friends Service Committee, "Speak Truth to Power."

[24] Ibid.

[25] See for example, the Speak Truth to Power Project at the Robert F. Kennedy Center for Justice and Human Rights, http://rfkcenter.org/speak-truth-to-power

[26] American Friends Service Committee, "Speak Truth to Power."

[27] Jeffrey M. Jones, "Confidence in U.S. Public Schools at New Low," *Gallup Politics*, August 6, 2012, http://www.gallup.com/poll/155258/Confidence-Public-Schools-New-Low.aspx

[28] Sharon D. Welch, *A Feminist Ethic of Risk* (Minneapolis: Fortress Press, 1990), p. 115.

[29] Welch, *Sweet Dreams in America*, p. 34.

[30] See chapter 9 for a discussion of self-deception and its corrective, the application of Sissela Bok's principle of veracity/test of publicity.

[31] Margaret Urban Walker, *Moral Repair: Reconstructing Moral Relations after Wrongdoing* (New York: Cambridge University Press, 2006), p. 199.

[32] Welch, *Sweet Dreams in America*, p. 34.

[33] David Blankenhorn, "How My View on Gay Marriage Changed," *The New York Times*, June 22, 2012, http://www.nytimes.com/2012/06/23/opinion/how-my-view-on-gay-marriage-changed.html

[34] Ibid.

[35] Ethan Bronner, "Gay Marriage Gains Backer as Major Foe Revises Views," *The New York Times*, June 22, 2012, http://www.nytimes.com/2012/06/23/us/david-blankenhorn-drops-opposition-to-gay-marriage.html; Maggie Gallagher, "Bigotry, David Blankenhorn, and the Future of Marriage," *Public Discourse: Ethics, Law, and the Common Good*, June 25, 2012, http://www.thepublicdiscourse.com/2012/06/5759/; Richard Kim, "What's Still the Matter with David Blankenhorn," *The Nation*, June 24, 2012; http://www.thenation.com/blog/168545/whats-still-matter-david-blankenhorn

[36] Steve Almond, "Condoleeza Rice at Boston College? I Quit," *The Boston Globe*, May 12, 2006, reprinted at http://www.commondreams.org/views06/0512-20.htm

[37] Steve Almond, "Liberals Are Ruining America. I Know because I Am One," *The New York Times*, June 8, 2012, http://www.nytimes.com/2012/06/10/magazine/liberals-are-ruining-america-i-know-because-i-am-one.html

[38] Ibid.

[39] "NYT: If We Just Ignore Rush & Fox, They'll Disappear," *Daily Kos*, June 9, 2012, http://www.dailykos.com/story/2012/06/09/1098772/-NY-Times-If-We-Just-Ignore-Rush-Fox-They-ll-Disappear; James Johnson, "'It's the Economy, Stupid,' Is More Relevant Today than Ever," *Examiner.com*, June 12, 2012, http://www.examiner.com/article/it-s-the-economy-stupid-is-more-relevant-today-than-ever

[40] Almond, "Liberals Are Ruining America."

[41] William Vesterman, *Reading and Writing Short Arguments*, 3rd ed. (Mountain View, CA: Mayfield, 2000), p. 344.

[42] Annette T. Rottenberg, *Elements of Argument: A Text and Reader* (Boston: Bedford, 1997), p. 316.

[43] John A. Williams, *Classroom in Conflict: Teaching Controversial Subjects in a Diverse Society* (Albany: State University of New York Press, 1994), p, 165,

[44] Pema Chodron, "The Birthplace of Compassion: In the Gap between Right and Wrong," *Shambhala Sun*, January 1996, p. 22.

[45] Maria Lugones, "Motion, Stasis, and Resistance to Interlocked Oppressions," in S. H. Aiken, A. Brighman, S. A. Marston, and P. Waterstone (Eds.), *Making Worlds: Gender, Metaphor, Materiality* (Tucson: University of Arizona, 1998), pp. 51–52.

46 Williams, *Classroom in Conflict*, p. 35.

47 For a detailed exploration of these and other strategies for refutation, see Richard D. Reike, Malcolm O. Sillars, and Tarla Rai Peterson, *Argumentation and the Decision Making Process*, 8th ed. (Boston: Pearson, 2013), chapter 10.

48 Katie Hafner, "In Ill Doctor, a Surprise Reflection of Who Picks Assisted Suicide," *New York Times*, August 12, 2012, p. 1.

49 Ibid., p. 4.

50 Ibid.

51 Judith A. Boss, *Ethics for Life: A Text with Readings*, 4th ed. (Boston: McGraw-Hill, 2008), p. 10.

52 Fung, "Deliberation before the Revolution," p. 398.

53 Ibid., p. 401.

54 Ibid.

55 Ibid., pp. 402–403.

56 Ibid., p. 403.

57 Ibid.

58 Ibid.

59 Ibid., p. 408. Importantly, the use of shame is a highly contested form of communication among communication ethicists. For a deeply insightful exploration of this issue, see R. L. Johannesen, K. S. Valde, and K. E. Whedbee, *Ethics in Human Communication*, 6th ed. (Long Grove, IL: Waveland Press, 2008), pp. 240–251.

60 Pamela Morgan with Susan Bales, "Competition, Cooperation, and Connection: How These Metaphors Affect Child Advocacy," *Frameworks Institute: Changing the Public Conversation about Social Problems*, n.d., http://www.frameworksinstitute.org/ezine11.html

61 Ibid.

62 Tarja Väyrynen, "Medical Metaphors in Peace Research: John Burton's Conflict Resolution Theory and a Social Constructionist Alternative," *The International Journal of Peace Studies*, 3.2 (July 1998), http://www.gmu.edu/programs/icar/ijps/vol3_2/Vayrynen.htm

63 Morgan and Bales, "Competition, Cooperation, and Connection."

64 Ibid.

65 Will Friedman, "Reframing 'Framing,'" Occasional Paper #1, Center for Advances in Public Engagement, n.d., http://www.publicagenda.org/files/pdf/Reframing%20Framing_0.pdf

66 Alison Kadlec and Will Friedman, "Framing for Deliberation," CAPE Working Paper, Center for Advances in Public Engagement, Summer 2008, http://www.publicagenda.org/files/pdf/CAPE%20Working%20Paper%20Framing%20for%20Deliberation.pdf

67 Carolyn M. Hendriks, John S. Dryzek, and Christian Hunold, "Turning Up the Heat: Partisanship in Deliberative Innovation," *Political Studies*, 55 (2007): 362.

Chapter 12

1 James Bohman, *Public Deliberation: Pluralism, Complexity, and Democracy*, (Cambridge: MIT Press, 2000), p. 4.

2 Ibid., p. 241.

3 In crafting our overview of guidelines for evaluating the deliberative value of arguments, we have drawn from our previous exploration on the subject appearing in Josina M. Makau and Debian L. Marty, *Cooperative Argumentation* (Long Grove, IL: Waveland Press, 2001), pp. 228–278.

4 Monroe Beardsley, *Thinking Straight*, 4th ed. (Englewood Cliffs, NJ: Prentice-Hall, 1975), p. 72.

5 Bernard Yack, "Rhetoric and Public Reasoning: An Aristotelian Understanding of Political Deliberation," in Derek W. M. Barker, Noelle McAfee, and David W. McIvor (Eds.), *Democratizing Deliberation: A Political Theory Anthology* (Dayton, OH: Kettering Foundation, 2012), pp. 39–56.

[6] John Warner and Evan Bayh, "Can Civility Be Returned in Governing Our Nation?" The Panetta Institute for Public Policy, May 23, 2011, http://www.panettainstitute.org/programs/lecture-series/webcast-video-archive/2011-protecting-the-american-dream-for-our-children/can-civility-be-returned-in-governing-our-nation/

[7] Ibid.

[8] Martha C. Nussbaum, *Upheavals of Thought: The Intelligence of Emotions* (Cambridge, UK: Cambridge University Press, 2001), p. 3.

[9] Ibid., p. 46.

[10] Ibid., p. 117.

[11] Ibid., p. 441.

[12] Ibid., p. 140.

[13] Ibid., p. 141.

[14] Ibid., p, 177,

[15] Ibid., p. 404.

[16] Quoted in Jay Lindsay, "Study: Less Religious States Give Less to Charity," *Monterey County Herald*, August 21, 2012, p. A-4.

[17] Ibid.

[18] Noelle McAfee, "Three Models of Democratic Deliberation," in Derek W. M. Barker, Noelle McAfee, and David W. McIvor (Eds.), *Democratizing Deliberation: A Political Theory Anthology* (Dayton, OH: Kettering Foundation, 2012), p. 32.

[19] Ibid., p. 33.

[20] Jonathon Haidt, "How Do Conservatives and Liberals See the World?" *Moyers and Company*, PBS, February 5, 2012.

Index